ANTIGONES

ANTIGONES

BY

GEORGE STEINER

New York   Oxford
OXFORD UNIVERSITY PRESS
1984

Copyright © 1984 by George Steiner

Library of Congress Cataloging in Publication Data

Steiner, George, 1929-
Antigones.

Includes index.
1. Sophocles. Antigone—Addresses, essays, lectures.
2. Sophocles—Influence—Addresses, essays, lectures.
3. Antigone in literature—Addresses, essays, lectures.
4. Antigone in art—Addresses, essays, lectures.
I. Title.
PA4413. A7S76   1984   882'.01   83-25267
ISBN 0-19-812665-4

Printing (last digit):   9 8 7 6 5 4 3 2 1

Printed in the United States of America

For Deborah

ὦ τέκνον, ἦ πάρει;

In den Gebieten, mit denen wir es zu tun haben, gibt es
Erkenntnis nur blitzhaft. Der Text ist der langnachrol-
lende Donner.

WALTER BENJAMIN, *Das Passagen-Werk*, N. 1. 1

(In the areas with which we are concerned, insight only
occurs as a lightning-bolt. The text is the thunder-peal
rolling long behind.)

ANTIGŎNE, a daughter of Œdipus, king of Thebes, by his mother Jocasta. She buried by night her brother Polynices, against the positive orders of Creon, who, when he heard of it, ordered her to be buried alive. She however killed herself before the sentence was executed; and Hæmon, the king's son, who was passionately fond of her, and had not been able to obtain her pardon, killed himself on her grave. The death of Antigone is the subject of one of the tragedies of Sophocles. The Athenians were so pleased with it at the first representation, that they presented the author with the government of Samos. This tragedy was represented 32 times at Athens without interruption. *Sophocl. in Antig.—Hygin. fab.* 67, 72, 243, 254.—*Apollod.* 3, c. 5.—*Ovid. Trist.* 3, *el.* 3.—*Philostrat.* 2, c. 29.—*Stat. Theb.* 12, 350.

Bibliotheca Classica or *A Classical Dictionary*, by J. Lemprière, DD (3rd edn., London, 1797)

PREFACE

THE idea for this book goes back to, at least, 1979, and the Jackson Knight Memorial Lecture on 'Antigones' which I gave at the University of Exeter. The publication of two brief surveys, Simone Fraisse's *Le Mythe d'Antigone* (1974) and Cesare Molinari's *Storia di Antigone* (1977), had rendered repetitive the notion of any chronological–systematic account of the Antigone motif in western literatures. My own aim has been, from the outset, to place this motif in the more general context of a poetics of reading, of a study of the interactions between a major text and its interpretations across time.

But Sophocles' *Antigone* is not 'any text'. It is one of the enduring and canonic acts in the history of our philosophic, literary, political consciousness. Incipient in this book, and central to it, is an attempt to answer the question of why it should be that a handful of ancient Greek myths continue to dominate, to give vital shape to our sense of self and of the world. Why are the 'Antigones' truly *éternelles* and immediate to the present?

My thanks go to the many students and colleagues who have, over the intervening years, listened, more or less patiently, to the work in progress and responded critically; to Elda Southern's scepticism; to the editorial guidance and encouragements of David Attwooll, Henry Hardy, and Hilary Feldman. John Waś has been far more than an authoritative copy-editor, and I owe much to his suggestions. Hugh Lloyd-Jones's reading of the typescript was generous precisely by virtue of its severity and ironies. The errata which now remain in the work are, therefore, compounded by obstinacy.

The iconography could not have been assembled without the tireless help of Evelyne Ender and the kindness of Oliver Taplin.

No element in this book is separable from its dedication.

G. S.

Geneva, November 1983

CONTENTS

ACKNOWLEDGEMENTS

The author wishes to thank the following for giving permission to reproduce photographs (plate numbers in brackets):

(1) British Museum; (2) Deutsches Archäologisches Institut, Rome; (3) Photos Lipnitzki-Viollet, Roger-Viollet, Paris; (4) Fotos Berlau, from *Antigone-Modelle* (Henschel Verlag, Berlin, 1948); (5) Dr F. Tornquist; (6) Photos Lipnitzki-Viollet, Roger-Viollet, Paris; (7) Foto Mara Eggert, Frankfurt-on-Main; (8, *top left*) Photos Lipnitzki-Viollet, Roger-Viollet, Paris; (8, *bottom*) Henri-Pierre Garnier, Nantes; (9) Susan Schimert-Ramme, Zurich; (10) Dr Oliver Taplin; (11) Crown Copyright, Victoria and Albert Museum (Theatre Museum), Houston Rogers Collection; (12) Centro Nazionale di Studi Alfieriani, Asti; (13) SPADEM; (14) Sammlung Georg Schäfer, Schweinfurt; (15) Mansell Collection, London.

CHAPTER ONE

I

WE are 'only the interpreters of interpretations'; so Montaigne—who is himself echoing Plato's description of the rhapsode as ἑρμηνέων ἑρμηνῆc in the *Ion*.

Between *c*.1790 and *c*.1905, it was widely held by European poets, philosophers, scholars that Sophocles' *Antigone* was not only the finest of Greek tragedies, but a work of art nearer to perfection than any other produced by the human spirit. The argument was concentric. Fifth-century Athens had housed and brought to expression the pre-eminence of man. It had marked the noontime of his secular genius in its philosophic, poetic, and political realizations. This supremacy was a commonplace to Kant and to Shelley, to Matthew Arnold and to Nietzsche. It is only an overemphasis to say that the history of thought and of feeling throughout the nineteenth century draws essential force from a reflection on Hellenism, from an attempt at once analytic and mimetic to grasp the sources of the Attic achievement and to clarify its political fragility. German Idealism, the Romantic movements, the historiography of Marx and Freud's mythography of the mind, with its roots in Rousseau and Kant, are, at cardinal points, active meditations on Athens. Ernest Renan spoke for his century when he recorded the revelation of sensibility which he had experienced when first visiting the Acropolis in 1865: it was that of 'le miracle grec, une chose qui n'a existé qu'une fois, qui ne s'était jamais vue, qui ne se reverra plus, mais dont l'effet durera éternellement, je veux dire un type de beauté éternelle, sans nulle tache locale ou nationale' ('the Greek miracle, a thing which has existed only once, which had never been seen before, which shall not be seen again, but whose effect will be everlasting, I mean to say an eternal type of beauty, with no local or national flaw'). 'Sage, wo ist Athen?' ('Oh say, where is Athens?') asked Hölderlin in his hymn, 'Der Archipelagus'. Renan answered that it lay hidden in modern man, that the

world would be saved only when it came home to the
Parthenon and broke its links with barbarism—'Le monde ne
sera sauvé qu'en revenant à toi, en répudiant ses attaches
barbares'.[1]

Baroque and neo-classical sentiment had located the heart of
'the Greek miracle' in the Homeric epic, in the enduring
capacity of Homer to instruct civic man in the arts of war and
of domestic order. The nineteenth century identified the
essence of Hellenism with Athenian tragedy. The motives for
this identification go far beyond aesthetic or didactic bias. The
major philosophic systems since the French Revolution have
been tragic systems. They have metaphorized the theological
premiss of the fall of man. The metaphors are various: the
Fichtean and Hegelian concepts of self-alienation, the Marxist
scenario of economic servitude, Schopenhauer's diagnosis of
human conduct as harnessed to coercive will, the Nietzschean
analysis of decadence, Freud's narrative of the coming of
neurosis and discontent after the original Oedipal crime, the
Heideggerian ontology of a fall from the primal truth of Being.
To philosophize after Rousseau and Kant, to find a normative,
conceptual phrasing for the psychic, social, and historical
condition of man, is to think 'tragically'. It is to find in tragic
drama, as did Nietzsche in *Tristan*, the *'opus metaphysicum* par
excellence'. This means that formal philosophic discourse,
from Kant to Max Scheler and Heidegger, will imply or
articulate a theory of tragic effect and that it will draw, almost
instinctively, on passages from tragedy for decisive illustration.
The terms of reference are set out in the famous Tenth Letter of
Schelling's *Philosophische Briefe über Dogmatismus und Kriticismus*
of 1795. Greek tragedy 'honours human freedom in that it
allows its heroes to struggle against the superior, the exceeding
power of destiny' (*die Uebermacht des Schicksals*). The 'constraints and bounds of art' demand man's defeat in this
struggle, even where the error or guilt which brings on such
defeat is, rigorously, 'fated' (*auch für das durch Schicksal begangene
Verbrechen*). *Fatum*, in Greek tragedy, is an 'invisible might,

[1] Nineteenth-century Hellenism is a vast topic which has been extensively studied.
Cf. G. Billeter, *Die Anschauungen vom Wesen des Griechentums* (Leipzig and Berlin,
1911), and E. M. Butler, *The Tyranny of Greece over Germany* (Cambridge, 1935). Cf. also
W. Rehm, *Griechentum und Goethezeit* (3rd edn., Berne, 1952). For a recent treatment,
particularly relevant to this chapter, cf. J. Taminiaux, *La Nostalgie de la Grèce à l'aube de
l'idéalisme allemand* (The Hague, 1967).

inaccessible to natural forces', and imperative even upon the gods. But man's defeat crystallizes his freedom, the lucid compulsion to act, to act polemically, which determines the substance of the self. Schelling's categories, 'freedom', 'destiny', the dynamics of the 'ego', the economy of mortal strife which he adduces, are the constants of post-Kantian metaphysics and psychology. To precisely these categories, to this dialectic of self-realization, the Greek tragic plays had given primary and lasting form.[1]

The Idealist, the Romantic imagination elevated Sophocles to supremacy among Greek tragedians. In so doing it was, as in much of its vitalist biology and its aesthetics, Aristotelian. In his fragments towards a *History of Attic Tragedy* of 1795, the young Friedrich Schlegel had asked himself: 'Thus, is Sophocles alone perfect, complete?' (*Also nur S ist vollkommen?*) He had replied affirmatively: 'The greatest of Greek poets are like a chorus in harmony, S. is the leader of the chorus, like Apollo Μουϲηγέτηϲ leading the chorus of the Muses.' In his lectures on the history of classical literature, first given between 1796 and 1803, A. W. Schlegel characterized Sophocles as the foremost of his peers in 'excellence and fulfilment'. He was— the original is in italics—a poet 'of whom it is almost impossible to speak except in adoration' (*anbetend*). To Schelling, in his lessons on *The Philosophy of Art* (1802–5), this judgement had the authority of self-evidence: 'The high morality, the absolute purity of the works of Sophocles has been the object of wonder throughout the ages.' Whatever the genius of Shakespeare, Sophocles remains 'the veritable summit of dramatic art'. F. Schlegel's *Geschichte der alten und neuen Literatur* (1812–14) goes further: 'Sophocles stands supreme not only in drama, but in the entirety of Greek poetry and spiritual development' (*Geistesbildung*). Goethe had made canonic the opinion that Sophocles had moulded to eternal perfection those agencies of terror and suffering which Aeschylus had woken to tremendous but sometimes enigmatic and arbitrary enactment, and that he had mastered and contained those psychological insights which were to insinuate into even the best of Euripides an element of aestheticism and of

---

[1] Cf. P. Lacoue-Labarthe, 'La césure du spéculatif', in Hölderlin, *L'Antigone de Sophocle* (Paris, 1978), an essay which is itself a commentary on Peter Szondi's *Die Theorie des bürgerlichen Trauerspiels* (Frankfurt-on-Main, 1973).

spurious modernity. To George Eliot, writing on 'The Antigone and its Moral' (1856), Sophocles was 'the single dramatic poet who can be said to stand on a level with Shakespeare'.

In the constellation of the seven extant tragedies of Sophocles, the first magnitude was assigned to *Antigone*. This estimate, often hyperbolic, pertained to the figure of the heroine, to the play itself, or to an indistinct fusion of both. 'You are right about Antigone—', wrote Shelley to John Gisborne in October 1821, 'how sublime a picture of woman! and what think you of the choruses, and especially the lyrical complaint of the godlike victim? And the menaces of Tiresias and their rapid fulfilment? Some of us have in a prior existence been in love with an Antigone, and that makes us find no full content in any mortal tie.' In the lectures on aesthetics (1820–9), Hegel addresses himself to the play as 'one of the most sublime, and in every respect most consummate works of art human effort has ever brought forth'. His lectures on the history of philosophy, delivered between 1819 and 1830, invoke the heroine, 'the heavenly Antigone, that noblest of figures that ever appeared on earth'. Throughout the 1840s, these sentiments abound. Friedrich Hebbel, who regarded his own play *Agnes Bernauer* as 'an *Antigone* for modern times', described Sophocles' tragedy as 'das Meisterstück der Meisterstücke dem sich bei Alten und Neueren Nichts an die Seite setzen lässt' ('the masterpiece of masterpieces, next to which there is nothing that can be set either old or new'). This verdict occurs in Hebbel's essay 'Mein Wort über das Drama!' of 1843, and he may or may not have been aware of Hegel's influential judgement. It is unlikely that Thomas de Quincey was, when he wrote his lengthy review of 'The Antigone of Sophocles as Represented on the Edinburgh Stage' (1846), but the tone is no less ecstatic. Everlastingly, this play 'wears the freshness of morning dew'. No other Greek drama 'towers into such affecting grandeur'; this despite the fact that 'the austerity of the tragic passion is disfigured by a love episode'. As to the persona of Antigone:

Holy heathen, daughter of God before God was known, flower from Paradise after Paradise was closed . . . idolatrous yet Christian lady, that in the spirit of martyrdom trodst alone the yawning billows of the grave, flying from earthly hopes, lest everlasting despair should settle upon the grave of thy brother.

Dissenting notes were few. Matthew Arnold had published his 'Fragment of an "Antigone"' in 1849. But in the 1853 Preface to the first edition of his poems, Arnold ruled that 'An action like the action of the Antigone of Sophocles, which turns upon the conflict between the heroine's duty to her brother's corpse and that to the laws of her country, is no longer one in which it is possible that we should feel a deep interest'. George Eliot, in the inward fabric of whose *Middlemarch* the figure of Antigone was to play so subtle and formative a role, riposted. Arnold had misread the meaning of the play. The conflict staged by Sophocles was of a timeless urgency. It dramatized clashes of private conscience and public welfare of a nature and seriousness inseparable from the historical, social condition of man. Indeed, George Eliot read the Sophoclean text as possessing an insistent closeness to her own most absolute concerns. The Greek play enacts 'that struggle between elemental tendencies and established laws by which the outer life of man is gradually and painfully brought into harmony with his inward needs'. When Cosima Wagner recorded in her journal for 18 June 1869 that the Master had designated Sophocles' *Antigone* as 'the incomparable *par excellence*', such assessment was conventional. Hofmannsthal's 'Vorspiel zur Antigone des Sophokles', a verse-prologue to a production of the play in Berlin in 1900, crowns a century of ecstatic vision:

> Dies strahlende Geschöpf ist keines Tages!
> Sie hat einmal gesiegt und sieget fort.
> Da ich sie sehe, kräuselt sich mein Fleisch
> wie Zunder unter einem Feuerwind:
> mein Unvergängliches rührt sich in mir:
> aus den Geschöpfen tritt ihr tiefstes Wesen
> heraus und kreiset funkelnd um mich her:
> ich bin der schwesterlichen Seele nah,
> ganz nah, die Zeit versank, von den Abgründen
> des Lebens sind die Schleier weggezogen ...

> (This radiant being belongs to no given time!
> She has vanquished once and continues to be victorious.
> As I look upon her, my flesh quivers
> as does tinder under a fire-wind:
> that which is imperishable within me is roused:
> from these beings their deepest essence steps forward
> and circles about me luminously:

I am near to the sisterly soul,
very near, time has sunk away, from the abysses
of life, the veils are drawn away . . .)

And in a curiously Mosaic trope, Hofmannsthal sees Antigone as one before whom the 'translucent, frozen waves of life step back in reverence':

> Sie geht durch eine Ebbe. Links und rechts
> tritt in durchsichtigen erstarrten Wogen
> das Leben ehrfürchtig vor ihr zurück!

Encomia and invocations continue after the turn of the century. In the *Alcione* of 1904, d'Annunzio turns to

> Antigone dall'anima di luce,
> Antigone dagli occhi di viola . . .
>
> ('Antigone of the lit soul,
> Antigone of the violet eyes')

Charles Péguy's 'Note sur M. Bergson' (1914) remarks in passing that 'for a semi-chorus from the *Antigone* I would give the three *Critiques* and a half-quarto of *Prolegomena*' (by Kant). In the summer of 1927, André Gide is rereading a number of Greek tragedies. He notes in his diary that nothing more beautiful has been written 'in any literature' than Aeschylus' *Prometheus* and the *Antigone*. But after 1905, and under pressure of Freudian reference, critical, interpretative focus had shifted to the *Oedipus Rex*.

Sophocles' *Antigone* had held pride of place in poetic and philosophic judgement for over a century. Why this predilection?

There is no ready answer. If adaptations and translations of the play go back to the 1530s, the same is true of other Greek tragedies. In his fragmentary biography of Sophocles, a compendium of standard *vitae* (1760), Lessing attributes no particular pre-eminence to *Antigone*. In his *Hamburgische Dramaturgie* (1767–9), Sophocles is passed over altogether. There are more than thirty operas on the Antigone theme known to have been composed between Alessandro Scarlatti's *Creonte* of 1699 and Francesco Basili's *Antigona* exactly one hundred years later. But operas on antique tragic themes were legion and there are no 'Antigones' in the western European theatres, certainly from the early eighteenth century to the time of the French Revolution. Strikingly, no painting on any motif in the Antigone legend is exhibited in the annual Paris *salons* between 1753 and 1789. Yet shortly thereafter, Sophocles' text and the figure of Antigone have become talismanic to the European spirit.

Mutations of this kind can spring from contingent, even casual occasion. Now unread, the Abbé Jean-Jacques Barthélémy's *Le Voyage du jeune Anacharsis* (1788) is one of the major works in the history of European taste.[1] This pedagogic fantasy, with its moralistic–topographical reconstruction of post-Periclean Greece through the rapt eyes of a young traveller, was the source of much of Romantic Hellenism and of the philhellenic policies and illusions of the nineteenth century. In chapter XI, the hero is taken to see his first Attic tragedy. It is Sophocles' *Antigone* and the young Anacharsis is overwhelmed: 'Quel merveilleux assortiment d'illusions & de réalités! Je volois au secours des deux amants . . . Trente mille spectateurs, fondant en larmes, redoubloient mes émotions & mon ivresse' ('What a marvellous composite of illusions and realities! I flew to the help of the two lovers . . . Dissolving in tears, thirty thousand spectators redoubled my emotions and my ecstasy'). There follows a substantial citation from Antigone's mortal lament and adieu. Other, more 'recent' and imaginary dramas are being staged, but Anacharsis 'has no more tears to shed, no more attention to give'. This is, I believe, the seminal passage in the Antigone vogue. We find it echoed for a hundred years.

The second decisive hazard was that of the simultaneous presence in the theological seminary at Tübingen, the *Stift*, of Hegel, Hölderlin, and Schelling. Hegel and Hölderlin were fellow-students and intimates from 1789 to late 1793. Schelling, five years their junior but already an academic prodigy, joined them in 1790. The complicity of ideals, the reciprocity of heuristic energies, which marked the intimacy of these three young men, were to have an effect on European thought and sensibility which it is not easy to exaggerate. Enthusiasts for the French Revolution, in its dawn stages, acolytes of Kantian Idealism as seen through the eyes of Schiller's poetry and aesthetic essays, equally determined to

[1] Cf. M. Badolle, *L'Abbé Jean-Jacques Barthélémy (1716–1795) et l'Hellénisme en France dans la seconde moitié du XVIIIe siècle* (Paris, 1927), 180–216, 328, 341–70.

restore to the enlightened soul what Hölderlin called 'that golden age of truth and of beauty which was Greece', Hegel, Hölderlin, and Schlegel turned to identical imperatives and models of radiance.[1] We cannot reconstruct the exact motions of symbiosis, but Hölderlin's cult of Sophocles and Schelling's conviction that tragedy was the essential discourse of being probably derived, in the first instance, from Hegel. As early as July 1787, Hegel had attempted to translate Sophocles, notably the *Oedipus at Colonus*. This text would refer him to the incomparable pathos of Antigone. He communicated the vital aura of this encounter to his two companions in ardour. Even across subsequent polemics and silences, the *Antigone* was to remain a bond between the three men. Severally, they were to set it at the pivot of consciousness.

The third cause of the *Antigone* predominance may well have been one of theatrical history. Goethe's presentation of the play, in Johann Friedrich Rochlitz's infirm and truncated version in 1808 and 1809, was no great success. But that staged on 28 October 1841 proved a triumph and a landmark. Directed by Ludwig Tieck, the choruses set to music by Mendelssohn, J. J. Chr. Donner's translation of Sophocles was acclaimed as the first authentic re-creation of classical Greek tragedy in modern Europe. *Pace* Heine's acerbic sniping in 'Der Neue Alexander', the 'Mendelssohn' *Antigone*, with its attempts at antique costumes and choreography, swept Europe. Less than a year after the Potsdam première, the play was mounted in Berlin. Paris followed suit in 1844, making of *Antigone* the first Greek drama to be produced in antique style on the French national stage. London and Edinburgh came next. We know from the recollections of the eminent Orientalist and mythologist Max Müller that throughout the 1840s the Mendelssohn choruses from the *Antigone* were a staple of family and amateur chorales. It was this production which gave impetus to the numerous poetic, philosophic discussions of the play (some already quoted) around the mid-

---

[1] The literature on this triad of genius is voluminous. Cf. E. Staiger, *Der Geist der Liebe und das Schicksal. Schelling, Hegel und Hölderlin* (Leipzig, 1935); M. Leube, 'Die geistige Lage im Stift in den Tagen der französischen Revolution', *Blätter für Württembergische Kirchengeschichte*, NF xxxix (1935); despite numerous errata, F. G. Nauen, *Revolution, Idealism and Human Freedom. Schelling, Hölderlin and Hegel and the Crisis of Early German Idealism* (The Hague, 1971); and O. Pöggeler, 'Sinclair–Hölderlin– Hegel', *Hegel-Studien*, viii (1973).

century. Similarly, what scholars have called a 'veritable cult of Sophocles' in France in the closing years of the century reflects a celebrated staging of the Oedipus–Antigone cycle in the Roman theatre at Orange in August 1894. Yet in both cases the theatrical fact is as much a product as a cause. The singular aura of *Antigone* in German metaphysics and poetics predates the Mendelssohn version by half a century; and the sanctification of Sophocles in French schooling and ethical–political reference gathers strength already ten years before Mounet-Sully's and Julia Bartel's legendary performances (Péguy was in the spellbound audience).[1]

Agencies more radical, more diffuse, were at work. To guess at these is, almost certainly, to get values and connections wrong. Analytic accounts of the history of feeling (*histoire des mentalités* is the more exact term) are fictions of logic after the fact. But conjectures are worth making—if only to honour Lessing's sovereign distinction between the inert assemblage of information and the elicitation of the vital lineaments of a phenomenon.

The rhetoric, the programmatic mythologies, and ceremonials of the French Revolution addressed themselves, also, to the status of women. Women are to assume those hallowed burdens of civic presence, those duties and licences of public utterance, which the *ancien régime* has denied them. The rights of man, as 1789 voiced them, are, emphatically, the rights of women. Even domesticity and the routines of the nursery are to be recognized and rewarded as instrumental to the health, to the historical fortunes of the nation-state. The exploitation and trivialization of eros which characterize the economic injustice and licentiousness of the old order are to be eradicated. From *libertinage* the legislators of 1789 and of 1793 are resolved to recuperate the lost stem, *liberté*. The presiding images are those of Lacedaemonian women, 'companions in arms' to their heroic husbands, or of the matrons of republican Rome, Brutus' and Cato's equals. The supposition, therefore, lies at hand that the programme of feminine emancipation and political parity between the sexes professed by the French Revolution and its Utopian or pragmatic sympathizers across Europe made of *Antigone* an emblematic text. And the lives of certain women do seem to bear out this resonance: witness

[1] Cf. S. Fraisse, *Péguy et le monde antique* (Paris, 1973), 64–6.

Madame Roland, Mary Wollstonecraft, Madame de Staël. There were, indeed, isolated comparisons drawn between Antigone's bold folly and that of Charlotte Corday, avenging assassin of Marat.

But the evidence is thin and, on balance, contradictory. The rhetoric of liberation was sonorous; the practice almost wholly conservative. Where the status of women in respect of certain legal and social dependencies was amended, this occurred within the general context of humane reform. Paradoxically, the constraints on feminine behaviour and intellectual nurture, imposed by the Napoleonic system and the ethos of the nineteenth-century mercantile bourgeoisie, were more stringent than those of the Hanoverian and Bourbon dispensation. Except at the sacrificial, terrorist fringe, as in certain small Russian revolutionary covens, where the figure of Antigone does play a symbolic part, young women hardly figure in nineteenth-century politics or political debate. The delicate but uncompromising domestication of female courage, of female initiative and acumen central to Manzoni's *I Promessi Sposi*, is fully representative. Thus there is the suspicion that the exaltation of Sophocles' heroine after 1790 is, in some degree, a surrogate for reality. Philosophers, poets, political thinkers acclaim an act of feminine grandeur and echo the affirmation of certain feminine principles over civic power and expediency. But they do so *en fausse situation*: in the knowledge, remorseful and/or complacent, that the contract offered in 1789 has not been observed at all or only marginally. Antigone belongs, hauntingly but safely, to the idiom of the ideal.

Yet, in a larger focus, the French Revolution *is*, one feels, key. More than any other surviving Greek tragedy, except for the *Bacchae* of Euripides—a text which, despite commentaries by Gilbert Murray and E. R. Dodds, continues to be radically reinterpreted and revalued, notably since the 1960s— Sophocles' *Antigone* dramatizes the meshing of intimate and public, of private and historical existence. It is the historicization of the personal which is the commanding truth and legacy of the French Revolution. There is a sense, though histrionic, in which the promulgation of a new calendar, the nomination of a Year One to mark the *incipit*, the *novum* of the human condition, was defensible. Time *had* changed. The inner temporalities, the orderings of remembrance, momentariness, and, above all, of futurity by virtue of which we compose our grasp of self, had altered. Goethe's observation of this formidable discontinuity at the occasion of the battle of Valmy, the closely argued metamorphic relations between the Revolution and the new densities of personal time in Wordsworth's *Prelude*, are famous evidence. But there is scarcely a recorded life or body of experience in the 1790s, in the Napoleonic era, in the decades of explosive urbanization, technological change, and social challenge that followed, which does not bear witness to the irruption of the political into the private. The uniformed marauders of history broke into Blake's garden. Napoleon and his staff passed under Hegel's window, as in a whirlwind, in the dawn hours before the battle of Iena. It was the very moment (October 1806) in which Hegel was completing the manuscript of the *Phenomenology*. The concatenation gives to that book, to the theory of personal consciousness in and through history expounded throughout the argument, and to Hegel's enigmatic conviction that Iena signified the 'end of the historical', the authority of felt meaning. Stendhal's novels are a single reflection of and on the new immersion of the private individual in historical extremity. Every man and woman who had known the Terror or who was to witness the coming of the modern factory, every man who had marched from Corunna to Moscow and back, carried the burn of history in his or her humble bones. By contrast, it is nearly a definition of the *ancien régime* that direct engagement with the historical–political sphere and the self-expression which such engagement compels had been the perquisite of the mighty and the professionals. As Goethe and Carnot saw, it was not only the great armies of the Revolution and of the nineteenth century that were mobilized by the *levées en masse*: it was European man.

In *Antigone* the dialectic of intimacy and of exposure, of the 'housed' and of the most public, is made explicit. The play turns on the enforced politics of the private spirit, on the necessary violence which political–social change visits on the unspeaking inwardness of being. At the hinge between the nineteenth and twentieth centuries, Yeats turns to *Antigone* because his own person, his poetry, his public ways, are charged with this mortal interplay. After 1789, the individual knows no armistice with political history. 'A terrible beauty is

born' or, more frequently, a terrible ugliness. In its articulation
of both, Sophocles' tragedy seemed matchless.

The motive for this articulation is sorority. Of all creatures
earthly or feigned, Antigone possesses the 'most sisterly of souls'
(Goethe's invocation of her in his 'Euphrosyne Hymn' of
1799). She incarnates sisterhood. The opening, untranslatable
line of the play compacts the final essence of identity, of human
relation, into sisterliness. In doing so, it foreshadows and
underwrites a perception of priorities at the core of Idealism
and Romanticism.

The theme is so vast as to rebuke summary. It pervades the
psychology, the letters (*belles-lettres*), the personal rhetoric of
the late eighteenth and nineteenth centuries. The subtlest
epiphany, the epilogue to the *figura* of woman as sister, to the
persuasion that the love between brother and sister is at once
the heart's heart and the transcendence of the erotic, is set out
in Musil's *The Man Without Qualities*. This finale takes its
authority, by explicit ingathering and echo, from more than a
hundred years of speculative obsession. Material abounds at
the biographical and expressive surface. In its early and major
phases Wordsworth's poetry, the innovations of phenomenal
awareness which organize this poetry, are the immediate yield
of a symbiotic duality. As often as not, the poem is the arrest
and notation of Dorothy Wordsworth's sensory flashes. The
prodigal complexity of Wordsworth's coming into being grows
from a brother–sister intimacy so profound as to comport—the
poems, the journals make this manifest—a near-fusion of
identities. Shelley's 'I am not thine: I am a part of *thee*'
precisely states the condition. Charles Lamb's relation to his
sister, Hegel's, Macaulay's intimacy with his sisters, are of a
vehemence, of a quality of tragic need which reduce all other
kinships, familial or conjugal, to a minor key. Throughout his
staged life and works, Byron intimates the centrality of desire,
of psychic correspondence between brother and sister. The
Gothic novel and melodrama make a cliché of brother–sister
incest. So do high literature and art and those haunting
intermediary modes—the verse and tales of Poe—in which
popular, mendacious forms take on the light of esoteric vision.
Shelley's 'Revolt of Islam' turns on the passion of brother for
sister. His 'Epipsychidion' defines the sorority of ardent souls
as the paradigm of all love, the Platonic and gnostic *amorosa*

idea which either leaves behind the raptures of wedded union
or gives to these their true character:

> Would we two had been twins of the same mother!
> Or, that the name my heart lent to another
> Could be a sister's bond for her and thee,
> Blending the beams of one eternity!

In Wagner's *Ring*, the mystery of psychic recognition and
mutual identification which knits brother to sister in Hagen's
black house, the consummation of this mystery prior to the
dawn of death, literally frees the energies of the world:

> Die bräutliche Schwester
> befreite der Bruder;
> zertrümmert liegt,
> was je sie getrennt;
> jauchzend grüsset sich
> das junge Paar;
> vereint sind Liebe und Lenz!

> (The sister-bride
> is freed by the brother;
> what kept them apart
> now lies in ruins;
> the young couple
> greet one another in delight;
> Love and Spring are united!)

Moreover, only one born of the union of brother and sister can
bring on the twilight of the gods which is also the morning of
man (only he can, in Hegelian terms, close history).

The existential and literary–artistic documentation is massive. It is also deceptive. So many biographies and fictions, from
*c.*1780 to 1914—the moment at which Musil locates his great
coda—direct us towards incest. Consequently, the exaltation
of sisterliness has been seen in this pathological perspective.[1]
Much of the thinking that needs to be done about this
phenomenological crux has stopped at the level of anecdote
and prurience. We have no worthwhile evidence as to the
actuality or frequency of incest in Idealist and Romantic lives,
let alone in society at large. Where such evidence is proffered

[1] Otto Rank's *Das Inzest-Motiv in Dichtung und Sage* (2nd edn., Vienna and Leipzig,
1926) remains the standard compendium. Cf. also M. Praz, *The Romantic Agony* (2nd
edn., London, 1970).

(as in the case of Byron), it is doubly suspect. The pressure of
meaning which attaches to Shelley's trope, 'Sister-Spouse', is of
an entirely different order. No literalism, no psychoanalytic
labelling, will elucidate the utter seriousness, the period-magic
of Baudelaire's call to 'mon enfant, ma sœur' ('my child, my
sister'). But it is just this magic and this seriousness, irrelevant
as they may be to Sophocles' meaning, which must be grasped
if we are to make sense of the special lustre of *Antigone* in
nineteenth-century feeling.

The co-ordinates of Idealism are exile and attempted
homecoming. Thus the epistemology of Kant is one of stoic
severance. Subject is severed from object; perception from
cognition. Even the imperative of freedom is promulgated at a
distance. Western metaphysics after Kant stems from the
negation of this distance or from any attempt to overcome it.
In Fichte the negation is made absolute: subject and object are
one. In Schelling (as in Schiller and Hölderlin) truth and
beauty are equated. This radiant tautology invites man, via
the conceptual imagination, to grasp, to internalize, the
principle of perfect oneness. The pulverization of the world
into discrete fragments is a phenomenological illusion. Where
it participates in truth–beauty, the individual spirit comes
home to a long-lost but primal unity. Hegel seizes upon the
forbidding dualism in Kant's ethics and model of perception;
he identifies the stasis inherent in aesthetic Idealism. His
dialectic is one of process, of the deployment and self-
realization of consciousness in and through history. But here
also the teleology is homeward bound: towards that synthesis
and 'end of history' when Spirit shall have harvested to itself
the dynamic, errant splinters of totality. (Nothing is more
taxing for the modern reader than to seek to recapture the
substantive intensity, the almost carnal presentness which
these abstract terms carry for the thinkers and poets of the
Revolutionary period and nineteenth century. But it is precisely this lived concreteness in philosophic debate and critique
which makes Idealist thought elemental to Romantic art and
poetry. The fusion is as vital to Coleridge and Shelley as it is to
Hölderlin.)

The causes of exile, of the scission of the subject from the
world, are arguable. Throughout Idealist speculation, there
are more or less open variants on Rousseau's postulate of man's

fall from a state of nature, from the sensory immediacy which is the innocence of intellect. The Hegelian intuition of a lost at-homeness in existence, of a necessary voyage through alienation and self-division, is graphic but, logically, indeterminate. At certain stages in the argument, the source of estrangement seems historical—some secular parallel to the theological fall. At other points, and more challengingly, self-exile seems implicit in the life of consciousness, in the capacities of the human ego to think 'outside' and 'against' itself, to perceive itself in an adversary mode. The great tragic current of 'exilic' sentiment after Kant is summarized in Heidegger's image of man as 'a stranger in the house of Being'. To this current, the entire Marxist critique of classic individualism is a consequent footnote.

To some Romantics, 'sublation' (Hegel's *Aufhebung*) from the condition of banishment out of the vital unity of being, seemed possible in moments of illumination. Because he is a compulsive seeker after such moments, soliciting the lightning-bolt, the poet, says Hölderlin, is the 'homecomer' *par excellence* and the most vulnerable of mortals. The early deaths, the madness, which ambush so many lives in the Romantic generations, are the price of the poet's impatient odyssey. Another homecoming, though only provisional and immanent, is that of intimacy with another human being, of the rare break out of the solitary confinement of the ego into the total acceptance of or, rather, 'accepting totality' of another. No philosophic tradition surpasses the wealth and nuance of Idealist reflection on friendship (Schiller's 'eines Freundes Freund zu sein' ['to be the Friend of a Friend']). None examines more insistently the unstable wonder of elective intimacy and the knife-edge between the trust of friendship and the final trust of hatred. Kant's ethical prescript as to the absolute valuation which one human being must assign to another, Fichte's heroic epistemological struggle with the 'counter-presence' of other selves and the paradoxical necessity of this presence to any intelligible system of freedom and society, Hegel's famous dramaturgy of the achievement of self through agonistic encounter with 'the other'—all are derived from the axiom of aloneness and the hope that this axiom can be, partially, rescinded. The cult of friendship in Romantic lives and literature is a direct echo.

But the epistemology and its emotional correlate are suspect. As Hegel insists, the roots of exile, of self-division, are internal. They are a fatal constant of self-consciousness. It is to ourselves that we are strangers. However absolute the empathy which knits friend to friend, however symbiotic and self-sacrificial the uses of amity—as they are enacted in the theme of Utopian conspiracy so frequent in Romantic poetry and drama—there can be no true homecoming to the self through another. Montaigne's definition of friendship, 'parce que c'était lui, parce que c'était moi' ('because it was he, because it was I'), keeps its distance. In this, it is the counterpart to the Idealist ontology of fusion. Rigorously considered, such fusion, such re-entry of the self into 'at-oneness with the world', is the ingathering of Narcissus. Fichte is stringent enough to see this. So, in the humorous vein, is Byron when, in 'Don Juan', he descants on Romantic 'egoism' and 'egotism' as categories of self-love. Is there, then, no escape from the haunted solipsism, from the *conscience malheureuse*, of post-Kantian, alienated man?

The Romantic answer is an apocalypse of desire, an erotic consummation so complete that it annuls the autism of personal identity:

> Du Isolde,
> Tristan ich,
> nicht mehr Tristan,
> nicht Isolde;
> ohne Nennen,
> ohne Trennen,
> neu Erkennen,
> neu Entbrennen;
> endlos ewig
> ein-bewusst . . .

> (Isolde you,
> Tristan I,
> no longer Tristan,
> not Isolde;
> without naming,
> without parting,
> new recognition,
> new consuming;
> endless everlasting
> single-consciousness . . .)

But this solution too is imperfect. The logic of the equation is that of death. It is the morbid facility of this resolution which vulgarizes Romantic art even at its apex, in Keats, in Baudelaire. The philosophic objections are even graver. Self-annulment is not self-realization (only Schopenhauer will hold it to be so, hence Wagner's adoption of Schopenhauer's doctrine). Apocalyptic eroticism is not a homecoming of and to the self, but a kind of final dispersal, a dissemination of the ego—however compacted the act of love, however unitary—to the *bufèra*, the whirlwind in which Dante encloses lovers. Indeed, the more ecstatic the self-surrender, the more acid are the mechanics of self- and of reciprocal corrosion. We yield of ourselves essential moral and perceptual components. We take into ourselves the 'otherness' of the beloved, but this incorporation is only falsely analogous with the mystery of incarnation. It is in fact a deeper estrangement and fragmentation in the centre of being. Kierkegaard is the incomparable diagnostician of these 'intimate alienations'. Contrary to what is superficially supposed, the Idealist critique of the human person is anti-Platonist. The *Symposium* views eros as a transition to oneness; Idealist psychology sees it as a barrier.

Now we are at the nub of the dialectic. There is only *one* human relationship in which the ego can negate its solitude without departing from its authentic self. There is only *one* mode of encounter in which the self meets the self in another, in which ego and non-ego, the Kantian, the Fichtean, the Hegelian polarities, are made one. It is a relation between man and woman, as it surely must be if primary rifts in being are to be knit. But it is a relation between man and woman which resolves the paradox of estrangement inherent in all sexuality (a paradox which incest would only enforce). It is the relation of brother and sister, of sister and brother. In the love, in the perfect understanding of brother and sister, there is eros and ἀγάπη. But both are *aufgehoben*, 'sublated', in φιλία, to the transcendent absoluteness of relation itself. It is here, and here only, that the soul steps into and through the mirror to find a perfectly concordant but autonomous counterpart. The torment of Narcissus is stilled: the image is substance, it is the integral self in the twin presence of another. Thus sisterliness is ontologically privileged beyond any other human stance. In it, the homecomings of Idealism and Romanticism are given vital form. This form receives supreme, everlasting expression in Sophocles' *Antigone*.

Between the 1790s and the start of the twentieth century, the radical lines of kinship run horizontally, as between brothers and sisters. In the Freudian construct they run vertically, as between children and parents. The Oedipus complex is one of inescapable verticality. The shift is momentous; with it Oedipus replaces Antigone. As we saw, it can be dated *c.*1905. But it is the earlier paradigm which concerns us now.

A fourth, presumably minor, motive suggests itself for the *Antigone* predominance. The subject of live burial harrows and enthralls late-eighteenth- and early-nineteenth-century imaginings. It is ubiquitous throughout Gothic fiction and theatre; it is common in the graphic arts and in high and low verse and prose-fantasy (again, Poe stands representatively at the meeting-point of these currents). But the topic also turns up, sometimes obsessively, in scientific and philosophic speculation.[1] One is tempted to make larger connections. Does the motif of the entombment of living persons codify an awareness of arbitrary judicial power? Is it, in other words, a fictional correlative to the facts of imprisonment in the convents and Bastilles of the old order? The iconography of July–August 1789, with its depictions of the emergence into daylight of the 'long-buried' victims of royal, ecclesiastical, and familial relegation, certainly suggests this overlap. But an altogether different context may also have been instrumental. It is that of the almost hysterical interest of both educated and popular levels of society, from the 1760s to the close of the nineteenth century, in so-called galvanic phenomena of nervous and muscular 'reanimation', in Mesmerism, in extra-sensory contacts with the departed. The dread of being sepulchred alive may relate to complex uncertainties as to the determination and finality of decease, to widespread intimations of psychic energies still active after clinical demise and burial. The cat's-cradle of meaning and sensibility is one which historians of thought and of letters have not, until now, unravelled satisfactorily. But there is no doubt that it concentrates diverse, deep-seated strands of feeling. These are unforgettably drama-

---

[1] Cf. M. Patak, 'Die Angst vor dem Scheintod in der zweiten Hälfte des 18. Jahrhunderts' (Dissertation submitted to the Faculty of Medicine of the University of Zurich [Q. 80. Z.], 1967).

tized in Sophocles' play and in the whole Antigone myth. Here was classical sanction for a present concern. Antigone's descent into living death spoke to Revolutionary and Romantic generations with an immediacy rivalled only by the finale of *Romeo and Juliet*. Comparison of the two plays in respect of the entombment motif are frequent.

But even if we add up the occasional and the internally crucial factors which I have listed, the status accorded to Sophocles' *Antigone* during more than a century of European thought and literature remains challenging. Why did Barthélémy choose just this tragedy for seminal reference? Why did Shelley, Hegel, Hebbel see in the mythical persona of Antigone the 'highest presence' to have entered the world of men? What intention attaches to the repeated hints (in de Quincey, in Kierkegaard, they are more than hints) that Antigone is to be understood as a counterpart to Christ, as God's child and messenger before Revelation? Complete answers elude us. Only the judgement of supremacy is clear. From it arise some of the most radically transformative interpretations and 're-experiencings' ever elicited by a literary text. It is four of these, comprised between the 1790s and the 1840s, which I want to look at now.

2

Hegel's prose does offer difficulties of a peculiar sort. Much of the work after the *Phenomenology* has come down to us in the form of lecture-notes imperfectly taken. A good many of the texts which precede 1807, on the other hand, were not meant for publication. They embody juvenilia, sketches, rough drafts, and fragments of self-address. Their publication is a result of posthumous glory. Yet it is these early, essentially private writings which are now regarded as vital to an understanding of Hegel and subjected to exhaustive commentary. However, even if we had only those works which Hegel himself saw into print, the inhibitions to understanding would be real. The fragmentary character of the early texts, indeed of the *Phenomenology* itself, together with the provisional, didactically self-revising format of the Berlin University lectures, are no biographical accident. Hegel's whole discourse enacts a refusal of fixity, of formal closure. This refusal is cardinal to his method and makes the notions of 'system' and of 'totality', customarily attached to Hegelianism, elusive. In Hegel, reflection and utterance are in constant motion on three levels: the metaphysical, the logical, and the psychological—the last of which encompasses the other two in so far as it seeks to make explicit the processes of consciousness which generate and structure metaphysical and logical operations. These three conceptual levels interpenetrate (this is the case at almost every point in Hegel's readings of *Antigone*). Hegel rigorously subverts the naïve linearities of common argument in order to communicate the simultaneities, often conflicting, and inward recursions or self-corrections of his proposals. But he did not have available to him those typographical and syntactical dislocations we are familiar with since Mallarmé. Hence the tension between vertical, 'chordal' compositions of meaning and the external conventions of an eighteenth- and early-nineteenth-century prose.

Yet, as we learn to trust Hegel's style, it takes on a paradoxical transparency. 'Hegel semble, en effet, avoir réussi *à se regarder penser* et même à noter, peut-être au fur et à mesure de leur déroulement, les étapes et les démarches successives de sa pensée' ('In effect, Hegel seems to have succeeded in *looking at himself thinking*, and even in registering, step by step, during the actual process of their development, the successive stages and motions of his thought').[1] This is an acute observation. But we can go further.

Hegel, and this is rare, was able to *think against himself*, and to observe and record himself doing so. The essence of Hegel's method and thought is self-polemic. Negation, sublation (*Aufhebung*) with its simultaneous reciprocities of dissolution, conservation, and augment, the coil and recoil of the dialectic mode, are the immediate theoretical instruments of Hegel's

---

[1] A. Koyré, 'Hégel à Iéna, in *Études d'histoire de la pensée philosophique* (Paris, 1971), 152 n. This essay first appeared in 1934. Together with the 'Note sur la langue et la terminologie hégélienne', first published in 1931 and also included in the *Études*, it constitutes the most enlightening discussion we have of the difficulties and virtues of Hegel's style. Cf. also T. W. Adorno, 'Skoteinos oder Wie zu lesen sei', *Drei Studien zu Hegel* (Frankfurt-on-Main, 1963), for a witty, subtle gloss on Hegel's fundamentally oral techniques of persuasion. In approaching the problem of how to read Hegel one cannot, particularly with reference to early writings, overlook a certain deliberate pride in opaqueness: 'Philosophy is by its nature something esoteric, neither made for the mob nor capable of being prepared for the mob,' wrote Hegel in 1802.

principle of adverse or 'counter-thought'. This principle is obsessively at work in Hegel's model of divided consciousness and alienation. Only Plato rivals Hegel as a dramatist and self-dramatist of meaning. But in the Platonic dialogues it is the tactics of argument which are dramatic rather than the substance. The latter can be, indeed it often has been, presented without its dialectic form. This is not so of Hegel. For Hegel, to think, to realize and articulate the dynamics of identity, is to 'think against'. It is to 'dramatize' in the root-sense of the verb, which is one of pure action. Spirit *is* action, proclaims the *Phenomenology*, action of an inherently agonistic or 'conflictual' kind. A sovereign passage from the Introduction to the *Lectures on the Philosophy of Religion* summarizes the dramatic–polemic ethos of Hegel's method:

Ich erhebe mich denkend zum Absoluten über alles Endliche und bin unendliches Bewusstsein und zugleich bin ich endliches Selbstbewusstsein und zwar nach meiner ganzen empirischen Bestimmung. Beide Seiten suchen sich und fliehen sich. Ich bin und es ist in mir für mich dieser Widerstreit und diese Einigung. Ich bin der Kampf. Ich bin nicht Einer der im Kampf Begriffenen, sondern ich bin beide Kämpfende und der Kampf selbst.

(Through thought, I raise myself to the Absolute above all finality; I am unbounded consciousness and at the same time I am finite self-consciousness, and this in accord with my whole empirical present-ness and constitution. Both sides seek each other and flee from each other. I am, and there is in me and for me, this mutual conflict and this unison. I am the combat. I am not one of the combatants; rather, I am both combatants and the combat itself.)

Given this ethos, drama, and tragic drama in particular, occupies a privileged place in the growth of Hegel's thought. A theory of tragedy is not an adjunct to Hegel's construct. It is a testing ground and validation for main tenets of Hegel's historicism, for the dialectical scenario of his logic, and for the central notion of consciousness in progressive conflict. Certain Greek tragedies, the *Antigone* pre-eminently, are as functional to the Hegelian thought-world as are certain expressionist lyric poems and the odes of Hölderlin to the ontology and language-mystique of Heidegger.[1]

[1] The secondary literature abounds in references to Hegel's views on tragedy. For the English-speaking reader, the best-known treatment is, of course, A. C. Bradley, 'Hegel's Theory of Tragedy' (first published in 1909), in *Oxford Lectures on Poetry*

Hegel's fascination with Sophocles dates back to an attempted translation of *Oedipus at Colonus* in the summer of 1787. But one cannot order in any neat temporal sequence the stages of reflection which lead to the first specific citation of *Antigone* in the late winter of 1795 or early spring of 1796. Hegel's nascent thought is a close weave in which multiple strands cross and recross synchronically.[1] Three main skeins or loops of argument bear on later readings of *Antigone*. Hegel's idealization of ancient Hellas is, as we saw, representative of his generation.[2] In one of the fragments composed while he was still at Tübingen, Hegel remarks on the 'schmerzliches Sehnen' ('the poignant, painful longing') which draws the modern soul to the remembrance of Greece. Only amid the 'happy people' of Periclean Athens were political liberty and religious faith concordant. This concordance was not abstract. The young Hegel insists on the singularly 'concrete' and 'immanent' quality of the Attic genius—an insistence in which are implicit the first moves in the Hegelian critique of Kant. The Greek πόλις will never signify for Hegel a contingent moment in human affairs. The ideal which the πόλις embodied, and the problem of the inadequacies or inherent self-destructiveness of

(London, 1950). This lecture, together with the principal discussions of tragedy in Hegel's writings, is available in Hegel, *On Tragedy*, edd. A. and H. Paolucci (New York, 1962). Cf. also L. A. McKay, 'Antigone, Coriolanus and Hegel', *Transactions of the American Philological Association*, xciii (1962); and O. Pöggeler, 'Hegel und die griechische Tragödie', *Hegel-Studien*, Beiheft 1 (1964).

[1] The writings of the young Hegel are the object of an extensive industry of exegesis and revaluation. They have been made available to us by H. Nohl, *Hegels theologische Jugendschriften* (Tübingen, 1907); G. Lasson, *Hegels Schriften zur Politik und Rechtsphilosophie* (Leipzig, 1913); F. Rosenzweig, *Hegel und der Staat* (Munich and Berlin, 1920); J. Hoffmeister, *Dokumente zu Hegels Entwicklung* (Stuttgart, 1936). Among the most useful elucidations are the following: J. Stenzel, 'Hegels Auffassung der griechischen Philosophie', *Kleine Schriften zur griechischen Philosophie* (Darmstadt, 1956); A. Negri, *Stato e diritto nel giovane Hegel* (Padua, 1958); J. Taminiaux, 'La pensée esthétique du jeune Hegel', *Revue philosophique de Louvain*, lvi (1958); A. Massolo, *Prime ricerche di Hegel* (Urbino, 1959); A. T. B. Peperzak, *Le Jeune Hegel et la vision morale du monde* (The Hague, 1960); H.-G. Gadamer, 'Hegel und die antike Dialektik', *Hegel-Studien*, i (1961). A number of these monographs themselves contain bibliographies of further secondary material.

[2] Hegel's attitudes to Greek antiquity have been extensively studied. Cf. J. Hoffmeister, *Hegel und Hölderlin* (Tübingen, 1931); L. Sichirollo, 'Hegel und die griechische Welt. Nachleben der Antike und Entstehung der "Philosophie der Weltgeschichte"', *Hegel-Studien*, Beiheft 1 (1964); A. Banfi, *Incontro con Hegel* (Urbino, 1965); J. Glenn Gray, *Hegel and Greek Thought* (New York, 1941; 1968); J. d'Hondt (ed.), *Hegel et la pensée grecque* (Paris, 1974); D. Janicaud, *Hegel et le destin de la Grèce* (Paris, 1975).

this ideal, will persist at the core of Hegel's teachings. To ask philosophically is (as it will be for Heidegger, that great reader of Hegel) to ask of Minerva. But during the Berne period, and certainly in 1794–5, the Utopian–lyric image of Athens, which the young Hegel had shared with Hölderlin and Schelling, alters.

In early 1795, if Nohl's datings of the theological juvenilia are correct, Hegel perceives the contrarieties latent in what he had taken to be the Attic concordance of the political–civic and the religious–ritual spheres. At roughly this point, in a threefold, overlapping consideration of the life of Christ, of the persona of Socrates, and of the oligarchic conditions of government in Berne, Hegel is possessed, to use Lukács's striking phrase, by 'the contradictoriness of being itself'.[1] He now labours to resolve this contradictoriness or, more exactly, to activate it into productive tension. In a text written at the beginning of 1795, Hegel designates religion as 'the nurse' of free men and the state as 'their mother'. It is in this specific context, in Nohl's fragment 222, that Sophocles' *Antigone* is first invoked. But the duality between religion and state is itself the consequence of an earlier alienation. There is, as Rousseau had seen, a tragic, though necessary and progressive, mechanism of rupture in the origins of the body politic: that of man's 'Entzweiung mit der Natur' ('scission from nature'). It is this estrangement which contains the source of ethical positivity. *Contra* Fichte, Hegel argues for the fundamentally social condition of the integral human individual, for the vanity of moral self-fulfilment in isolation from a social–civic fabric of values and options. Against Kant, Hegel is beginning to emphasize the concrete historicity and 'collective' character of the ethical choices which the individual is compelled to make, a compulsion which divides and, therefore, advances consciousness on its teleological path. Rosenzweig assigns this phase in Hegel's development to the Frankfurt period, 1796–1800. He points to the influence of Montesquieu and to Hegel's strained attempts to combine a qualified Kantian idealism with a 'Jacobin–absolutist' model of the nation-state.[2] Shortly before the decisive move to Iena, in 1800, Hegel makes yet

[1] G. Lukács, *Der junge Hegel* (first published in 1948; now vol. viii of the *Werke* [Neuwied and Berlin, 1976]), 494.
[2] Cf. F. Rosenzweig, *Hegel und der Staat*, p. 114.

another attempt at dynamic conciliation. Man can attain no
authentic ethical and self-conscious posture outside the state.
But the latter is a 'thought totality', a totality conceived and
inhabited by the intellect, almost in the sense of Kant's
praktische Vernunft ('practical reason or understanding').
Religion, on the other hand, derives its vitality from the
human imagination, 'als ein lebendiges, von der Phantasie
dargestellt' ('as a living presence, represented by fantasy').
There need be no conflict.

Interwoven with these concerns, in chronologically opaque
fragments, are the germs of a theory of tragedy. One of these,
which will become vital when we come to Kierkegaard's
'counter-Hegelian' Antigone, relates to the figure of Abraham.
Abraham has cut himself off from his homeland, from his
kindred, from nature itself. His monotheism is alienation and
the blind acceptance of dictates whose moral imperative and
rationale is wholly, inaccessibly external to himself (again,
there is here a polemic against Kant). Judaism incarnates this
abandonment of man's inmost 'to an alien transcendence'. It
is, in consequence, the antithesis to the Greek ideal of 'unison
with life'. In particular, Abraham's concept of destiny is
antithetical to that of the ancient Greeks (fragments 371–2 in
Nohl's edition). It is a destiny which comports the pathos of
sterile alienation, not the essential fruitfulness of tragedy.
Hence the arresting fact that Judaic sensibility, with its
millennial immersion in suffering, does not produce tragic
drama.

The latter hinges on certain particular, Hellenic conceptions of *Gesetz* ('law') and *Strafe* ('punishment'), conceptions
grounded in the uniquely agonistic relation of Athenian man
to himself, to nature, and to the gods. It is in the period from
1797 to late 1799, in such fragments as N. 280 and N. 393, that
a theory of tragedy is incipient. It is to μοῖρα, with its dynamic
impersonality but existential immanence, that Hegel seems to
attach the paradoxical but decisive category of 'fated guilt', of
an order of culpability in and through which an individual
(the tragic hero) comes wholly into his own—comes home
fatally to himself without relinquishing, as does the Jewish
sufferer, his at-oneness with life. Hegel ponders Sophocles,
Hölderlin's early experiments in tragic form, Shakespeare's
Macbeth, and the treatment of the collision between familial

bonds and civic ritual in Goethe's *Iphigenie*. It is difficult to schematize successive moments or motifs in Hegel's thought at this stage. The principal points are these: all conflict entails division and self-division. Conflict and collision are necessary attributes of the deployment of individual and public identity. But as 'life' cannot, finally, divide itself, as unity is the goal of authentic being, conflict causes tragic guilt. For a time (the notion dates back to Berne), Hegel seems to suggest that this inevitable culpability can be transcended by 'die schöne Seele' ('the beauteous soul'), of which Christ or Hölderlin's Hyperion are exemplary. In the 'beauteous soul', conflict and suffering even unto death do not comport an alienation from existential unity. But Hegel soon relinquishes this suggestion. If it is to find self-realization, human consciousness, certainly in the 'heroic' and, therefore, historically representative man or woman, must first pass 'par ce crépuscule du matin qu'est la conscience malheureuse' ('through that morning twilight which is the unhappy conscience and consciousness').[1] In doing so, it will risk, indeed it will assure, its own ruin. In the midst of 'the silence of the oracles and the chill of the statues rises the voice of tragedy'.[2] But such ruin is instrumental in the preservation and animation of the equilibrium between religion and state. It is an indispensable moment in the self-realization of Spirit in history. Though in a more tentative formulation, these appear to be the lineaments of a theory of tragedy as Hegel sketches it immediately before and during the start of his Iena period. Almost self-evidently, they point to Aeschylus' *Eumenides*.

It is, in fact, this play which Hegel refers to in his first more extensive text on tragedy. The passage is to be found in the treatise *Ueber die wissenschaftliche Behandlung des Naturrechts* of 1802.[3] It is of extreme obscurity. It seems to reflect that 'apocalyptic sense of contemporary events' which Rosenzweig ascribes to Hegel's thought between 1800 and Napoleon's temporary destruction of Prussia in 1806. The fundamental issue is plain enough: it is that of the possibility and nature of the dynamics of mediation as between the individual and the nation-state. Kant and Schelling had remained in the

---

[1] J. Wahl, *Le Malheur de la conscience dans la philosophie de Hegel* (Paris, 1929), 188.
[2] Ibid. 67.
[3] G. Lasson (ed.), *Hegels Schriften zur Politik und Rechtsphilosophie*, pp. 384–5.

idealized, inert sphere of universalized legalism. But by 1801, in
the *Schrift ueber die Reichsverfassung*, Hegel had come to identify
the highest human freedom with the most comprehensive and
organic form of civic community ('die höchste Gemeinschaft').
But this identification also entailed a polemic, agonistic, self-
divisive relation between man as a 'state-being' (*staatlich*) and
as a 'burgher' or citizen-bourgeois with essentially familial,
economic, and self-conservative motivations. How is the
philosopher, the thinker of dialectical totality, to integrate
these two axes of being? He does so by looking to Greek
tragedy, in which both the conflict and its dynamic resolution
are, incomparably, delineated.

The internal division of the πόλις into colliding interests
(*Stände* or *états* in the sense dramatized by the French
Revolution) is equivalent to, is the source of, 'the enactment of
tragedy in the ethical sphere'. In this sphere, there must be a
staatsfreier Bezirk, a domain free from the absolute authority of
the state, though definable and meaningful only within the
state's larger compass. The state, which Hegel now sees as a
Kriegstaat, a 'war-state', is in creative conflict with the domain
of *Privatrecht*, 'private right', whose primary impulses are not
those of war and of civic sacrifice in battle, but of the
preservation of the family. Inevitably, the state will seek to
absorb this familial sphere into its own governance and order
of values. Yet if it did so completely, it would destroy not only
the individual but the procreative units from which it draws
its military–political resources. Thus the state, even in the
moment of conflict, will 'concede divine honours' to the
domestic, ethically private dimension of existence.

This is a suggestive and intelligible scheme. Hegel now
obscures it to the point of near-impenetrability by attaching it
to a tentative metaphysical or ontological design. The division
between πόλις and individual itself reflects the engagement of
'the Absolute' in temporality and in phenomenal contin-
gencies. Of this engagement, the antique deities are, as it were,
the vehicle and symbol. Their implication in human moral
conflicts causes a self-scission in the nature of the divine: as
between the concrete dictates and executive powers of justice
represented by the Eumenides, and the 'indifferent light' or
dispassionate oneness of the Absolute which is symbolized by
Apollo. Athena's intervention in the trial of Orestes, and the

fact that the votes cast are equally divided, make possible two
decisive moments in the dialectic: the reconciliation between
unity and division (or 'embodiment') in the nature of the
divine, and the acceptance and recognition by the πόλις of its
own relation to the 'harmonious opposition' of the gods.

The convolution of this text results not only from the
imposition of an essentially immanent–political discourse on a
transcendent symbolism awkwardly poised between strands in
Hegel's thought which go back to Berne and even Tübingen
on the one hand, and the as yet diffuse idiom of his mature
philosophy on the other. The obscurity results from the
interference-effects of two very different literary sources. The
ontological–symbolic nebulosities and the motif of divine
commingling in human polemics (a motif central to Hölderlin)
do point to the *Eumenides*. The scenario of collision between
Kriegstaat and *Privatmensch* springs directly from *Antigone*. It is
the latter, moreover, which pervades the context of Hegel's
discussion and which is ubiquitously implicit even where
Aeschylus' drama is alluded to.

Immediately prior to the passage we have been looking at,
Hegel makes a major point: *Sittlichkeit* ('ethics', 'morality
grounded in custom') concedes an important portion of its own
rights to 'the subterranean powers, relinquishing something of
itself to them, and offering them sacrifice'. This concession and
offering fulfils a complex dual function: it recognizes the *Recht
des Todes* ('the rights of Death') and, at the same time,
discriminates, distances these rights from the ethical–political
arbitration of the living. Somewhat later in Hegel's essay, we
learn that the family is the highest totality 'of which nature is
capable', that the generation of children within the family is
the modus of reproduction of 'totality' itself, a modus constantly and legitimately challenged by the bellicose ideals of the
state. All this directs us not to the *Eumenides* but to *Antigone*. As
does the proposition, at the most opaque point in the passage
cited, that only the death of the tragic hero can make
intelligible (can bring about?) the unification of the riven
nature or duplicity of the gods when these are enmeshed and
disseminated in mortal collision ('in die Differenz verwickelt').

In other words: at the point in 1802 in which he is writing
about natural law, Hegel is profoundly involved in those
specific themes of conflict between nation-state and family,

between the rights of the living and those of the dead, between
legislative fiat and customary ethics, which will be fundamental to the *Phenomenology*. And it is in Sophocles' *Antigone*
that these conflicts are, primordially, set forth. It may be, as
Lukács argues,[1] that the *Eumenides* reference and the related
darkness in the text represent a last attempt to 'dehistoricize'
the political issues, to establish a continuity between antique
and modern as Hölderlin was striving to do. After 1802,
however, no such 'dehistoricization' is possible for Hegel. The
Napoleonic adventure, to which Hegel assigns an absolute
metaphysical singularity, has made of the new nation-state the
Apollonian *Lichtgott*, 'the Light-god' who must find fulfilment
and self-renewal in war. πόλεμος, on the Napoleonic scale, is
the public radiance of man. But what, in this imperial scheme,
are the rights of the subterranean and nocturnal agencies of
familial kinship and of death? Tragedy stems from the postulate and sublation of these antinomies. In *Antigone* the
logic of revelation in tragic form is consummate. Thus the
passage from the *Eumenides* to *Antigone* is neither accidental nor,
in any primary sense, autobiographical. It articulates the
essential step from Hegel's juvenilia to the *Phenomenology*.[2]

The presence of Antigone in the *Phenomenology* has often been
noted.[3] It has not been studied in detail. Yet it constitutes no
less remarkable an incorporation of a work of art into a
philosophic discourse than does that of Homer in Plato or of
Mozart's operas in Kierkegaard. As such, Hegel's uses of
Sophocles are not only immediately pertinent to a study of the
'Antigone' motif in western thought; they document the whole
central issue of hermeneutics, of the nature and conventions of
understanding. Here, in the face of a rarely equalled force of
appropriation, we can attempt to follow the life of a major text
within a major text and the metamorphic exchanges of
meaning which this internality brings about. If the
Phenomenology itself is, notably in its first six sections, dramatically constructed, it is, in significant degree, because it has
great drama as its core of reference.[4]

---

[1] Cf. G. Lukács, op. cit. 500–1.

[2] For further discussion of this obscure, transitional text, cf. F. Rosenzweig, *Hegel
und der Staat*, pp. 162–7.

[3] Cf., *inter alia*, W. Kaufmann, *Hegel: Reinterpretation, Texts and Commentary* (New
York, 1965), 142–6.

[4] The *Phenomenology* has, of course, generated a large secondary literature. It has, in

With Jamesian obliqueness, Hegel will name Antigone twice
only. But beginning with section V (c, a), her presence is vivid.
It is in this segment that Hegel spells out the axiom of
existentialism. Being is a 'pure translation' (*reines Uebersetzen*)
of potential being into action, into 'the doing of the deed' (*das
Tun der Tat*). No individual can attain an authentic knowledge
of himself 'ehe es sich durch Tun zur Wirklichkeit gebracht
hat' ('until it has brought itself into actuality through action').
The translation is one from 'the night of possibility into the day
of presentness'; it is an awakening into the dawnlight of the
deed of that which was the latency, the slumber of the self. This
is the break of morning and of action for Antigone. The
purpose of the existential act must be that of a total 'coming
into being', of an accomplishment so central that it cannot be
mere external 'facticity' (*eine Sache*). If the deed is merely self-
interested, if to act is only to 'busy oneself', 'others will hasten
to it as flies to a freshly set out bowl of milk' (with which image
Ismene seems to enter the argument). The authentic act of self-
realization is equivalent to 'die *sittliche Substanz*'—the 'ethical
substance' or 'morality as substantive performance'. To en-
quire of the justification or compass of this ethical substance, to
challenge its enactment in the name of external criteria, is
vanity. Enter Creon.

Yet, 'in its purest and most meaningful form', in its most
evident rationality, ethical action is the 'intelligible, general
doing of the state' (*das verständige allgemeine Tun des Staats*). The
result is an ambiguity of necessary guilt. Translation into
authentic individual being demands the existential deed. Man
is nothing but 'l'œuvre qu'il a réalisée' ('the work he has
fulfilled').[1] But in so far as individual action is not that of the

particular, induced two of the most important acts of close reading in modern
philosophic literature: J. Hyppolite, *Genèse et structure de la Phénoménologie de l'esprit de
Hegel* (Paris, 1946), and A. Kojève, *Introduction à la lecture de Hegel* (Paris, 1947). In its
fragmentary form—the text, though massive, is made up of the notes taken by
members of Kojève's famous Hegel seminars between 1933 and 1939—this masterpiece represents both an acute commentary on and a virtual parallel to the
Phenomenology. A further attempt at 'counter-statement' in the guise of marginal
commentary is made by Jacques Derrida in *Glas* (Paris, 1974). Often wildly self-
indulgent and arbitrary, Derrida's 'gloss' does, at several points, offer important
insights. Together, these three books, and the reticulations of their positions towards
Hegel, almost make up a history of post-war French philosophic and stylistic
sensibility.

[1] A. Kojève, *Introduction à la lecture de Hegel*, p. 92.

rational state, it may or may not have substantive reality, it may or may not be justifiable. Being quintessentially *his*, the deed of the individual will bring him into collision with the rational norm of realized purpose ('policy') in the state. In riposte, the latter will oppose law ('Gesetz') to inner imperative ('Gebot'). Where this opposition is forced to extremity, there will be a violent emptiness or 'formality' in the law and a self-destructive autonomy, an imperative of and for the self alone, in the individual. Let Sophocles' play begin.

The collision has its concrete source in two dialectical moments. The one is 'the tyrannical blasphemy or sin which makes of wilfulness a law' and which would compel the ethical substance to obey this law. The second moment is a subtler evil: it is the 'testing of the law' through 'the blasphemy or sin of knowing' (*Frevel des Wissens*, a formidable phrase) which 'reasons itself free from the law' and takes the latter to be a contingent, alien arbitrariness. Note the deliberate ambivalence of Hegel's formulation. If the first moment applies unmistakably to Creon, the second tells of both Creon *and* Antigone, though the verb *räsonieren* points to Creon rather than to Antigone. This pointer becomes a brilliant stab of light in the portrait of Antigone with which section V of the *Phenomenology* closes.

Ethical substance can only be grasped by self-consciousness; it can only become self-substance, in the individual human person. Ethical substance and personal being are made tautological in men or women who are 'lucid unto themselves, who are unriven spirits'. Such men or women are 'makellose himmlische Gestalten, die in ihren Unterschieden die unentweihte Unschuld und Einmütigkeit ihres Wesens erhalten'. The sentence is of an exalted density and theological tonality which makes translation halting: 'immaculate celestial types or presences, who preserve within their differences and divisions of self the never-deconsecrated innocence and integrity of their being.' Such men and women simply *are* ('Sie *sind*, und weiter nichts'—a lapidary proposition which contains the heart of Heideggerian and Sartrian ontology). Now, for the first time, Hegel names and cites the play (lines 456–7). And reiterates: 'Sie *sind*.' For such men and women, the right (*das Rechte*) is the absolute, disinterested substance of existence. The section closes imperatively: 'dieses aber ist *ihre Wirklichkeit* und

Dasein, ihre *Selbst* und *Willen*' ('but this [the right] is *their actuality* and *being*, their *self* and *will*'). Antigone stands before us as she had not done since Sophocles.

She is, of course, a Hegelian Antigone. Pellucid to herself, in possession of and possessed by the deed which is her being, this Antigone *lives* the ethical substance. In her, 'the Spirit is made actual'. But the ethical substance which Hegel's Antigone embodies, which she *is* purely and simply, represents a polarization, an inevitable partiality. The Absolute suffers division as it enters into the necessary but fragmented dynamics of the human and historical condition. The Absolute *must* descend, as it were, into the contingent, bounded specificities of the individual human ethos if that ethos is to attain self-fulfilment, if the journey homeward and to ultimate unity is to be pursued. But in the process of 'descent', of polemic deconstruction, the 'ethical world' is riven between immanent and transcendent polarities (*die in das Diesseits und Jenseits zerrissene Welt*). 'Sie spaltet sich also in ein unterschiedenes sittliches Wesen, in ein menschliches und göttliches Gesetz' ('It divides itself and crystallizes around the antinomies of human and of divine law'). Because he is the medium of this scission, man must undergo the agonistic character of the ethical–dialectical experience and be destroyed by it. Yet it is precisely this destruction, Hegel reminds us, which constitutes man's eminent worth and which allows his progression towards the unification of consciousness and of Spirit on 'the other side of history'.

Hegel's next step is not primarily logical; it is a conjecture essential to his poetics of individuation and historicism. The division between divine and human laws does not assume the form of a direct confrontation between men and gods, as it may be said to do in Aeschylus' *Prometheus* or Euripides' *Bacchae*. Because it is now entirely immanent in the human circumstance, the ethical substance polarizes its values and its imperatives as between the state and the family. It is in the family that divine law has a threefold status: it is 'natural', it is 'unconscious', it is of the 'folk-world' (the key phrases are: '*natürliches* Gemeinwesen', '*bewusstloser* Begriff', and 'das Element der Wirklichkeit des Volks dem Volke selbst'). This status is unavoidably adversary to that of the divine law as it functions in the religion of the πόλις. 'La Famille s'oppose à l'État comme les Pénates aux Dieux de la cité' ('The family is opposed to the state as are the Penates to the gods of the city').[1] This opposition finds its pivotal manifestation in the burial of the dead. It is around this motif, and its dramatization in *Antigone*, that Hegel now concentrates the existential dualities of man and society, of the living and the dead, of the immanent and the transcendent, which underlie the *Phenomenology*.

Within the family, the commanding agencies of consciousness are those of relationship to individualized particularity. It is the specific persona which is conceived as totality. To it is assigned a weight of presentness denied to the 'generalized individuality' of the citizen in the perspective of the state. Death, as it were, 'specifies this specificity' in the highest degree. It is the extreme accomplishment of the unique (as in the Kierkegaardian–Heideggerian postulate of one's *own* death, inalienable to any other). 'Death is the fulfilment and highest labour' an individual takes upon himself. As we shall see, this 'achieved totality' may be, indeed ought to be, expressly civic, such as is death in the war-service to the nation. But *in death*, the individual reverts 'immensely'—the epithet is meant to suggest the radical vehemence of Hegel's vision—to the ethical domain of the family. The πόλις, moreover, 's'intéresse au Tun, à l'*action* de l'individu, tandis que la Famille attribue une valeur à son Sein, à son *être* pur et simple' (the state 'concerns itself with the deed, with the *action* of the individual, whereas the family attributes value to his being, to his *existence* pure and simple').[2] It is this root-difference between a political and an ontological valuation which determines the primacy of burial.

In this primacy, the question of the actual preservation of the body from physical decay (Polyneices' unburied corpse) takes on a fundamental role:

The dead individual, by having detached and liberated his being from his action or negative unity, is an empty particular, merely existing passively for some other, at the level of every lower irrational organic agency. . . . The family keeps away from the dead the dishonouring of him by the appetites of unconscious organic agencies and by abstract [chemical] elements. It sets its own action in place of theirs, and it weds the relative to the bosom of the earth, the elemental presence which does not pass away. Thereby the family

[1] A. Kojève, op. cit. 100.   [2] Ibid.

makes of the dead a member of a communal totality (*eines Gemeinwesens*) which is stronger than, which maintains control over the powers of the particular material elements and lower living creatures, both of which sought to have their way with the dead and to destroy him. . . . This final duty thus constitutes the complete *divine* law or positive *ethical* act towards the particular individual.

The esoteric concreteness of Hegel's vision reanimates, as does almost no other commentary on *Antigone*, the primal dread of decomposition, of violation by dogs and birds of prey, central to the play. It knits the family to precisely the two sources or moments of Antigone's deed: 'the essence of divine law and the realm below the earth.'

Inside the family, continues Hegel, one relationship is privileged above all others by virtue of the immediacy and purity of its ethical substance. It is that between brother and sister. Again, Hegel's contracted, lyric argument is shot through with the presence of Antigone. Brother and sister are of the same blood, as husband and wife are not. There is between them no compulsion of sexuality or, if there is such compulsion (Hegel implicitly concedes the possibility), it has been overcome. In the relation between parents and children there is reciprocal self-interest—the parents seek a reproduction and continuation of their own being—and inevitable estrangement. This relation, moreover, is ineluctably organic. Brother and sister stand towards each other in the disinterested purity of free human choice. Their affinity transcends the biological to become elective. Femininity itself, urges Hegel, has its highest intimation, its moral quintessence, in the condition of sorority (*Das Weibliche hat daher als Schwester die höchste* Ahnung *des sittlichen Wesens*). The sister's view of her brother is ontological as no other can be: it is his being, his existence in and of itself, to which she assigns irreplaceable worth. Correspondingly, there can be no higher ethical obligation than that which a sister incurs towards her brother.

But in fulfilling his identity as citizen, in performing the deeds which realize his manhood, the brother must leave the sphere of the family. He leaves the hearth (οἶκος) for the world of the πόλις. Woman stays behind as 'head of the household and guardian of the divine law' in so far as this law is polarized in the household gods, the Lares and Penates. The ethical kingdom of woman is that of the 'immediately elemental'. It is

a kingdom of custodianship (of 'negativity', in Hegel's special
vocabulary) necessarily antinomian to the destructive positivity of the political. 'La loi *humaine* est la loi du *jour* parce
qu'elle est connue, publique, visible, *universelle*: elle règle non
pas la famille mais la *cité*, le gouvernement, la guerre; et elle est
faite par l'*homme* (*vir*). La loi humaine est la loi de l'homme. La
loi divine est la loi de la femme, elle se cache, ne s'offre pas dans
cette ouverture de manifestation (*Offenbarkeit*) qui produit
l'homme. Elle est nocturne . . .' ('*Human* law is the law of *day*
because it is known, public, visible, *universal*: it does not
regulate the family but the *city-state*, the government, warfare;
and this law is made by *man* (*vir*). Human law is man's law.
Divine law is the law of woman; it hides itself, it does not body
itself forth in that openness of appearance (*Offenbarkeit*) which
produces man. It is of the night . . .').[1] Derrida's gloss is
eloquent; but it also reflects a common misunderstanding. It
is only on the 'historical' level that the agonistic encounter is
between 'human' and 'divine' laws. The polarization merely
'phenomenalizes' the self-scission of the Absolute. If there is
divinity in the household gods, under feminine guard, so there
is also in the gods of the city and in the legislature which
masculine force has established around them. Hence the tragic
ambiguity of collision.

Hegel is now ready to take his final dialectic step. In death,
the husband, son, or brother passes from the dominion of the
πόλις back into that of the family. This homecoming is,
specifically and concretely, a return into the primal custody of
woman (wife, mother, sister). The rites of burial, with their
literal re-enclosure of the dead in the place of earth and in the
shadow-sequence of generations which are the foundation of
the familial, are the particular task of woman. Where this task
falls upon a sister, where a man has neither mother nor wife to
bring him home to the guardian earth, burial takes on the
highest degree of holiness. Antigone's act is the holiest to which
woman can accede. It is also *ein Verbrechen*: a crime. For there
are situations in which the state is not prepared to relinquish its
authority over the dead. There are circumstances—political,
military, symbolic—in which the laws of the πόλις extend to
the dead body the imperatives of honour (ceremonious
interment, monumentality) or of chastisement which, ordi-

[1] J. Derrida, *Glas*, p. 161.

narily, pertain only to the living. Hence a final, supreme clash
between the worlds of man and of woman. The dialectic of
collision between the universal and the particular, the sphere
of the feminine hearth and of the masculine forum, the
polarities of ethical substance as they crystallize around
immanent and transcendent values—is now compacted into
the struggle between man (Creon) and woman (Antigone)
over the body of the dead (Polyneices). The mere fact that such
a struggle takes place defines the guilt of woman in the eyes of
the πόλις. 'La Femme est la réalisation concrète du crime.
L'ennemi intérieur de l'État antique est la Famille qu'il détruit
et le Particulier qu'il ne reconnaît pas; mais il ne peut se passer
d'eux' ('Woman is the concrete embodiment of crime. The
family is the internal foe of the antique state; the family which
this state destroys and the private person which it does not
recognize; but it cannot do without them').[1]

Innocence is irreconcilable with human action; but only in
action is there moral identity. Antigone is guilty. Creon's edict
is a political punishment; to Antigone it is an ontological
crime. Polyneices' guilt towards Thebes is totally irrelevant to
her existential sense of his singular, irreplaceable being. The
Sein of her brother cannot, in any way, be qualified by his *Tun*.
Death is, precisely, the return from action into being. In taking
upon herself the inevitable guilt of action, in opposing the
feminine–ontological to the masculine–political, Antigone
stands above Oedipus: her 'crime' is fully conscious. It is an act
of self-possession even before it is an acceptance of destiny.

Schicksal (*fatum*) now enters Hegel's reading of the play.
Antigone and Creon must both perish inasmuch as they have
yielded their being to the necessary partialities of action. It is
in this exact sense that character, that individuation *is* destiny.
'The opposition of the ethical powers to one another, and the
process whereby individualities enact these powers in life and
deed, have reached their true end only in so far as both sides
undergo the same destruction. . . . The victory of one power
and its character, and the defeat of the other side, would thus
be only the partial, the unfinished work which progresses
steadily till equilibrium is attained. It is in the equal subjection
of both sides that absolute right is first accomplished, that the
ethical substance—as the negative force consuming both

[1] A. Kojève, op. cit. 105.

parties, in other words, omnipotent and righteous Destiny—
makes its appearance.' The identification of this reading with
the schematic triad of thesis–antithesis–synthesis is an over-
simplification (this triad is Fichte's rather than Hegel's).
Nevertheless, we recognize in this metaphysics of fatal equilibrium the essence of the Hegelian concept of dialectic, of
historical advance through tragic pathos. Kojève's summation
renders the poignant rigour of Hegel's 'Antigone': 'Le conflit
tragique n'est pas un conflit entre le Devoir et la Passion, ou
entre deux Devoirs. C'est le conflit entre deux plans
d'existence, dont l'un est considéré comme sans valeur par
celui qui agit, mais non par les autres. L'agent, l'acteur
tragique n'aura pas conscience d'avoir agi comme un criminel;
étant châtié, il aura l'impression de subir un "destin",
absolument injustifiable, mais qu'il admet sans révolte, "sans
chercher à comprendre"' ('Tragic conflict is not a conflict
between duty and passion, or between two duties. It is a
conflict between two planes of being, which one of those who
acts regards as valueless, but which is recognized by others.
The tragic agent, the tragic actor will not be conscious of
having acted as a criminal; being punished, he will have the
impression of suffering a "destiny" which is absolutely unjustifiable, but against which he does not rebel, which he
accepts "without seeking to understand"').[1]

Thus there is, in the calm of doom, parity. But the equation
is not one of *indifference*. Antigone possesses an insight into the
quality of her own guilt which is denied to Creon. The body of
Polyneices *had* to be buried if the πόλις of the living was to be
at peace with the house of the dead. Derrida's conjecture, so
far as it bears on the Hegel of the *Phenomenology*, is tempting: if
the role of God in the speculative dialectic is, most probably,
masculine, God's irony and self-division, the infinite disquiet of
his essence are, possibly, those of woman.[2] All honour to
Antigone.

---

[1] Op. cit. 102. Cf., by contrast, Derrida's fantastications regarding the dangers of
cannibalism and vampirism to which Polyneices' corpse is exposed. These suppositions
lead to the identification of Antigone with the love-and-death goddess Cybele (op. cit.
163–6, 210).

[2] Cf. J. Derrida, op. cit. 211.

ANTIGONES
37

3

Ironically, it is not with this profoundly original, delicate exegesis that one commonly associates Hegel's general theory of tragedy or particular interpretation of *Antigone*. It is later readings which achieve notoriety and which initiate debates that continue to this day. These later readings are, doubtless, related to the *Phenomenology*. But they represent a more abstract, silhouetted mode of understanding. The canonic text comes in Part Two (II. 3. a) of the *Lectures on the Philosophy of Religion*:

Fatum is that which is stripped of thought, of the concept; it is that in which justice and injustice disappear in abstraction. In tragedy, on the contrary, destiny operates within a sphere of *ethical Justice*. We find this expressed in its noblest form in the tragedies of Sophocles. In these both fate and necessity are at issue. The fate of individuals is represented as something incomprehensible, but necessity is not a blind justice; it is, on the contrary, perceived to be true justice. Just for this reason, these tragedies are the immortal 'works of Spirit' (*Geisteswerke*) of ethical understanding and comprehension, and the undying paradigm of the ethical concept. Blind fate is something unsatisfying. In these Sophoclean tragedies, justice is grasped by thought. The collision between the two highest moral powers is enacted in plastic fashion in that absolute *exemplum* of tragedy, *Antigone*. Here, familial love, the holy, the inward, belonging to inner feeling, and therefore known also as the law of the nether gods, collides with the right of the state (*Recht des Staats*). Creon is not a tyrant, but actually an ethical power (*eine sittliche Macht*). Creon is not in the wrong. He maintains that the law of the state, the authority of government, must be held in respect, and that infraction of the law must be followed by punishment. Each of these two sides actualizes (*verwirklicht*) only one of the ethical powers, and has only one as its content. This is their one-sidedness. The meaning of eternal justice is made manifest thus: both attain injustice just because they are one-sided, but both also attain justice. Both are recognized as valid in the 'unclouded' course and process of morality (*im ungetrübten Gang der Sittlichkeit*). Here both possess their validity, but an *equalized validity*. Justice only comes forward to oppose one-sidedness.

It is from this passage that derives the notion of tragedy as a conflict between two equal 'rights' or 'truths' and the belief that Sophocles' *Antigone* illustrates, in some obvious way, the dynamics of collision and 'synthetic resolution' in the Hegelian dialectic. The flat proposition, moreover, that 'Creon is not a tyrant', that his person and conduct embody *eine sittliche Macht*, is often cited to evidence Hegel's turn to an *étatiste* or 'Prussian' philosophy of the nation-state.

The text is highly condensed (resulting, as it does, from the transcription of lecture-notes). It presumes knowledge of the symbolic ontology of the self-scission of the Absolute as it is expounded in the *Phenomenology*, and of Hegel's early theory of punishment as a 'tragic necessity' in the dialectic of heroic self-fulfilment. And if there is, undeniably, a turn to authoritarian prudence in Hegel's personal–philosophic stance, there is, also, an attempt to articulate a logic of active poise, of what Kierkegaard will call 'motion on one spot'.

Napoleon's defeat or, rather, self-defeat, Napoleon's recession from a metaphysical into a political–contingent force, signifies the adjournment (the end?) of the original Hegelian finality. Spirit and history are not yet (are never?) to be made one. Man cannot pass from the realm of the state to the realm of the Spirit. It is within the realm of the state that he must pursue his homeward journey. But the impulse to this pursuit is, as we know, polemic. It is solely in and through conflict that (heroic) man or woman initiates those explorations of moral values, those sublations (*Aufhebungen*) of rudimentary contradictions into subtler, more comprehensive dissents, which alone activate human ethical advance. Antigone *must* challenge Creon if she is to be Antigone, if he is to be Creon. Her 'ethical superiority', in respect of the immediacy, of the primal character and purity of familial–feminine law, must both be made manifest *and* destroyed by the law of the state.[1] If Antigone were to triumph, if the private dimension of human needs were to demolish the public, there could be no progress. There could, quite simply, be no locale for meaningful, which is to say tragic, collision.

The young Hegel had perceived the inherent contradictoriness of being itself. After the *Phenomenology* and in the years of self-debate which lead to the Heidelberg *Encyclopaedia* of 1817, Hegel centres this general concept of internal contradiction in the notion of the state and in that of the relations between state and individual. It is only *within* the *Staat* and by virtue of tragic conflict *with* the state—the two being logically bound—that

[1] Cf. G. Lukács, op. cit. 511.

external and internal morality can be defined, actualized, and thus brought nearer to the unity of the Absolute. Rosenzweig's formulation is rhetorical but accurate: 'At the outset stood the birth-pangs of a human soul, at the end stands Hegel's philosophy of the State.'[1]

Hence the imperative of equilibrium, of equalization as between the univocal or one-dimensional parties to moral collision (Marcuse's idiom is, of course, explicitly Hegelian). If Creon was only or essentially a tyrant, he would not be worthy of Antigone's challenge, he would not, in Heidegger's transcription, be authentically 'questionable' (*frag-würdig*). If he did not incarnate an ethical principle, his defeat would possess neither tragic quality nor constructive sense. In Sophocles' exemplary rendition, this defeat, in exact counterpoise to Antigone's, entails progress. *After* the deaths of Antigone and of Creon, new conflicts will spring from the division within the πόλιϲ of the 'ethical substance'. But these conflicts, so far as they concern the private and the public, the familial and the civic, the prerogatives of the dead and those of the living, will be enacted on a richer level of consciousness, of felt contradiction, than that which arose from the corpse of Polyneices. In other words: in his *Lectures on the Philosophy of Religion*, Hegel is attempting to spell out the paradox of 'divisive unity' essential to his whole logic of the positivity of negation. He seeks to articulate the device of a conflict *in extremis* which, at the same time, vitalizes, strengthens the object of its mortal provocation (the state). He is trying to preserve two opposing categories indispensable to the dialectic: primordial stasis, the realm of the underworld and of woman, and the dynamics of history. The result is a deceptively brutal reading.

The formal and structural compulsions which underlie this reading translate readily into aesthetic judgement. In the *Aesthetik* (Part Three, III, ch. 3, iii. a), Hegel proclaims Sophocles' *Antigone* to be 'of all splendours of the ancient and of the modern world . . . the pre-eminent, the most satisfying work of art'. The context makes plain that this supremacy stems directly from the precise equipoise of motive and destiny as it is realized in the executive form and content of the play. It is in the absolute parity of tension and disaster achieved by

---

[1] F. Rosenzweig, op. cit. 188. Cf. also pp. 99–101 for an inspired, if somewhat uncritical, summation of Hegel's concept of the state.

Sophocles that Hegel finds harmonious proof of his central postulate of the agonistic nature of human consciousness. Like no other text, *Antigone* makes 'actual and true' the symmetries of significant deaths. But despite its logical and aesthetic strength—a strength which will make of it the official Hegelian interpretation—this whole analysis is radically at odds with the sensibility of the later Hegel, with the bias of spirit which he brings to the play. The sentiments voiced about the fate and stature of Antigone herself in the *Lectures on the History of Philosophy* (I. 2. b. 3) have a hyperbolic poignancy. They hint at emotional identifications irreconcilable with the dialectic impartiality of the canonic gloss.

Hegel is considering the phenomenological meaning and role of Socrates. He finds a contradiction in Socrates' attitude towards his own death. The sage has refused the possibility of escape because it seems preferable to him to submit to the laws of the πόλιc. Yet at the trial itself and throughout his imprisonment, Socrates has maintained his innocence. In fact, he accepts neither the legitimacy of the sentence nor of the judicial proceedings against him. Antigone's response to her doom is altogether higher. It enacts the homecoming of individual, fragmented consciousness to the coherence of the Absolute. Hegel cites lines 925–6: 'If this seems good to the gods, | We shall, in the course of suffering, be made to understand, to avow our error.' These are the sublime perceptions with which 'the celestial Antigone, the most resplendent (*herrlichste*) figure ever to have appeared on earth' goes to her death. The sacramental overtones in Hegel's idiom are unmistakable. Antigone is set above Socrates, a formidable elevation if we bear in mind the literally talismanic status of Socrates as the wisest and purest of mortals throughout Idealist thought and Romantic iconography. But 'the most resplendent figure ever to have appeared on earth' takes us further. The phrasing 'makes it almost impossible not to think of Jesus, and to note that Antigone is here placed above him'.[1] Kierkegaard, too, will sense the blasphemous pathos of this suggestion, only to negate it. This much is clear: Hegel's exaltation of Antigone, whatever its covert 'autobiographical code', whatever its covert affinities to the lasting ambivalence with which

---

[1] W. Kaufmann, *Hegel*, p. 273.

Hegel treats Christian revelation, goes beyond even his
aesthetic celebration of the play. And it undermines
thoroughly the dialectic of perfect equilibrium between Creon
and Antigone.

However, it is the latter which achieves rapid and commanding influence. In substance, both the theory of tragedy
and the specific analyses of *Antigone* as we know them after the
mid-nineteenth century derive from the debate on Hegel. To
be more precise: they derive from the contrast between the
view put forward by F. Schlegel when he sees Antigone as
making 'visible' the divine agency in human guise and by
A. W. Schlegel when he pronounces Creon to be criminally at
fault on the one hand, and Hegel's symmetrical reading on the
other (the latter becomes generally available after the publication of the third part of the *Aesthetik* in 1838).[1] From H. F. W.
Hinrich's *Das Wesen der antiken Tragödie* of 1827 and August
Boeckh's *Ueber die Antigone des Sophokles* of 1824, 1828 onward,
the Hegelian current is dominant. It is massively expounded in
Fr. Th. Vischer's celebrated *Aesthetik, oder Wissenschaft des
Schönen* (1846–58). The Hegelian apologia for Creon will not
be fundamentally challenged before O. Ribbeck's *Sophokles und
seine Tragödien* of 1869 and Wilamowitz-Möllendorff's designation of Antigone's death as that of a religious martyr in his
studies of Greek tragedy towards the end of the century.
Modern scholars incline to reject Hegel's interpretation in the
seemingly dogmatic, simplified form in which most of them
have come to know it. They find it discordant with the spirit of
Sophoclean drama and with the literal meanings of the Greek
text.[2] But this rejection is far from unanimous. A number of the
most penetrating of recent studies of *Antigone* are couched in
the very terms of the Hegelian scenario. Creon is 'no old fox
using his cunning on behalf of might and *raison d'état*'—he is a
man 'entranced' (*begeistert*) and wholly possessed by a vision of
civic law. This law determines nothing less than the existence
of Thebes ('ein Gebot, mit dem die Existenz Thebens nun

[1] Cf. E. Eberlein, 'Über die verschiedenen Deutungen des tragischen Konflikts in
der Tragödie "Antigone" des Sophokles', *Gymnasium*, lxviii (1961).
[2] Cf. C. M. Bowra, *Sophoclean Tragedy* (Oxford, 1944), 67; K. Reinhardt, *Sophokles*
(3rd edn., Frankfurt-on-Main, 1947), 78; W. Jens, 'Antigone-Interpretationen', in
Satura. Früchte aus der antiken Welt. Otto Weinreich zum 13. März 1951 dargebracht (Baden-
Baden, 1952), 47 and 58; V. Ehrenberg, *Sophocles and Pericles* (Oxford, 1954), 31; H.
Lloyd-Jones, *The Justice of Zeus* (University of California Press, 1971), 116 ff.

einmal steht und fällt').[1] 'Des deux attitudes religieuses que l'*Antigone* met en conflit,' write J.-P. Vernant and P. Vidal-Naquet in the most influential of recent readings, 'aucune ne saurait en elle-même être la bonne sans faire à l'autre sa place, sans reconnaître cela même qui la borne et la conteste' ('of the two religious attitudes which *Antigone* sets at odds, neither could by itself be the right one without reserving a place to the other, without acknowledging the very thing which constrains and opposes it').[2]

I know of no serious modern reflection on the nature of tragedy, on the paradox of harmony out of terror, which does not have to come to terms with Hegel's 'dualism' (which is both obvious and undeclared in Nietzsche's scheme of Apollonian and Dionysian principles). Max Scheler's well-known statement of the insolubility of essential conflicts within the texture of reality itself and his definition of the tragic are Hegelian to the core: the tragic, says Scheler in his 'Zum Phänomen des Tragischen' of 1914, is a primary 'component of the universe itself'. When we experience tragic drama, an ineluctable constituent 'of the *World*—and not of our ego, of its feelings, of its encounters with pity and fear' is revealed to us. When Scheler speaks of the 'radiant dark which seems to encircle the head of the "tragic hero"', he is echoing Hegel's image of the 'elect of suffering' and of Antigone in particular.

Thus we find in Hegel's successive and, at decisive points, internally contrasting interpretations of the *Antigone* of Sophocles one of the high moments in the history of reading. Here 'response' to a classic text engages 'responsibility' ('answerability') of the most vivid moral and intellectual order. The Hegelian Antigone(s) stand towards Sophocles' heroine in a relation of transforming echo. It is this relation, with its paradox of fidelity to the source and autonomous counter-statement, which constitutes the vitality of interpretation. On this rare level one can, without irony, compare the hermeneutic with the poetic act.

[1] G. Nebel, *Weltangst und Götterzorn: eine Deutung der griechischen Tragödie* (Stuttgart, 1951), 181.
[2] J.-P. Vernant and P. Vidal-Naquet, *Mythe et tragédie en Grèce ancienne* (Paris, 1977), 34.

4

In Goethe, the two are never far apart. Goethe's literary criticism and interpretation are almost invariably practical. Their occasion, their field of reference relate directly to the needs of his own production. The latter, in turn, will often incorporate movements of theoretic and functional discourse. The celebrated considerations on *Hamlet* are integral to the fiction of *Wilhelm Meisters Lehrjahre*. The most penetrating of Goethe's reflections on the spirit of classical art and literature are set out, in scenic form, in the 'Helena Act' of Part II of *Faust*. It is cardinal to Goethe's sovereign pragmatism, as it is to the epistemology of Kant, that critique is action and that action interprets.

Goethe's initial reading of Greek tragedy, with the aid of Latin and of German translations, goes back to 1773. He extends his knowledge of the tragedians in the summer of 1781 and the autumn and winter of 1782. It is, probably, at this time that he read Sophocles. He rereads him, thoroughly, and with a new German version to hand, in the late summer and autumn of 1804. *Shakespeare und kein Ende* (1813) contains a magisterial comparison between classical and modern drama and dramaturgy. The period from 1823 to 1827 sees Goethe closely concerned with the theory and practice of Greek tragedy in the light of Aristotle's *Poetics* and of his own attempts to solve the formal problems posed by *Faust* II. The dramatic torso *Elpenor* (1781–3) and the *Helena* fragment written in September 1800 are among the most inward pastiches of Greek tragedy in modern western literature.

But any such register trivializes the main point. Goethe's life and work are inseparable from the informing authority of the antique and of Attic art and letters in particular.[1] Goethe's testimonies to this authority are legion. His remark to F. von Müller (30 August 1827) summarizes the strategy of a lifetime: in order to face the challenges of the modern world, a man

[1] It would be fatuous to attempt to list even a fraction of the books, monographs, and articles on Goethe's relations to antiquity. For the English-speaking reader, B. Fairley, *Goethe as Revealed in his Poetry* (London, 1932), and H. Trevelyan, *Goethe and the Greeks* (Cambridge University Press, 1941), remain enlightening. Cf. W. Schadewaldt, *Goethestudien: Natur und Altertum* (Zurich and Stuttgart, 1963), 23–126, for a shorthand but acute survey of the whole vast topic. The relevant texts are masterfully assembled in E. Grumach, *Goethe und die Antike* (Berlin, 1949).

must guard his back 'and so he leans on the Greeks'. In the essay of 1805 on 'Winckelmann and his Century' Goethe had crystallized his sense of the Greek paradigm (though 'crystallized' is the wrong word; because there are central fibres of Winckelmann's personal existence which Goethe chooses to disguise, this great essay remains at once, and characteristically, both translucent and hermetic). Of the races of men, only the ancient Greeks achieved *natürliches Glück*, a 'native, an organic felicity'. If Greek poets and historians endure everlastingly as a wonder for the insightful and the despair of those who would toil after them in rivalry (*die Verzweiflung der Nacheifernden*), it is because they brought the sum of their energies to bear on the realities of their own time and place. They realized their potential for action on both the personal and communal planes. For the ancient Greeks, actuality was the criterion of worth; for the moderns, values reside solely in what has been thought and felt. For the ancients even 'imaginaries' (*Phantasiebilder*) are 'of bone and marrow'. Sensibility and concept are not fragmented, they are not severed from the daylit fact. A 'scarcely curable' dissociation between reality and perception mars the modern temper. With it has lapsed the 'naïve' presentness of supreme art. The terms of Goethe's dichotomy and of the sorrow which attends them are very nearly Hegelian.

It is precisely a concordance between internality and the world which gives to Homer and the three tragedians their exemplary pre-eminence. In the *Iliad* and in Greek tragedy, word and world are fused under pressure of clear action. If Homer is the sun of all western poetry (Goethe will never waver from this conviction), the three tragic poets are the ranking planets. Goethe's judgement as to their respective magnitudes is not uniform. He finds in the *Oresteia* an incomparable, a primal immensity of poetic means. Euripides is the principal source for modern experiments in lyric pathos and subtlety of motivation.[1] Sophocles matches neither Aeschylus' 'enormity' nor the nervous virtuosity of Euripides. In the last analysis, however, and just by virtue of his harmonic, median position in the triad, he is the most

---

[1] From 1823 to 1825, Goethe is actively engaged in a possible restoration of Euripides' *Phaethon*. He will return to this project in 1827. He publishes observations on the *Cyclops* in 1823 and 1826; on the *Bacchae* in 1827.

satisfying of the three.[1] More exactly, he is the touchstone of ideal tragic form. It is in the *Philoctetes* that tragic pathos is most perfectly rendered.[2] The problematic notion of catharsis is made radiantly obvious in the calming of terror at the close of *Oedipus at Colonus*. The final transfiguration of Faust is closely modelled on that of blind, aged Oedipus. In his person, moreover, in his civic eminence and poetic mastery, Sophocles embodies Goethe's own ideal of the concordance of thought and deed. And it is because it explores the rare quality of this concordance that *Torquato Tasso* seems so Sophoclean.

Apparently, the *Antigone* plays only a muted part in Goethe's argument on tragic drama. One might suppose that the relentless catastrophe of the play repelled Goethe, that what is involved is the notorious question of Goethe's avoidance of conclusive tragedy. This supposition would, however, be shallow. Goethe saw deep and unflinchingly into human disaster. He did feel that *Versöhnung* ('reconciliation', 'the making of amends' on an almost cosmic scale of values) was the most mature outcome of tragic drama. Aristotle, for one, had shared this sentiment. But it could, it often had to be, reconciliation at the cost of human immolation and self-immolation. Goethe's formulation in the 1827 *Nachlese zu Aristoteles Poetik* is uncompromising. *Versöhnung* may have to wait on 'eine Art Menschenopfer' ('a kind of human sacrifice') either direct or by surrogate, 'as in the case of Abraham and of Agamemnon'. There is no bridling at terror here. No, the seeming absence of *Antigone* from Goethe's explicit comments before 1818 reflects, paradoxically, the centrality of the play in one of Goethe's own foremost dramas.

The background to *Iphigenie* (1779, 1786) is manifest.[3] The general treatment of the myth of Iphigenia's sacrifice and

---

[1] Cf. W. Schadewaldt, *Goethestudien*, p. 33.

[2] Cf. Goethe's observations on the treatment of the Philoctetes theme in Sophocles as compared with that in the lost plays of Aeschylus, Euripides, and the Latin tragedian Accius (1826).

[3] The English-speaking reader will find valuable guidance in J. Boyd, *Iphigenie auf Tauris: An Interpretation and Critical Analysis* (Oxford, 1942), and E. L. Stahl, *Iphigenie auf Tauris* (London, 1961). Cf. U. Petersen, *Goethe und Euripides: Untersuchungen zur Euripides-Rezeption in der Goethezeit* (Heidelberg, 1974), for a thorough investigation of the status of the Iphigenia motif at the time. W. Rehm, *Griechentum und Goethezeit. Geschichte eines Glaubens* (3rd edn., Bern, 1952), and A. Lesky, 'Goethe und die Tragödien der Griechen, *Jahrbuch des Wiener Goethe-Vereins*, lxxiv (1970), contain valuable discussions of Goethe's attitude to the sources of *Iphigenie*.

translation to Tauris derives from Euripides. The heroine's
account in Act III of the inheritance of doom in the house of
Atreus stems from the *Oresteia*. Yet the fabric and spirit of
Goethe's play are neither Aeschylean nor Euripidean. The
presiding genius is that of Sophocles. Central to the drama is
the collision between archaic immediacies of human reflex and
the didactic sophistications of the civilizing process. 'Iphigenie
and Tasso', writes Adorno, 'are civilization-dramas (*Zivi-
lisationsdramen*).'[1] As in Sophocles' *Ajax* and *Philoctetes*, the
terms of the conflict are ambiguous. If 'civilization' prevails
over barbaric innocence or the irrational, it can do so only by
recognizing the impurities of motive and the part of illusion in
itself. In *Ajax* and *Philoctetes*, as in Goethe's *Iphigenie*, reason
and civic humanism resort to tactics which are mendacious.
The dialectics of the collision, the parity of bias and self-
deception as between antagonists, strongly suggest the
Hegelian contour of tragic form, a contour, as we saw,
patterned on Sophocles. The stature of Iphigenie largely
transcends the duplicities of the conflict in which she is
enmeshed; more exactly, Iphigenie enforces on these duplicities ethical insights of a rare, Kantian order. This enforcement refers us, repeatedly, to the precedent of Antigone.

It is Iphigenie who proclaims the quintessential Sophoclean
belief that

> Götter sollten nicht
> Mit Menschen wie mit ihresgleichen wandeln:
> Das sterbliche Geschlecht ist viel zu schwach,
> In ungewöhnter Höhe nicht zu schwindeln.

> (Gods should not
> Wander among men as with their peers:
> The race of mortals is far too weak
> Not to grow dizzy upon unaccustomed heights.)

It is from this fatal neighbourhood, of which Hölderlin will
make the focus of his image of Antigone, that sprang the
horrors suffered by Tantalus and his lineage. When Thoas,
alert to the inspired interest of Iphigenie's narrative, cautions:

[1] T. W. Adorno, 'Zum Klassizismus von Goethe's Iphigenie', *Gesammelte Schriften*
(Frankfurt-on-Main, 1974), xi. 499. This challenging essay, with its emphasis on the
Hegelian quality of Goethe's treatment of the collision between 'barbarism' and
'civilization', first appeared in 1967.

'No god is speaking; it is your heart', she responds as would
Antigone: 'The gods speak to us only through our hearts.' The
confrontation between the absolute monarch and the young
woman who opposes his decree, in Act V, sc. iii, intimately
echoes the Antigone–Creon clash. 'From childhood on',
declares Iphigenie, 'I have learned obedience; first to my
parents, then to a goddess. When in compliance, my soul is
most at ease and liberty. But neither in Argos nor here have I
learned to bend to the crass fiat of a man.' 'Ein alt Gesetz,
nicht ich, gebietet dir' ('an ancient law, not I, commands
you'), counters Thoas. Iphigenie's answer is Antigone's:

> Wir fassen ein Gesetz begierig an,
> Das unsrer Leidenschaft zu Waffe dient.
> Ein andres spricht zu mir: ein älteres,
> Mich dir zu widersetzen, das Gebot,
> Dem jeder Fremde heilig ist.

> (We seize eagerly upon a law
> Which serves as weapon for our passion.
> Another ordinance speaks to me, bids me
> Oppose you. A more ancient law:
> Which holds every stranger to be holy.)

In the moment of supreme bewilderment, knowing her own
values compromised by tactical falsehood, Iphigenie turns
inward, to the threatened sanctuary of the moral self, as does
Antigone: 'What means have I left to defend my innermost
self? Do I appeal to the goddess for a miracle? Is there no
strength in the depths of my soul?' Though it bears witness to
his humanity, to that which gives 'barbarism' its troubling
edge over civility, Thoas' solitude at the close of the play is an
echo of Creon's aloneness. The *Parzenlied* (the 'Song of the
Fates') is not only one of the summits of Goethe's art. It is
a metamorphic re-creation of the choral odes in *Antigone*. In
it are fused the celebrated first stasimon on the vulnerability
of man and the chorus's later reflections on the legacy of ruin
in the high house of Laius. 'Es fürchte die Götter | Das
Menschengeschlecht!' ('May the race of men go in fear of the
gods!') is 'translation' in the ideal sense of Novalis and of
Walter Benjamin. Goethe elicits the heart of meaning in
Sophocles; he communicates the sum of vision beyond the
literal parts. Metrically, also, the *Parzenlied* is one of the rare

equivalences we have in any modern tongue to the hammering pace and lash of a Sophoclean choral lyric.

Writing to Goethe in January 1802, Schiller commented that the primary action in *Iphigenie* was that of *das Sittliche*, of ethical consciousness. This was Hegel's express term in relation to *Antigone*. Goethe himself, in *Shakespeare und kein Ende*, saw in the determinism of ethical consciousness, in the imperative of moral choice (*das Sollen*) the root of Greek tragedy. This imperative, he added, had been most finely articulated in the person of Antigone. Antigone and Goethe's Iphigenie are sisters in spirit.

Between 1813 and 1818, Goethe recast the Latin and German versions of a text of the third century AD, 'The Paintings of Philostratus'. The original consisted of a description of a gallery of antique paintings in a Neapolitan villa. Goethe's motive was frankly didactic. By evoking the mythological depictions in Philostratus, he would furnish contemporary artists with exemplary subjects and conventions of representation. One of the antique works shows Antigone:

Heldenschwester! Mit einem Knie an der Erde umfasst sie den toten Bruder, der, weil er seine Vaterstadt bedrohend, umgekommen, unbegraben sollte verwesen. Die Nacht verbirgt ihre Grosstat, der Mond erleuchtet das Vorhaben. Mit stummen Schmerz ergreift sie den Bruder, ihre Gestalt gibt Zutrauen, dass sie fähig sei, einen riesenhaften Helden zu bestatten. In der Ferne sieht man die erschlagenen Belagerer, Ross und Mann hingestreckt.

Ahndungsvoll wächst auf Eteokles' Grabhügel ein Granatbaum; ferner siehst du zwei als Totenopfer gegeneinander über brennende Flammen, sie stossen sich wechselseitig ab; jene Frucht, durch blutigen Saft, das Mordbeginnen, diese Feuer, durch seltsames Erscheinen den unauslöschlichen Hass der Brüder auch im Tode bezeichnend.

Translation is by no means easy. Goethe's idiom here is oddly statuesque. It aims at tactile presence:

Sister of heroes, heroic sister! One knee touching the earth, she grasps, enfolds her dead brother who, because he perished threatening his native city, was to decompose unburied. Night conceals her magnanimous deed, the moon sheds light on her purpose. She seizes her brother with mute sorrow, her form and person give one confidence that she is capable of burying a hero of giant stature. In the distance one sees the slain assailants, steed and man, outstretched.

In solemn intimation, a pomegranate tree grows on Eteocles'
burial mound; further on, you see two flames burning opposite each
other in sacrifice to the dead; they repel each other mutually;
through its blood-juice, this fruit signifies the murderous beginning,
through their strange appearance, these fires signify the unquench-
able hatred of the brothers also in death.

Philostratus' source or, presumably, that of the picture, is a
well-known passage in Pausanias (IX. 25. 1). Not far from the
gates of Thebes, the traveller is shown a tumulus on which
grows a pomegranate. The tree is living still: 'you can
break open the ripe fruits and see that the inside of them is like
blood. . . . The whole area is called Antigone's Pull; she tried
hard to lift the dead body of Polyneices but it was too heavy, so
then she thought of dragging it, and managed to draw it along
and throw it into Eteocles' burning pyre.' Goethe's marmoreal
exercise makes plain that there is no dissent from a stylized
valuation of Antigone.

On 21 March 1827, Goethe invited Eckermann to look at
H. F. W. Hinrich's newly published monograph on the nature
of Greek tragedy. Discussion followed a week later. Goethe
deplores the fact that a natively robust North German
sensibility such as Hinrich's should have succumbed to the
abstruse convolutions of Hegelian thought and idiom. Certain passages, such as that on 'the collective certitude' of the
chorus in Greek tragedy, verge on the incomprehensible.
Prophetically, Goethe suggests that the Hegelian style will
bring German philosophy into disrepute. What will English
and French readers make of a jargon impenetrable even to
native German-speakers? The notion that collisions between
state and family engender tragic conflicts is, surely, well
founded. But Hegel's claim, adopted by Hinrich, that this is
the sole or the best source of all tragic conflicts is excessive.
Ajax is destroyed by the daemon of personal honour; Hercules
perishes through erotic jealousy. Eckermann counters: it is
Antigone whom Hegel and Hinrich have in view when
constructing their general scheme. It is the unique purity of
sisterly love they aim at. Goethe objects with brusque obvious-
ness: is the love between sisters not even purer, are there not
numerous instances in which the love between sister and
brother carries a sensual strain? No; Hegel–Hinrich's error lies
deeper: they regard a Sophoclean drama as the enactment of

an abstract idea. In reality, Sophocles simply resorts to some established, communal myth with the purpose of making it as theatrically effective as possible. He is not a metaphysician but a working playwright. The 'thought-element' is already implicit in the myth (Goethe was, at this time, immersed in the *Poetics*). In *Ajax* a brother strives to bury his brother; in *Antigone* a sister performs this same task. The difference lies in the hazard of legend.

Eckermann directs the conversation to the Hegelian image of Creon. In Hinrich's reading the Hegelian formulation is patent: Creon incarnates 'the tragic might' of the πόλις; he exercises the morality of public duty and virtue (*die sittliche Staatstugend*). Goethe is wholly dismissive. How can anyone believe such an interpretation? Creon's motive is hatred of the dead man. Polyneices' attack on Thebes has been sufficiently chastised by death in battle. His corpse is innocent. Indeed, Creon's decree, in that it causes the pollution of the whole city, is a *Staatsverbrechen*, 'a political crime'. All the personages, all the evidence in the play, testify against the tyrant. Creon plunges ahead in blasphemous obstinacy. He ends a shadow.

'Yet listening to Creon, one would suppose that he had a certain degree of justification' (Eckermann's qualification is merely meant to elicit the master's ruling). It is Sophocles' art as a dramatist, his rhetorical schooling, which confuse us. Such is Sophocles' rhetorical cunning that persuasion can become sophistic. Consider Antigone's apologia in lines 905 ff., her proof of the uniqueness of a brother in respect of familial love and duty. What could be more casuistical, more perilously close to bad comedy? In 1821, August Ludwig Jacob had argued that this passage must be spurious. In 1824, Boeckh, adopting the Hegelian emphasis on the Antigone–Polyneices relation, had pronounced the lines to be authentic. Goethe's wish is unqualified: may philology show them to be a base insertion.

The conversation resumes on 1 April. *Iphigenie* had been performed the night before. Unforcedly, in a manner which reflects the internal kinship of the two plays, attention reverts to *Antigone*. *Das Sittliche*, the ethical principle, has been divinely implanted in the human soul. In certain elect beings, it is made manifest through exemplary action. If a particular beauty of presence accompanies such action, the ethical and the aesthetic combine to inspire emulation. The morality of *Antigone* is not Sophocles' invention, 'sondern es lag im Sujet' ('it lay, rather, in the subject'). Creon is Antigone's foil. Her tranquil nature requires compelling provocation in order to exhibit its own latent grandeur. Creon's other function is ancillary: to make plain to us the hatefulness of his wretched error. In Ismene, the dramatist has rendered 'a beauteous measure of the ordinary' (*ein schönes Mass des Gewöhnlichen*). It is contrastively that Antigone develops and reveals to us the far greater heights of her own moral dimensions. In all this, there are no enigmas: only moral and poetic illuminations worthy of constant study. One must ponder 'die alten Griechen und immer die Griechen' ('the ancient Greeks and always the Greeks').

The third part of Eckermann's *Conversations with Goethe*, containing these passages, appeared in 1848. Implying as it does so much that is primary to Goethe's art and at-homeness in the world, the reply to Hegel and the gloss on *Antigone* seemed conclusive.

5

This gloss was, of course, unavailable to the young Kierkegaard. The initial reference to Sophocles in the *Papirer*,[1] dated 1835, is an oddity. The illegitimate offspring of Christianity, notably the rationalists, seek to show that the Church is now senile, that it ought to be made a ward of the courts: 'whereas its true children believe that in the critical moment and to the world's astonishment it will rise up like Sophocles in full power.' The allusion is to a spurious anecdote, almost certainly based on ancient comedy, which had been recorded by Cicero and passed on by Lessing. Haled before a tribunal by his greedy sons, Sophocles proved his competence to order his affairs even in high age by reciting from the last and most magical of his plays. The fable pleased Kierkegaard: he will repeat it in his *Concluding Unscientific Postscript* of 1846.

[1] Any discussion of Kierkegaard's thought must lean heavily on the *Papirer*, the notebooks and unpublished jottings. These are now available in an English-language version in H. V. Hong and E. H. Hong (edd.), *Søren Kierkegaard's Journals and Papers* (Indiana University Press, 1978).

But the role of Antigone in Part I of *Either/Or* (1843) does not arise from anecdote. It knits fundamental strands in Søren Kierkegaard's personal existence and discourse. Antigone is, for a time, one of the inmost guises of his being.

In seeking to interpret this fact and the version of 'Antigone' to which it gives rise, one meets with forbidding difficulties. Key terms in Kierkegaard's Danish will not translate, even into neighbouring German. The sense of affinity is, in fact, treacherous: Kierkegaard borrows heavily from the vocabulary of the German Idealists, but inflects his borrowings in a radically personal manner.[1] Moreover, though the impact of Hegel on *Either/Or* and on the 'Antigone' section in particular is pervasive, the question as to the nature of Kierkegaard's actual familiarity with Hegelian texts remains unclear. But severe as they are, these are only preliminary obstacles. Kierkegaard's 'Antigone' is embedded in 'indirect discourse', in the ironic–reflexive dialectic of hypothetical proposals and self-negations which is Kierkegaard's chosen mode of communication.[2] No proposition, however charged with evident persuasion, can be taken unequivocally. It is inwoven in a philosophic–rhetorical fabric of extreme idiosyncrasy. To what degree is this fabric autobiographical, to what extent is the entire Antigone excursus a confessional mask, a virtuoso piece of ironized self-disclosure? Kierkegaard's warnings are unmistakable. Truth makes its appearance via 'fragmentary prodigality'. Systematic exegesis, efforts at exhaustive interpretation, are vain. 'A completely finished work has no relation to the poetic personality': correspondingly, a 'completely finished' hermeneutic negates the dialectical and self-negating immediacy of the living script. 'Read me aloud', urges Kierkegaard, as would a trained actor. Kierkegaardian discourse is that of a dramatist playing voice against voice. The 'Antigone' in *Either/Or* is a fragmentary drama within a dialectical–dramatic medium.[3] Perhaps it is this medium which ought to be looked at first.

---

[1] On a number of linguistic points, I am indebted to the generous guidance of Dr R. Poole of the University of Nottingham.

[2] For a recent, massive study of the concept and uses of 'indirect discourse', cf. N. Viallaneix, *Écoute, Kierkegaard* (Paris, 1979).

[3] Despite its pietistic constraints, Emanuel Hirsch's treatment of Kierkegaard as a 'dramatist' remains classic. Cf. E. Hirsch, *Kierkegaard-Studien* (Gütersloh, 1933), i. 57–92.

There has, in recent studies, been a useful re-emphasis of Kierkegaard's Romanticism. Singular as he was in stature and strategic indirection, Kierkegaard had, certainly at the outset, been immersed in the Romantic mood and style. Even his polemics against Romanticism derive from the practices of self-mockery familiar to Byron and E. T. A. Hoffmann. Kierkegaard's 'Antigone' is part of 'The Ancient Tragical Motif as Reflected in the Modern: An Essay in the Fragmentary Read before a Meeting of the SYMPARANEKROMENOI'. As Walter Rehm has shown, each element in this format has its antecedent in Romantic letters and postures.[1] *Symparanekromenoi* is a mildly ungrammatical coinage which combines a turn of phrase in Hebrews 11 with a borrowing from Lucian's *Dialogues of the Dead*. It can be rendered, circuitously, as 'fellow-moribunds, companions in live burial, brethren in decease and mortuary readiness'. Fraternal covens of the night, brotherhoods of the sepulchral and macabre, are a commonplace in Romantic literature and biography. The aesthetic of the fragmentary, of the aphorismic, is a recurrent motif in Romantic rhetoric from Coleridge and Novalis to Nietzsche. The hybrid of direct address, personal memoire, philosophic discourse, fictive letters, pseudonymous interventions, and analytic commentary in *Either/Or* and the 'fragmentary lecture' belongs to a genre which Novalis entitled 'literary Saturnalia'. Kierkegaard, Baudelaire, Rozanov, are among its masters. Mirrors reflect, echoes splinter, in self-dividing mazes.

The ultimate model is that of Lucian and Petronius. But the particular *Verwirrungsrecht* ('the licence, the right to confuse and to employ confused forms') in *Either/Or* has its closer precedent. It is that of Friedrich Schlegel's *Lucinde* of 1794. This 'scandalous' mixture of intimate revelation, erotic dialogues, letters, and philosophic reflections, comparable only to Hazlitt's *Liber Amoris*, was thoroughly familiar to Kierkegaard. He had examined Schlegel's text in his own dissertation on Socratic and modern concepts of irony (1841). Though

---

[1] Any discussion of Kierkegaard's 'Antigone' must follow in the wake of Walter Rehm's penetrating essay 'Kierkegaard's "Antigone"', first published in 1954. This essay is reprinted in *Begegnungen und Probleme* (Berne, 1957). No other serious study of this theme is available. For a cursory reference, cf. R. J. Manheimer, *Kierkegaard as Educator* (University of California Press, 1972), 103–12.

Kierkegaard's judgement is marked by Hegel's distaste for the
work, the resonances of *Lucinde* in *Either/Or* are both general
and specific. When he writes of a 'gentle furioso and shrewd
adagio of friendship', Schlegel foreshadows the central self-
reference to music in Kierkegaard's idiom and aesthetic. When
he praises the beloved for the secrecy in which she enfolds her
passion during the bustle of the day, only to pour it forth in
the privacy of the night, Schlegel touches on a dominant
Kierkegaardian theme. Already in 1794 and 1795, moreover
(could Kierkegaard have failed to notice a monograph entitled
'On Diotima'?), Schlegel had exalted Antigone.

By the 1840s, a contrastive treatment of ancient and modern
tragedy was a banality. Undertaken, during the seventeenth
century, in Corneille's prefaces, argued anew by Voltaire,
central to Lessing's *Hamburgische Dramaturgie*, the comparison
had been given magisterial form by Goethe and Victor Hugo.
In each case, the touchstone of argument is Aristotle's *Poetics*.
So it is, also, in Kierkegaard's 'Essay', but it is Aristotle read in
the light of Hegel's *Aesthetik*. The latter is quoted directly and
the terms of Kierkegaard's discussion are those of Hegel's
theory of tragedy. As I mentioned, the question of whether or
not Kierkegaard had personal access to Hegel's actual writings
remains unresolved and disputed.[1] He may have derived much
of his knowledge of the Hegelian system from Schelling, from
the writings of the younger Fichte, and from the interpretations and didactic summaries offered by the Danish
Hegelians (B. Sibbern, P. Møller, M. L. Martensen). Where
Kierkegaard criticizes Hegel, he may be echoing Schelling's

---

[1] The literature on this topic is large. Cf. J. Wahl, 'La Lutte contre le hégélianisme',
in *Études Kierkegaardiennes* (Paris, 1938); K. Löwith, *Von Hegel zu Nietzsche* (2nd edn.,
Zurich, 1950); M. Bense, *Hegel und Kierkegaard, eine prinzipielle Untersuchung* (Cologne,
1948); W. Anz, *Kierkegaard und der deutsche Idealismus* (Tübingen, 1956). The ranking
authority in the field is Niels Thulstrup. His *Kierkegaard's Relation to Hegel* (Princeton
University Press, 1980) provides a detailed historiography of the problem as well as a
summarizing statement. Despite voluminous research, says Thulstrup, the essential
question as to Kierkegaard's direct knowledge of Hegel, as to what he did or did not
read of Hegel and when and in what versions, remains unanswered. What lies beyond
cavil is the fact that Kierkegaard himself 'devoted a significant portion of his
considerations and of his creation to the clarification of his relations to Hegel and the
latter's disciples'. In his scintillating chapter on 'Hegel, Kierkegaard and Niels
Thulstrup' (*Kierkegaard, The Myths and Their Origins*, trans. G. C. Schoolfield [Yale
University Press, 1980]), Henning Fenger goes much further. He argues, as I have,
that the Hegelian elements in the early Kierkegaard are pervasive. His case would
have been even stronger had he considered Kierkegaard's 'Hegelian' uses of Antigone.

notorious Berlin lectures of 1841.[1] All this is the case, and it has induced certain scholars to suppose that Kierkegaard knew almost nothing of Hegel in the original. It is my own belief that he did, and that there are moments in his 'Antigone' which force one to ask what he knew of the *Phenomenology* (early Hegel being more out of the way of general discussion).

Kierkegaard's opening move is purely Hegelian: historical development remains within the 'sphere of the concept' (Hegel's *Begriff*). Nevertheless, the notion of 'the tragic' has undergone drastic changes between antiquity and the current age. These changes are to be elucidated. But differential analysis is only a technique towards Kierkegaard's proper aim, which is 'an attempt to show how the particular character of ancient tragedy is taken up by, is embodied in, modern tragedy'. If this internalization can be demonstrated, the true essence of the tragic will come to light. Ours, notes Kierkegaard, is at once an epoch of individual isolation and of frenetic gregariousness. The interplay between these two currents generates comedy. Yet, in comparison with ancient Greece, our age is the 'more melancholy and, therefore, it is more deeply desperate'. It is this despair, as we shall learn, which enforces a grasp of individual responsibility. Spasmodic, cross-hatched as it is (a series of satiric political asides anticipates, uncannily, Kierkegaard's analyses of the 1848 crises), the argument follows a main thread. Tragedy is about responsibility, about the acceptance of guilt.

In antique tragedy, the individual agent, however free, is embedded in the 'substantive categories' of state, family, and destiny (*fatum*). Self-conscious, reflexive subjectivity is a determinant of modernism. Hence a primary difference: as between the 'epic', action-centred character of classical tragic drama and the psychological, introspective tenor of the modern. In ancient tragedy the hero *suffers* his fatal destiny, in modern drama 'he stands and falls entirely by his own acts'. All this, of course, is pure Hegel. The next stage in the argument is not. The transition from the aesthetic to the ethical, which lies at the heart of *Either/Or* and of Kierkegaard's sense of personal development, relates to the quality of tragic guilt. The latter is ethical precisely to the degree in which it is reflexively

---

[1] 'One must say this against Schelling: he diminished Hegel implacably, unjustly, and in vain' (K. Jaspers, *Schelling: Grösse und Verhängnis* [Munich, 1955], 282).

apprehended and consciously internalized by the solitary individual (modern man in his fragmented state). Accountability for one's own acts, the taking of guilt upon oneself, signifies the transcendence of the aesthetic; and because true evil, true culpability, are not 'aesthetic' but only 'ethical' categories, they can be handled fully only by modern tragedy. Rather, and here lies the 'synthetic' originality of Kierkegaard's method, full tragedy must 'sublate'—the dynamics are Hegelian still—the aesthetic components of classical tragedy into the ethical reflexivity of the modern. Moreover, however modern and solipsistic the individual, he remains 'a child of God, of his age, of his nation, of his family and friends'. Pure isolation is at once comical and desperate, a formidable premonition of the Kafka–Beckett aesthetic. It is by acquiescing in the relativity of ethical–familial relations that the individual enters into the tragic sphere. Yet only by virtue of this entry can there be 'healing'. For only in the tragic sphere is the aesthetic wholly instrumental in the ethical. It is just this instrumentality which gives to great tragedy 'an infinite gentleness'.

Now Kierkegaard's antinomies take an even subtler turn. The healing aesthetic of tragedy is like a 'mother's love' or feminine principle (the 'sublation' of tragedy at the end of Goethe's *Faust* seems implicit in the entire discussion). The harshness of the ethical is itself tempered by the religious. This temperance makes of the religious the 'expression of a paternal love'. Both are essential, both are functional, within secular limitations at least, in tragic drama. 'But what is human life when we take these two things away, what is the human race? Either the sadness of the tragic, or the profound sorrow and profound joy of the religious.' Echoing Winckelmann and his Romantic disciples, Kierkegaard speaks of the melancholy, of the consoling sadness, in the art, poetry, and even 'joy' of the ancient Greeks. (Already, 'Antigone' is actively inferred below the surface motion of the discourse.)

Having sketched this synthesis, this paradox of 'tragic grace' in which the aesthetic and the ethical are seen as necessary preliminaries to the religious, Kierkegaard now reverts to differentiation. The starting-point is a quotation from Hegel's *Aesthetik* on true compassion, which is empathy with the 'moral justification' (*sittliche Berechtigung*) of the tragic sufferer.

Kierkegaard applauds this definition but refines it. He proposes a fundamental distinction between the response, the
'com-passion' of the ancient and the modern spectator, and
between the enactments of tragic guilt to which he is
responding. The key terms are *sande tragiske Sorg* ('true tragic
sorrow') and *sande tragiske Smerts* ('true tragic pain'). In ancient
tragedy, the *Sorg* is deeper, the pain less. In modern tragedy,
the *Smerts* is sharper, the sorrow less. This difference hinges
immediately on the concept and presentation of guilt (*Skyld*).
Greek sorrow is 'so gentle and so deep' because it lacks the self-
conscious, reflexive understanding of guilt. It is a sorrow
bestowed on the suffering of the fated, erring hero. If there is
ambiguity in this suffering, if there is opaqueness (*Dunkelhed*),
and Kierkegaard will invoke Sophocles' *Philoctetes*, these are of
an aesthetic order. In modern tragedy, on the contrary, the
conception of guilt is manifest and personal. A merciless
transparency (*Gjennemsigtighed*) prevails. It is not sorrow which
dominates our response, but pain. Kierkegaard cites Hebrews
10: 31: 'It is a fearful thing to fall into the hands of the living
God.' To do so is to know and to live one's own *Skyld*. The
wrath of the Greek gods brings agony, but, as it were, from
outside, from an arbitrariness beyond or prior to good and evil.
Thus the pain is less. Only in the passion of Christ, in the
assumption of total guilt by total innocence, do these categories
of the dialectic 'neutralize themselves' and achieve
equilibrium.

    The dialectic leap follows. Tragic guilt is inherited guilt. But
'inherited guilt' (the human legacy of original sin) 'contains
the self-contradiction of being guilt, and yet not being guilt'.
The individual's acceptance of inherited guilt is an essential
act of piety. In this piety, guilt and innocence, transparency
and opaqueness, are indivisibly meshed. Thus the guilt of the
tragic personage 'has every possible aesthetic ambiguity'. We
have seen that this ambiguity marks the wrath of the gods in
Greek tragic drama. But the reflexive understanding of the
inheritance of guilt, and the terrible pain which springs from
this understanding, are not Greek. They are Hebraic.
Jehovah's visitations of the sins of the fathers upon the children
unto the third and the fourth generations embody the central
tragic paradox of 'innocent guilt'. If this embodiment has not
produced tragic plays, it is because Judaism 'is too ethically

developed', because it has set aside 'aesthetic ambiguity'. But both categories, both sets of terms in the dialectic, are requisite: Greek and Hebraic, epic and reflexive, aesthetic and ethical, sorrow and pain. Kierkegaard's conclusion has a synthesizing, combinatorial motion which is plainly Hegelian:

The true tragic sorrow consequently requires an element of guilt, the true tragic pain an element of innocence; the true tragic sorrow requires an element of transparency, the true tragic pain an element of obscurity. This, I believe, best indicates the dialectic wherein the categories of sorrow and pain come in contact with each other, as well as the dialectic which lies in the concept of tragic guilt.

Now the 'brothers in and towards death' can draw nearer, for Kierkegaard is ready to send into the world his 'daughter of sorrow', the one to whom he has given 'a dowry of pain . . . She is called Antigone'.

Kierkegaard's relation to the child of Oedipus is one of possessive irony, of a Don Juanism of the soul such as he himself has described in his analysis of Mozart. 'She is my creation, her thoughts are my thoughts, and yet it is as if I had rested with her in a night of love, as if she had entrusted me with her deep secret, breathing out this secret and her soul in my embrace.' In one sense, Antigone is the 'lawful possession' of the erotic ironist; in another, she is an autonomous being who has entrusted to the narrator-lover the integrity of her person. Kierkegaard is playing dialectically on the ambiguity of poetic invention (*invenire*: 'to find that which was not yet there'). He is playing on the power, more than metaphoric, of the 'created' persona to 'stand outside' and 'against' its creator in existential independence ('Anna Karenina has escaped from my control,' confides Tolstoy to his editor). That this 'ecstasy', this literal 'standing outside' of a major creation in language or the arts, is profoundly analogous to the relations of man to God—we are his creatures entirely, but in this entirety lies our independence from him—is a point evident to Kierkegaard. Antigone 'comes into existence only as I bring her forth', yet 'I must constantly look behind me to find her'. And it is through Antigone that the categories of *Sorg* and of *Smerts*, of sorrow and of pain, shall be united. 'The daughter of antique, unreflected sorrow shall have bestowed upon her the modern (poisonous) dowry of reflexive pain.'[1] As Johannes de Silentio will say in Kierkegaard's *Fear and Trembling*, like Oedipus, Greek tragedy was blind; modern tragedy is made 'seeing'.

In Kierkegaard's 'Antigone', all the primary relations are the same as in Sophocles 'and yet everything is different'. Antigone *alone* knows the truth of her father's incestuous condition, she alone knows the quality of the bond which united him to Jocasta. In Kierkegaard's reading, there is no Ismene (a 'disappearance' implicit in line 941 of Sophocles' drama—*if* this line is not corrupt). At some early age, Antigone was gripped by intimations of the appalling truth. These 'cast her into the arms of anxiety'. Anxiety, anguish (*Angst*), is the modern tragic element *par excellence*. Its probing, self-reflexive constancy, its intensification in time, convert sorrow, which is 'in the present tense', to pain. In the Greek version, claims Kierkegaard, Antigone 'is not at all concerned about her father's unhappy destiny'. No doubt, this destiny is re-echoed in the wretched death of her brothers, and the spectator sorrows 'infinitely' as he observes the fatal ramifications of Oedipus' inheritance. But the actual conflict arises from a purely human prohibition, from outside, as it were. Antigone's defiance of Creon's edict is 'a fateful necessity', a visitation of the sins of the fathers upon their children. And there is sufficient freedom of action in Antigone's conduct to compel our love and admiration. But there is, above all, blind 'necessity of fate . . . which envelops not only the life of Oedipus but also his entire family'. Had Creon not prohibited the burial of Polyneices, had *fatum* not found its contingent realization, Antigone's personal existence could have ripened into happiness. Nothing intrinsic to her character pre-ordained her fortunes. In the Sophoclean play, therefore, as Kierkegaard reads it, Antigone's relation to her father is at once 'objective' ('fated') and opaque.

Kierkegaard's Antigone, on the contrary, is one of the *symparanekromenoi*, of 'the living dead'. She carries inside her a dowry which 'neither moth nor rust can corrupt': that of her

---

[1] W. Rehm, *Begegnungen und Probleme*, p. 288. It is Kierkegaard's insistence on this 'transmission of pain' which, according to G. L. Luzzatto, profoundly influenced Ibsen's dramatic theory and practice (in 'Sofocle e Kierkegaard: L'Antigone Moderna', *Dioniso*, NS XX [1957], 99–105). Unfortunately, Luzzatto offers no evidence for this suggestion beyond assertions of the order of: 'Ibsen deve avere meditato questo passo . . .'

secret knowledge of Oedipus' catastrophe, and of her own
relation to this catastrophe. *Angst* has made the cup of pain
within her brimful. But nothing 'ennobles a human being so
much as keeping a secret', be it a secret painful unto death.
The Christological echoes lie very near: 'One says of a bride of
God that she has the inward faith and spirit in which she rests.
Our Antigone I should call a bride in a perhaps even more
beautiful sense, indeed she is almost more, she is mother, she is
in the purely aesthetic sense *virgo mater*, she carries her secret
under her heart, hidden and concealed.' The renown, the very
survival, in the spiritual sense, of the house of Oedipus lies in
the hands of her silence. She is wedded to that silence; 'she
knows not any man and yet she is a bride'. Sophocles'
Antigone, argues Kierkegaard, can almost rejoice in Creon's
edict: it allows her to publish to the world her grief over
Polyneices' death. *His* Antigone cannot give voice to her
sorrow; its cause must, forever, remain secret. She lives, as
Rehm puts it, in the *incognito* of her pain.

Oedipus is now dead. But even while he lived, Antigone has
not had the boldness to reveal her dread secret to her father.
'To confide it now to any living being would be to disgrace her
father.' By maintaining inviolable silence, she pays daily,
almost hourly, last honours to Oedipus. But even this silent
consecration is full of ambiguity. Antigone is not certain
whether Oedipus himself was aware of his parricidal, incestuous condition. In this uncertainty, urges Kierkegaard, lies the
modern twist of *Angst*. Knowing herself to be the offspring of
Oedipus and Jocasta, not knowing for certain whether her
father knows the truth of this begetting, Antigone 'feels herself
alienated from mankind'. She is, twice over, a stranger in the
house of being. Oedipus lives in glory, acclaimed by the πόλις.
Antigone joins in the celebrations of his high state. This
enthusiasm is, paradoxically, the only way in which she can
vent her sorrow. She dares not grieve openly over what she
knows to be his blighted identity. Sorrow suppressed or
paradoxically inverted is pain. 'Considered in this way,' offers
the virtuoso raconteur, 'I think that Antigone can really
interest us.'

The screw is given a last turn. 'Antigone is mortally in love.'
Given the depths of her soul, this can be no common love. She
must bring to her beloved Haemon the dowry of her inmost

being: her secret and the pain which springs from it. But can she justify to the sacred dead, to Oedipus, the sharing of her secret even with the beloved? This is the first half of the tragic 'collision' (Kierkegaard uses Hegel's term). The second half is dialectically correspondent: how can Antigone do justice to her lover, to the total love she feels towards him, if she withholds the very essence of her spirit, if she allows him no access to her inmost self? The lover presses his suit; he comes upon Antigone at the grave of Oedipus and adjures her to be his by virtue of the manifest love she bears her father. Unaware, he is closing a death-trap on Antigone. Now the *machine infernale* is exquisitely sprung. 'The colliding forces are so evenly matched that action becomes impossible for the tragic individual.' Antigone can find peace only in death. Only her death can arrest the pollution (the inherited guilt) which the disclosure of her secret and the consummation of her love would, fatally, transmit to succeeding generations. 'Only in the moment of death can she admit the intensity of her love; she can admit to the lover that she belongs to him only in the moment in which she does not belong to him.' Kierkegaard's simile comes from Plutarch: fatally wounded, knowing that he will die in the instant in which the spear is drawn from his wound, heroic Epaminondas waits for news of victory:

Thus does our Antigone bear her secret in her heart like an arrow which life has, unrelentingly, driven in deeper and deeper without killing her. For as long as it remains in her heart, she can live. But in the moment it is drawn out, she must die. The beloved must strive constantly to wrest her secret from her. And yet it is this which means her certain death.

'Who, then, has truly slain Antigone,' asks the ironist: 'the dead Oedipus or her living lover?' 'Both,' replies the dialectic. Twice a stranger in the house of the living, Antigone is sent twice over into the dark of death.

Kierkegaard's fantastication on 'Antigone' is many-layered. The formal surface is, as we saw, that of ironic parable in the Romantic mode. The key concept 'of that which compels interest' rather than, say, compassion or ideological adherence or even pragmatic intervention, had been expounded by Schlegel and by Tieck. 'Interest', sharpened to a razor's edge of psychological ingenuity, is the supreme aim of the narrative experiment. The net of the dialectic is drawn tighter and tighter so as to reduce Antigone to absolute extremity. In Rehm's accurate phrase, she is hounded to a sharp apex of isolation (*die isolierende Spitze*) on which either immobility or motion entails self-destruction. At this final pitch of interest, the stance of the contriver and of the *symparanekromenoi* is that of the *voyeur*. The theatre of pain dreamt by Sade is not far distant. Kierkegaard is perfectly conscious of this element of coercive scrutiny and spectacle. The blameless blindness of the Greek tragic vision is gone; modern dramaturgy depends on a most intense 'seeing'.

In this philosophic–psychological sport or *concetto*, the autobiographical features are, of course, drastic. There is a level at which every touch and twist in this version of 'Antigone' encodes precise references to what Kierkegaard took to be his most intimate existence. The *Papirer* for 1841–3, the six transparently autobiographical allegories of inherited taint and despair in the *Stages on Life's Way* of 1845, closely parallel the Antigone fable of *Either/Or* and even reduplicate its language and organization in a manner characteristic of Kierkegaard's method of indirect discourse.

Antigone's tortured relation with her father, the devouring immanence of the dead father in the living child, exactly mirror Søren Kierkegaard's image of his own circumstance. His father had cursed God: 'How appalling', he recalled in 1846, 'for the man who, as a lad watching sheep on the Jutland heath, suffering painfully, hungry and exhausted, once stood on a hill and cursed God—and the man was unable to forget it when he was eighty-two years old.' And there had been worse: some obscure but ineradicable wrong committed by Kierkegaard's father on that wholly shadowy, never-referred-to figure, his mother—a wrong to which the son bore secret witness. How, then, could Antigone-Kierkegaard speak the inmost truth of her/his being without bringing shame on the father, without revealing to the world a desperately tainted inheritance?

The other dominant relation in the code is that with Regine Olsen, with the beloved whom Kierkegaard abandons so publicly and with such apparent brutality. The 'Antigone' scenario literally transcribes this supreme crisis in the life and thought of Kierkegaard. The earliest 'Antigone' entry in the notebooks (1841?–2) sets out a simplified version. Antigone falls in love 'with all the energy of love, but in order to halt the vengeance of the gods she would not get married, she would regard herself as a sacrifice to the wrath of the gods because she belonged to the family of Oedipus, but she would not leave behind any family that could again become the object of the angry gods' persecution.' But soon the motive for renunciation becomes more specific and lacerating. 'No doubt', notes Kierkegaard on 20 November 1842, 'I could bring my Antigone to an end if I let her be a man. He forsook his beloved because he could not keep her together with his private agony. In order to do it right, he had to turn his whole love into a deception against her, for otherwise she would have participated in his suffering in an utterly unjustifiable way.' Antigone must flee Haemon, Søren Kierkegaard must repudiate Regine Olsen, because the lover cannot entrust to the beloved the secret which both constitutes and ravages his identity. The strands of anguish are wound tight in a passage written in Berlin on 17 May 1843 (*Papirer*, iv. A. 107):

But if I had to explain myself then I would have to initiate her into terrible things, my relation to my father, his melancholy, the eternal darkness that broods deep within, my going astray, pleasures, and excesses which in God's eyes are not, perhaps, so terrible, for it was dread which drove me to excess, and where was I to look for something to hold on to when I knew, or suspected, that the one man I revered for his power and strength had wavered?[1]

The autobiographical content, the vehemence and concreteness of self-projection which inform Kierkegaard's reading of 'Antigone', are beyond doubt. But even as the stylistic guise of the parable is brilliantly expressive of a wider Romantic convention, so the elements of self-portrayal are not only comparable with numerous contemporary documents (witness the intimate, early writing of Newman or of Pusey), but they are part of a thoroughly objective context. And it is, in the final analysis, the latter which matters, which alone gives to Kierkegaard's discourse its enduring theological, philosophic, and psychological claims to attention. *Either/Or* is not a memoir of infirmity, whatever pain underlies it, but a superbly controlled intellectual exploration and argument.

[1] Cf. E. Hirsch, op. cit. i. 104, and W. Rehm, op. cit. 407 and 460 ff., for attempts to elucidate the full meaning of this text.

The preliminary observations on ancient and modern tragic
drama make evident that Kierkegaard, like St Augustine and
Pascal before him, is wrestling with the paradox of 'innocent
guilt', of the legacy of original sin in the soul and flesh of the
individual. Christianity and reflexive modernity have assigned
to this paradox a visibility denied to Greek 'naïvety', to the
primitive notion of the hero's fated doom. Kierkegaard finds in
the relations of *his* Antigone to Oedipus a peculiarly graphic,
concentrated enactment (his later term will be 'embodiment')
of hereditary fatality in the antique sense and of a reflexive
apprehension of this fatality in the modern. Such a reading
promises insight into the mystery of the transmission of sin from
parents to children, a transmission ultimately negated by
Christ's promise of salvation, but none the less existentially
active in the human race. That the terror of a specific
inheritance of sinfulness, of what Rehm calls 'a negative
blessing', weighed on Kierkegaard is undeniable. But the
Antigone–Oedipus relation, as he pictures it, is representative
of a classical theological paradox and of the spiritual–
psychological consequences of this paradox, on a scale far
larger, far more objective, than that of private crisis.

This holds also for the haunting motif of secrecy. Juvenal
and the Church Fathers had propounded that in respect of
secrecy women were as a leaking vessel. This 'truism' had
nourished homily and satire throughout the centuries. It was
reversed by Romanticism. It was in woman that a secret found
its particular dwelling. It was through her capacity to guard a
secret even unto death that woman acquired a distinctive
pathos and nobility. The reasons for this reversal in the
dialectic and phenomenology of discretion are unclear. They
must touch on changes of mutual perception at the core of
erotic and social sensibility.[1] But the literary evidence is
unmistakable.

That the spell of secrecy and of the silence which is the voice
of secrecy lay heavy on Kierkegaard is obvious. Pseudonyms
such as Frater Taciturnus and Johannes de Silentio contain a
whole psychology of self-cloistering and mask. There is a
genuine sense in which the prolixity of Kierkegaard's published discourse is, in effect, an attempt to keep inviolate a
central zone of unspeaking secrecy. No less obvious are the

[1] Cf. P. Boutang, *Ontologie du secret* (Paris, 1973), 125–43.

degree and concreteness of Kierkegaard's identification with those 'brides of quietness', Antigone and Cordelia. The contiguity of the two personae in *Either/Or*, where Cordelia is the seducer's quarry, suggests that Kierkegaard may even have intuited the troubling affinities between the figure of Oedipus and that of Lear. And the tragic break with Regine Olsen is, indeed, seen by 'Antigone-Kierkegaard' as arising from an absolute and a compulsion of unspeakable secrecy. But Kierkegaard's treatment of this theme is no more delicate or obsessive than is that by other Romantics. It is on precisely this same pivot that turn the tales and dramas of Kleist: Alkmene, Kätchen, Penthesilea, the Marquise von O. are the tortured but sanctified carriers of a mastering secret. Kierkegaard's Antigone, therefore, together with her Romantic sisters of silence, tell of far more than private suffocation.

They belong, very probably, to a critique, eloquent and pervasive throughout the early decades of the nineteenth century, of the new technological, journalistic inroads on the spiritual autonomy of the individual. How is one to remain *hin enkelte* ('that individual'), that singular presentness without which there can be no integrity and self-recognition of spirit, in the face of a clamorous mass culture? The question is no more urgent in Kierkegaard than it is in, say, Carlyle or Emerson. One answer lies in the custody of a secret, a secret grave and spacious enough to guard the soul against dispersal.

One further point needs to be made. Kierkegaard's thought abounds in dramatic parables. It is around characters and episodes out of Scripture, out of classical and modern literature, out of historical narrative, that Kierkegaard compacts, that he gives 'indirect immediacy' to his meaning. Very often, the decisive mystery of relation between fathers and sons is argued in reference to David and Solomon and Abraham and Isaac.[1] The category of the aesthetic–sensual is incarnate in Don Juan. Faust allegorizes the imperfect modulation from the intellectual to the theological. Thus there is in the adoption of Antigone to represent Kierkegaard himself in relation to his father and to Regine Olsen an act of deliberate selection. The reason for this choice is, I am convinced, to be found in Kierkegaard's involvement with Hegel. It is the Hegelian

---

[1] At one point, Antigone and David and Solomon are brought into immediate proximity. See no. 5669, dated 1843, in the *Journals and Papers*, v, Part One.

Antigone which lies behind the tormented silhouette in *Either/Or*. Kierkegaard's antenae alerted him to Hegel's infatuation (the word is not too strong) with Sophocles' Antigone. They alerted him to a meditative passion which had elevated the daughter of Oedipus above Socrates and even, perhaps, above Christ. To mould the person of Antigone to his own anguished–ironic purposes, to make her most secretly *his*, was, for Søren Kierkegaard, to search out and challenge the Hegelian system at its nerve-centre. Contrasting, in certain respects antithetical, as they are, the *Antigone* readings and transformations proposed by Hegel and by Kierkegaard remain inseparable.

6

Hegel's relations with Hölderlin were among the most intricate and fragile of which we have record. Goethe's were among the more negative. His pained distaste when a passage from Hölderlin's version of *Antigone* was read to him and to Schiller in 1804, a reading itself motivated by condescension, is notorious. There is no reason to suppose that Hölderlin's name, let alone his interpretation of Sophocles, came to Kierkegaard's notice.

To Goethe and to Schiller, Hölderlin's treatment of the Greek text gave palpable evidence of mental collapse, of the *Umnachtung* (literally, 'benightedness') in which the poet endured from 1804 to his death in 1843. The same view is taken in Schelling's letter to Hegel of July 1804. The radiant being, possessed by Apollo and harried by personal misfortune, has lost his reason. The 1808 and 1846 editions of Hölderlin echo this diagnosis. The 'translations' from the ancient Greek are wild dark things which must be understood as the tragic indices of mental crisis and decay. Even Wilhelm Dilthey's careful remarks in *Das Erlebnis und die Dichtung* (1905) are in the same register. It will not be until Norbert von Hellingrath's inspired edition of Hölderlin's versions of Pindar in 1911 that the entire question of the intent and legitimacy of these translations from the Greek and of the decisive role they play in Hölderlin's later poetry is brought into a positive light. By the time of Heidegger's lectures on Hölderlin in the 1940s, revaluation was dramatic. Karl Reinhardt, the most eminent of 'Sophocleans', could declare in 1951 that Hölderlin's *Oedipus der Tyrann* and *Antigonä* were not failed experiments or the products of derangement, but 'the highest poetry, felicitous to the last'. And to Wolfgang Schadewaldt, Hölderlin's Sophocles represents a force of penetration into the antique original, an authority of understanding in depth, which no other translation or critique, in whatever language, can rival.[1]

These are the judgements of classical philologists and scholars. But the rediscovery of Hölderlin's 'translations' of Sophocles, and of his *Antigonä* in particular, has reached far beyond the sphere of classical studies. It is no exaggeration to say that this text is crucial to modern hermeneutics, to the theory and practice of semantic understanding. The *Antigonä* carries to extremity the radicalization of lexical and syntactic means, the shift from sequential–logical conventions and from the external reference of ordinary discourse to an internalized coherence of metaphor and image-clusters, which make of Hölderlin's late work a primary source of modernism. Sixty years before Mallarmé's *Hérodiade* (and Mallarmé, also, was acutely aware of Hegel's dramatization of language, of Hegel's concept of language as the privileged enactment of the subject 'hammering out' its own consciousness), Hölderlin's *Antigonä*, whose 'paratactic', which is to say 'discontinuous', 'elided', seemingly fragmented, modes of relation seem to prefigure Mallarmé's text, had posed those fundamental questions about the status of meaning which are the object of modern semiotics and 'grammatology'. Walter Benjamin's esoteric but indispensable essay of 1923 on the nature and limits of all translation is an excursus on Hölderlin's Pindar and Sophocles. Hölderlin's practice is both the source of Benjamin's reflections and the ambiguous ideal towards which these reflections strive—ambiguous because Hölderlin's ingress into the original is of such vehemence that, as Benjamin puts it, 'the doors of language close behind the translator'. Nor is it accidental that students of poetics and of language most in sympathy with Lacan, with Derrida, should assign to

---

[1] Cf. K. Reinhardt, 'Hölderlin und Sophokles', in A. Kelletat (ed.), *Hölderlin* (Tübingen, 1961), 303. This essay was originally published in 1951. Also W. Schadewaldt, 'Hölderlins Übersetzung des Sophokles', in J. Schmidt (ed.), *Über Hölderlin* (Frankfurt-on-Main, 1970).

Hölderlin's *Antigonä* an exemplary function in their analytics.[1] Precisely, moreover, to the degree to which current metaphysics and epistemology see in language the crux of their interests, Hölderlin's Sophocles has become a motif of philosophic argument. One cannot separate the 1804 *Antigonä* from important tenets in Heidegger's doctrine of man's exile from and attempted homecoming to a natural order of 'earthbound' and of civic being, and in Heidegger's model of the Λόγος, of the autonomous radiance of speech when 'it streams towards us' through great poetry.[2] In a more restricted, yet still spacious, compass, Hölderlin's adaptations of Sophocles are at the heart of the vexed theme of the evolution and crises of German sensibility. The modulation from an 'Attic idealism' as expounded by Winckelmann, Goethe, Schiller, and the young Hegel, to the violent, transformative appropriation of the ancient gods in Hölderlin's late hymns, Pindar versions, and translations from *Oedipus Rex*, *Antigone*, *Ajax*, and, so far as they survive, from *Oedipus at Colonus*, embodies a choice of extremity, an investment in obsession, which will find its logical consequence in Wagner's 'totalization' of the Aeschylean precedent and in Nietzsche's tragic Hellenism.

Thus there was in Goethe's flinching away from Hölderlin's text more than canonic scorn for amateurism and stridency. There was a perception of a degree of emotional nakedness, of an enlistment of the irrational, which, no less than Kleist's *Penthesilea*, an appropriation of the antique which Goethe found equally distasteful, could wake ominous chords in the German political and social temper. The contrasts between Goethe's relations to Sophocles in *Iphigenie* and Hölderlin's encounter with Sophocles are, very exactly, those between a European classicism, a code of stylistic poise derived from the humanism of the Renaissance, and a new, self-consuming

---

[1] Cf. P. Lacoue-Labarthe, *Hölderlin: L'Antigone de Sophocle suivi de la césure du spéculatif* (Paris, 1978).

[2] Important texts from Heidegger's work on Sophocles' *Antigone* and on Hölderlin's interpretation of Sophocles are, as yet, unpublished. But cf. the *Introduction to Metaphysics*, trans. R. Manheim (Yale University Press, 1959), and 'Hölderlins Erde und Himmel', in the *Hölderlin-Jahrbuch*, xi (1958–60) (Tübingen, 1960). Heidegger's views on Hölderlin's *Oedipus der Tyrann* and *Antigonä* are faithfully reflected in Jean Beaufret's preface to *Hölderlin: Remarques sur Œdipe/Remarques sur Antigone*, trans. and notes by F. Fédier (Paris, 1965). B. Allemann, *Hölderlin und Heidegger* (2nd edn., Zurich, 1954), remains the most sympathetic general treatment of this poetic–philosophic conjunction.

anarchy. The paradox of 'mastering submissiveness' in regard to the archaic original, as Hölderlin seeks to enforce it, carries within it seeds of destruction. That these should spring from Sophocles, the most balanced of artists, must have seemed to Goethe a peculiar violation.

Every facet of Hölderlin's enterprise has been closely investigated—though much remains to be done concerning Nietzsche's and Heidegger's precise indebtedness to Hölderlin's 'Hellenism', and concerning the actual word-by-word fabric of the Sophocles versions *per se*. There is no need to cover in detail familiar ground.[1] Our present focus is that of Hölderlin's account of the meaning of Sophocles' play and, especially, his reading of the characters of Antigone and Creon. How did he interpret their mortal conflict? What can be said of his interpretation in comparison with the readings put forward, at roughly the same period, by Hegel, Goethe, and Kierkegaard? But to answer these questions it will be necessary to consider, however summarily, the composition of Hölderlin's text and to define the main issues raised by his theory and practice of linguistic transfer. For the fundamental fact is that of unison, of indivisibility under pressure. No linguistic detail in Hölderlin's *Antigonä*, no aspect of the relations, consequent or contrastive, between this final work and Hölderlin's previous lyric, dramatic, and translational writings, is immaterial to the central question of interpretation. In Hölderlin's Sophocles, poetics and hermeneutics, philology and politics, are strictly inseparable. As we shall see, the very act of translation is a crucial moment in a larger design. The ideal is that of fusion, of a homecoming (tragically frustrated) to oneness between consciousness and the world. It is the same motion which we have observed in Hegel's *Phenomenology*. Philosophy and the lyric imagination after Kant are the record of a pilgrimage out of inner exile. The first stasimon in Sophocles' *Antigone* is its touchstone.

[1] The following are helpful: M. Corssen, 'Die Tragödie als Begegnung zwischen Gott und Mensch. Hölderlins Sophokles-Deutung', *Hölderlin-Jahrbuch*, iii (1948–9) (Tübingen, 1949); W. Schadewaldt (ed.), *Sophokles, Tragödien. Deutsch von Friedrich Hölderlin* (Frankfurt-on-Main, 1957); Fr. Beissner, *Hölderlins Übersetzungen aus dem Griechischen* (2nd edn., Stuttgart, 1961); W. Binder, 'Hölderlin und Sophokles', *Hölderlin-Jahrbuch*, xvi (1969–70) (Tübingen, 1970); R. B. Harrison, *Hölderlin and Greek Literature* (Oxford, 1975); B. Böschenstein, 'Die Nacht des Meers: Zu Hölderlins Übersetzung des ersten Stasimons der "Antingonae"', in U. Fülleborn and J. Krogoll (edd.), *Studien zur deutschen Literatur* (Heidelberg, 1979).

Hölderlin's endeavours to translate Sophocles most probably date back to the time of intimacy with Hegel and with Schelling in Tübingen. The translation of a choral ode from *Oedipus at Colonus* can be dated 1796. The autumn of 1799 produced a first version of the talismanic stasimon in *Antigone*.[1] Later in the same year, Hölderlin wrote the epigram which defines one significant aspect at least of his trust in Sophocles:

> Viele versuchten umsonst das Freudigste freudig zu sagen,
> Hier spricht endlich es mir, hier in der Trauer sich aus.

> (Many strove in vain joyously to express the highest joy,
> At last it speaks to me here, here in sorrow it expresses itself fully.)

Hölderlin worked on *Oedipus der Tyrann* and *Antigonä* from 1797 to 1804. The main spell of translation seems to fall between the spring of 1801 and the autumn of 1802. Both texts were certainly well advanced by June 1802, the moment of Hölderlin's desolate return from a period as house-tutor in Bordeaux. A certain number of revisions, principally affecting *Antigonä*, were made during the psychologically and materially catastrophic year 1803. Hölderlin secured a publisher in the summer of that year and dispatched the manuscript on 8 December. The two dramas, marred by numerous printing errors, again most particularly in *Antigonä*, were issued in April 1804. It may be that Hölderlin was working on *Oedipus at Colonus* and on *Ajax*, a play which, as we shall see, he saw as peculiarly contiguous to *Antigone*, immediately before his collapse in the summer of 1804. These latter texts had been meant to be volumes three and four in a complete rendition of Sophocles' tragedies.

At least three levels of translation, both programmatic and empirical, can be made out in the palimpsest of Hölderlin's Sophocles. They cannot, however, be discriminated neatly and any vertical, chronological division is a simplification. Such was the constant pressure of thought and of technical experiment which Hölderlin brought to bear on the problem of translation as a whole and on the relations, dramatic in translation, between an antique source and modern means of

---

[1] Cf. B. Böschenstein, op. cit., for an acute comparison between this early version and that of 1804.

transformative comprehension, that different strategies of understanding of transference interpenetrate virtually throughout. There is, very roughly, an early method of which the *Antigone* stasimon of 1799 and a translation of the prologue to Euripides' *Bacchae* may be said to be representative. This is the period of 'classic idealism' in which Hölderlin, often in observance of Schiller, seeks to convey the Greek original 'faithfully but also freely'. The aim is to produce a German text in which the sense and luminous force of the Greek tragedians is wholly evident, but whose idiom, cadence, and rhetorical conventions are natural to the native tongue. This transfer is possible precisely because the native tongue is now in a novel condition of national confidence. Important vestiges of this 'liberal fidelity' can be seen throughout Hölderlin's *Oedipus*. In *Antigonä* they are rarer. A second level—but is it not already operative in some of Hölderlin's own early poetry, in his treatment of German itself?—is that of intransigent literalism. The covert model is that of an interlinear primer, of word-by-word equivalence irrespective of the norms of word-usage, grammar, and style in the translator's native speech. It is on this fierce 'literality', and with reference to Hölderlin's treatment of the odes of Pindar, that Walter Benjamin bases his theory of absolute translation and of the confluence of all secular tongues towards a primal source of perfect unison and facsimile. Such literalism is practised, so far as is possible, in the translation of sacred and liturgical texts and in the word-by-word, phrase-by-phrase commentary they inspire. Thus it is likely that Hölderlin's pietist background, like Benjamin's 'Talmudism', plays a definite role in this paradoxical design. The coercive but often penetrative 'Atticization' of German which results, with its contrivance of a 'transparent' idiom and its dislocation of sentence structures, clause dependencies, participial agreements, is visible in *Oedipus der Tyrann* and emphatic in *Antigonä*. Hölderlin's adoption of literalist techniques and of a consequent estrangement from 'natural' German seems to have been dominant in 1801–2. But here, as well, there is precedent in his own verse and in those elements of the young Hölderlin's style which derive from the lyric extremism of Klopstock.

It is after his return from France and in a time of uttermost personal stress that Hölderlin articulates and puts into practice

a third mode of metamorphic transfer. That there may have
been implicit in this mode and in its application to Sophocles
after the summer of 1802 symptoms, symbolic markers, of
Hölderlin's *Umnachtung* is plausible. But this is not the point.
Even in its imperative extremity, this third level of theory
and of practice, which may be the most fascinating and
epistemologically challenging in the history of the arts of translation, represents an intelligible, self-consistent development
in Hölderlin's views on language and society. It embodies
a fundamental part in his portrayal of man's condition in a
natural, civic, and religious context. To consider it as 'only'
a theory of poetic translation, let alone a pathological phenomenon, is to excise it from a vital entity.

This final concept of the motion of meaning between the
original Greek text and its German version, between Sophocles
and Friedrich Hölderlin, assigns to the temporal distance
between   fifth-century   Athens   and   nineteenth-century
Germany a dynamic, teleological character. Time itself, to
which the late Hölderlin ascribes a mystery of purpose and of
generative energy closely related to the nature of the divine—
Zeus, Dionysus, Christ as he comes after them, are 'fathers of
Time' and preside over Time's revolutions—is transformative
of the classical text. But not merely transformative in the sense
in which we might argue that Sophocles' meanings are qualified, altered, possibly enriched by centuries of receptive interpretation, by the echoes and reflections which they have
instigated in later works. Hölderlin's notion of the transformational agency of time is radical and ontological. It addresses
itself to the very being of the original, to what Heidegger will
call its 'presentness' and existential durance (*Da-sein, Wesen*).
Latent in the original text are certain truths, certain orders
of signification and performative potentialities which are un-
realized when it appears in its initial embodiment. This
embodiment is, in some respects, only an annunciation,
however well wrought, of forms of being yet to come. It is the
'translator's' sacred, if paradoxical and even antinomian, task
to call into life these indwelling but hitherto unfulfilled
latencies, to 'surpass' the original text in the exact spirit of this
text. This violence of loving elicitation, this 'knowing the
author better than he knows himself' (out of which 'scandalous' perception Borges spins his fable of the 'translator' Pierre

Menard), is made possible, indeed compelling, by the revolutions of time and the change of languages. It is these which
empower the 'translator' to act as the legatee and, in the
strongest sense, as the executor of the antique poet's heritage
and 'will'. Hölderlin's late hymn, 'Patmos', expresses this vision
of an epiphany of understanding. It refers us immediately and
illuminatingly to the function of the apostle as the 'translator'
and, therefore, 'achiever' of the Word under the imperative of
revelation. In this drama of linguistic transfer, the apocalyptic
and the pentecostal are closely inwoven.

The application of this programme to *Oedipus der Tyrann*
and to *Antigonä* is argued in a letter which Hölderlin sent to
his (presumably bemused) publisher, Friedrich Wilmans,
in September 1803. Its cryptic formulation of the
'Orientalization' of the Greek original, of the amendments
which the translation is to make where there are *Kunstfehler*
('artistic flaws') in Sophocles, presumes an understanding of
Hölderlin's entire theory of history and of the special relations
between the Attic and the German–occidental spirit (between
das Griechische and *das Hesperische*). Even given such pre-
requisites, however, much in Hölderlin's model remains
opaque and seems to reach deep into private obsession.
Hölderlin is polemicizing, obliquely, against Schiller's idealization of the harmonic universality of Greek art and against
F. W. Schlegel's insistence on the never-to-be-rivalled perfection of the classical. Hölderlin, who sees both Sophocles and
himself as poets in times of crisis, of temporal dislocation and
revolution, is persuaded that there are 'suppressions', 'constraints on totality', in Sophocles' dramas which he, the later
and 'Hesperian' heir and interpreter, can discern and amend.
By virtue of which discernment and *Verbesserung*, literally
'correction and improvement', he will be truer to Sophocles
than Sophocles himself has been. What, then, have time and
the modulation from Greek to German brought to light?

Apollonian fire, the primordial ecstasies and purities of
divine inspiration, blazed freely in the Greek world, notably in
its archaic stages. To this, Plato's *Ion* bears somewhat ironic
witness. But native to Attic sensibility was a gift of temperance,
of 'Junonian sobriety' (*junonische Nüchternheit*). This esoteric
phrase may point to the 'cool', counter-erotic role which Hera
(Juno) plays in the *Iliad*. This sobriety, graphic in Plato's

condemnation of poetic irresponsibility, dampens the naked flame. It imposes on Sophoclean tragedy a certain 'excess of form'. Apollonian lightning is, as it were, prevented from damaging, but also from informing ecstatically, the shaped order of Sophocles' *Antigone*. This order is threatened, as we shall see, by the 'wild world of the dead', by the daemonic agencies dwelling in the earth. We 'Hesperians' come after the immense turn in the wheel of time, after the dual dispensation of Dionysus and of Christ with its roots in the 'Oriental'. Thus our condition of spirit is precisely the reverse of that of the ancient Athenians. Our 'Zeus' is a 'native–national principle' (*vaterländisch*) who has rooted us in native ground, in the immanence of the earth-bound. He is truly a *Vater der Erde*, an Earth-Father, as the Attic Zeus was not or, more pertinently, as the Sophoclean Zeus was on the way to becoming in the very deed of Antigone. Being, therefore, terrestrial, 'of the earth earthy', we can expose ourselves, indeed we must expose ourselves, to the radiant terror of Apollonian fire. We can, we must, nourish the holy flame of poetic inspiration, of revelation past reason, for it will not consume our earthy, firmly embedded nature. Hölderlin's ode 'Wie wenn am Feiertage . . .' provides an incomparable account of the modern poet's exposure to the 'paternal lightning-bolt' of Apollonian visitation. The dialectic of history, of the 'contrast in continuity' between the Greek and the Hesperian which makes this exposure necessary, is expounded in a much-commented letter to Böhlendorff in December 1801.

In terms of this dialectic, Hölderlin must translate Sophocles 'against himself', against that in Sophocles which dampened the primordial flame of visionary menace and mantic insight by means of a deeply ingrained, culturally defensive sobriety. The translation will make 'shimmeringly transparent' the 'Apollonian-passionate foundations' (*apollonisch-leidenschaftlicher Urgrund*) covert, constrained within the 'Junonian-sober governance and self-control' (*junonisch-nüchterne Beherrschtheit*) of Sophoclean classical form. In doing so, Hölderlin's translation will bring to the fore the 'Oriental' substratum and well-spring stifled in fifth-century Greek art, and will amend those 'faults', those cases of self-censorship, albeit subconscious, which are *now* manifest in the very perfection of the Sophoclean text. This motion of amendment is itself dialectical. The arrows of temporality speed in opposite directions. Overall, Hölderlin is 'fulfilling' the potentialities of future being, of deployment in and through historical time, latent in *Oedipus Rex* and *Antigone*. He is, by virtue of his much later historical condition—most subtly, the term 'Hesperian' has connotations both of westward progress and of twilit decline—bringing to the Greek text that which 'was already there' but could not, at the time, be made visible. But Hölderlin can only generate this 'realization' by going 'behind' Sophocles, by proceeding 'upstream' and 'eastward' to those archaic fonts of tragic meaning and of tragic gesture which Sophocles' continence, Sophocles' Periclean addiction to temperance, had, to some degree, stifled. This return to the occult source is embodied in the etymologizing thrust of Hölderlin's practice as a translator. It is in the often concealed or eroded roots of words that Apollonian lightning has left its authentic mark. It is to these roots that we must force our way if we are to liberate the charge of primal inspiration and the meanings of Sophoclean meaning. Only thus can we induce the classical text to exhibit its full genius and the bearing of this genius on our age and needs of spirit. 'Jetzt komme, Feuer!' ('Come now, Fire!') This summons, at the beginning of 'Der Ister', is Hölderlin's talismanic rite both as poet and as translator. The two are made one in the act of total translation, in the obeisant megalomania of the ecstatic.

There would be much more to say about Hölderlin's myth of history, from which Nietzsche's famous dichotomy of Dionysian and Apollonian evidently derives. The hallucinating doctrine of translation which this historiography underwrites is absorbing in itself. But what I want to show here is the intimate concordance between this doctrine and Hölderlin's theory of tragedy as it is set out in the three successive versions of his *Der Tod des Empedokles*, in the paper he wrote on the 'fundamentals' of this lyric drama (the 'Grund des Empedokles' of August–September 1799), in the letters to Böhlendorff, and, above all, in the two sets of 'Annotations' or 'Observations', the *Anmerkungen*, with which he prefaced *Oedipus der Tyrann* and *Antigonä*. It emerges that Hölderlin's theory of translation is a 'tragic theory' exactly mirroring Hölderlin's model of tragedy and that the latter, in turn, is founded on the same dialectic of encounter, of

self-destructively creative collision, which is central to Hölderlin's precepts and techniques of translation. The 'tragedy of
understanding in and through translation' on the one hand,
and 'tragic drama as the transfer into discourse of otherwise
untranslatable collisions' on the other, are facets of the
identical crystal. Sophocles' *Antigone* is made to carry a double
weight: it is the source of Hölderlin's final paradigm of tragedy
and also its decisive proof. Thus the play is as central to
Hölderlin's poetics and symbolic metaphysics as it is to the
logic of human relations and to the aesthetics of Hegel. More
so, perhaps, for the Sophoclean text seems to take almost
complete possession of Hölderlin's sensibility in its twilight.

   The concept of tragedy which Hölderlin affirms in successive
versions of his *Empedokles* and in related analyses is that of a
Gottesgeschehen, of a 'God-event' or existential manifestation of
the imminence and proximity of the divine at signal hours and
in privileged settings in mortal affairs. God and man, writes
Hölderlin during the winter of 1799–1800, a moment charged
with secular intimations, meet *per contrarium*, in contrariety.
The resulting encounter is, in the Heraclitean–Hegelian sense
of the word, a πόλεμος, a fierce grappling. In this collision, the
divine assumes the quality or form of the 'organic', this is to
say of the life-principle in its natural and civic lineaments, in
its 'boundedness'. In man, on the contrary, there is an
unbounded, formless, subconscious, and potentially all-
consuming life-force which Hölderlin designates as the 'aorgic'
(*das Aorgische*). The parallel with the antinomy between
Apollonian fire and 'Junonian sobriety' in the theory of
translation is patent. In certain mortals, at the apex of ecstatic
consciousness, the 'organic' and the 'aorgic' *seem* united: 'Der
Gott und Mensch *scheint* Eins' ('God and man *seem* one'). But
this resolution of an almost Hegelian dialectic, this synthesis, is
illusory or, at best, momentary. The divine plane is inevitably
superior. Inherently aggressive, the attempt at symbiosis
between mortal and divine can only lead to a more lucid
insight into the abyss which separates both. But from the
compulsion to leap across this abyss, literally the *salto mortale* in
human consciousness, stems, one ought to say 'springs', the
tragic action. The 'polemic' between God and man, the
process of transcendental collision, entails the death or, more
rigorously expressed, the self-destruction of the protagonist

(Empedocles' suicide, his leap into the divine fire). Yet only in such death can there be a restoration of equilibrium. The 'organic' now takes on universal validity for the individual and the 'aorgic' which rages in the singular spirit is made subject to rational understanding and to integration in nature and society. What is not entirely clear, either in the *Empedokles* torsos or in Hölderlin's gloss, is whether the tragic agent, the 'wrestler with the divine', is chosen by fatality or is self-appointed. Empedocles' foes cite his arrogant egotism. The philosopher-prince himself tells of a sense of exile from the organic and the universal so acute, so contrary to his ecstatic intimations of unity, that he has no choice but to strive for a homecoming to that which is divine in man even at, pre-eminently at, the risk of death. But unmistakably, it is Hölderlin's conviction that even beyond the stature of the 'tragic individual' there is a temporal factor. The 'polemic' between man and God, the attempt, inherently agonistic, to overcome the separation between 'organic' and 'aorgic', can only occur fruitfully in moments of more or less catastrophic social–historical transformation.[1] Revolutions, in their secular guise, are the public enactments of such mysteries of collision— of the *Gottesgeschehen*. That there are in this 'Empedocles-model' of the nature and format of tragic drama notable analogies with Hegel's analysis of tragedy is evident. The common source is Sophoclean.

It is to this source that Hölderlin now turns. The observations on *Oedipus* are transitional as between Hölderlin's first concept of tragedy and the esoteric doctrine which he expounds in respect of *Antigone*. But even so, the commentary on *Oedipus*, with its compressed syntax and turns of Swabian dialect, is as awkward to paraphrase as are some of the explanatory glosses of Mallarmé, whose method Hölderlin so curiously prefigures. According to Hölderlin (whose interpretation here finds no support in the text), Oedipus interprets the message brought from the Delphic oracle *zu unendlich* ('too limitlessly', 'too far in excess of its boundaries'). The oracle could, ought to have been understood as calling on Oedipus to rule firmly in Thebes, to exercise a just and pure rule of law in order to restore civic stability as it is threatened by the plague. Instead, Oedipus immediately adopts the voice and status of

---

[1] This point is argued convincingly in M. Corssen, op. cit. 150.

priesthood, of ritual retribution. It is *he*, urges Hölderlin, who directs Creon's thoughts to the long-past murder of Laius. It is *he* who ascribes to this murder an unending legacy of pollution and who makes of the pursuit of the unknown assassin an imperative 'without limitations'. In so doing, Oedipus succumbs to the temptations of *nefas*. The term signifies 'enormity', more exactly, an enormity sprung from opposition to the gods, from some violence done to natural destiny. Hölderlin would have known the term from Virgil and from Lucretius, in whom it is specifically associated with the world of the Furies. That in Oedipus which yields to, which in fact solicits, the seduction of *nefas* is characterized, memorably, as 'die wunderbare zornige Neugier' ('the wondrous, admirable incensed curiosity') which fires knowledge when the latter has broken through its natural constraints—when rationality is in an 'aorgic' state. Free of 'organic' constraints, Oedipus' lust for insight is, as it were, 'drunk' (like Hegel, again, the late Hölderlin has a hauntingly sensory concept of the spell of abstract and analytic thought). But even this inebriation and the raging curiosity which drive Oedipus doomward retain their 'resplendent harmonic form' (*seine herrliche harmonische Form*). Oedipus is now trapped in an 'autonomous'—the epithet will be crucial with regard to Antigone—logic of self-scission and self-ruin. Knowingness, at this pitch of limitless thrust, elicits knowledge which mortal man cannot contain. In his fury of clairvoyance, Oedipus the king-priest has made of himself the literal monster, the hybrid born of an attempted coupling between man and God, of that coercive fusion between 'organic' and 'aorgic' of which Hölderlin had given a first version in *Der Tod des Empedokles*. Note how Hölderlin radicalizes, makes transcendent, the incest motif in the Oedipus legend. Now 'a limitless parting' must follow, which is to say the destruction of the 'tempter and attempter of enormity'. Oedipus is doomed.

In a momentous aside, Hölderlin argues that through its very fabric the dramatic dialogue in Sophocles' *Oedipus* acts out the collision between the antithetical agencies of mortal and divine, of 'aorgic' and 'organic', of boundless and rule-governed. There is a sense, itself 'monstrous', in which a dramatic dialogue, particularly in the Greek form of 'sticho-mythia' (the exchange, in alternate verses, of attack and defence, of proposition and riposte), seeks reciprocal annihilation. In Sophocles, says Hölderlin, 'Rede gegen Rede', 'discourse *contra* discourse', aims, violently, at synthesis, at oneness of meaning. This it cannot achieve. On the contrary, the more closely the personages engage in agonistic dialogue, the more cutting the separation, the more irremediable the alienation which results. The pious mendacities, the compassions, the lamentations enunciated by the chorus, labour, to the point of exhaustion, to temper the suicidal dialectic of the dialogue. But in vain.

Oedipus' overreaching lunge towards *nefas* is not an isolated act or an accident of private psychology. He follows, he 'takes on', the 'curve' of 'lacerating Time' (*der reissenden Zeit*). The hour is one of catastrophic dislocation: there is, in Thebes, pestilence, sensual anarchy, febrile divination—Hölderlin's reading, here, being far more Senecan than it is Sophoclean. In such hours, mankind will fall into 'unremembrance of the gods'. The gods will seem to have receded out of reach and thought. Such recession could 'open a breach', could cause 'lacunae' in the continuity of the cosmic order (at this point, Hölderlin's vocabulary is almost private). To prevent this breach, to fill the gap, certain human beings—Oedipus—must be made, must make of themselves, *Verräter*, 'traitors to God'. They must, as it were, commit treason against the natural, against the ontological boundaries which separate mortal beings from the divine. By committing such treason, 'assuredly in a sacred way', these sanctified and self-sacrificial betrayers *compel* the divine to manifest its offended, overwhelming power and thus restore it to man's awareness. Is Hölderlin evoking, subconsciously perhaps, the 'betrayal to epiphany' which Judas visits on Christ? This evocation could throw light on the development of his argument. For in the revolutionary hour, in the 'moment of categorical reversal', to use Hölderlin's famous phrase, there is 'treason' on both the human *and* the divine plane.[1] Zeus has become 'nothing but time'; because time is involved in a dynamic of total change,

---

[1] J. Beaufret, op. cit. 25–6, argues that Hölderlin's idiom and analysis at this point derive immediately from Kant's use of the notion of 'categories' and, perhaps, from the Kantian critique of time. Hölderlin's early enthusiasm for Kant is certain, but by the time of the *Anmerkungen* the differences between his own tragic metaphysics and Kantian Idealism are drastic.

Zeus 'makes no sense'. Pure temporality is tantamount to incomprehensible crisis. Man, in turn, is forced to follow, to move with this incomprehensible, seemingly 'senseless' whirl of time. Thus he becomes fragmented into a succession of broken-edged moments and impulses, and is severed from the responsible roots and limitations of his being. Whatever its application to Sophocles' *Oedipus*, this analysis is brilliantly diagnostic of the condition of spirit of a truth-obsessed individual (Friedrich Hölderlin) under the pressures of the French Revolution. What fulcrum there is in this 'chaos of time', what understanding, lodges with Teiresias, as it will also in *Antigone*.

In wilful error, Hölderlin makes of *Oedipus der Tyrann* the earlier of the two plays. He does this so that Antigone's persona and her deed can make manifest, in final form, the *mysterium tremendum* of the agonistic unison between God and man, between the 'organic' in the natural world and the 'aorgic' in the individual, between cataclysmic time and common temporality, between antique and Hesperian. This manifestation is enacted in the polemic collision and coercive fusion between language and meaning which we call translation. It is from a 'translation' of Sophocles' *Antigone*, from a transmutation of the Greek original into its 'wholeness', that is to emerge, in a well-known phrase of Salvatore Quasimodo, whose context is also one of entombment and resurrection, 'the image of the world' (*dove esita l'immagine del mondo*). To this transfiguration, the notes on *Oedipus der Tyrann* and the actual techniques of translation in Hölderlin's version are a prologue. So much is evident.

What remains debatable is the actual provenance and reach of the *Anmerkungen zur Antigonä*. Much of this commentary, whose date of composition is late but not exactly known, can be decoded both in the light of Hölderlin's idiom after 1801 and in terms of his theory of tragedy, as well as with concrete reference to the play as he renders it. But there are components which remain almost unintelligible, and this despite extensive and often ingenious modern exegesis. However tangential, the factor of nervous disorder cannot be ruled out. In 1803–4, Hölderlin characterized his own condition as that of a man blasted by divine fire. There is in the compaction of the *Anmerkungen* a wild haste. Hölderlin is grasping at 'revealed' insights; the spirit is blazing through the letter while giving to the letter, as in the Johannine parable of 'Patmos', an incomparable aura of literality. But insight and communication are simultaneously threatened by and inseparable from the nearing darkness of unreason. There are, I believe, elements in these annotations, as there are in the *Antigonä* proper, where night intrudes. The exalted status which twentieth-century philosophic and literary criticism assigns to Hölderlin's 'Sophocles' ought not to obliterate altogether the touch of truth in the reactions of the poet's contemporaries. There is derangement here and a solicitation of chaos.

More drastically, even, than *Oedipus*, Sophocles' *Antigone* is, according to Hölderlin, a play set in, and representative of, a moment of 'national reversal and revolution' (*vaterländische Umkehr*). The hour is that of a dramatic revaluation of moral values and political power-relations. From the fatal collision of tragic agents and world-views there will emerge a 'republikanische Vernunftsform' ('a republican rationality', 'a reasoned structure in the republican mode'). 'This is particularly evident at the close when Creon is almost manhandled by his knaves' (a motif wholly invented by Hölderlin). Throughout the Haemon–Creon debate, the coming of republican institutions is foreshadowed. The French Revolution has brought to expressive fulfilment certain republican, 'insurrectionary' elements—Hölderlin uses the actual term *Aufstand*—of which Sophocles, himself witness of Periclean 'democracy' and incipient crisis, was aware, but which his sovereign formality left muted. In short, and with connotations close to those of Spinoza's title, *Antigone* is, to Hölderlin, a 'theological–political' document.

It is in this historicist and revolutionary perspective—what could be more kindred to Antigone than a career such as that of the young Saint-Just executed in 1794 for his Utopian fanaticism?—that we must interpret the clash between Creon and Antigone. The dialectical markers which Hölderlin had previously identified now come into play. Creon incarnates 'das Förmliche', that which is both 'shapely' and 'formalistic', that which in Attic sensibility and statecraft, as well as in the conventions of Sophoclean drama itself, reflects 'Junonian sobriety'. His sphere is the universalizing, harmonious compass of the 'organic'. It is, also and essentially, that of the law, of *Gesetz*, in the strongest sense of the 'statutory' and 'rule-bound' as it is dominant in a pre-revolutionary πόλιc. By virtue of antithesis, *Anti*gone (does her very name not declare as much?) embodies 'das Unförmliche', the 'formless', with all its implications of primal infinity, of undifferentiated generative energies. In her, the 'aorgic' is uncompromisingly unleashed; Apollonian fire possesses every fibre of her being. She is *gesetzlos*, 'lawless', but in a sense which is yet to be defined and which will only become entirely visible in Hölderlin's reading of the fourth stasimon in the play.

Analogies with Hegel's view of the conflict between state and individual, between coercive legalism and instinctive humanism, in *Antigone* are undeniable. At the outset, Hegel and Hölderlin had travelled the same road. But the differences are trenchant. Despite its argument for perfect dialectical equilibrium, Hegel's interpretation makes of Creon a false or superficial pietist and of Antigone's religiosity an authentic inspiration. In Hölderlin's conception, *both* figures are radically religious. They worship the same heavenly powers but experience their relations to these powers, their respective 'god-nearness' or 'god-distance', in irreconcilably opposite ways. Hence one of the most famous moments in Hölderlin's translation: his reading of οὐ γάρ τί μοι Ζεύc in line 450 as 'Darum, *mein* Zeus . . .' ('Because, *my* Zeus . . .'). It is through this 'possessive pronoun'—certainly a grammatical error on Hölderlin's part—that we are to enter into Antigone's true nature.

She is the quintessential *Antitheos* of whom the poet had written in his seminal letter to Böhlendorff of December 1801. This is to say that she is one whose stance before God or the gods (Hölderlin uses these designations interchangeably) is contrary, adversative, polemic. But this contrariety and agonistic attack is sublime piety. The *Antitheos* is one who '*in Gottes Sinne*, wie *gegen* Gott sich verhält'—who 'comports himself as if *against* God, *in a godly sense*'. This divinely possessed 'God-counterer' becomes the holiest of heretics, a figure who will become central in Dostoevsky's scenario of the 'holy sinner' and loving challenger of Christ. Hölderlin's points of reference are philosophical. Precisely like Empedocles and like Rousseau, as Hölderlin portrays him in his ode 'Der Rhein', Antigone is a 'holy fool' (*törig göttlich*). To an even more exalted degree than Rousseau, she is *gesetzlos*, 'lawless'. In both instances, however, this 'lawlessness' is a divinely inspired judiciousness. It enacts

an espousal of absolute and also of historically evolving justice
which not only exceeds legalism and the statutory but is in
inevitable antithesis to them. The letter of the law (Creon) is
challenged by the primal spirit and nascent future of the law
(Antigone). As in Hegel's dialectic, so in Hölderlin's interpretation, the radical and the revolutionary, that which is at the
roots and which reaches into futurity, presses its claims against
the spurious fixity—spurious because contingent—of present
institutions. In this 'Streit der Liebenden', 'quarrel, combat of
the loving and of lovers', the *Antitheos*, be it Empedocles-
Rousseau, be it the child of Oedipus, speaks 'the language of
the purest'—an ecstatic, unworldly idiom which, in his Rhine
hymn, Hölderlin characterizes as Dionysian, hence 'aorgic'.
Such enunciation and the intimacy with the divine sought,
suffered, by the 'God-wrestler' are literally suicidal. The
Begeisterter, 'he whom the Spirit informs and possesses', must
perish in his wild progress towards the divine, even as the
translator's native tongue will perish in its wild motion towards
a complete appropriation and 'ingestion' of the numinous
source. The 'cannibalistic' note is there: the *Antitheos*, in
Hölderlin's account to Böhlendorff, is granted 'too large a
portion' of the divine presence or 'becomes more of a portion of
this presence' than can be contained—*mehr von Göttern ward* is a
suggestively ambiguous phrase. The *Antitheos* perishes of a
surfeit of transcendence. This suicidal consummation is
Hölderlin's answer to the question posed by Schelling in the
last of his *Letters on Dogmatism and Criticism* of 1795–6: how can
we endure, how can we assign rational meaning to, the
destruction, often self-destruction, of the Greek tragic hero by
virtue of a 'destined crime' or inevitable error? It is the
resolution of this seeming outrage in the 'just lawlessness' and
'holy crime' of the *Antitheos* which makes of tragedy 'the most
rigorous of poetic forms', the executive genre most central to
man's understanding of his condition in respect of God, of
himself, and of society. And because it reveals the *Antitheos* in
his/her fullest self-awareness and articulate force, Sophocles'
Antigone is unquestionably the highest example of the supreme
literary–linguistic art form. It is to Hölderlin, as *Tristan und
Isolde* will be to the early Nietzsche, not only the greatest work
of art, but the *'opus metaphysicum* par excellence'.[1]

---

[1] This illuminating parallel is drawn by P. Lacoue-Labarthe, op. cit. 208.

But this awesome reading, together with the interpretation
of Haemon, the rhetoric of tragic speech, the subtle view of the
functions of the chorus, all of which Hölderlin points to
hermetically in his *Anmerkungen*, only take on arguable substance in his actual 'translation' of the play. Here, assuredly,
'God lies in the detail'. What, then, are the orders of relation
between Sophocles' *Antigone* and Hölderlin's *Antigonä*?

7

The mechanics of these relations were defective. None of the
editions of Sophocles apparently available to Hölderlin (texts
had been published in 1739, 1760, 1777, 1781, and 1786) was
sound by modern standards. The best edition, issued by R. F. P.
Brunck in 1786–9, was either overlooked by Hölderlin or
inaccessible to him on grounds of cost. Thus he relied
principally, though not exclusively, on an Italian recension of
1555, the so-called 'Iuntina'. This is a notoriously infirm piece
of work whose misreadings and spurious conjectures visibly
account for a good many of Hölderlin's errors. At other points
in *Antigonä*, the crux is that of Hölderlin's command of ancient
Greek. His passion for the language, his involvement with it
from the time of his school-days, are certain. His intimacy with
Homer, Pindar, Sophocles, and Plato was vivid and authentic.
Witness the felicity, the sharpness, of his quotations and subtle
misquotations from these writers throughout his own writings.
Time and again, Hölderlin's penetration of the antique text,
his ability to 'get behind' words and phrases in order to isolate,
to elicit their core of meaning, far surpasses routine philological competence. But it is just the latter which is often lack-
ing. Whether out of ignorance, carelessness, or haste, Hölderlin
frequently misunderstands what Sophocles is saying. Where a
corrupt text and Hölderlin's misprision of a Greek compound
form come together (in lines 604 ff., for instance), the result
will be arbitrary or chaotic. But even where his text is passable,
Hölderlin may confuse neighbouring cases and modes, misread
word-endings, and overlook diacritical accents. Such lapses
become drastic when he is seeking to enforce his ideal of
absolute literalism, of lexical and grammatical facsimile, on a
Greek original which he is either reading in a false recension or

1. (*Top*) Antigone brought in front of Creon by two guards. Lucanian nestoris by the Dolon Painter *c.*380–370 BC (London BM F 175).

2. (*Bottom*) Antigone, Heracles, Creon, Ismene, represented on a Greek vase of the mid-fourth century BC found in Italy.

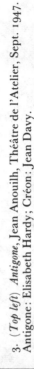

3. (*Top left*) *Antigone*, Jean Anouilh, Théâtre de l'Atelier, Sept. 1947. Antigone: Elisabeth Hardy; Créon: Jean Davy.

4. (*Top centre*) *Antigone*, Bertolt Brecht, Stadttheater von Chur, Switzerland, 15 Feb. 1948. Antigone: Helene Weigel. Production: C. Neher and B. Brecht.

5. (*Left*) Szenenskizze (stage-drawing) by Caspar Neher for Brecht's *Antigone*.

6. (*Top right*) Sophocles' *Antigone*, translated into French by A. Bonnard, Comédie Française, 1951. Antigone: Renée Faure; Créon: Jean Davy.

which he is, quite simply, reading falsely. There is, at such points, no escape into the approximate stylishness which protects normal literary translation. Many of these textual and interpretative deficiencies—glaring to Hölderlin's contemporaries—have been identified and glossed.[1] Obviously, they impinge on central issues of understanding. Often, e.g. in lines 245 ff., it is almost impossible to distinguish literal error from deliberate transformation and 'fulfilment'. Given Hölderlin's purpose and method, the two will overlap. But these technical failings, cumulative as they are, are not the compelling issue. What matters is Hölderlin's agonistic grappling with what he took to be the ultimate principle and genius, the 'revealed' character, of the original. What counts is the reading of Sophocles 'against Sophocles' in the light of an imperative of transcendent fidelity.

Totus locus vexatus, says the textual critic of the opening lines of the play. Why does Antigone invoke Ismene's 'head'? What is the exact force of the rare epithet αὐτάδελφον? How are we to gauge Antigone's phrase, if the text in fact authorizes it, 'no evil is to be spared us even, still in our lifetime'? The note of august terror is Aeschylean, but the composition of a prologue in dialogue form may have been a Sophoclean innovation (the one other example being that of the problematic *Prometheus*). More than in any other Sophoclean tragedy, as we shall see, we are plunged immediately not only into extreme dramatic tension but into the category of polemic as enacted in dialogue. That which pierces undeniably through the uncertainties of the words is the crowding, almost breathless, insistence and imperiousness of Antigone's appeal. The opening word of *Antigonä* is a willed monster: *Gemeinsamschwesterliches!* The adjective constitutes a visual, auditive, semantic welding of all the connotations of sorority, shared destiny, blood-relation, forced 'oneness', which are set out serially and discretely in the Greek. And where ordinary translators seek circumlocution and some 'rational' idiom of affection, Hölderlin is nakedly literal: *o Ismenes Haupt!* It is Ismene's 'head', with every implicit physicality and 'primitivity', to which Antigone turns and addresses her fatal plea. Such carnal immediacy is appropriate to one who has, just before dawn, confronted, given swift and spontaneous sacrament to, the *body* of her

---

[1] Cf. R. B. Harrison, op. cit. 187–206.

brother. *Zeus* in Sophocles; *der Erde Vater* in Hölderlin. He is thus made the Hesperian deity of Antigone-Hölderlin's specific possession and recognition, but also a god whose title directs us to the chthonian theme of the play, to the bestowal in earth, underground, of the dead, to Antigone's live interment, to the primal agencies of justice and of retribution who dwell in the subterranean realm. Hölderlin's motion of translation is, itself, an intense 'uncovering' and breaking of surfaces.

Sophocles' Antigone cites the legacy of pain and disgrace which she and Ismene have inherited from Oedipus. Which has come upon them since Oedipus' fall. Hölderlin makes of this neutral, temporal marker a miniature drama: *seit Oedipus gehascht ward*—'since Oedipus was seized upon'—in which phrase the verb *haschen* might, most accurately, be rendered as 'mugged'. Several imaginings are at work here: the sense of ambush, of Oedipus' innocent collapse into a prepared trap; also, I think, a hint at the great Aeschylean motif of Clytemnestra's net as it ensnares the unsuspecting Agamemnon. Principally, however, Hölderlin communicates Antigone's unyielding view of her father's guiltlessness and the fierce intimation she harbours of the murderous house in which she and her sister are now left defenceless (a *Häscher* is an officious man-hunter). Her reference to Creon as *Feldherr* is precisely Sophoclean: he is no more than the στρατηγός who has come to power by virtue of brute victory in the bloody battle of the previous day. And where the Greek has κήρυγμα in the ordinary sense of an edict and herald's proclamation, Hölderlin uses the Christological–Pauline 'Uns kundgetan' (as implicit in 'kerygmatic' theology). The point is not arbitrary. A mere 'general' has assumed priestly, revelatory functions. In doing so, Creon re-enacts the fatality of overreaching which Hölderlin had identified in the Oedipus of *Oedipus der Tyrann*. The one play is beginning to shimmer ambiguously through the other.

Hölderlin may be eliding, compacting, or reading uncertainly in his version of the awkward passage which closes this fierce address. The original alludes to the harm which Creon's decree purports against 'those beloved, those lovable to us'. Why the plural? Perhaps, suggest the commentaries, because Antigone is dividing the Theban world into 'them' and 'us', because it is the whole house of Oedipus which is aimed at by Creon's commandment. Hölderlin reinforces the suggestion. *Feindesübel*, literally 'enemy-evil', or 'the evil carried by a foe', is now marching upon 'die Lieben', 'the loved ones'. In almost every instance, Hölderlin concretizes, gives a heightened physical tenor to, the more neutral, abstract Greek verb. His Antigone, a vehement bodily presence, a being to whom family and blood-kinship are a transcendent totality, stands before us as Oedipus' unflinching advocate and, perhaps, as his would-be avenger. Already in the background, moreover, there is *her* Zeus, the Father of Earth.

Ten lines later occurs one of the 'scandalous' touches in Hölderlin's translation. The scholiasts had, from the start, worried over Ismene's καλχαίνουϲ. They and their modern successors are more or less agreed that this bizarre epithet (one parallel is to be found in Euripides) signifies 'sombre', 'ominous', 'solemnly portentous'. The Greek seer at Troy is *Kalch*as; κάλχη is an ancient, obscure term probably referring to the purple limpet or murex. From it a dark-red, purple dye was made. 'Du scheinst ein rotes Wort zu färben' ('You seem to colour a word red' or 'to colour a red word'), says Hölderlin's Ismene. Schiller laughed aloud. Reasonable and academic versions paraphrase: 'You seem to be harbouring some dark, some portentous or garish proposition.' Hölderlin is seeking to break open the classic surface in Sophocles' art, the 'poetic' aura and indistinction of his adjective. He is gambling, as it were, on the archaic resources of a more immediate, bodily condition of human utterance. Like archaic statues, distressing to classical taste, words once wore the strident colours of their intent.

Line 45 looks straightforward, but editor-scholars quibble, and properly so. Is there a waspish note in Antigone's 'I will bury my brother, and yours too'? Or is the Greek grammar one of rhetorical stress on the simultaneous unity and diversity (psychological) of kinship? Hölderlin inclines to the latter: 'Von dir und mir mein ich' ('I mean this brother of yours and mine'). The phrase is Swabian. Antigone is compounded of native earth. Ismene's retort, ὦ ϲχετλία—a term which belongs specifically to the vocabulary of tragic drama—connotes both unyielding obstinacy and misery. Hölderlin puts *verwildert*. The epithet is manifold and trenchant. Principally, it signifies 'that which has been allowed to run wild', which has reverted to

wilderness and solitude. In Hölderlin's gloss, Ismene is antici-
pating the 'solitary desert' in which Antigone will find herself
when on the point of death. But the term is also applied by
Hölderlin to characterize the madness and subsequent aloneness of Sophocles' Ajax. At several important turns in *Antigonä*,
the presence of Ajax, in the grip of divine and destructive
possession, is tangible. Hölderlin seems to have perceived in
Ajax a more rudimentary formulation of the 'aorgic' spirit.

As to Creon's edict: what right has he 'to keep me from my
own?' Antigonä's phrasing is densely ambiguous: 'Mit diesem
hat das Meine nichts zu tun.' 'That which is mine', not only in
the sense of familial intimacy and even property but in that of
essential inwardness and personal identity, 'has nothing to do
with Creon' or 'has nothing to do with this proclaimed statute'.
Mit diesem allows either or both readings, a duality which will
recur whenever Antigonä 'abstracts' Creon by making him
interchangeable with his hollow, inhuman prescriptions.
κείcομαι (line 73) is tricky. The verb is current in Greek erotic
epigrams. 'For I shall rest beside him', as offered in one of the
standard English versions (H. D. F. Kitto's), is evasive. The
whole passage is charged with expressions of uncompromising
love. Antigonä's language, like that of Rousseau's *Confessions*,
has the licence and purity within licence of the ecstatic. 'Lieb
werd ich bei ihm liegen, bei dem Lieben' ('lovingly I shall lie
with him, by the loved, lovable one's side'). To rejoin
Polyneices thus, Antigone must commit 'holy transgression'.
Sophocles' terminology at this decisive moment is taut to the
point of untranslatability. P. Mazon simply borrows from
Racine: Antigone qualifies herself as *saintement criminelle*.
Hölderlin is as darkly compacted as the Greek: 'Wenn Heiligs
ich vollbracht' ('when I have accomplished it sacredly/in
holiness'). This is the maxim of the *Antitheos*. And when Ismene
resorts to the word *Aufstand*, she points not only to the mystery
of 'pious rebellion' but initiates what Hölderlin takes to be the
theme of political revolution along republican lines.

With its reiterative (anaphoric) construction, Creon's anathema on Polyneices is more than twice as long as his laudation
of Eteocles. Polyneices had returned from just exile to ravage,
to put to the torch γῆν πατρῴιαν καὶ θεούς, 'his fatherland, the
sanctuaries of his native gods'. Throughout, Hölderlin underlines the organic–political impetus, estimable in itself, of

Creon's hammering rhetoric. 'Vom Gipfel an' is obscure and haunting. What is Hölderlin 'mis-reading'? Does he mean to say that Polyneices will burn, will lay waste 'from the roofs down', or that he and his mercenaries came 'down from the heights' (both touches being more Euripidean than Sophoclean)? The latter sense is hinted at by the conflict in *Empedokles* as between the ordered sphere of the πόλις and the formless, primal quality of the mountain heights. The suggestion of untamed Arcady is made poignant in Hölderlin's rendition of the Guard's narrative. No human trace near Polyneices' corpse: 'Und auch des Wilds Fusstritte nirgend nicht.' The line is exquisite, redoubling the terse original to achieve an aura of bemused innocence. No spoor of a wild animal 'nowhere nothing'. And we think back on Ismene's use of *verwildert*.

Heidegger's sentiment that the second choral ode or first stasimon (choral song uninterrupted by dialogue) in Sophocles' *Antigone*, together with Hölderlin's mature translation, could provide a sufficient basis for western metaphysics, is plausible. In the present context, I want to look at two aspects only of Hölderlin's celebrated text, both of which are all-important for his interpretation of the play as a whole. Hölderlin is perfectly aware that the opening phrase, πολλὰ τὰ δεινά, exactly echoes the opening of a choral ode in Aeschylus' *Choephoroe*. The Aeschylean resonance, with its implicit evocation of Clytemnestra's crime and of the criminal vengeance which awaits her, is one of terror and enormity in human affairs. Sophocles' usage, to judge not only by the appearance of δεινός in lines 243 and 1046 of *Antigone* but also by closely comparable uses of the word in *Oedipus Rex* (545), *Philoctetes* (440), and *Oedipus at Colonus* (806), is more ambiguous. If there is in δεινός the concept of 'terror' and of 'excess', there is also, as in Herodotus' use of the term—Herodotus' idiom being often analogous to Sophocles'—or in Plato's in the *Protagoras*, the notion of 'sagacity', of 'practical wisdom' and 'canniness'. Our own 'uncanny', in fact, points to a similar congruence of associations. Hölderlin's first version proposes 'Vieles gewaltige giebts', in which *gewaltige* closely resembles the twofold Sophoclean sense, 'violent' and also 'of great magnitude, of an ingenuity which commands awe'. *Gewaltige* is retained by J. Chr. Donner in his 1839 translation which, as we

have seen, was used in the influential staging of the play in
1841. Several French versions use *les choses merveilleuses*, further
inflecting the sense towards a positive value. But in his second,
definitive reading, Hölderlin changes to 'Ungeheuer ist viel'.
The shift in prosody and word order achieves a lapidary and
oracular effect. But the differences between *gewaltige*, the
adjective, and *Ungeheuer*, the adjectival noun, cut far deeper.
Ungeheuer literally means that which is 'monstrous', whose
uncanniness derives from alien enormity. Emil Staiger will
adopt the word in his 1940 translation, Brecht will do so in
1948, Schadewaldt in 1974. Karl Reinhardt, in 1949, prefers
des Unheimlichen, with its connotations of eerie unhousedness
and its echo of Freud's famous argument on 'the uncanny'.
What does Hölderlin's revision purport? It is, undoubtedly, a
part of the strategy of extremism throughout his late vocabulary and syntax, of the enforcement of vehement hyperbole
on a Sophoclean style which he judges as too reticent and
sophisticated. The mutual slaying of Eteocles and Polyneices,
Creon's edict, the inexplicable violation of this edict as
recounted by the terrified Guard—all these evoke the mystery
of boundless life-forces and of fatal cunning in man which lies
at the roots of the multiple meanings of δεινός. But *Ungeheuer* is
now used radically, concretely. When it is made 'self-polemic',
when it attempts suicidal commerce with the divine, man's
nature becomes literally 'monstrous'. It reverts to the status of
a doomed hybrid, such as were the heroic half-gods, Centaurs,
and Titans before the imposition of an 'organic' and Olympian
order. Thus the word points directly at Antigone when she
assumes the role of an *Antitheos*.

Lines 367–8 in the second antistrophe concentrate the
fundamental elements of the tragic debate. They contain four
key terms: νόμουc, χθονόc, θεῶν, and δίκαν. Sophocles' conceptions of 'law', of 'native earth', of 'divinity', and of 'justice',
together with the subsequent history of these designations,
have provoked voluminous commentary. These are the elementary particles of philosophical–political matter in the West.
The overall sense is unmistakable (owing, as it happens, to
a famed emendation in line 368): 'let man, in his awesome
magnitude and intensity of cunning and of knowing, assign
their due portion to the law of his native land and to the justice
of the gods.' Should he fail to do so, he will end dishonoured

and ἄπολις, literally 'citiless'. May no such unhoused being find a welcome at my hearth, says the chorus. For he is polluted and contagious. Hölderlin's transfer, touching as it does on the inmost of his own condition, is lexically and syntactically compressed and involuted almost to the edge of nonsense. Hölderlin seems to be reaching back not to Sophocles but to the more ancient master of absolute immediacy, Pindar. Yet the passage is, at the same time, revelatory. The 'laws' which are being offended by mortal enormity and invention are 'those of the Earth'; violence is being done to 'conscience in its commitment to, in the oath which it has sworn to, the natural order' (*Naturgewaltger | Beschwornes Gewissen*). Misreading or recasting the Greek, Hölderlin fuses into an ambiguous continuum the Sophoclean antithesis between ὑψίπολις ('high in civic standing') and the sinister ἄπολις. According to Hölderlin, *both* the high public man *and* the ostracized fugitive come to ruin in the hour of man's unguarded excess. This reading is tersely distributive: Creon, highest in the city, Antigone, soon to be torn from her civic condition, are both hurtling towards ruin. Neither will achieve homecoming. In this way Hölderlin resolves at a stroke the factitious but vexed question as to whether this first stasimon is aimed at Creon, at Antigone, or at both.

What is more, he does so in a manner which rigorously exemplifies his understanding of the singular function of the chorus. According to the *Anmerkungen*, the chorus embodies the divine as it is present in and a witness to human secular conflict. This embodiment occurs on an essentially rational, conceptual plane. Being, as it were, the 'suffering, passive organ of a body (the body politic) which is caught up in suicidal conflict', the chorus, by virtue of its thematic invocation of the gods, by its reflection on and of their presence, communicates a sense of *das Ungeheure* in the human circumstance. It communicates it more abstractly and formally than does the tragic protagonist, but also with more dispassionate intelligence. Thus this sovereign ode is, among many other things, an act of inspired self-definition by the chorus of elders of Thebes. And it is beautifully right that it is these elders who should cry out to us the approach of Antigone, bound.

Hölderlin's gloss on lines 405 ff. is at once among the most

emphatic and esoteric in the *Anmerkungen*. 'The most audacious
moment in man's works and days (*Taglauf*) or in a work of art'
is that in which the spirit of time and of nature, the celestial
(*das Himmlische*), seizes upon him. Thus possessed, a human
being finds himself in 'wildest' confrontation with the sensory,
material object of his concern. The wildness of this confrontation stems from the fact that the object, the 'counter-
presence' (this being the exact construction of the word
Gegenstand), is only half animate with the energies of the spirit.
Whereas both halves of the human protagonist, the natural
and the mantic, the instinctual and the civic, are now in the
grip of spiritual totality. I believe, but am not certain, that this
is what Hölderlin is saying. Even in its own terms, however, its
application to the encounter between Creon and Antigone is
enigmatic. Antigone's blazing spirituality, the ecstatic temper
of her address, are plain to see. But what is the 'object' of her
polemic interest? Is it the burial of Polyneices, is it Creon? Can
we say of either that a sensory, material (*sinnlich*) presence or
phenomenality is now 'half in reach of spirit' or—Hölderlin's
phrasing is ambiguous—'reaches only half-way towards' the
spiritual? What is evident in Hölderlin's exegesis and in his
text is the inference of a violent imbalance or even rupture of
harmonic relations between spirit and matter, between the
transcendent freedom of the totally spiritual, a concept highly
suggestive of Hegel and of Schelling, and the adversative
'object'—Polyneices' corpse, Creon's edict?—which, in
Freudian terminology, one would call 'the reality principle'. It
is in such a moment of imbalance and confrontation, pursues
Hölderlin, that a human being must 'cling most closely to
himself', must 'hold on' to his identity with greatest firmness.
In so doing, he or she will most fully deploy his or her authentic
character. In the present instance, the 'wild' time-spirit
(*Zeitgeist* taken literally) which tears man from his common
roots and compels him to follow in its turbulent wake is that
of 'der ewig lebenden ungeschriebenen Wildnis und der
Totenwelt'. This resplendent phrase anticipates exactly
Antigone's speech. The *Zeitgeist*, as it overwhelms Antigonä,
has two sources: 'the eternally live, unwritten wild primacy of
being' and 'the world of the dead'. We are in Nietzsche
country and at the heart of Heidegger's existentialism.

We have noted Hölderlin's '*Mein* Zeus' in line 450. The

ordinary reading is: 'It was not Zeus who issued this decree' or
'who proclaimed this edict to me'. A third reading seems to
hover on the far edge of grammatical possibility. If we treat the
article as wholly indefinite or as ambiguous, it would be
conceivable to construe Antigone as saying that 'neither Zeus
nor the goddess of Justice enthroned among the nether powers
($\Delta i\kappa\eta$) have commanded *this*'—i.e. her disobedience, her
twofold attempt to bury Polyneices! The impulse, the deed
would be entirely Antigone's own and *autonomous* in just the
sense in which this epithet is used about her in the play. This
reading for radical ambiguity, for subconscious or rhetorically
masked paradoxicality, is, we must presume, foreign to the
passage in its Sophoclean tenor. But it will, as we shall see,
sanction 'absurdist' and existentialist versions of the fable.
Moreover, implausible as it is, this reading concurs intimately
with the notion of the *Antitheos*, of the 'God-*provocateur*', which
lies at the centre of Hölderlin's *Antigonä*. In lines 278–9 the
chorus, on hearing the Guard's description of the token burial
before dawn, had at once raised the question of divine agency.
Creon rejects the conjecture with sarcastic fury. And we learn
that it *is* a mortal hand, Antigone's, which has sown gentle dust
on Polyneices' torn flesh. But what if it *had* been the gods,
what if Zeus and Justice were already signalling their intent
to chastise Creon and repair his blasphemy? Hölderlin's
Antigone would, one suspects, try to outstrip their coming. Her
'aorgic' impatience, like that of Saint-Just at the slowness of
history, would challenge the gods. Why wait for *them*, for the
cumbersome unfolding of the 'organic', when the flame of
absolute life and perception consumes her? This impatience
almost defines the figure of the *Antitheos*. It is distinctly
possible, therefore, that the flicker of grammatical undecidability in the Greek text may have caught Hölderlin's rapt
attention and strengthened his general interpretation.

His actual rendition of Antigone's reply is richly idiosyn-
cratic. The writ of the *Todesgötter*, of 'the Death-gods'
(Hölderlin's designation of Justice), runs 'hier im Haus', a
specification which derives either from a false reading or, more
likely, from the implicit dialectic between the 'earthy' and
familial on the one hand and the public–political on the other.
Coercing German into a word order and pace as close as
possible to Sophoclean Greek, Hölderlin gives to the famous

'unwritten laws' (ἄγραπτα νόμιμα) a tremendous physical weight. Throughout, Antigone's diction, so elevated in the original, is on the borderline of a rough and populist colloquialism. It invokes ultimate values in a key of almost perfunctory, vulgate speech. The turn of phrase, 'Das eins der sterben muss' ('A creature, an anyone, which must die'), is already Brechtian. This Jacobin note not only undermines Creon's rhetoric but signals, in gruff pathos, Antigone's acceptance of her own fate, her willed entry into the neuter case of death. *Satzungen* is a complex word. It relates, of course, to 'laws' (*Gesetze*). But according to Antigone the 'postulates', the 'unalterable imperatives' posited by the powers of Justice in the underworld and by 'her Zeus', Father of Earth, have an authority, a 'foundational' timelessness, beyond any written and (therefore) *ad hoc* legislation. Here Antigone is a Kantian *in extremis*, but her notion also recalls some of Plato's disconcerting speculations on the decay of felt meaning when oral propositions pass into writing. Nearly all translators skimp ἀνδρὸς φρόνημα. Hölderlin makes the point with Sophoclean incisiveness: Creon's edict is nothing but 'eines Manns Gedanken'—'one man's thought/the thought of a (singular) man'. In this tag there is, again, the stroke of casual anonymity, of contingent devaluation in respect of Creon's lofty person. 'Das würde mich betrüben' is wonderfully understated. Had she not performed burial rites for 'her mother's son', Antigone would have been *betrübt*, which is to say little more than 'saddened', 'dejected'. Once more, Creon's vengeful pomp is deflated. We are beginning to hear that note of noble mockery, of sublime flyting, *erhabener Spott*, which Hölderlin, in one of the most acutely original parts of his reading, assigns to Antigonä.

In his commentary on *Oedipus der Tyrann*, Hölderlin cites Haemon as one who is engaged in the heart of the tragic action not through native inclination but because he has no choice. He is caught up in the cataclysmic motion of time and thus loses touch with his natural and composed being. An individual essentially at peace with his condition or, as Hölderlin puts it, at home in the 'organic' sphere, is whirled into violent and 'senseless' action. The temporal *Umkehr* now compels him to make decisions alien to his true nature. Haemon, to whom filial obedience and civic order are profoundly natural, must choose between his father and his bride. Lines 744–5 are, pursuant to the *Anmerkungen*, the pivot of the play. They mark the instant in which time alters, in which the revolution of temporality (one thinks of Yeats's doctrine of great time-cycles spinning to a catastrophic point) 'objectifies and clarifies' all conflicting issues. In sarcastic anger, Creon challenges Haemon: 'So I offend Justice, do I, when I exercise my functions, my prerogatives as ruler?' Haemon's reply is textually somewhat problematic. One can read: 'Is it to exercise these functions well when one spurns Justice?', or 'Scorning divine Justice you devalue your own rights'. Hölderlin recasts the exchange: 'Do I lie', asks Creon, 'when I remain true to my primal beginnings?' (*Wenn meines Uranfangs ich treue beistehe?*) By these 'primal beginnings' we are, I believe, meant to understand Creon's 'organic' relations both to his identity as ruler and to the civic, 'legal' Zeus whom he rigidly honours and represents. Creon is a *Protheos*, one absolutely unwilling to challenge, to seek insurgent intimacy with, his god. 'You are not being true to your *Uranfang*', counters Haemon, 'hältst du nicht heilig Gottes Namen'—'if you do not hold God's name to be holy/if you do not hold it in holiness' (the phrase is italicized in the *Anmerkungen*). This is a frankly 'Hesperian' transformation, mirroring that of time itself. Creon, intimates Haemon, is actually betraying Zeus because he fails to observe Zeus' involvement in and generation of the great turn—Yeats's word, and he will translate parts of *Antigone*, is 'gyre'—in the wheel of time. Creon remains fatally 'Greek-classical' and pre-Dionysian.

With its accelerando towards disaster, the word-duel between father and son throws into relief what Hölderlin characterizes as the key to Greek tragic discourse. 'Das griechischtragische Wort ist tödlichfaktisch' ('the *Greek-tragic word is factually-deadly*'). It seizes upon the human body and kills it. In Greek tragic drama there occurs 'der wirkliche Mord aus Worten' ('real murder through words'). We 'Hesperians' know of the terrible hurt words can do to mind and soul, but we do not experience, except metaphorically, the 'athletic, plastic' (Hölderlin's adjectives) immediacy of physical destruction through an act of speech. Theseus' curse literally slays Hippolytus. Oracular and prophetic utterances tear through human flesh. Even as Creon's spoken command murders

Antigone, so the words which Haemon has been compelled to
hurl at his father and their fierce rebound, words sprung from
the 'aorgic' and revolutionary crisis of the moment, are
bringers of death. And now it is death itself which enters in the
person, in the voice, of Antigone.

There is little in literature to rival Antigone's death-song
(κομμός) and the multiplicity of levels, formal and conceptual, on which take place the exchanges between herself
and the chorus. No commentary—and this scene has inspired
linguistic and philosophical exegesis since Alexandria—
matches Hölderlin's 'practical criticism', the understanding in
action of his translation. It is here that he deploys his utmost
genius as poet-reader, matching vision to vision, syllable to
syllable. Antigone sings of Antigone, the supple discipline of
the lyric convention being such that it allows a terrible
dispassion, a 'far-off intimacy'. She sings herself and of herself
as one wedded to Acheron, to the black river of extinction. To
the chorus's offer of consolation, at once elegant and
insensitive—'you go to a famous death, unmarked by sickness
or the sword'—she replies with the high, comely mockery in
which Hölderlin sees the noblest trait of her being. Her tone,
her stance, bear witness to 'the superlative of the human spirit
and of heroic virtuosity'. Antigonä's *geheimarbeitende Seele* ('the
soul in secret labour') will, in the very instant before its mortal
grappling with the opposing god, 'sidestep' (*ausweichen*) the
final totality of confrontation. It will tease fate and the deity
with an irony, with a dark merriment so lofty that this teasing
may become actual blasphemy. Such high scorn, like the ritual
flyting before a combat unto death or the ceremonial flourish
and doffing of blades before a fatal duel, enables heroic
sensibility to define, to declare itself one last time before its self-
consuming and 'monstrous' collision with the immortal. On a
wholly *secular* level, this prelude has its analogue in Hamlet's
mockery of Osric.

Such declaration of sensibility in the face of death is
quintessentially human. It is indeed the apex of the existential.
As such, says Hölderlin, Antigonä's *erhabener Spott* will entail a
comparison with the inorganic, with those orders of creation
which can neither 'mock' nor wrestle with God. Hence
Antigone's evocation, in aeolic verses whose unison of unbearable poignancy with a breath of ironic provocation no

translation, no commentary, can fully recapture, of Niobe and
of Niobe's metamorphosis into eroded stone. Sophocles'
Antigone does not refer to Niobe by name. She calls her
'daughter of Tantalus'. Hölderlin goes even further in stressing
the extinction of personal being. By the emphatic placing of
the word 'Wüste' ('desert') in line 823, Antigonä not only
proclaims Niobe's lifeless sterility after the hideous visitation of
the provoked gods, but echoes Haemon's anguished taunt:
'Thebes shall be made a desert under Creon's absolute rule.'
Unnamed, Niobe is made central to Hölderlin's interpretation
of the whole passage. Reacting to Antigone's lofty jibes, the
Sophoclean chorus invokes Niobe's divine origins in officious
anapaests—the metre is, at every moment, sharply revelatory
of the underlying complex of feelings. Hölderlin's 'heilig
gesprochen, heilig gezeugt' ('declared a saint, born a saint') is
a strangely 'Hesperian' modulation. So also is the transmutation in Antigone's incensed riposte of the Greek formulaic
phrase 'the gods of my fathers' into *Vaterlandsschutzgeister*
('guardian spirits of the fatherland'). In Hölderlin's reading,
Niobe, by virtue of her mockery of the Olympian gods, is 'das
Bild des frühen Genies' ('the image of early, of primitive,
ingenium'); she is an *Antitheos* of a rudimentary kind but
ancestral to Antigonä.[1]

Fury is now the keynote. Only in 'fury' (*Zorn*, a word which
Hölderlin uses in the *Anmerkungen* and twice adds to the actual
text of the play) can the impassioned God-challenger relinquish the 'organic' composure of her being and cast off her
secular and civic moorings. *Zorn* seizes upon her as she recalls
the murderous mystery of the death of Oedipus. The chorus,
forced to clairvoyance by the overpowering pressure of
Antigone's lament, rules that it is 'self-willed passion', a wild
autonomy of impulse—the word αὐτόγνωτος is graphic—which
has driven Oedipus' child to her ruin. Hölderlin's version is:
'Dich hat verderbt | Das zornige Selbsterkennen' ('it is furious,
raging self-recognition which has ruined you'). In sacred fury,
the *Antitheos* comes to know himself, not in his Socratic
rationality but, on the contrary, as one consumed by the
primal wildfires of vital energy which relate him to the gods,
which compel him to seek out the gods in deadly wrestling. It

---

[1] Cf. R. B. Harrison, op. cit. 177–9, for the suggestion that the Niobe passage points
also to Hölderlin's doctrine of the perilous human progress from 'Nature' to 'Art'.

is, as the first stasimon foresaw, these wildfires which bar heroic man from the harmonious but tamed flame of the hearth. As Bernard Böschenstein has emphasized, the political inferences are drastic. 'Self-recognition in fury' is a magnificently concise formulation of the Jacobin–Utopian demon of revolution and revolutionary terror. Autobiographical strands are implicit as well. Hölderlin had recognized himself as a spirit 'made furious' by inspiration and the philistine deafness of the society around him.

Sophocles' heroine goes the way to death 'unwept, friendless, unwed, wretchedly alone'. Antigonä goes *trübsinnig*. The term is ambivalent. It signifies both 'gloomy of spirit' and 'mentally bewildered' or even 'deranged'. Again it is difficult to exclude altogether the personal reference. But supreme throughout the whole passage is the invocation of elemental forces, of fatalities inwoven with the dark springs of human identity. To elicit these, Hölderlin translates 'against Sophocles' in precisely the loving sense in which Antigonä hurls herself against 'her Zeus':

Die zornigste hast du angeregt
Der lieben Sorgen,
Die vielfache Weheklage des Vaters
Und alles
Unseres Schicksals,
Uns rühmlichen Labdakiden.
Io! du mütterlicher Wahn
In den Betten, ihr Umarmungen, selbstgebärend,
Mit meinem Vater, von unglücklicher Mutter,
Von denen einmal ich Trübsinnige kam,
Zu denen ich im Fluche
Mannlos zu wohnen komme.
Io! Io! mein Bruder!
In gefährlicher Hochzeit gefallen!
Mich auch, die nur noch da war,
Ziehst sterbend du mit hinab.

This defies retranslation.

No section of the play has drawn more commentary or controversy than the fifth choral ode, with its seemingly extraneous mythological allusions and its bewilderingly varied pace of trimeter and tetrameter lines. I will come back later to the problems which it poses. Hölderlin seeks to enforce on the

figure and fate of Lycurgus, as these are evoked in the first
antistrophe, an absolute parallelism with those of Antigone.
He too is imprisoned in a rocky cave. He too challenged a
god, Dionysus, in 'begeisterter Schimpf' (a very nearly untranslatable phrase signifying 'a possessed scolding', i.e. the
flyting of the mad but holy *provocateur*). Lycurgus now laments
his madness (*Wahnsinn*) and his 'flowering rage' (*blühender
Zorn*), an incomparable half-line for which there is no
authority in the original, but whose Antigonä-echo is manifest.
The close of the ode, on the other hand, is pure Sophocles. The
word 'child', παῖς, knells twice in the chorus's farewell to
Antigone. 'Even a child of the gods [the high, tragic personae
cited in the ode] was not safe against the long-living Furies, the
Μοῖραι.' The reiteration is liturgical in its pathos: 'Even she, oh
child [or, perhaps more specifically, 'oh daughter'] . . . was not
safe.' Hölderlin's one modernization is too slight, too faithful in
spirit, to be un-Sophoclean: 'Das grosse Schicksal' ('the great
Fate') has the sombre gravity of Μοῖραι. The cadence matches
to perfection the haunting original: 'Doch auch auf jener | Das
grosse Schicksal ruhte, Kind!' ('But also on her, on that
one | The great Fate rested, child!')—in which *ruhte*, with its
note of gentle repose, of sanctified calm, seems to penetrate the
Sophoclean text to the heart of its meanings. Hölderlin's
treatment of Antigone's κομμός and of the choral response
justifies hyperbole. To him, the tragic dramas of Sophocles
were indeed 'rediscovered holy books'. Their 'rediscovery', as
it is made possible by Hölderlin's version, is itself an annunciation of 'a new nearness of the gods'.[1] It is a theophanic act
whose risks, whose radiance, are beyond those of any other
literary translation or exegesis. Except, qualifies Walter
Benjamin, of the interlinear version of Scripture.

Only in Teiresias is there concordance between 'aorgic'
prophecy and the rational, civic piety of the 'organic'.
Necessarily, however, this concordance is achieved on a
mundane, existential level. It is not the fusion of spirit sought
by the tragic agent. Hence Hölderlin's stress on the physical,
sensory elements in Teiresias' narrative of burnt offering and
pollution. The Sophoclean passage, notably in lines 1000–15,
does exhibit those qualities of physical shock which Euripides
will heighten even further. In *Antigonä* the touches of carnal

[1] K. Reinhardt, op. cit. 292.

disorder are maximalized. The 'wet odour' of the blighted
sacrifice sweats and wallows on the unburnt flesh. Where the
Greek cites 'mute' or 'puzzling' omens, Hölderlin 'translates':
'Der zeichenlosen Orgien tödliche Erklärung'—'the fatal, the
killing pronouncement of orgies which are signless, which
refuse signification.' The 'signlessness' of the omens is literally
murderous in just the sense which Hölderlin ascribes to Greek
tragic speech, and subtly echoes Antigone's appeal to 'unwritten laws'. Where Teiresias addresses Creon as 'my child',
Hölderlin prefers 'o Kind!' in exact parallel with the chorus's
adieu to Antigone. And when, in a question which may echo
the archaic lyric and satiric master, Archilochus, the
Sophoclean seer asks of Creon what sense there is, what
chivalric prowess, in slaying a dead man twice over, Hölderlin
contracts the phrase to a formidably laconic, Latinate three
words: 'Zu töten Tote' ('To slay the slain').

Teiresias' prophecy of impending horror richly underwrites
Hölderlin's model and idiom of total reversal in time and in
the architecture of reality. Already, the sun over Thebes is
'swift', 'impatient' in its offended course. Hölderlin writes
eifersüchtig, 'jealous', thus endowing cosmic retribution with
animate motive. There can be no more cataclysmic *Umkehr*
and inversion of values than the exposure of the stinking dead
on the earth's sunlit surface and the relegation of the living to
the lightless underground of death. Unburied, Polyneices is
schicksallos, literally 'without destiny'. This argument, which
Hölderlin grafts on the text, is very close to the Hegelian gloss:
unless he can return to earth within a fabric of familial custody
and remembrance, a man has not lived 'his authentic essence'.
He is stripped of fulfilment. There shall soon be bitter
lamentations 'in your houses', foretells Hölderlin's Teiresias.
The plural is arresting. Either he is misreading, or he wishes to
suggest something of Creon's regal opulence and of his
hubristic identification with the πόλις as a whole. 'You shall
not escape the wrath of my arrows,' warns the departing
Teiresias in *Antigonä*. Hölderlin is compacting a triple allusion:
to the dread arrows of Apollo which slew Niobe's children, to
Hölderlin's mythography, god of the 'Asiatic' elements which
rained upon Agamemnon's host when an earlier seer had been
mocked.

The final choral ode is, as we shall see, one of the most

dramatically tense and contradictory in the play. The call to Dionysus—god of Thebes, patron of tragic drama, and, in Hölderlin's mythography, god of the 'Asiatic' elements which will bridge the time-chasm between the Olympian world and Christ's epiphany—is at once frenetic and sumptuous, ecstatic and ceremonious. The intricate metrics 'act out' these contrasting and combinatorial tonalities.[1] The fundamental division, exactly reflecting the chorus's false hopes of imminent delivery from death and from hatred in the city, is that between Dionysus the protector and Dionysus the elemental agent of inhuman logic (as he will be in Euripides' *Bacchae*). Hölderlin's dialectical sense is consummate. He makes of Dionysus a hybrid, jubilant and menacing, a true half-god born of Zeus' lightning and of the dark earth as it is represented by Semele's womb. The analogy with Christ and his mortal mother lies close. So, also, does the theme of monstrous begetting in the house of Oedipus. Hölderlin's idiom takes on a wild lyric density. The god dwells near Ismenus' 'cold brook'. Hölderlin imports the epithet to achieve dramatic contrast with the hot breath of the dragon whose murdering teeth Cadmus had sown when Thebes began. This dragon 'gasps for, mouths for' breath. Hölderlin says *haschet*, the very verb used by Antigonä when she recalls her father's cruel entrapment at the start of the play. Dionysus is hailed as 'Freudengott'. But in this nomination, the overtones of 'joy' (*Freude*) are almost Nietzschean in their superhuman energy and archaic impersonality. In 'Lapis Lazuli', Yeats communicates a comparable sense of icy fire. Now the city is mortally ill—unmistakably, the Greek text echoes the visitation of the plague at the outset of *Oedipus Rex*. The chorus implores the coming of the god. Dionysus is, literally, the χορηγός, the chorus-leader 'of the blazing stars'. There is thus at the close of Sophocles' *Antigone*, as throughout Euripides' *Bacchae*, an enacted meditation on the nature of tragic theatre itself, on the relations between the formal modes and ritual vestiges in tragic drama and the society and cosmos in whose framework the drama is performed. Dionysus is hailed as 'guardian of nocturnal cries' or 'appeals in the night'. This attribute is at once mysterious and pertinent. In our

---

[1] Cf. the invaluable metrical analysis in G. Müller, *Sophokles. Antigone* (Heidelberg, 1967), 242–3.

night-words, in the discourse of our sleep, there is ecstasy
and desolation, eros and nightmare. Dionysus is receiver of
both. He is also sentinel over secrecy, over the sacred discretion
of Antigone's resolve as she harbours and acts upon it before
dawn. Hölderlin's reading is precisely inspired: 'Chorführer
der Gestirn' und geheimer | Reden Bewahrer!' And he renders
unfailingly the crowning ambivalence in the ode. The god is to
reveal himself amid the rout of the 'Delirious Ones' (Θυίαιϲιν),
of the frenzied Maenads whose merciless joy had brought
ecstasy to Thebes and death to myopic Pentheus. Hölderlin
meshes insanity and jubilation: 'die wahnsinnig | Dir Chor
singen, dem jauchzenden Herrn' ('who, crazed, are a chorus to
you, exultant Master', where the Greek has 'to you, bountiful
deity'). The exultant frenzy, the somnambular revel, are
Friedrich Hölderlin's own in these, almost the last lines he
wrote for publication. Aptly, they take us back to the invocation of fiery Dionysus in the very first of his Pindaric odes.
    There are characteristic strokes in Hölderlin's handling of
Creon's desperate lament. Where Sophocles alludes to the
'infernal, the everlastingly impure haven of the Underworld',
Hölderlin translates with implacable literalness: 'du schmut-
ziger Hafen' ('you dirty harbour'). This suggests that Acheron
and its dark landings are clogged and sullied by the victims of
Creon's folly. The queen has slain herself cursing Creon, the
killer of her sons (I will come back to the theme of the death of
Megareus in line 1310). Hölderlin's expression *Kindermörder*
('childkiller') is a pitiless colloquialism out of the world of
Herod and of *Faust* I. Hölderlin closely parallels the strident
reiterations of ἐγώ and μοι throughout the last forty lines of
Creon's desolation, reiterations which are themselves a sinister
echo of the egotism, of the obsessive self-reference, of the
doomed king at the opening of *Oedipus Rex*. The choral maxims
which close the play, in normal Sophoclean fashion, are shot
through with Hölderlin's particular vision. In the Greek, it is
not 'wisdom' or 'sagacity' which are the highest felicity, as
most English-language translations have it. It is φρονεῖν, 'das
Denken' ('the act, the process of thought'). One must not,
urges Hölderlin, *entheiligen* ('desecrate') that which is
'heavenly'—a 'Hesperian' inflection of the original which
simply bids us commit no impiety against the gods. 'Proud men
see their arrogant words struck by great blows of fate, and it is

only the passage of years which teaches them to think sagely.'
So Sophocles. Hölderlin's turn is gnomic: 'high shoulders'
must suffer the 'fine', must bear 'compensation for' (*Vergeltung*)
'high looks'. Only such suffering can, in old age, teach us 'zu
denken' ('to think'). Hölderlin, on the verge of going into
night, had come to regard the bare act of thought as a far-off
benediction. Nowhere, perhaps, was he closer to Sophocles.

8

It is not obvious that there is another work of literature which
has elicited the strengths of philosophic and poetic interest
focused on Sophocles' *Antigone* during the late eighteenth and
the nineteenth centuries. The touchstone would be *Hamlet*. But
there is nothing in the enormous interpretative, variant, and
mimetic legacy of the play to equal Hölderlin's *Antigonä* nor, it
may be, the quality of philosophic obsession which a Hegel and
a Kierkegaard brought to the Greek text.

The condition of the poetic in respect of philosophic
discourse is classically elusive. Plato's negative vehemence on
this matter suggests the force of the undertow which draws
metaphysical and political argument towards the more open
ground of literary metaphor. Because it isolates and enacts
summary moments in human uncertainty, because it stresses
behaviour to the breaking-point of disaster—disaster being the
final logic of action—tragedy has, pre-eminently, attracted
philosophic 'use'. The utilitarian impulse is already evident
in Aristotle's *Poetics*. Tragedy serves to embody, to instigate
to visible presentness, perennial metaphysical–ethical–
psychological considerations of the nature of free will, of the
existence of other minds and persons, of the conventions of
contract and transgression between the individual and transcendent or social sanctions. Because it resorted to a dramatization of the very processes of thought—there is a theatrical
touch even to Hegel's logic—Romanticism sought to efface the
demarcations of category as between philosophic and poetic
discourse. It conceived of both as intuitively grounded and dialectically performed (it is in the Faustian dissociation between
the 'grey' of theory and the 'green' of imaginative action that
Goethe is most anti-Romantic).

Hegel uses Sophocles' *Antigone* to test and to exemplify successive models of religious–civic conflict and of historical coming-into-being. But these models have themselves been put forward by the concrete universality of the play. Kierkegaard's use is desperate in its needful arbitrariness. Seeking to arrive at an explicit but bearable formulation of his own circumstance and of the general status of inwardness and secrecy in a modern community, Kierkegaard makes of *Antigone* an open-ended precedent. The room for reconsideration, for judicial and psychological appeal, in poetic form is more supple, more richly indeterminate than it is in philosophic demonstration. The unknown retains a greater measure of healing authority. Kierkegaard's 'Antigone' is one of the possibilities in Sophocles', a possibility available to subsequent construction precisely in so far as it had been classically discarded. To the degree that philosophic inquiry is a recapture of freedom, of liberal spaces lost to dogma, to formal logic, to the mandate of the pure and the applied sciences, to the degree that philosophy *is* freedom, in Schelling's arch-Romantic equation, the poetic will be its chosen terrain. 'But can philosophy become literature and still know itself?'[1]

The high readers of *Antigone* whom we have considered would, I think, answer by shifting from the ideal of 'self-knowing', weakened as it had been by Kant's critique, to that of 'being itself'. Philosophy after Hegel often 'is itself' not by becoming literature, a danger which, ironically, presses on Plato's dialogues, but by using literature as its licence for free motion. There is an order of finality in the 'textual fact' of Sophocles' *Antigone*. But there is also undecidability in regard to archaic intent and the turbulence which history brings to the reach of meaning. This is so of all serious literature. But the dialectical openness of relation between text and enacted sense is peculiarly heightened in drama. At the start of this chapter, I put forward provisional answers to the question: why *Antigone*? I want to come back later to the underlying pattern of the economy of myth in western thought. Hegel, Kierkegaard *might* have made of some other tragic play the elect of argument and self-mirroring.

The issues raised by Hölderlin's *Antigonä* are more difficult to circumscribe. I have shown elsewhere that there are indeed

[1] S. Cavell, *The Claim of Reason* (Oxford, 1979), 496.

translations which betray the original via 'transfiguration', this is to say, whose verbal virtuosity, depth of sentiment, or historical impact surpass that of the primary text. Such 'transfigurations' tend to occur in lyric poetry or over this or that stretch of a longer work. For a full-length translation or adaptation to challenge its source and 'stand in its way' is loving treason of a rare kind. As we have seen, however, the concept of 'translation', even in its most extended sense, hardly comprises the interactions between *Antigonä* and *Antigone*. The consequences of Hölderlin's hermeneutic metamorphosis of Sophocles are, necessarily, reciprocal. We read, we experience Sophocles differently after Hölderlin. This effect of dislocation is common to major literary criticism and to the entire lineage of internal reference and active echo in western letters. We read Shakespeare differently after Samuel Johnson or Coleridge; *Bleak House* has altered under pressure of its own influence on the parables of bureaucracy in Kafka. But the *Antigonä–Antigone* osmosis is far closer, the point-to-point mapping far more paradoxical. I am aware of only one parallel: it is that of the relations between Verdi's *Otello* and *Falstaff* and the Shakespearean texts from which they derive formally and existentially. *Otello* is arguably, *Falstaff* is most certainly, superior to its source in regard to dramatic concision and emotional 'adultness' (Verdi's Moor, his Iago, cohere and come upon us whole, while Shakespeare's do so only by virtue of poetry and even then at levels which adult sensibility must labour to accept). Boito's omission of Act I in Shakespeare's *Othello*, and the storm-opening on Cyprus, are an upward stroke of genius. Nearly at every juncture, the forced mechanics of *The Merry Wives of Windsor* are made inexhaustible wonder by a hurt forgiveness of life, of time, granted to Verdi in high and Sophoclean age. Here, as in reference to Hölderlin's *Antigonä*, the common practices of judgement fumble. In *Antigonä*, moreover, the mystery of 'derivative autonomy' is at once clarified and complicated by the fact that Hölderlin's model of the 'God-challenger' and of the 'loving–destructive fusion' which he aims at coincides with his theory and practice of actual translation. Thus there is, as we saw, in Hölderlin's Sophocles a 'tragedy of translation' as well as supreme tragedy 'in translation'. But these are only obtuse phrases. It makes (almost ominous) sense to ask: suppose the

Greek original had been lost *after* Hölderlin's version—such cases are known in the Middle Ages and even the early Renaissance—what then? We would be in possession of one of the supreme tragic plays in literature. It would be a play, in certain respects, 'beyond', 'in excess of', Sophocles. It is not easy to elucidate the singular and hyperbolic status which Hegel, Kierkegaard, Goethe perhaps, assigned to Sophocles' *Antigone*. But one way of doing so is just this: to know the Greek play as having been, as being, the efficient cause of Hölderlin's *Antigonä*.

In the act of philosophical interpretation, in the poet's recasting, we confront the fundamental constancy of homecoming, the backbone of theme and variation in western sensibility. The Antigone myth reaches unwavering across more than two millennia. Why should this be?

CHAPTER TWO

I

THE earliest representation we have of Antigone being brought before Creon is a vase-painting which scholars assign to the late fifth or early fourth century BC. Theatrical, operatic, choreographic, cinematic, narrative versions of 'Antigone' are being produced at this very moment. The line of philosophical, political, ethical–jurisprudential, and poetic analyses and invocations of the myth and of the variants on Sophocles which have followed through the ages, shows no sign of being broken. No register of 'the matter of Antigone', from the *Odyssey* (XI. 271 ff.) to Liliana Cavanni's film *I Cannibali* of 1972 or to Kemal Demirel's *Antigone* and Athol Fugard's *The Island*, both produced in 1973, the one in Turkey, the other in South Africa, can hope to be complete.

Numerous treatments are lost to us: among them the archaic epic cycles on the House of Laius and the destiny of Thebes; Euripides' *Antigone*, which is cited in lines 1182 and 1187 of Aristophanes' *Frogs*; the Latin *Antigone* of Lucius Accius, dated mid-second century BC; rococo and neo-classical operatic versions of the Antigone-tragedy of which merely the titles or fragments of the libretti survive. Currently, there are 'Antigones' which circulate only in clandestine, samizdat form. At a rough estimate, the catalogue of Antigone dramas, operas, ballets, pictorial and plastic representations in post-medieval European art and literature alone runs into the hundreds. Maurice Druon produced his own variant, *Mégarée*, in 1944. In his 1962 preface to the play, he puts the question self-deprecatingly: 'What schoolboy, if he has had the luck of being educated by sound humanists, has not dreamt of writing an Antigone? . . . a hundredth, a thousandth Antigone?'

No inventory of the poems in which Antigone makes her appearance, either *in propria persona* or in the lit shadow of allusion, will be anywhere near exhaustive. It stretches from the implicit presence of Polyneices in Pindar's Ninth Nemean (line 24) and Sixth Olympian (line 15) Odes to Ovid's *Tristia*, 5; from the mid-twelfth-century *Roman de Thèbes* to Canto XXII of the *Purgatorio* and chapter twenty-three of Boccaccio's *De claris mulieribus*, not itself, of course, a poem, but the immediate source of innumerable poetic reprises. The Antigone motif passes from the Renaissance to Goethe's *Euphrosyne*, and from Goethe to Hofmannsthal and to Yeats. Donald Davie's mordant poem, 'Creon's Mouse', appears in 1953. Antigone's constancy in the western poetic repertoire is literal. As is that of the Creon–Antigone confrontation and dialectic in their political, moral, legal, sociological ramifications. Named or implicit, the two figures and the mortal argument between them initiate, exemplify, and polarize primary elements in the discourse on man and society as it has been conducted in the West. Again incomplete, the bibliography would extend from Aristotle's *Rhetoric* to the exultant apologia for Creon in Bernard-Henri Lévy's *Le Testament de Dieu* of 1979. No less than 1943–4, 1978 and 1979 were, in fact, years of 'Antigone-fever'. The Hölderlin version is translated into French and staged in Strasbourg. An *Antigone Through the Looking-Glass* surfaces in London. At least three major new productions, modulating on Sophocles, Hölderlin, and Brecht, are mounted in Germany. Heinrich Böll, aiming to characterize the German condition in a time of terrorist attack and suicide, does so in terms of the Antigone story and of the unwillingness of official culture and the media to allow its radical implications (in the film *Der Herbst in Deutschland*). Over and over again, western moral and political consciousness has lived what Helmut Richter calls, in one of his political sonnets, *Antigone anno jetzt*, 'Antigone year-now'.

Even more pervasive, and altogether impossible to index, has been the role of the matter of Antigone in the actual lives of individuals and communities. It is a defining trait of western culture after Jerusalem and after Athens that in it men and women re-enact, more or less consciously, the major gestures, the exemplary symbolic motions, set before them by antique imaginings and formulations. Our realities, as it were, mime the canonic possibilities first expressed in classical art and feeling. In his diary for 17 September 1941, the German novelist and publicist Martin Raschke recounts an episode in Nazi-occupied Riga. Caught trying to sprinkle earth on the publicly exposed body of her executed brother, a young girl, entirely unpolitical in her sentiments, is asked why. She answers: 'He was my brother. For me that is sufficient.'[1] In December 1943, the Germans descended on the village of Kalavrita in the Peloponnesus. They rounded up all the males and did them to death. Against explicit orders, in peril of their own lives, the women of the village broke out of the school in which they had been imprisoned and went *en masse* to lament and to bury the slain. Many years later, Charlotte Delbo commemorated their action in a poem entitled, justly and inevitably, 'Des Mille Antigones' (1979). But also in humbler circumstances, in the spasms of the young when faced with the unctuous imperative of the old, in the daily rub of Utopian or anarchic impulse against the mildewed surface of 'realism' and expedient routine, the Antigone gesture is made, the polemics spring out of an ancient mouth. Indifference to the theme, rejection of its universality, are so rare as to appear an eccentric provocation. I have quoted Matthew Arnold's doubt. In Book III. 37 of *The World as Will and Representation*, Schopenhauer, determined on anti-Idealist and anti-Hegelian originality, refers to the 'ekelhafte Motive' ('the repugnant motifs' or 'motivations') in 'such tragedies as *Antigone* and *Philoctetes*'. These have remained isolated cavils. Since the fifth century BC, western sensibility has experienced decisive moments of its identity and history in reference to the Antigone legend and to the life in art and in argument of this legend. Overwhelmingly, it has felt women in the face of arbitrary power and of death to be, as Romain Rolland called them in his desperate plea for an armistice and a burial of the dead during the hecatombs of 1914–18, 'les Antigones de la terre'—'the Antigones of the earth'.

Such economy of imagining challenges understanding. No century has been more attentive than ours to the theoretical and descriptive study of myths. The concept of 'the mythical' occupies a central place in modern psychology, in social anthropology, in the theory of literary forms. Fascinatingly, the intensity and range of investigation since Frazer, Freud, and Cassirer has been such as to mythologize certain aspects of its own method and form. I mean by this that the analytic–

---

[1] Cf. D. Hoffmann (ed.), *Hinweis auf Martin Raschke* (Heidelberg and Darmstadt, 1963), 81.

descriptive study of myths and the inquiry into the functions of the mythological in human consciousness and social institutions have, in themselves, taken on a 'mythical' cast. Claude Lévi-Strauss's *Mythologiques* (so akin, in this regard, to Frazer's *Golden Bough*) is both a 'logic of myths' and a lyric discourse whose modes of argument and of representation generate the kinds of narrative, of symbolic and ritual device, proper to the myths under discussion. The 'demythologizing' movement in twentieth-century Protestant theology and exegesis stems precisely from an awareness that the category of myth had subverted that of revealed historicity. In short, the assertion that myth is the conceptual common denominator in our current readings of collective psychology and social structure, that it animates our understanding of narrative and symbolic codes, and even of such would-be 'scientific' constructs as the Marxist analysis of alienation and millenarian redemption, is almost banal.

None the less, the fundamental questions remain. How do myths originate, if this notion of inception in observable time is, indeed, applicable? What processes of canonization and of discard are at work to bring about the acceptance and transmission of certain myths and the obliteration of others? Again, the question itself may be misconceived. It could be that any sensible definition of 'myth' entails the fact of survivance. There would, strictly considered, be no 'forgotten myths'. Why, then, is the canon of major myths in western culture so relatively restricted (compare the compendia which anthropologists have assembled of Australasian or Amazonian mythologies)? And, this being the crux of my present argument, why should a return to these same key myths be the constant reflex in western art and literature, from Pindar to Pound, from the wall-paintings of Pompeii to Picasso's Minotaur? How are we to make intelligible the fact that our psychological and cultural condition is, at signal points, one of uninterrupted reference to a handful of antique stories? It is not, I think, unfair to suppose that our grasp of these several and close-knit questions has not advanced conclusively since Vico's initiation of the modern experience of the mythical in the *Scienza nuova* of 1725.

Scholarly opinion today has it that the tragic tale of Antigone, as we know it, was most probably Sophocles'

invention. In this context, it remains entirely unclear what is to
be understood by 'invention'. Pausanias (IX. 25) mentions a
piece of terrain outside Thebes, a furrow in the ground, which
the local inhabitants ascribed to Antigone. This, they assured
the traveller, was the indelible spoor left by Polyneices' corpse
as Antigone dragged it to the funeral pyre. We have no way of
telling whether this scenic marker precedes the literature or
comes after it in illustration. It is supposed, with a fair measure
of confidence, that the disasters of the clan of Laius and their
effect on the early history of Thebes and of Argos were the
subject of epic treatment as early as the second half of the
eighth century BC. But nothing save small fragments of an
Oidipodeia or *Thebais* has come down to us. A recently
published and much-discussed papyrus assigns to Jocasta a
commanding role in the Eteocles–Polyneices quarrel, but gives
to this fratricidal affair a judicial and dynastic framework
which differs markedly from Sophocles' (Polyneices has
renounced his claims to alternating kingship in Thebes in
exchange for the wealth, the treasures of the οἶκος, bequeathed
by Oedipus).[1] It has been suggested that we have here an epic
fragment or 'dramatic lyric' by Stesichorus, which would take
us back to the late seventh or early sixth century. The
obscurities in the arrangement of rotating kingship implicit in
Sophocles' handling of the Eteocles–Polyneices conflict, the
vestigial ambiguities in Creon's claim to legitimacy in Thebes,
have led certain classical scholars and anthropologists to argue
that the entire saga of Oedipus and his children mirrors a
violent, obscure transition from a native matrilineal system
to the patrilineal conventions of dynastic succession and
property-division brought by the Dorian invaders.[2] Far echoes
of this crisis would emerge in Euripides' *Phoenician Women*,
notably in lines 1586–8.[3]

The survival of Oedipus and Jocasta into old age, as shown

---

[1] Cf. P. J. Parsons' discussion in the *Zeitschrift für Papyrologie und Epigraphik*, ii (1975),
and C. Meillier, 'La Succession d'Œdipe d'après le P. Lille 76a + 73, poème lyrique
probablement de Stésichore', *Revue des études grecques*, xci (1978). The papyrus in
question was first published in 1976.

[2] Cf. G. Devereux, 'Sociopolitical Functions of the Oedipus Myth in Early Greece',
Psychoanalytic Quarterly, xxxii (1963). This reading has, however, met with little assent.

[3] Cf. the illuminating discussion of the whole mythical background and the possible
variant traditions in F. Vian, *Les Origines de Thèbes* (Paris, 1963). Vian notes that in
both Aeschylus and Euripides Creon would seem to be 'en concurrence avec des
souverains plus authentiques' (p. 184).

in Euripides' drama, Homer's famous allusion in the *Iliad*, IV. 394, to a son of Haemon, Pindar's reference, in his Second Olympian, to Polyneices' male heir, the Euripidean *Antigone*,[1] and a disputed passage in a commentary by the Byzantine scholiast Aristophanes, demonstrate that Sophocles' version was not, or not at the outset, the only available or accepted one. This points either to variants in the legendary material or to liberties of invention taken by individual poets. The latter may have been greater than neo-classical and even nineteenth-century critics supposed. Knowing nothing about the part which Antigone may or may not have played in such epic texts as the *Thebais*, the *Oidipodeia*, the *Epigonoi*, the *Amphiarai Exelasis*, we can make no sensible guess as to relations between the extant myths and our play. What is, on present evidence, quite plausible is the hypothesis that Antigone's defiance of Creon's edict on the very night after the murderous battle, and the tragic collision provoked by this defiance, were Sophocles' 'idea'. The representation of this theme at the close of Aeschylus' *Seven Against Thebes*, with its strong hints of a fortunate resolution, is now thought, though not unanimously, to be a post-Sophoclean addition to an earlier play. It would signal the success and fascination of Sophocles' invention.

But this tells us little of the relations of such invention to the orders of authority, of 'historical truth', of symbolic suggestion in the corpus of myths. The very status of the term 'myth' in fifth-century Athens is largely inaccessible to us. Despite hints in Herodotus, we do not know the relations which Greek thought at the time of Sophocles saw between 'myth' and what we call 'history'. We are not in a position to assign to what we know of classical Greek the kinds of discrimination we draw in current English between, say, 'myth', 'legend', 'fable', and 'saga'. Certain scholars and interpreters have perceived archaic elements in *Antigone*. They see the presence of a 'magical' or astronomical–numerological motif in seven-gated Thebes and in the twice-seven champions who assail and defend these portals. Vestiges of very old, pos-

[1] For a discussion of the evidence, cf. L. Séchan, *Études sur la tragédie grecque* (Paris, 1926), 289–90, and J. Mesk, 'Die Antigone des Euripides', *Wiener Studien*, xlix (1931). The publication of the Oxyrhynchus papyrus of Euripides' play has rendered these earlier discussions out of date. It now looks probable that this *Antigone*, like Sophocles', ended unhappily. But the plot-lines diverge.

sibly totemic associations have been ascribed to the heraldic devices and the gloss put on these devices in Aeschylus' *Seven Against Thebes*. Other classicists reject such conjectures out of hand.

What seems more than probable is the echo in the knot of incest around Oedipus, in Oedipus' encounter with the riddle of the Sphinx, of elements of uncertainty, of trial and error, in the evolution of western kinship systems and of the civic institutions which these systems generate and underwrite. I will argue, though only in a preliminary, tentative form, that this evolution, as well as the root sense of certain other primary Greek myths, is intimately associated with and registered in the fundamental features of our syntax (gender, nomination, verb tenses and modes). In the story of the House of Laius, the anthropological, the sociological, the linguistic origins and lines of descent are most probably inseparable.

What we cannot define is Sophocles' awareness of and attitude to this archaic inheritance. We cannot, to put it crudely, guess plausibly as to Sophocles' view of 'the Oedipus complex' (if this phrase corresponds to any reality). We cannot know whether Sophocles attached any particular formal or psychological aura to the Greek dual, an inflected form which specifically expresses a double agency. Its use at the start of *Antigone*, its absence thereafter, have suggested to modern anthropologists and comparative grammarians some reference to archaic kinship codes and representations. Sophocles himself comes very late. He is far closer to our own concept of literature than he is to the 'origins' of the saga of Laius and his fatal clan. These origins and the formation of an *Oidipodeia* over a millennium, perhaps, or more, take place in a purely oral context. Owing to modern ethnographic and linguistic studies, we do seem to know rather more—we know 'differently'—of such a context than did Aristotle and his contemporaries. We sense something of its collective matrix and formulaic techniques. It may well be that there is in the oral elaboration and mnemonic transmission of myths a postulate of 'real presence', a suspension of temporality in favour of an always-renewed immediacy such as we find in the language and gestures of the sacraments. Whatever his origins in one place and time, the Saviour is epiphanically present 'here and now'. In contrast, narrative time, the ambiguity of that which is recounted or performed now but which 'actually took place' in the past, may well be a literary and epistemologically critical concept. It may be the late and necessary condition of 'fiction', as Aristotle already knows the term, in distinction from 'myth'. That this distinction, depending as it does on writing, can be seen as inhibiting, that the passage from the mythical to the fictive can be experienced as a derogation and a loss of truth, emerges clearly from Plato's critique of μίμησις and from his constant uneasiness in respect of Homer. Thus there is a haunting sense in which 'literature', be it of the highest quality, is only an epilogue to the native acts of the imagination.

This, however, does not tell us how these acts were originally performed or why it is that some of them—the fistful of Greek myths which have shaped western consciousness—should have outlived others. The social historian, particularly after Fustel de Coulanges and Marx, will answer that there are material determinants. We know of the royal house at Mycenae, we know of the Theban dynasty, because the power-relations between patron and bard, between the teller of tales and his audience, were such as to favour certain epic cycles over others. The individual imagination is embedded in social circumstance and its inventions survive or are obliterated with the institutions in which it found expression. Pindar says as much even when he is already feeling his way towards the proud scandal of the survivance of the poem long after the city in whose honour and pay it has been sung will have perished. Obviously, there is truth in all this. The affair at Troy involved patrician and regional mafias eager for ennobling commemoration. But, again, this is a late truth. The essential modes of the mythical ordering of the world far antedate Mycenae. And how is it that Sophocles, so much on our side of the calendar of western history and sensibility, could recapture or, indeed, add to these modes?

The theme of burial touches on elemental chords in private and public sentiment. The practices attached thereto are as various and fantastic as are the different alphabets. Each comports a wealth of semantic and symbolic values. These seek to balance the dualities, the contradictions, which Hegelian terminology calls 'dialectic' and which recent structural anthropology designates as 'binary'. In other words: the rites of bestowal of the dead attempt to satisfy, to stylize inherently opposed impulses and social reflexes. They labour to remove the dead from sensory intrusion on the living while, at the same time, they would enforce on remembrance a tactile, durable incitement and focus. The sepulchre is meant to house and contain the dead within or very close to the city of the living; πόλις and *necropolis* are contiguous. Simultaneously, interment or the ritual exposure of the departed are aimed at inhibiting the dread errancy and visitation of the dead, their return, except perhaps one day and night of the year, to the streets and houses of the living. As Hegel noted, there is a motion of fusion and of recoil in respect of the earth, an espousal and repudiation of the bonds between flesh and dust which are explicit in the very name of Adam in the western image of the mortal body. The shroud, the coffin, the burial chamber guard man from casual dissolution in the ground. At the same time, however, the grave-shaft, the charnel-pit, the cemetery ensure the homecoming of the flesh to the dark earth, the absorption of the individual by the organic cycle of devolution and fertility. The elements and the cardinal points on the map play their functional, emblematic role in this dialectic. The disappearance of a dead body in the weltering sea—Palinurus, Lycidas—impresses western sensibility as peculiarly desolate. Many cultures incinerate their deceased; others keep them jealously from the cleansing anonymity of fire. In one code of grief, tombs are oriented westward; in another, the chance of resurrection depends on an eastward lie.

Classical antiquity expounds the specific belief that non-burial prevents access to the realm of the dead. The spirit of the unburied man or woman will haunt the near shores of Lethe in a passion of remembrance and reminder. In the framework of this belief, animals play an ambiguous part. There is an emphatic horror in Hebraic and Graeco-Roman feelings at the thought of the exposure of dead bodies to the appetites of vultures and of dogs (whereas there are other ritual–social traditions in which precisely such exposure ensures the natural disappearance of corrupt flesh and the swift passage of the deceased to the purity of the spiritual). In the Judaic–Hellenic view, it is as if the human person were peculiarly, almost obscenely, vulnerable to animality, as if the exit of the spirit at the hour of death drew towards it the solicitations of the beasts who come now to claim, to assert their own part in man. Yet, by virtue of the characteristic dialectical or binary movement of consciousness, animals can also be seen as the sentinels and retinue of the departed. If dogs lick Jezebel's accursed blood, they also, in other symbolic episodes in the western legacy, stay even unto death by their fallen masters and protect them from scavengers. The damned are given in pasture to birds of prey. But the famous dirge in Webster's *The White Devil* instructs us to

> Call for the robin redbreast, and the wren,
> Since o'er shady groves they hover,
> And with leaves and flowers do cover
> The friendless bodies of unburied men.

Indeed, in Webster's invocation—and he was a master of the ceremonies of death—the actual animals which are thought to gnaw at corpses, which are thought to avenge the gross intrusion of the dead into their own subterranean lodging, are the protectors of the dead body:

> Call unto his funeral dole
> The ant, the fieldmouse, and the mole,
> To rear him hillocks that shall keep him warm.

Thus, from the mutilation and burial of Hector to Sartre's *Morts sans sépulture*—that 'Antigone' title—central but often contradictory sentiments about the proper treatment of the dead have busied western societies. 'Earth to earth' is a complex motion.

Especially when the cadaver is that of a criminal or of an enemy. In which case instincts and arguments are tensely poised. There can be prudential magic in capturing the flesh and bone of a mighty foe, in 'ingesting' in the πόλις the numinous virtues of a slain adversary. In turn, the remains of the sanctified, of those whom the gods have visited even in ambiguity, as in the case of Oedipus at Colonus, can bestow lasting good fortune on the ground and bounds in which they have been honourably sepulchred. Classical reflexes and legal prescriptions waver. So, to be sure, do those of the Christian community: witness the fury over dead Ophelia's 'maimed rites'. Plutarch attributes to Solon a law which 'forbids men to speak evil of the dead'. It is piety, held Solon, to consider the

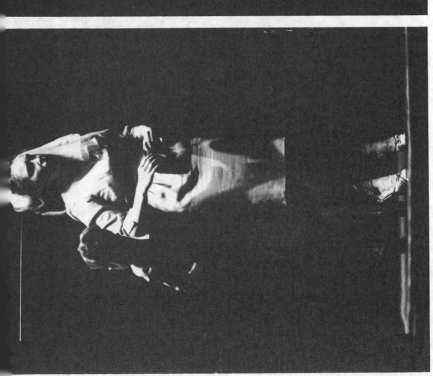

7. *Antigonä*, Hölderlin, first performed in Frankfurt-on-Main, 4 Nov. 1978, directed by Christof Nel. (*Left*) Antigonä: Rotraut de Neve. (*Right*) Creon: Axel Wagne.

8. *Antigone*, opera composed by Arthur Honegger. (*Top left*) Paris, Feb.
1952—Antigone: Hélène Bouvier; Créon: Clavère. (*Bottom*) Angers, 20
March 1981—Antigone: Rosane Crepield; Créon: Julien Haas.
9. (*Top right*) *Antigonae*, opera composed by Carl Orff, Zurich, 29 Jan.
1983. Conductor: Ferdinand Leitner; Producer: August Everding.
Antigonae: Rose Wagemann; Kreon: Roland Hermann.

deceased as sacred. It is justice not to meddle with those who are gone. And it is 'politic' (Dryden's astute translation) not to dishonour the enemy dead lest such disgrace renew and perpetuate familial blood-feuds or civic discord. Thucydides, however (I. 126), reports a homicidal imbroglio in which a party of Athenians lured fugitives away from sanctuary with promises of safety and then slew them. Those guilty of this outrage were punished even beyond death: their bones were disinterred and their bodies cast forth. In I. 138, Thucydides tells us that after Themistocles' death in banishment his remains were returned secretly to Attica for, as Thomas Hobbes translates, 'it was not lawful to bury one there that had fled for treason'. Xenophon's *Hellenica* (I. vii) appears to echo this legislation. In 406, after a botched naval engagement against the Spartans off Mytilene, accusations are launched against the son of Pericles and the commanders responsible. The indictment, as Xenophon renders it, cites a law whereby convicted temple-robbers (we shall hear Creon's charge against Polyneices) and traitors shall not be allowed burial on Athenian soil. The harshest text of all is to be found in that pitiless register of crime and punishment, of impiety and nocturnal retribution, so Venetian in atmosphere, of the Tenth Book of Plato's *Laws* (909 a ff.). Atheists and sorcerers, God-deniers and those 'who in their contempt of mankind bewitch so many of the living by the pretence of calling forth the dead', shall be executed and barred from access to the other world in so far as such access depends on due burial. Observe the grim symmetry which Plato posits as between the nature of the trespass and that of the chastisement. Whoever denies the gods or seeks to raise spirits 'shall be cast out beyond the borders without burial'. If any free citizen have a hand in seeking to give the condemned clandestine funeral rites, 'he shall be liable to prosecution at the suit of any who cares to take proceedings'.

Our evidence is, therefore, both selective and contradictory. What seems unquestionable is Sophocles' fascination with the topic. It informs *Ajax*, *Antigone*, and *Oedipus at Colonus*, to list only plays which survive. The entombment and transfiguration of Oedipus reach back, even in Sophocles' reasoned and supremely discreet treatment, to far vestiges of the totemic. The debate on burial rites in *Ajax* is at once more abstract and more comprehensive than that in *Antigone*. Menelaus argues crassly but coherently. Ajax has been made mad by a god, and in this madness he has sought to massacre his liege-lords and companions-at-arms. It would be wholly unreasonable and offensive to social justice to honour such a man with funeral rites and a lasting sepulchre. Let the sea-birds have their fill of him. True, this is a fearful commandment. But Dread, *Φόβος*, a demon of battle and of civic order, has his shrine in Sparta, and no man, however grand in his sometime heroism, is above retribution. Should Teucer seek to bury his half-brother, he too may find himself 'in need of a grave'. The chorus of Salaminian sailors, while faithful to self-slain Ajax, sees 'wisdom' (*coφία*) in the general humanitarian sentiments with which Menelaus has prefaced his pronouncement. But they go on to ask: should just claims of reparation and of exemplary judiciousness extend to a corpse?

Teucer's objections are neither ethical nor legal. He detests the sons of Atreus for the lordly bullies they are. He denies their sovereignty over Ajax, who came to Troy freely and who saved their hides on more than one blood-soaked field. Agamemnon now enters to press the attack. Ajax's murderous delusions had their roots in overweening and anarchic pride. He would not accept the award to Odysseus of the arms of Achilles, though this award was deliberated upon and voted in ripe council. Ajax's madness, like Teucer's will to give him burial, is a defiance of *νόμος*, of law rationally arrived at and supreme over all. Without this supremacy, there will be social chaos and that individual descent into animality so clearly manifest in Ajax's end. Teucer's fraternal passion, and this is a significant touch, is voiced in 'a barbarian tongue' which Agamemnon professes not to understand. Teucer has a Trojan mother (line 1263). Odysseus intervenes. His rhetoric is charged with subtle humanity. Compassion and piety reside, literally, in the tenses of the verb. Ajax *was* a deadly foe, Odysseus *had* himself found him hateful and dangerous. But this odium, this menace, do not encompass the presentness of his remains. To disgrace the corpse is not so much to dishonour Ajax as it is to offend divine law (*θεῶν νόμους*). It is not right, it is not equitable—*δίκαιον* seems, at this point, to carry values which range all the way from formal justice to instinctive decorum and courtesy of spirit—to injure a valiant man in death even if he *was* your enemy. Line 1347 is sophisticated yet poignant: the key-phrase is μισεῖν καλόν, '(when it was) seemly to hate'. There is a season for such hatred. With Ajax's terrible death, this season is ended. To hate him now would be to demean the high and perilous loathing which had divided the living. A strong ruler (the word used is τύραννος), confesses Agamemnon, does not find it easy to observe such niceties of pity. Odysseus' final argument is one of broad humanity: 'I too shall be in need of decent burial', the clear hint being that such need comes, swiftly perhaps, to all mortals. Agamemnon yields. But there is one further motif of consummate tact in the epilogue. In his gratitude, Teucer begs Laertes' wise and eloquent son not to take part in the funeral rites which he has secured for his dead foe. Let him be an honoured guest only, lest Ajax's torn spirit take offence. Odysseus acquiesces; and as we learn from the *Odyssey*, Ajax's 'great shade is burning still' when Odysseus seeks parley with it in Hades. There is an uncanny logic in the fact that Ajax, unlike Odysseus, hates *after* death, that sorrow and madness have made his hatred corrupt. Moreover, as Jebb points out in his edition of the play, the whole debate has ritual grounds which differ from those in *Antigone*, which penetrate more directly into civic life and history. Ajax is a 'hero' in the full technical sense, a tutelary spirit and guardian example to the brave. Such formal status can only be realized and made efficient if there is a visible sepulchre and locale for commemorative rites. To deny Ajax burial—this is not the issue with Polyneices—would be to despoil generations yet to come of sanctity. As always, there is in Odysseus' humaneness a touch of clairvoyant gain.

It is an evident challenge for a great dramatic poet to engage language closely with the essentially speechless which is death. The debate in *Ajax*, the dramatization of Oedipus' transfiguration and passage into everlastingness in *Oedipus at Colonus*, Antigone's invocations of the underworld, are acts of circumscription. They enclose the unspoken enigma of death within the grammars of religious, psychological, political, moral, and poetic discourse. Something central to Sophocles' art and vision is involved. But the coincidence in dates of composition of *Ajax* and *Antigone*—the former is now generally held to be the earlier of the two plays—is arresting. It does raise the distinct possibility that the shared theme of disputed interment points to a specific historical situation and conflict.

It has been proposed that the Sophoclean treatment of the relations between the living πόλις and the claims of the dead, particularly in *Antigone*, reflects the atmosphere and style of Athenian politics as declared in Pericles' celebrated funeral oration which was delivered in the winter of 440 BC.[1] Some scholars find evidence for a new spate of familial tombs in Athens at about this time. *Ajax* and *Antigone* would constitute a pointed advocacy for the freedom of familial burial practices at a moment when the state, under pressure of war and internal polemic, was seeking to control, indeed to regiment, private piety.[2] It has been urged that the burials of Ajax and of Polyneices stand for the return of Themistocles' remains to the Piraeus, as it is mentioned in Thucydides. This return would, in precise concordance with the Sophoclean tragedies, signify the victory of θεςμός —traditional, divinely sanctioned custom—over νόμος understood as legal ordinance.[3]

The historical evidence is tenuous, and Professor H. Lloyd-Jones rejects it altogether. Nevertheless, the general point is credible. In assuming executive and lasting form, the diffuse matter of myth will often crystallize around a concrete node, around a contingent 'impurity' in the affairs of the city. Without losing its universality, the legend takes on a local habitation and a temporal focus. Paradoxically, it may be this concentration around a core of timely and spatial specificity— the instauration of a tribunal and jury system on the Areopagus, the consecration of a shrine at Colonus, discord, perhaps, over the bestowal of Themistocles' bones in Attic ground—which gives to myth its supple durability. The

---

[1] This association emerges strongly from the larger argument in V. Ehrenberg, *Sophocles and Pericles* (Oxford, 1954). Cf. in particular pp. 64 ff. and 146–72.

[2] Cf. D. Marmeliuc, 'Reflectări ale contemporaneităţii in tragediile lui Sofocle', *Studii Clasice*, viii (1966), 28–9.

[3] Cf. J. Carrière, 'Communicazione sulla tragedia antica greca ausiliaria della giustizia e della politica', *Dioniso*, xliii (1969), 171–2. In his concise review of all the available historical and literary evidence, Giovanni Cerri ('Ideologia funeraria nell'*Antigone* di Sofocle', in G. Gnoli and J.-P. Vernant (edd.), *La Mort, les morts dans les sociétés anciennes* [Cambridge University Press, 1982], 121–33) concludes that Sophocles' play must be seen against a situation of rapidly evolving debate and conflict. Neither Creon's edict nor Antigone's challenge can be identified with any static polarities in Attic usage or belief. Different precedents, diversely interpreted, gave to the Sophoclean treatment 'una problematica attuale'. Cerri argues that no real progress will be made in our understanding of the Creon–Antigone dialectic until we have 'decodified' the exact idiom, the context of allusion, in which their debate is couched.

underlying process would not be, as most modern scholars and 'mytho-logists' suppose, one of a rational re-examination and critique of the mythical foundations.[1] On the contrary: the poet, the dramatist, calls upon, compacts, the disseminated energies and authority of myth in order to give to a current, circumstantially bounded event or social conflict the 'visibility', the compelling dimensions, the inexorable logic and extremity of the mythical. The myth precipitates and purifies the agitated, opaque elements of the immediate situation. It enforces on them distance and the dignity of the insoluble. But to do this it must internalize the local occasion. It is willed attempts at 'timelessness', such as we find them in neo-classical art or in nineteenth-century epic sublimity, which bring on rapid datedness. Universal texts and works of art guard within themselves a life-giving parochialism.

This may enlighten us as to how Sophocles grafted on to the general, dispersed material of an *Oidipodeia* a plot tightly drawn from local circumstance and current dispute. And it may suggest that it was the permeability of the high myth to the pressures of political and social immediacy which ensured the great success of the play (for which there is solid evidence). But it does not tell us why the graft 'took' on the millennia; why it is that Antigone, together with a handful of other figures—Orpheus, Prometheus, Heracles, Agamemnon and his pack, Oedipus, Odysseus, Medea—should constitute the essential code of canonic reference for intellect and sensibility across western civilization. It does not explain the dynamics of antique theme and constant variation, of Hellenic source and successive recomposition, which have, to this day, been fundamental to our arts and letters. Why a hundred 'Antigones' after Sophocles?

A question so banal yet central is difficult to focus. At one level, it addresses itself to the singularly recursive character of western thought and style as a whole. It asks nothing less than why this thought and style should have developed via a sequence of recapitulations of the classical, beginning with the Roman reprise of the Greeks (the Ciceronian moment may be the key to the history of the western order) and with the 'pre-Renaissance' of the Carolingian empire. At a more specific

[1] For a representative summation of this approach, cf. M. Détienne, *Dionysos mis à mort* (Paris, 1977), 34–5.

level, the question aims at 'the tyranny of Greece over the western mind', a 'tyranny' as manifest in Joyce's *Ulysses*, in the *Cantos* of Pound, in the parodistic classicism of Picasso and Stravinsky, as it was in the explicit *imitatio* of the Renaissance, of the Enlightenment, and of Romantic and Victorian Hellenism.[1] To ask so largely is to risk platitude. Yet simply because it is ubiquitous, simply because it underwrites at almost every point the codes and conventions of our literacy, the phenomenon ought not to be taken for granted. There are other cultures which exhibit no comparable energy of reiteration, in which there is no analogous reversion to the *auctoritas* of a classic precedent. Even more striking is the fact that this reflex of recapitulation should have survived the radical impulses of nihilism, of apocalyptic cleansing and innovation, which have played so drastic a part in the crises of modernity. Well before Voznesensky, men had cried out exultantly for 'a fire in the Architectural Institute', for a great purgation to sweep away the marmoreal sovereignty of the past. Instead, the twentieth century has been one of the most 'neo-classical'.

Ought there not, by now, to be a spate of 'Hamlets', of 'Macbeths', or of 'Lears' (Edward Bond's *Lear* variant is one of the very few we have)? When there are 'repeats' of Molière's *Amphitryon*, as in Kleist and in Giraudoux, why should these themselves be so patently a part of a chain of echoes which leads back to Plautus and to Plautus' Greek sources? Is it so very difficult to devise new 'stories'? Writing in 1961, Rolf Hochhuth seeks to call into view the hellish climate of life in Berlin in the spring and summer of 1943. Innumerable 'true stories' and emblematic possibilities must have lain to hand. *Die Berliner Antigone* is, as its title proclaims, our hundredth, our two-hundredth, variant on Sophocles. Again, I ask: why should this be?

Both in its general and more specific forms, this question seems to underlie major aspects of the Marxist theory of history and of culture. It is explicit in Freudian psychoanalysis, in the Jungian argument on archetypes, in the structural anthropology of Lévi-Strauss. But I am not certain whether it has

---

[1] For recent studies of the theme, cf. M. L. Clarke, *Classical Education in Britain, 1500–1900* (Cambridge University Press, 1959); R. M. Ogilvie, *Latin and Greek* (London, 1964); R. Jenkyns, *The Victorians and Ancient Greece* (London, 1980); F. M. Turner, *The Greek Inheritance in Victorian Britain* (Yale University Press, 1981).

been asked directly, insistently, enough. I am not certain that we have registered an appropriate astonishment, even, perhaps, a condign sense of scandal, at the persistently repetitive and 'epigonal' tenor of so much of our consciousness and expressive forms. Did the nerve of symbolic invention, of compelling metaphor, die with Athens?

It is in his *Introduction to the Critique of Political Economy* that Marx seeks to refine the naïve, the sociologically vulgar, model of the relations between the ideological–aesthetic 'superstructure' in a culture and its economic and social base. These relations, urges Marx, cannot be formulated in any simplistic, one-to-one equation. They are much subtler, both in regard to the quality of the ideological or artistic climate of a given community and in regard to the temporal stages of social evolution. The need for refinement had forced itself upon Marx. He shared with the whole of nineteenth-century high literacy and with the philosophic Idealism of his German generation the conviction that the achievements of ancient Greece stood unsurpassed. Not even Marx's beloved Shakespeare had excelled the abiding genius, the exemplary universality, of Homer, Aeschylus, or Sophocles. Yet how could such intrinsic eminence and its persistent dominion over the western imagination—the latter being the more arduous part of the question—be reconciled with the undoubted truth that Athenian economic and social structures, slavery in particular, represented a 'primitive', long-surpassed phase in social development? The dialectical nature of the normal reciprocities between spirit and society seemed, in this vital instance, strained to the utmost if not negated. Marx's well-known solution is a poignant *non sequitur*.

The genius of Greek art and literature is that of 'the childhood of man'. The immediacy of perception, the truth to nature, the confident breadth of Greek sculpture, architecture, lyric verse, epic, and drama are those of an inspired child, of the young 'seer blest' in the radiance of daybreak. Our incessant fascination with the Greek achievement, the compulsion which draws us to these ancient things, is one of enlightened nostalgia. We know that we cannot go back to the childhood of our being (Hölderlin's *Umkehr*), we know that we have long since diagnosed and surmounted the vicious conditions of economic production and political power which attended this childhood. But we know also that we cannot recapture its heroic innocence of sensibility, its trust in the ordering and performative energies of art. Rationally, Marx must have realized that the concept of 'the childhood of mankind' is untenable, that ancient Greece was as much a late product of historical evolution as any other culture of which we have record. His own work on classical materialism and atomic theory shows that he did not usually ascribe to Greek thought any spirit of immaturity. But the authority of the *Iliad*, of the *Oresteia*, of *Antigone* over the modern temper was irrefutable. This paradox demanded explanation even where the explanation is itself an 'analytic myth'.

Both the mythical motion in Marx's diagnosis and the bearing of this diagnosis on the question of beginnings are characteristic of modernity. There is a demonstrable sense in which metaphoric scenarios of inception, of psychological and sociological genesis, have determined the style and substance of modern psychology, social anthropology, aesthetics, and linguistics. The *sciences de l'homme*, as Durkheim and Lévi-Strauss call them, represent a common endeavour to substitute for a metaphysics of 'creation'—no longer viable once its theological premises had been eroded—an immanent model of 'process'. But in this endeavour—and it is this which makes Marx, Freud, Heidegger, the anthropologists, the comparative grammarians and grammatologists (witness Derrida on Plato) such evident heirs to the Renaissance and the Enlightenment—the Greek 'case' continues to be the crucial one. The matter of Oedipus and of Antigone, the pre-Socratic fragments, Greek social institutions and the theoretic debates which these institutions generated, are the source of the process of western philosophic and social inquiry and give to this inquiry its shorthand.

Freud's attempt to accord his genetic psychology with the findings of Darwinism on the one hand and of modern cultural anthropology on the other, are intricate and unstable. No less than Marx, Freud resorts to the Greek precedent via an intuitive sense of its imaginative–formal decisiveness. It is self-evident to Freud that the Greek myths and their enactment in Greek art and literature have given to western cultural and symbolic codes their dynamic foundation. Oedipus, Narcissus, Orestes, Kronos devouring his children, Prometheus the

fire-thief, are the psychically richest yet most economic crystal-
lizations of elemental impulses and configurations in the unconscious and subconscious fabric of the race and of the individual.
It is in these 'prime' myths that our consciousness finds its ever-
renewed homecoming to the opaque comforts and terrors of its
origins, a homecoming made compelling and endurable by the
formality, by the narrative coherence, by the lyric and plastic
comeliness with which the Greek spirit invested the uncanny
and the daemonic. The fratricidal symmetry of Eteocles' and
Polyneices' death-struggle, their return to the womb of the
earth, to the maternal aspects of θάνατος, the menace of
bestiality which the prohibition of such return entails (the
unburied corpse), the ambiguities as to the value-order of
fraternal, filial, and exogamic or erotic love as they run
through the entire play—all these are the compaction and
intelligible dynamism of 'elementary particles' in the constitution and development of human identity. They are
susceptible of psychoanalytic interpretation. But such
interpretation—Freud was scrupulous on this point—depends,
in turn, on the symbolic density, on the 'essentiality of gesture
and utterance, on the *unselfconscious* sophistication'—here
Freud is very close to Marx—of the initial Greek statement.
We return always to Oedipus or Icarus or Antigone as we
return to ourselves when our fingers brush, with unknowing
alertness and recognition, across our own face and body.
Implicit in Freud's method is the assumption—it defines his
conservatism—that the indispensable mapping has been done,
that the contribution of modern psychology and social thought
to our understanding of the springs of man is a methodological
and possibly a therapeutic one, but not a refutation of the
antique. Freud insists that we do not know 'more' of human
motive and illusion than did Sophocles. Our knowledge is self-
consciously theoretic and evidentially armed as his was not.
But it is, even at its best, a knowingness which comes after the
radical wonder of knowing.

Though his 'advance' is latent in Freud's *Interpretation of
Dreams* and quite explicit in an oddly perfunctory footnote in
Freud's *Totem and Taboo*, Jung does go further. Jung's whole
approach, moreover, bears immediately on art and poetry,
both of which—witness the paper on 'The Poet and Day-
Dreams'—Freud had treated in a cautionary, not to say

condescending, vein. Jung knows that the phenomenon of the fascination, of the spell across time, and formal transformations which are exercised by great art and literature, is crucial in any theory of the individual psyche and of culture. He sees in the question of why it is that an 'Antigone' should lodge ineradicably and via incessant replication in our private and public sensibilities over the millennia not only a legitimate, but a fundamental, object of inquiry. Jung's model of the genesis of consciousness is historicist. Archaic levels of the psyche are within us 'like an old river-bed in which the water still flows'. Nothing, posits Jung, 'is ever lost'. Seeking to achieve integration with certain aspects of its primally amorphous, undifferentiated self, the human psyche generates mythical configurations and personae. These act as an essential *speculum mentis*, a dynamic mirror in which are reflected and given recognizable shape the innermost experiences of consciousness. It is from this process of 'self-detachment' (Thomas Aquinas defines 'spirits' as animate fragments of the human psyche), it is from this activity of mirroring perception, that the enduring myths originate. Jung defines the mythical personage either as a *psychologem* or as an 'archetypal psychic structure of extreme antiquity corresponding to levels of consciousness which have hardly left the animal sphere'. This personage is not only or even principally individual. It is a collective embodiment (Karl Kerényi, the mythographer and adherent of Jung, uses the term 'transpersonal').

Thus a mythical figure would be 'a collective personification' giving bearable, joyous, explanatory forms to archaic collective fantasies and phases in the elaboration of the psyche. Under the pressure of civilization, in the course of the evolution of individual mentality towards more analytic and 'rational' types of representation, the collective figure gradually breaks up. It passes into the profane level of secular and deliberate art. This art, however, and Jung's suggestion here is persuasive, can exercise its lasting spell, can survive and indeed foster repetition and variation over the ages, *only* if it conserves and makes palpable its links with those archaic, fundamental instinctive patterns ('archetypes') from which human consciousness grew and which continue alive in folklore and in ritual. We revert to 'the archetypal analogies', to the primal constellations of gesture and image in art, because the conscious mind, however emancipated and secularized, is both repelled by and drawn towards its earlier stages of existence. Confronting these, it 'remembers', it 'knows that it has been here before'. It is precisely this *déjà vu* within formal and executive originality which makes of our experience of great art and poetry a homecoming to new remembrance.

There are vital elements in Jung's theory, notably the constitution and transmission of specific memories through 'the collective unconscious', which I find difficult to grasp. But the supposition that the major work of art or text or musical composition derives its compelling 'repeatability', its constantly novel yet entirely expected shock of recognition—we know what awaits Agamemnon in the house of death but our spirit cries out in startled terror each time this knowledge is fulfilled—from archaic levels and exercises of psychic life, is plausible. At the least, it focuses directly on the fact that this is how enduring art, music, literature do work on and inside us, and it is not afraid to see in this fact a central challenge to understanding. The application of the Jungian hypothesis to folklore, to ritual vestiges in folk-ways and liturgy, to the 'authorless' myths narrated in primitive cultures, is often straightforward. Its application to a very 'late' and profoundly intellectualized product such as Sophocles' *Antigone* is more problematic. Yet Jung would, I think, want to argue that the millennial magnetism of the play and of the myth it enacts draws on much older sources of psychic energy. The images and behaviour associated with the burial motif, the hints of seasonal kingship rituals which glimmer still in the Eteocles–Polyneices conflict and in the configuration of seven-gated Thebes, the uncertainties over the respective claims of blood-kinship and of wedded love, may indeed be 'archetypal'. More particularly, Jung would, I imagine, observe in Antigone, and in the spell which she has cast on the western imagination, an instance of the youthful *anima* hiding, guarding, as it does in countless dreams and symbolic representations, the archetype of the wise old man, of the sage, magician, and king who is Oedipus.

In 'To Juan at the Winter Solstice', Robert Graves makes a 'hyper-Jungian' statement:

> There is one story and one story only
> That will prove worth your telling,
> Whether as learned bard or gifted child . . .

Are archetypes and the myths in which they find articulate
figuration indeed restricted in number? Does their instauration belong, necessarily, to 'a primitive or barbarous consciousness'? I am not certain that Jung arrived at any firm
conclusion. But structural anthropology, particularly with
Lévi-Strauss, poses the question again. It argues that the key
myths in our culture correspond to certain primordial social
confrontations and to the evolution of the mental 'sets' and
material institutions in which these confrontations—the exchanges of women and goods, the division of labour, the
adaptation of familial to communal practices—could be
'imaged', contained, and, to some degree, resolved. Thus
dynastic ambiguities, the control of burial rites within the
confines of the πόλις, the distribution of power and of the
means of symbolic affirmation as between men and women,
youth and age, are given 'conflictual' space in Sophocles'
Antigone and in the body of myths on which he drew. There is a
sense, therefore, in which it is both natural and economic to
return to 'Antigone' each time conflicts of a historically and
psychologically analogous order—as in the religious wars of
the sixteenth century or in the Paris of 1940-4—recur. Being
historical, arising, as they do, from the biological and social
realities of the human condition, such conflicts and the myths
which give them intelligible, debatable expression are not
unlimited in number or in kind.

   In Lévi-Strauss's 'mytho-logic', the principle of constraint
may lie even deeper. The ways, essentially polarized, essentially dualistic or binary, in which the imaginings and
grammars of man seem to organize and narrate their sense of
the world—Eteocles against Polyneices, Antigone against
Creon, family against state—could reflect the axial, the
symmetrical, structure of the brain and of the body. Kerényi's
reading of the play shows what close affinities there are
between Jungian and Lévi-Straussian approaches. Antigone
and Creon signify 'the two sides of total world-reality'
(*Weltwirklichkeit*).[1] They are composed respectively of the two
'hemispheres of being and non-being'. It is Antigone's function, rare under normal conditions of Greek reticence and
oblique representation, to articulate, to evoke unreservedly,
the world of the dead. This evocation brings her near to the

[1] K. Kerényi, *Dionysus und das Tragische in der Antigone* (Frankfurt-on-Main, 1935), 9.

Dionysian, with its ecstatic bent to self-destruction. Hence, argues Kerényi, the presence of Dionysus throughout the later and fatal movements of Sophocles' play. Creon embodies a mode of mortality which cannot come to terms with death, which seeks to bar from the secular city the sacred energies of the chthonic, of the underworld. But these, as line 1284 instructs us, are threatening to engulf the πόλις. Only Antigone's sacrificial death, only her union with Dionysus, can restore the mystery of symmetry in mortal being. 'Thus *Antigone* continues to be, in aesthetics, the touchstone for every theory of tragedy.'[1]

These are almost hermetic speculations. What is clear and arresting is the fact. We have added very few indeed to the seminal presences given us by Hellas. Our labours are those of Heracles. Our rebellions look to Prometheus (Marx wore his image as talisman). The Minotaur inhabits our labyrinths and our flyers plummet from the sky like Icarus. Even before Joyce—*heureux qui comme Ulysse*—our peregrinations and home-comings were Odysseus'. The incensed hurt of women continues to find voice via Medea. The Trojan women speak our lament over war. The drug culture and the flower-child looked to the Bacchae. Oedipus, Narcissus are enlisted to dignify, in fact to define, our complexes. Mirror looks to mirror, echo calls to echo—and these, also, are similes out of Greek myths.

The staple rejoinder is that the western imagination after Christ has also generated archetypal personae and plots which possess the self-replicating drive of antique mythology. Four are cited: Faust, Hamlet, Don Juan, Don Quixote. They are, to be sure, very different in origin and after-life. Hamlet and Don Quixote appear to represent specific acts of authorship, of particular contrivance. Their sources of being, most evidently with regard to Cervantes's novel, are local and historical. Both have crystallized and, in turn, perpetuated certain stances, 'typologies', self-recognitions, mimetic styles, in western sentiment and behaviour. 'Hamlets', 'Don Quixotes' are familiar encodings of idiom and gesture throughout western society since the seventeenth century. And both have, of course, led multiple lives in art, music, drama, ballet, and film. But two questions need to be asked about Hamlet. To what extent is he, as Freud and Gilbert Murray noted, a variant on Orestes?

[1] Ibid. 17.

To what extent does the imaginative power which the motifs of fratricide, usurpation, incest, and filial vengeance in Shakespeare's play exercise upon us derive from the statement of these motifs already made in Aeschylus', Sophocles', and Euripides' dramatizations of the House of Atreus? The second question is this: what significant 'Hamlets' after *Hamlet*? There are fitful brilliancies of recall in Musset's *Lorenzaccio*. Laforgue's *Hamlet* is an intriguing fragment, tangential to its source. Hamlet, as a persona, as a complex of attitudes, is vividly present in Russian poetry from Pushkin to Pasternak. But there is little here to match the legacy of *imitatio* and variant, of recapitulation and pastiche, which follows on Agamemnon, on Helen of Sparta, on Laius and his breed. As to Cervantes: Smollett's variant, *The Adventures of Sir Launcelot Greaves*, remains both a rare example and a curiosity. Borges's ingenious parable on 'Pierre Menard' makes the point: there is only one way to re-create Don Quixote adequately, to achieve a 'truly modern' version—this is, says Borges, to recopy Cervantes's text word for word.

The dynamics of myth in the matter of Faust and of Don Juan are closer to 'the primary' and more suggestive of the Greek example. It may well be that the figure of Juan Tenorio embodies the *only* case we can document of the invention of an 'archetypal fiction' by an individual author. Uncertainties persist as to the initiative taken by the pseudonymous 'Tirso de Molina'. But once his *Burlador de Sevilla* had been launched, its protagonist and the motif of the avenging statue took on the energies and metamorphic ease of the anonymous. Imitations, reprises, parodies are myriad. Via Molière, Da Ponte–Mozart, Byron, Pushkin, Shaw, the legend has known the manifold, disseminated lives which we associate with classical myths. And it may be, as Kierkegaard suggests, that the theme of absolute erotic desire, quintessentially expressive in music, is modern in a radical psychological and social sense. In which case it would constitute the only major addendum western sensibility has made to the fundamental mapping of impulse in Greek art and thought. The self-reproductive vitality of the Faust motif, as it emerges in Germany during the 1580s, seems to rival that of the master myths of Hellas. The Faust sequence from Marlowe and Goethe to Bulgakov, Valéry, and Thomas Mann rivals the inheritance of Mycenae and of Troy. What

one would wish for, however, is a better understanding of the
ways in which the legend of Doctor Faustus is a Christian
variant on the archetype of Prometheus. In what measure and
across what modulations of uncertain remembrance is the
Faustian lunge for knowledge a variant on the Promethean
theft of fire? Where the myth enters literature, in Marlowe, in
Lessing, in Goethe, the Promethean analogue is present.
Moreover, whatever their transformational force, neither the
Don Juan nor the Faust motifs and the hybrids which have
come of them have in any way lessened the hold of the archaic
and Hellenic over western culture. And the Shakespearean
heritage offers no true parallel to the classical. There ought, by
now, to be a pride of 'Hamlets', 'Macbeths', 'Othellos', and
'Lears', related to the canon as are the numerous great versions
of 'Greek' tragedy since Rome. A play such as Edward Bond's
Lear is striking precisely because it represents so rare an
experiment. There is in Shakespeare's stature and range of
achievement just that quality of the anonymous, of the
nationally collective, which should have engendered imitation
and metamorphic reprise. It is, on the contrary, Oedipus and
Electra, Antigone and the Eumenides, who have been given
incessant voice in twentieth-century high theatre and poetry.
Again one asks: why should this be?

   Here Heidegger's analyses are the most radical and the most
in tune with the problem of the inaugural (the *instauratio magna*
in western consciousness). Heidegger's ontology is, in essence,
a theory of beginnings. He ascribes to the Greek spirit and to
the Greek language in their pre-Socratic phase a specific,
unique proximity to the 'presentness and truth of Being'.
Anaximander, Heraclitus, and Parmenides experienced, were
in some measure able to articulate, a primordial equation
between the 'being of Being'—the hidden but also radiant
principle of all existence—and the capacity of speech, of the
spoken Λόγος, to be meaningful. They apprehended, they were
possessed by, language in its original state of truthful nomination and concealment. Thus they could both 'say the world'
and perceive that which speech guarded inviolate within its
own autonomous strengths. As does the pulsing light of the
Apollonian sun, when it both reveals and masks ('blinds') the
essence of reality, so does the human word as the first Greek
thinkers and poets knew it. The Socratic–Platonic turn to

metaphysics, says Heidegger, following on Nietzsche, divorced
sensory perception from ideal and abstract authenticity. The
Aristotelian view of language was functional and pragmatic.
These philosophic developments mark the irreparable fall of
the western spirit from the numinous grace and immediacy
of the word. We have never 'spoken Being' again as did
Parmenides in his identification of oneness and existence,
as did Heraclitus when he saw the world as 'harvested,
ingathered by lightning'.

But in the great poets something of the auroral presence of
direct saying endures. It is they who can suffer and then
communicate the consuming visitation of naked Being, of truth
in its unconcealment (ἀλήθεια). The gods and their fire-speech
are still neighbours to Pindar. Being and meaning are fused
still in the second choral ode in *Antigone*. Even in its
metaphysical and instrumental modes, the Greek language
remains uniquely endowed with the afterglow of its ontological
source. It is Greek, ancient Greek—Heidegger's argument is
radically anti-Hebraic—which has determined the essential
destiny of western man. It is, states Heidegger flatly, from the
successive 'experiencings' and interpretations by philosophers,
poets, translators, of the Greek verb 'to be' that this destiny
takes form. It is, to a more or less conscious degree, from Greek
grammar and from the vocabulary of Greek philosophic and
lyric expression that we continue to derive the markers of our
communal and personal identity in the West. Hence the
persistent authority of Greek motifs and of the drama, poetry,
and speculative discourse in which these are enunciated or
enacted, over our art, literature, and thought. Each recursion
to a Greek mythical theme, even in variant or antinomian
guise, represents, in Heideggerian terms, a literal homecoming: to the *Lichtung* ('the clearing') in which Being made itself
manifest. It is a return to the locale of 'the gods', of those
elemental truths and forces which inform our encounter with
the overwhelming fact that *we are*. No subsequent mythologies,
assuredly not those of Hebraic Christianity, can draw us back
to the great dawn of meaning, of consciousness, of language
itself. But without such motion of return, imperfect, obstructed
as it inevitably is—Plato, Descartes, technology, positivistic
science stand between us and the Λόγος—western man would
perish altogether. Greek myths, what stays alive in our culture

of the Greek lyric–existential idiom, are our fragile moorings to Being. Thus it is that those poets in whom Heidegger makes out the most intense, the most necessary presentness of Being and of truth, are closest to the Greek root and most 'mythological' in their themes and executive means. It is Hölderlin above all, it is Rilke, who are the 'shepherds of Being' in our desolate state.

I want to work forward from Heidegger's argument without, necessarily, adopting its Arcadian ontology and suppressed religiosity. We have no access to the origins either of speech or of that disinterested and selective mode of speech we call 'literature'. The most archaic of Chinese inscriptions, the *Gilgamesh* epic, Miriam's song of triumph in Exodus (*if* it is the oldest text in the Pentateuch), the fragments of the pre-Socratics are, on the time-scale of linguistic and formal evolution, modern. They stand far nearer to us than they do to the origins of discourse and of genre. There is an undoubted truth in the assertion that the Homeric poems represent a very late, even a 'decadent' state of the art of oral formulaic narrative. The techniques of narration, of lyric invocation, of epic encomium and gnomic instruction, as we find them in Homer and the early rhapsodes, may constitute an epilogue to the long history of the heroic imagination. Yet from the perspective of western sensibility after Rome, the Greek language and Greek literature *are* primary (as from a theological–liturgical point of view is Hebrew). We know, when we give it thought, that the speech and expressive conventions of Heraclitus, Archilochus, or Pindar are late products of processes of development and selection which we cannot trace. But to *us* they convey the authority of morning. It is by their light that we set out. It is they who first set down the similes, the metaphors, the lineaments of accord and of negation, by which we organize our inward lives. It is they who first saw the wine-dark in the sea and the green flame in the laurel. Our lion-heart and fox-cunning are theirs. To come home to the Greek world and its myths is to attempt to give to our resources of expression something of the lustre and knife-edge of beginnings. New metaphors, in particular, are hard come by. How many are there in Shakespeare?

The question of the sense of historical time in early Greek mentality is a vexed one. But whatever may have been their awareness of a far more ancient provenance, the authors of the oldest Greek lyrics and cosmological dicta gave to their utterances an unmistakable aura of innovation. A formidable instrument had been acquired and brought into willed practice. Writing had given to poetic inspiration and to abstract thought a new contract with time. The act of discourse need no longer be ephemeral or collective. The odds against oblivion had shortened immeasurably. Thus the intricately refracted life of the *Iliad* inside the *Odyssey*—the song of the minstrel about Troy in the hearing of disguised Odysseus—seems to point to the new dimensions of textual reference. Pindar's odes can invoke, with the gusto of discovery, the scandalous durability of words, the fact, carnally, ethically paradoxical and even outrageous, that the poem will live beyond the hero which it celebrates, beyond the city in which it is sung. There is in the abstruse but lapidary register of the pre-Socratic fragments the proposal, itself not without enormity, that discourse, set down, susceptible of exact transmission, can speak, can contain, the world. In short: Greek language and literature, at a level which is not merely one of a foreshortening illusion on our part, do feel and declare themselves as primal. They are, certainly in the sixth and early fifth centuries, new and revelatory to themselves. Something of this novelty and epiphany are ours each time we make contact with them via mythical substance and rhetorical form. We do not, I think, secure a comparable 'reinsurance' for the imaginative and the speculative, a comparable energy of incipience, after Dante.

If we leave to one side the Hebraic component—and this is, *pace* Heidegger, an arbitrary move—it follows that we are a ζῷον φωνῆεν ('language animal'), Greek not only by designation but in substance. By this I mean not only in respect of the repertoire of primary metaphor, but with reference to Greek grammar or to the adaptations which this grammar made of its Indo-European sources. The gamut of past and future tenses, of optatives and subjunctives, which empower remembrance and expectation, which allow hope and counter-factual supposition to create room for the spirit in the midst of the crowding imperatives of the biological—are organized along Greek lines, in which very phrase the indispensable notion of 'the organic' as that which has vital logic of form is Greek through and through. So are the syntax of deduction and of inference, of proof and of negation, which are the alphabet of rational thought. 'To live death', 'to die life', the oxymoronic yoking of infinitive and direct object in Heraclitus (fr. A 62 Diels–Kranz), is one example among many of the 'grammatology of thought' or 'thought-grammar' discovered and/or first formulated by archaic Hellas and without which our philosophy and our poetics are inconceivable. There is, in consequence, in a sense related to Heidegger's but on a more secular, pragmatic level, indeed a motion of 'homecoming to ancient Greece' in western thought and speech. To articulate experience grammatically, to relate discourse and meaning as we do, is to 'be Greek'. It is in this fundamental sense that I should want to cite Shelley's assertion: 'We are all Greeks.' Most visibly, most consciously so, in respect of philosophical, political, and poetic utterance. And it is because literary form grows out of the suggestions and demarcations of the grammatical that all our principal literary genres, the entirety of Polonius's inventory, with the exception of the full-length prose novel, have their Greek models.

But I want to go further so as to bring myth and grammar into seminal relation. Many of the ways in which the Greek language and our inheritance of this language inform, abstract, make symbolic, analogize, or metaphorize the components of our mental experience and of our presence in the natural and the social worlds seem to me inseparable from certain key myths. It is in intimate conjunction with these myths that the semantic encoding, the expressive means of our grammars of thought and of feeling, can be most vividly construed. I believe that Greek evolved the prodigality and dialectical spirit of its syntax and its conviction that language is the distinctive function of man, in generic interaction with the evolution and 'fixation', with the conscious verbal statement, of myths. There is, I am persuaded, an underlying sense in which 'initial' and determinant Greek myths *are myths in and of language*, and in which, in turn, Greek grammar and rhetoric internalize, formalize, certain mythical configurations. Thus the 'figure of speech' will, at its inception, have been the literal persona in the mythological construct. Language and myth develop reciprocally. They are correlative 'spaces' in which the nascent capacities for metaphor and reasoned imagining come into articulate being. In their linguistic and in their mythical encoding, these capacities originate from or work from a common source. They stem from those areas of ripening consciousness and of collective happening where the pressures of inquiry, of conjecture, of taboo, of sublimation are brought to bear on the initially inchoate intake of perception. 'Les mythes se pensent dans les hommes,' says Lévi-Strauss. I would want to anchor this process of 'thinking themselves' in the grammar, in the language-forms, in which it takes place. 'Myths speak themselves in men', human speech is instinct with myths. The imprint has a twofold root; but the articulate forms are fused.

I would not want to dissociate the primary set of myths which make visible, which dramatize uncertainties of kinship (the incest motif) from the evolution of the grammar of cases. Vestiges of this interaction can be made out in the very designations of the 'nominative'—consider the dramatic grammar of uncertain identity in the Oedipus theme, in Odysseus' syntactical ruse in the cave of the Cyclops—the 'genitive', the 'vocative'. The case system is no less a chronicle of opaque and territorial encounters than are the myths of the first heroes on their forays into the border countries of chaos. Relatedly, I would argue that the myths of hybrid species and human animality, considered to be among the most ancient, enact and, dialectically, help to generate what must have been the laboured development in language of stable categories of gender, of the first classifications, at the base of grammar, of inorganic and organic, of bestial and human (the ambiguities, the retardations in this process are profoundly played upon in Pavese's *Dialoghi con Leucò*).

How are we to interpret the mythological elevation of Memory above all other Muses? The answer may lie with the lexical–grammatical generation of preterites and with a concomitant insight into the role which past tenses play in the creation of art and of argument. Conversely, I would suppose that the discovery of the paradoxical capacity of language to secrete knowledge rather than to reveal it, together with the linguistic leap into unconstrained futurity—the mere fact that we can speak of, that we can in speech postulate and describe events a million years hence—had their informing counterpart in the Prometheus motif. Inextricably mixed are the arts of keeping fire going against tomorrow's night or the winter to come and the 'forward-dreaming' in the futures of the

grammatical code. There is no purer articulation of counter-
factuality, of the licence of grammar to unsay the past and to
construe alternative realities, than the conceit of Helen's
translation to Egypt during the Trojan war. 'She was never in
Troy,' says one version of the myth, meeting, imaging in this
negation the metaphysics or grammatology of absence implicit
in optatives of the verb. I read in Narcissus the long history of
the demarcation of the first person singular, together with the
solicitations and menace of solipsism, of the withering of
utterance to monologue, as these are latent in the grammar of
the ego. In the myth of Echo—and the two are related—we
can make out the archaic experiencing of the suggestive
sterility of the synonymous and the finding, perhaps vertiginous, of the tautological.

The essential point would be this: addenda to the primary
corpus of (Greek) myths, primary in that it literally underwrites the semantic means and reflexes of our cultural
condition, are as rare as substantive addenda to the structure of
our Indo-European syntax. What significant tenses, conjuga-
tions, pronominal forms, have we added to classical grammar? In what notable ways are our instruments of metaphor
and of metonymy, of analogy and of inference, different from
those available to Homer or to Plato? Genuine additions to the
basic range of cultural encodings, to the psychological and
symbolic mapping by which a civilization locates itself, are
exceedingly rare ('Don Juanism' may, conceivably, be such
an addition). The *myths in and of language* of archaic Hellas
delineated and covered much of the native ground of our
being. The principle of return to the Greek sources, the *ricorso*
which is so central an impulse in western literature and
thought, is implanted, as it were, just below the surface of our
speech-acts.

No body of myth after the Greeks has possessed a comparable inherence in the actual fabric and syntactic markers of
language. No fable after Hellas, not even that of Faust, benefits
from this order of genetic logic: this is to say from so close a
kinship with the modes of discourse in which it is narrated and
transmitted. Compared to the Greek 'myths in language', even
the most haunting and anonymous of our legends are, to
some degree, linguistically contingent and of the surface.
Shakespeare 'enters the language', a suggestive idiom, as

master and innovator. But his plots do not spring from inside it, they are not the record of how this language and its context of consciousness came into being, as are the cry of Pan, the riddle of the Sphinx to Oedipus, or Narcissus' address to the mirroring pool. It is only in music, where 'plot' and 'form' are one, that post-classical western civilization has created works of mythical necessity and universality. Wagner is sometimes 'Aeschylean' as no other artist in the personalized, reflective tradition of invention after the Renaissance is. This is why 'literature' as we know and practise it does not compel replication, does not engender a lineage of thematic reprise and variation as did Homer, Pindar, or the Attic tragedians.

Whenever, wherever, in the western legacy, we have found ourselves engaged in the confrontation of justice and of law, of the aura of the dead and the claims of the living, whenever, wherever, the hungry dreams of the young have collided with the 'realism' of the ageing, we have found ourselves turning to words, images, sinews of argument, synecdoches, tropes, metaphors, out of the grammar of Antigone and of Creon. Indwelling in our semantics, in the fundamental grammar of our perceptions and enunciations, the Antigone-and-Creon syntax and the myth in which they are manifest are 'specific universals' transformative across the ages.

It is, I believe, this actual incision of the mythical situation in the semantic base which explains the economy of dominant motifs in western art and literature. It is this incision which makes intelligible the mechanism of 'eternal return' to the Greek roots. 'Those who speak truth', says Paul Celan, 'speak shadows.'

2

To Robert Garnier, magistrate, such shadows had a brutal immediacy. He travelled France, witnessing dynastic and religious civil wars whose horrors were long remembered. Unburied bodies, fratricidal encounters, the extirpation of ancient families, were no literary–academic trope in late-sixteenth-century France, but a matter of everyday experience. Garnier's lyric dramas are obsessed by the sense and

spectacle of a society in dissolution.[1] The Antigone theme lay
to hand. It had been popular throughout the Renaissance.
The Sophoclean version was available in Italian, in Luigi
Alamanni's translation, as early as 1533. Three Latin renditions followed between 1541 and 1557. Garnier is obviously
familiar with the adaptation of Sophocles in French made by
the poet Jean-Antoine de Baïf in 1573. Renaissance poets,
grammarians, and mythographers regarded Sophocles'
Antigone as inseparable from the two other plays in the 'trilogy',
Oedipus Rex and *Oedipus at Colonus*. Aeschylus' *Seven Against
Thebes* and Euripides' *Phoenician Women* were considered out-
riders to this central bloc. This view was given authority by
Seneca's conflation of these several sources in his own *Phoenissae*
—one of the most imitated texts in the history of western
drama. Garnier's *Antigone* of 1580 draws liberally on this whole
cluster.

The historicism of Garnier and his contemporaries is
synchronic. A constancy of human suffering and of the
malpractices from which this suffering inevitably springs
foreshortens history. The desolate Argos lamented by Jocasta is
France. The formal topics of her grief—menacing pikes in
place of ripening grain, the shepherd's Arcadian hut used as a
guard-room by brawling mercenaries—are concrete universals.
The House of Laius intimately parallels that of the Valois or
of the Guises. No artifice of transfer is required as between the
antique and the contemporary. Humanist tragedy, whether
classical or biblical, is a sustained analogy, unifying time
through an invariance of *exemplum* and moral meaning. For
Garnier, this meaning is naturally Christian. The paganism of
the Sophoclean or Senecan sources is to sixteenth-century
humanists (the elusive, guarded exception being Montaigne)
an ornamental accident.

The subtitle to Garnier's tragedy reads *ou la piété*. The word
is arch-Virgilian. It is emblematic of that in Virgil's *Eclogues*
and *Aeneid* which was seen as manifesting the mysterious yet
necessary deployment of Christian values, the successive
dawnings before Christ, in ancient art and civilization.
In *pietas* there is both worship and compassion. Sixteenth-
century thought and eloquence touch often on the

[1] Cf. G. Jondorf, *Robert Garnier and the Themes of Political Tragedy in the Sixteenth
Century* (Cambridge University Press, 1969).

near-interchangeability of *piété* and *pitié*, of piety and pity. Both
are embodied, quintessentially, in the person of the *mater dolorosa*
as she prepares for entombment the tortured flesh of the Son.
Renaissance sensibility experienced the analogies with
Antigone as unforced. The Sophoclean motifs of virginity, of
nocturnal burial, of sacrificial love, the Sophoclean sense of
action as compassion, of heroism as freely shared agony, all
these are exact annunciations or prefigurations of Christian
truths.

Against Créon's *loy*, Garnier's Antigone sets *l'ordonnance de
Dieu, qui est nostre grand Roy*. Her phrasing fuses a dual
authority: God's ordinance and that of legitimate kingship.
'God' here is in the Judaeo-Christian singular (as, in fact, he
can be said to be at certain points in Sophocles' grammar).
His commandments can be made law only by his anointed.
To Garnier's heroine, Créon represents the fundamentally
anarchic, because arbitrary, because dynastically suspect,
impositions of military–despotic rule characteristic of civil war.
Yet her justification is also secular or, more exactly, 'humanistic' in a very precise sense inherited from Cicero via St
Augustine. Good conduct must be in accord with *l'humaine
piété*. Créon's edict commands *toute inhumanité*. I do not know of
any much earlier use of this term in its threatening immensity.
In Antigone's mouth its propriety is very nearly that of a play
on words. We hear in *inhumanité*, as Garnier will have heard,
the verb 'to bury': *inhumer*. Deeper still, and radical to both,
lies the necessary kinship of the 'humane' and of the 'earthly',
of *humanitas* and *humus*. To deny earth to the dead is to negate
their humanity and one's own. Antigone invokes a 'natural
humanity': *Je n'ay rien entrepris que d'amour naturelle*. This
imperative, implicit in antique piety, is made categorical by
the Judaeo-Christian God and the analogue of Golgotha. Thus
Polynice's burial and Antigone's living descent into the tomb
are part of a destined motion of meaning which leads to
universality through Christ's entombment and resurrection.
The instrumentality of this motion is woman. The child comes
to being in the dark and enclosed centre of her body. It is she
who bears the Son of Man to his grave. The frequent echoes of
ventre and *antre* in Garnier's *Antigone* precisely parallel those
between 'womb' and 'tomb' in English baroque poetry and
sermons.

Garnier saw corpses exposed by the score, perhaps by the hundreds. Military historians put at anywhere between a quarter and a third of a million the number of men left unburied between the trenches during the battle of Verdun. This unimaginable condition underlies Créon's taunt in Anouilh's *Antigone* (1944). In no man's land the unburied bodies are soon pounded to an indiscriminate *bouillie* ('mash'). There can be no way of distinguishing between Étéocle and Polynice, between the would-be traitor or deserter and the Unknown Soldier honoured by the eternal flame. Virginia Woolf's vision of the scene is the most hallucinatory, the most knowing in its macabre sexuality. It occurs in a dream sequence in *The Years* (1937), an episodic family chronicle threaded by the reading, by the translation into English verse of, by recurrent allusions to, Sophocles' play: 'The unburied body of a murdered man lay like a fallen tree-trunk, like a statue, with one foot stark in the air. Vultures gathered. . . . Quick, quick, quick with repeated jerks they struck the mouldy flesh.'[1]

For Romain Rolland, as for Sophocles' Teiresias, but on a far vaster scale, the nakedness of the dead between the barbed wires meant an outrage not only against humanity, but against the cosmic order. More specifically, it signified the collapse of masculine ideals and masculine domination in a world gone mad. Only women could now rescue mankind from man. This is the burden of Rolland's 1916 appeal *A l'Antigone éternelle*. The mothers, sisters, wives, daughters of the slain must stop the massacre and bring due burial to the charnel-house. Between the lines of Romain Rolland's pamphlet flickers the fantastic possibility that women would invade the professional sanctum of the battlefields, that they would simply swarm between the barrages and the bayonets to bury their fathers, their husbands, their sons and brothers. So far as we know, no women's movement, however pacifist, however radical, ever contemplated this healing folly. But the Antigone gesture is magnetic: 'Soyez la paix vivante au milieu de la guerre, — Antigone éternelle, qui se refuse à la haine et qui, lorsqu'ils

---

[1] Virginia Woolf's involvement with the Antigone theme is recurrent. It begins with *The Voyage Out* in 1915. It is taken up in 'On Not Knowing Greek', *The Common Reader*, 1st series (1925), and given a feminist–political twist in *Three Guineas* (1938). Cf. G. Joseph, 'The *Antigone* as Cultural Touchstone: Matthew Arnold, Hegel, George Eliot, Virginia Woolf, and Margaret Drabble', *PMLA* xcvi. 1 (1981).

souffrent, ne sait plus distinguer entre ses frères ennemis' ('Be living peace in the midst of war—everlasting Antigone, who does not yield herself to hatred, who, when they suffer, no longer knows how to distinguish between her rival brothers').

For all their murderousness, Napoleonic battles, when commemorated in art or lyric verse, tended to be stylized neo-classically. Garnier looks to antiquity in order to accentuate, to validate the universal status of contemporary happenings. Pierre-Simon Ballanche, the Utopian–socialist illuminate, invokes the classical background in order to achieve distance. His *Antigone*, a prose epic in six books, Ossianic and ceremoniously cadenced in the manner of Chateaubriand, appeared in 1814. Europe lay at war. But the fatal ground before Thebes is, in Ballanche's narrative, a star-lit pastoral where the dead slumber in moon-blanched repose. Polynice seems to salute his sister with a gesture of tranquil pathos. It is only from the far-off woods that we hear the mournful roar of wild beasts woken by the scent of carrion. Garnier knew just what it meant for human bodies 'to be pasture to wolves'. Ballanche's *bêtes féroces* are incised at the edge of a cameo. This, too, is where we shall find them in Romantic and Victorian paintings of Antigone's deed of mercy. It is with a funerary urn on her shoulder—a traditional *figura* of classic sorrow—that Antigone crosses the darkened stage in the Potsdam–Mendelssohn production. Gérard de Nerval saw this presentation at the Odéon in May 1844. Its marmoreal grace drew from him a touch of prophetic irony: 'But our religion, as well, prohibits burial rites for the bodies of the self-slain.'

Modern warfare abolishes the difference between the πόλις and the plain. Already in Marguerite Yourcenar's modish vignette 'Antigone' (in *Feux*, 1936), the streets of Thebes are shaken by the passage of tanks. Within the walls, Créon's war against his subjects is, ideologically, and through its uses of police terror, even more savage than is the struggle at the seven gates. Creon's household cavalry tramples the hungry Theban crowd in Walter Hasenclever's *Antigone* of 1917. Yet even this episode, inspired by world war and the *misère* of German cities on the eve of revolution, falls far short of the urban hell of the 1940s. Deserters, adolescents half out of their senses with fear, soldiers separated from broken units, were strung up on Berlin lampposts. Any attempt to cut down their fly-blown bodies was punishable by instant execution. This is the lurid starting-point of Brecht's *Antigone*, a variant on Sophocles and on Hölderlin's Sophocles, first performed in 1948. A body swings before the door. One of the two sisters is clutching a knife. The Gestapo man makes his entry.

Between 1939 and 1945, the cadavers of 269 women executed in Gestapo cellars for crimes against the state were handed over for dissection to the anatomy departments of Berlin's teaching hospitals. Implicated in the 1944 plot against Hitler, Anne's brother has been hanged and consigned to dissection. But just after the air raid his remains have been removed, carted through fire and ruin, and given loving burial. Now Anne is to be beheaded and her own body is to take the useful place of her brother's. How can the judge even dare hint to the Führer that the intolerable young woman is secretly affianced to his son, that the latter is threatening mutiny if the sentence is carried out? Rolf Hochhuth's novella, *Die Berliner Antigone* (1958), perhaps the finest achievement in his uneven work, enlists the Sophoclean model with unsparing economy. As for Garnier, so for Hochhuth time has stood still in the seasons of the inhuman. Anne had vomited at the sight of her brother in the anatomy theatre. Now she avoids looking at his tortured features. But the 'dark acre' is an 'island of peace' in the surrounding sea of flames. The moss is cool, there is a world of peace in the unkempt forsythia. This Antigone not only inters Polyneices at the cost of her own life: she literally substitutes her body for his. This is Hochhuth's intensification of the established motif of joint burial.

But poignant as they are, and hauntingly apposite to their own temporal–political circumstance (the only known performances of Garnier's *Antigone* took place in Paris in 1944 and 1945), these several treatments of Antigone's encounter with the desecrated remains of her brother and of her entombment of Polyneices do not add essentially to Sophocles. The dumb show at the outset of Athol Fugard's *The Island*, first staged in 1973, does. It is a harrowing addendum to the Sophoclean font.

We are on Robbens Island, the special inferno in the South African police state:

The long drawn-out wail of a siren. Stage-lights come up to reveal a

moat of harsh white light around the cell. In it the two prisoners—
John stage right and Winston stage left—mime the digging of sand.
They wear the prison uniform of khaki shirt and short trousers.
Their heads are shaven. It is an image of back-breaking and
grotesquely futile labour. Each in turn fills a wheelbarrow and then
with great effort pushes it to where the other man is digging, and
empties it. As a result, the piles of sand never diminish. Their labour
is interminable. The only sounds are their grunts as they dig, the
squeal of the wheelbarrows as they circle the cell, and the hum of
Hodoshe, the green carrion fly.

John and Winston are preparing to present *Antigone* for the
Christmas entertainment of the prison staff and honoured
white guests. I will come back to their subversive, dialectical
readings of Sophocles. What matters here is the torturing
parody of burial enacted in the punishment drill of the two
convicts. The back-breaking weight trundled to the ditch, the
hopeless attempts to fill the sand-pit, the Furies' song of the
carrion fly, these are desperate mockeries of Antigone and her
high task. 'The piles of sand never diminish.' The living toil to
bury the unnumbered dead, only to be caught up themselves in
the never-ending spiral of violence and injustice. 'I told you,
man, Antigone buried Polyneices. The traitor! The one who I
said was on *our* side. Right?' Now she too, 'A bastard of a lady
that one, but a beautiful bitch', is dragged to burial. But the
wolves will dig and the sands blow away. Beyond the blank
desolation of the close of Sophocles' play, there now stretches
pure waste. Emptiness is not a Sophoclean or, indeed, a fifth-
century Attic perception. Fugard's is the satyr play to all
preceding 'Antigones'.

3

We saw that Kierkegaard annuls Ismene. She is often absent:
in Euripides, in Seneca, in that greatest reader of Euripides
and Seneca, Racine, who omits her from *La Thébaïde* (1664).
She does not figure in Alfieri's *Antigone* of 1782, nor in the ballet
Antigone, composed by Theodorakis and choreographed by
John Cranko for Covent Garden in 1959. Iconography and
staging have not been kind to Ismene. She is the blonde, hollow
one. But already the scholiasts and early rhetoricians noted
a striking fact. In Sophocles' extant dramas, the Antigone—

Ismene pairing has its precise counterpart in Electra–
Chrysothemis. Sophocles resorts twice to the same asymmetry
of sisterhood and conflict.[1] Reflecting on George Eliot's *Adam
Bede*, Freud suggests that the contrastive intimacy between the
small dark and the taller fair-haired young women in the
household stands for a primal symbolic dissociation between
fundamental tenets in the feminine psyche or, rather, in this
psyche as imagined and represented by men. Chrysothemis, of
course, means the 'lit' or 'golden' one. She does not contest the
terrible legitimacy of Electra's purpose. She simply seeks to
weigh the cost of murder. She senses the barren automatism of
violence which will come of Electra's vengeance. Electra, in
turn, flings at her the word οἶκος: 'Go back into the house,' she
says. Domesticity is to be the contemptible sphere of pale
Chrysothemis. Electra will dance her dance of death in the
public courtyard of the house of Atreus. Yet if there is
'blondeness' and, perhaps, 'pallor' in her sister's name, there is
also θέμις, signifying 'Justice'.

In the pseudo-Aeschylean epilogue to the *Seven Against
Thebes*, Antigone and Ismene intone a formal lament over the
bodies of their slain brothers. The ritual phrases echo each
other precisely. Conceivably, one might read a nuance of self-
pity into Ismene's threnody, a hint of weakness absent from
Antigone's strident outcries. But no real difference emerges.
The Herald enters and proclaims Creon's edict. At once,
Antigone voices defiance: she will carry Polyneices to his
forbidden tomb. Ismene joins Antigone. She has said nothing.
This silence may be due, quite simply, to Aeschylean stage
practice. Or it may dramatize, with subtle economy, the

---

[1] Thematic and formal analogies between the two 'cautious sisters' are present in
Yannos Ritsos's dramatic monologue 'Ismene'. In Ritsos's version, an ageing Ismene
recalls Antigone in terms which come close to the 'Anouilh-prototype :

> She never wore a piece of jewellery; she even stuck away
> her engagement ring in a chest, carrying about
> her dark arrogance among our young friends,
> brandishing her surly look over our laughter
> like a bare sword of futility.
>   And if, sometimes,
> she made an effort to help at table, to bring a dish, a jug of water,
> you would think she carried on her palms a bare skull
> and set it among the amphorae. Nobody got drunk after that. . . .

First published in 1972, Ritsos's 'Ismene' has been translated into English by Rae
Dalven (in *The Fourth Dimension* [Boston, 1977]).

difference in the stance of the two sisters as it had been set out by Sophocles.

Most medieval, baroque, and Renaissance allusions to and treatments of the Antigone material derive from Statius' first-century epic, the *Thebaid*. In it, oddly, it is Antigone who begins by being *flebilior*, 'the more tearful', and Ismene who is characterized as *rudis*, 'plain, direct of speech' (VII. 535–6). Only when her husband, Atys, is borne from the field mortally hurt, and dies in her arms, does Ismene yield to wild, connubial sorrow. However, as Creon turns tyrannically upon aged Oedipus and his harrowed brood, Statius' Ismene fades. It is now Antigone whose temper becomes that of a *virgo lea*, 'a virgin lioness'. And she finds an ally in Argia, Polyneices' widow, who has come from Argos, through night and peril, to reclaim her husband's corpse. In Rotrou's *La Thébaïde* (first performed in 1638), in Racine's version, in Alfieri's, it is the figure of Argia which replaces that of Ismene. The same is true of numerous baroque operatic treatments. Antigone–Argia duets, united in pathos, replace the tense dialectic of the two sisters. It is not until the modern period and the eclipse of Statius that playwrights and commentators restore to Ismene her Sophoclean presence.

In Hasenclever's *Antigone*, Ismene's appeal to her sister carries an undeniable moral weight:

> Durch neues Unrecht stürzt das alte nicht;
> Du rührst den ewigen Jammer sinnlos auf . . .
> Sei Mensch mit allen Menschen!

> (Old injustice is not brought low by new;
> Senselessly, you stir to life eternal sorrow . . .
> Be human among humans!)

She strikes at the bitter core of Antigone's motives: 'You hate Creon, daughter of Oedipus!' This, to one who proclaims that she knows nothing of hatred, that she is made solely for love. Later, it is Ismene who interprets for the citizens of Thebes the sacrificial, insurrectionary logic of Antigone's death: 'Thebans! Antigone is dead. | Come to her grave. She died for you!'

'Dialogues of the deaf', *dialogues des sourds*, between the possessed and the 'reasoners', are familiar to the French stage.

Certain thrusts and parries in the exchanges between Anouilh's Antigone and Ismène recall, inevitably, the exasperations of Molière's Alceste, the Misanthrope, and his Philinte. But there is also a cunning hint at Hedda Gabler's treatment of little Thea Elvsted: like fierce Hedda, Antigone, when they were children, bullied Ismène and cut off her beauteous hair. Anouilh's Ismène is, distinctly, the older sister. In a crazed family, she has made sanity her business.[1] Hence she 'has some understanding' for Uncle Créon's position: 'je comprends un peu notre oncle' (in which the thoughtful *un peu* is a master touch). Ismène's vocabulary is precisely that of 'reflection', of 'ponderation', of 'understanding'. Antigone contemns these words. Yet Ismène's last exit is ambiguous, as is every feature of Anouilh's device. Spurned by Antigone, Ismène assures Créon that tomorrow it is *she* who will steal from the city to bury Polynice. It is the name of doomed Antigone which she cries twice as she leaves the stage.

In 1944, the year of Anouilh's *Antigone*, Maurice Druon, then a very young writer, published his *Mégarée*. So far as I am aware, this is the only work in the great range of Antigone variants which turns on the character and fate of Creon's son, Megareus. He is known to Aeschylus, and Sophocles refers to him once, crucially (line 1303). At the climax of the assault on Thebes, Creon, under compulsion of Teiresias' prophetic bidding, sacrifices Megareus to the gods and thus obtains salvation for Thebes. In Euripides' and Statius' versions, it is Menoeceus, another of Creon's sons, who is sacrificed or who commits voluntary, ritual self-immolation by plunging from the beleaguered walls. Megareus and Menoeceus overlap obscurely in the Theban cycle.

In Druon's play, Mégarée is Ismène's lover. He knows that Thebes has been betrayed from within, that Créon is secretly treating with the enemy so as to ensure his own succession. He knows that Tirésias is a political trickster. A clairvoyant, existentialist nausea drives him to his suicidal gesture. Even

[1] In *The Madness of Antigone* (Heidelberg, 1976) Gerald F. Else argues that the true subject of Sophocles' play is literal folly, the madness which has come, literally, of pollution and incest. Ismene must disappear from the latter half of Sophocles' drama because hers is the only 'normal mind' (p. 29), the only mind not possessed by ἄτη. In a more traditional reading, André Bonnard notes that Ismene's successive interventions sharply bring to light the 'identical obsessiveness' in the characters of Antigone and Creon (*La Tragédie et l'homme* [Neuchâtel, 1951], 49).

Ismène's love and frank vitality seem to him irremediably
sullied by civic corruption and the blind egotism of a dying
society (Druon wrote much of the play in 1942). Mégarée tells
Ismène to visit the battlefield at evening so that she too may
learn that human flesh is mere carrion when men die without
the buttress 'of an enterprise, of a struggle, of an act of will'.
Learning of Mégarée's death, Tirésias says, memorably, that
'he has gained victory at the eighth gate, that through which
the gods enter into the city'.

Throughout the literature, Antigones bid Ismenes stay alive,
lest the clan of Oedipus be totally eradicated. Mythographers
waver as to Ismene's end. Archaic rumour was that she had
been murdered by one of the seven Argive champions during
the onslaught on Thebes. Another tradition tells of how
Antigone and Ismene took refuge in a temple which is then put
to the torch by Eteocles' vengeful son, Laodamas. A small
stream, a hillock, a hamlet near Thebes, at various times bore
the name of Ismene. We know of a river-nymph Ismene, and of
rites for Ismenian Apollo. In Sophocles' *Antigone*, Ismene alone
survives—a licence of mercy inadmissible to Kierkegaard. The
motif of an aged Ismene, at peace with her monstrous
begetting, perhaps reminiscing on the House of Laius as she
knew it, is seductive. But only Yannos Ritsos has, until now,
attempted it.[1]

'We are only women,' says Ismene to Antigone in extenua-
tion of her terrors, of her conviction that Antigone's resolve is
a mad impropriety. Unavoidably, the debate between the two
sisters focuses on the question of the role of women in the city,
of women in politics. Chrysothemis' objections to Electra's
plans are of a more contingent, private order: 'If I had
strength . . .' In poignant allusion to the fate of Antigone,
Chrysothemis sees Electra immured in everlasting darkness,
underground (line 382). But she does not, even for a moment,
deny Electra's conception of justice and the moral compulsion
by which she is driven. Ismene's doubts are generic. And the
western tradition of social sensibility, of political usage, has
found them difficult to refute.

Garnier sets the tone:

> Considérez, ma Sœur, notre sexe imbécile,
> Aux périlleux dessins de ce monde inhabile . . .

[1] See above, p. 145, n. 1.

Ismène's use of *imbécile* is one which is still current in Pascal:
'unsuited by nature to the world's business.' The second line
concisely paraphrases her meaning. Women are 'imbeciles' in
matters of state. Shakespeare lavishes courage, wit, tenacity,
mental virtuosity on his young heroines. Androgynous in their
disguises, his Rosalinds, Portias, Violas, Helenas traverse the
masculine order like shooting stars. But only once do
Shakespeare's liberalities of imagining extend to women's
claims on the political:

> I grant I am a woman, but, withal,
> A woman that Lord Brutus took to wife;
> I grant I am a woman, but, withal,
> A woman well-reputed, Cato's daughter.
> Think you I am no stronger than my sex,
> Being so father'd and so husbanded?
> Tell me your councils, I will not disclose 'em.
> I have made strong proof of my constancy,
> Giving myself a voluntary wound
> Here, in the thigh: can I bear that with patience
> And not my husband's secrets?
>
> (*Julius Caesar*, II. i. 292–302)

The politics of Lady Macbeth are 'stronger than my sex' to the
precise degree of 'unsexed' monstrousness. The supernatural,
this time positive, is apparently the only permissible medium
for the political woman: it alone enables Saint Joan to take
heroic action and to challenge her judges in terms which echo
Antigone's. Especially so in Shaw's great trial scene: Joan will
obey canon law only if such law accords perfectly with the
commandments of her inner light. What her Voices have
imparted, she will defend, she will act upon 'alone and against
all'. There is more than a hint of Creon in the avuncular,
exasperated Cauchon.

It is only very slowly that history falls into step with
Antigone. Certain women—Mme Roland, Charlotte
Corday—performed heroically and sacrificially during the
French Revolution. They referred themselves to Plutarch
('Cato's daughter') rather than to the anarchic solitude of
revolt in Antigone. Populist legend and hostile propaganda
both accentuate the role of women during the Commune, of
women who fought on the barricades and who sought to shield

the bodies of their husbands and sons from the fury of the victors. Memories of 'red viragos', of *les Pétroleuses*, will haunt those French publicists and conservative thinkers who are, to this day, Creon's advocates. In the late 1870s and early 1880s, women play a dramatic part in Russian nihilist circles, in the terrorist attacks on the regime carried out by *Zemlya i Volya* ('Land and Liberty'). I suspect that Vera Zasulich's trial elicited occasional parallels with and allusions to Antigone. But it is only very recently, with 'women's liberation', that Ismene's prudential stand, that the 'Ismene bias' in western treatments of the Antigone myth, are being refuted.

It was in Germany, in 1967, that the Living Theatre (out of New York) first staged its 'anarcho-pacifist' adaptation of the Sophocles–Hölderlin–Brecht *Antigone*. Between them, a blonde, sensuous Ismene and an ascetic, dark Antigone divide the whole gamut of available politics: acceptance or negation. Judith Malina's Antigone is the embodiment of millennially outraged, patronized, excluded womanhood. No man could undertake her mission or match her lucid despair. Masculine blindness and barbarity have brought humanity to the verge of self-destruction. It is time for women to act, to force anarchic, intemperate life on the conventions of death as these are enacted in wars, in capitalism, in male-dominated 'reality-principles'. The wild Bacchic round which accompanies and, therefore, masks Antigone's execution in the Living Theatre staging, is a symbol of the false coupling of men and women in a traditional social order. Only women's authentic liberation, only the utter refusal of Ismene's *notre sexe imbécile*, will break the infernal circle.

George Tzavellas's film version of Sophocles' *Antigone* (1961) is full of epic sound and fury, but Irene Papas's interpretation of the figure remains traditional. In Cavanni's *I Cannibali*, nine years later, the women's movement is aggressively manifest. Antigone, daughter of a Greek- or Latin-American-style 'colonel', who tyrannizes the city, seeks to lead a popular insurrection. At her side is the mysterious, almost sexless hippy who stands for Teiresias. But Antigone is fatally in advance of her times. The 'Milanese', i.e. the citizens of the modern metropolis, prefer safe despotism. Men prove unworthy of the women who would lead them to freedom.

By far the subtlest collage of the antique and the contemporary, of Antigone–Ismene and the 'woman question', is achieved in Heinrich Böll's script for *Der Herbst in Deutschland* (1979). The question is this: can Sophocles' *Antigone* be screened on television just when the 'Red Fraction' and the Baader–Meinhof gang have almost brought the country to its knees, at a time when acts of brutal terror are being carried out in the name of absolute justice? Imprisoned, almost literally buried alive in isolation cells, Ulrike Meinhof (Antigone?) finds means of committing suicide. Andreas Baader (Haemon?) does so a year later. The state refuses to return their bodies to their families. Is Creon not justified in defending the survival of society against merciless killers? What *really* came to pass in Antigone's death cell? In Böll's parable, as in several of his novels, women's voices are key. The Antigones are now on the march. Is there a place left for the classical femininity of Ismene, for her avoidance of death?[1]

4

In a well-known article, Kurt von Fritz argues vigorously that no private, erotic element enters into Haemon's plea for Antigone.[2] Any such element would gravely trivialize and compromise the moral–political thrust of Haemon's debate with Creon. It is in the course of this high polemic that Haemon 'loses his father'. Having failed to cut down the tyrant at the mouth of the tomb, Haemon has nothing left but suicide. It is precisely Haemon's disinterestedness, his freedom from personal passion, which make of him one of 'the comeliest

---

[1] Cf. G. Lukács, 'Antigoné mellett—Ismené ellen', *Híd*, i (1968). Lukács's repudiation of Ismene can be usefully compared with the outright advocacy in W. Jäkel, 'Die Exposition in der Antigone des Sophokles', *Gymnasium*, lxviii (1961). Here Ismene is seen not as a mere foil to Antigone, but as one whose moral vision is unblinded by evil. Ismene provides the norm of sane and ethical conduct against which to measure all other personages. Jäkel's assessment itself echoes the valuation of Ismene as 'heroic' in a profoundly feminine way which is argued in H. Weinstock, *Sophokles* (Wuppertal, 1948). Yet it is precisely this attribution of 'heroism' which is criticized by I. M. Linforth, *Antigone and Creon* (University of California Publications in Classical Philology, 15. 5, 1961). Ismene 'is a pitiable figure, but she cannot be called heroic. On a frantic impulse she proposes to throw away her life, but she has no higher purpose; she can do nothing to save Antigone' (p. 211). 'My sympathies have always been with . . . heroic, painfully reasonable Ismene,' writes Donald Davie in *Thomas Hardy and British Poetry* (London, 1973), 87. The debate persists.

[2] K. von Fritz, 'Haimon's Liebe zu Antigone'. First published in 1934, this article is included in the author's *Antike und moderne Tragödie* (Berlin, 1962).

figures' in Sophocles. The celebrated choral ode to Eros
(lines 781 ff.) relates to the situation of Antigone and Haemon
solely by virtue of vulgar misunderstanding. It underlines,
once again, the myopia of the Theban elders and the spiritual solitude in which the protagonists suffer their destinies.

Other readers have seen in Haemon's love for Antigone and
in the likelihood that this love is reciprocated a mainspring of
the catastrophe. 'Haemon's threat to die with this girl is the
product not only of anger but also of deep love.'[1] With
Haemon's entry, the flavour of the play changes markedly. It
comes near to being 'romantic tragedy'.[2] Cross-echoes between
the sepulchral suicides of Antigone and Haemon on the one
hand, and of Romeo and Juliet on the other, suggest themselves
compellingly. Nineteenth-century depictions and *tableaux* of
the episode illustrate the overlap.

It is uncertain whether the 'engagement' between Creon's
son and heir and the sister-child of Oedipus is Sophocles'
invention.[3] Hyginus' *Fabulae*, a second-century AD compendium which proved a constant source for western literatures and iconography, may be giving the plot of Euripides'
Antigone. Creon hands over Antigone to Haemon for punishment, such being the archaic privilege of the eldest son or of the
husband-to-be or of both: 'Ille iam Haemoni filio cuius sponsa
fuerat dedit interficiendam.' Unwilling to carry out the
sentence, Haemon turns on his father. The *Iliad* (IV. 394)
knows of a son born to Haemon. Nothing justifies the belief
that Antigone is his mother. But just such parentage constitutes
one of the main themes in Euripides' *Antigone*—a play from
which only a few fragments survive, and whose relation in time
to Sophocles' drama cannot be determined. It may be,
however, that the brevity of Haemon's role in Sophocles, and
the indeterminacy of his actions, dramatic as these are,[4] gave
to later playwrights, and to readers such as Kierkegaard, room
for invention.

---

[1] G. H. Gellie, *Sophocles: A Reading* (Melbourne University Press, 1972), 44.
[2] A. J. A. Waldock, *Sophocles the Dramatist* (Cambridge University Press, 1966), 125.
[3] Cf. the careful discussion of this 'engagement', more exactly rendered as
accordailles, in P. Roussel, 'Les Fiançailles d'Haimon et d'Antigone', *Revue des études
grecques*, XXXV (1922).
[4] Cf. the shrewd discussion of Haemon's indeterminacy in T. von Wilamowitz-
Möllendorff, *Die dramatische Technik des Sophokles* (Philologische Untersuchungen, 22,
1917), 21–3.

Excessive claims ought not to be made for Racine's *La Thébaïde*. This is a very early work, heavily indebted to Rotrou.[1] But there are premonitions of the magic to come. Exiled from Antigone's presence so as to prove the constancy of his love (*ardente amitié*), sent by Antigone to be a fighter for Polynice, Hémon is now at her feet. Antigone's concession to his ardour has a muted musicality which, like mature Racine, mocks translation:

> Je souhaitais, Hémon, qu'elle vous fît souffrir,
> Et qu'étant loin de moi quelqu'ombre d'amertume,
> Vous fît trouver les jours plus longs que de coutume . . .
>
> (I did wish, Haemon, that absence made you suffer,
> And that, being far from me, some shade of sadness
> Would make you find the days longer than of wont . . .)

Dispatched by Antigone to separate her two murderous brothers, Hémon is slain by their insensate fury. He dies in Créon's arms, joyous (*trop heureux*) in the knowledge that he does so at the behest of the beloved. His sacrifice leads to a baroque twist. Créon lays his diadem and his amorous person at Antigone's feet (some years later, Saint-Simon will reflect archly on the not altogether rare marriages, for reasons of state and of estate, between ageing uncles and virginal nieces). Again, there is in Antigone's reply, a reply which merely conceals and gains time for her mortal resolve, a note of pure Racine:

> Adieu, nous ne faisons tous deux que nous gêner,
> Je veux pleurer, Créon, et vous voulez régner.
>
> (Adieu, we do nothing but intrude upon each other,
> I wish to weep, Creon, and you to govern.)

But the affair ends in Senecan bathos. Créon threatens to pursue Antigone to Hades where, 'everlasting object of her hatred', he will still be rival to his son.

Alfieri had 'a palpable design' on the Italian language—he was resolved to give its modern literature European status—and on contemporary drama, which he strove to restore to

---

[1] Though it is inclined to be too laudatory, a thorough critical–textual treatment of the play is to be found in M. Edwards, *La Thébaïde de Racine* (Paris, 1965).

classical dignity and didactic efficacy. In their willed intelligence, Alfieri's tragic plays much resemble those of Voltaire, whom he studied faithfully. The *Antigone*, written in Turin in 1776 and first acted, by noble amateurs, in Rome, with Alfieri in the part of Creonte, in 1782,[1] all but presumes knowledge of *Polinice* (also composed in 1776). In this latter play, it is made manifest that Creonte has hounded the two brothers to fratricidal combat, thus causing the ruin of the House of Oedipus and his own elevation. Whence the strident detestation of Alfieri's Antigone for her uncle. Now, Creonte is determined to marry Emone to Antigone, thus establishing the legitimacy of his dynasty. This configuration derives directly from Voltaire's *Oreste*, and it is Voltaire's Élèctre who is the close model for Alfieri's unbending heroine.

But Alfieri is a poet, and there are genuine accents in the despairing love of Antigone and Emone. How could the shade of tortured Edipo endure knowledge of their union, how could Creonte, once he is apprised of Antigone's mutiny? The two raging presences loom over the condemned lovers. 'Misero padre, padre inuman'—these two phrases hammer across the dialogue. Love and death are poised in a way at once entirely traditional—'lascia ch'io mora, se davver tu m'ami' ('let me die, if truly you love me') could be a quote from Petrarch—and in a way which announces the intensities of Romanticism. Alfieri's Emone is no probing dialectician. He threatens Creonte with the might of his sword. He heaps scorn on 'the king, the father, the man'. At the melodramatic close, it is the sudden sight of Antigone's body which crushes him, which unnerves his rebellious purpose. He has only one vengeance left on Creonte: 'Ecco, a te rendo il sangue tuo' ('There, I give back to you your own blood').

It is not only Alfieri's idiom which recalls opera: it is the way in which the action is grouped, vocally, into aria-like monologues, duets of mounting intensity, and combative trios. From Giuseppe Maria Orlandini's *Antigona* (1718, 1727) to Rossini's incidental music to *Edipo a Colono*, almost exactly one hundred years later, the Antigone theme is an operatic 'regular'. Even a very selective catalogue would include 'Antigones' or

---

[1] Paul Sirven's multi-volume study of Alfieri is almost unreadably garrulous and jocose. But vol. iii, *Vittorio Alfieri* (Paris, 1938), contains much of the relevant material. Cf. in particular pp. 8–47.

'Creontes' by Baldassare Galuppi (1751), Giovanni Batista Casali (1752), Giuseppe Scarlatti (1756), Ferdinando Gasparo Bertoni (an *Antigona* in 1756, a *Creonte* in 1776), Michele Mortellari (1776), Niccolò Antonio Zingarelli (a setting of Marmontel's version of *Antigone* in 1790), Peter von Winter (1791), Francesco Bianchi (1796), and Francesco Basili (1799). Among these forgotten works, Tommaso Traetta's *Antigone*, first staged at St Petersburg in 1772, was widely held to be the apex of the entire *opera seria* style, and Antonio Sacchini's *Œdipe à Colone*, whose posthumous première was in 1787, held the stage of the Paris Opéra until 1844, and was revived in Naples in 1977. Only detailed study could demonstrate the extent to which baroque and neo-classical operatic treatments accentuate the Antigone–Haemon element, and how greatly the importance of Haemon benefits from the simple fact that his register is that of the 'first tenor' in the ensemble.[1] Time and again, Antigone and Haemon, whom Sophoclean tragic economy keeps strictly apart, are joined in cantilenas and duets of desolate ecstasy, false hopes, and adieu.

Much later, this blighted unison will find lyric consummation in one of the strangest texts in the whole repertoire: Houston Stewart Chamberlain's *Der Tod der Antigone*.[2] Severed from her lover, Antigone embraces a Wagnerian *Liebestod*, a death in and through Eros. Her cadence, her words almost, are Isolde's: 'Who has lived like Antigone, cannot live longer; | Who has loved like Antigone, cannot love again.' Suddenly, Haemon appears in the dark of the rock-tomb (the finale of Verdi's *Aida* is not far off). The lovers echo each other's cries of ecstatic longing, of hunger for death. Creon, like King Mark, will burst too late upon their rapturous sleep.

In Matthew Arnold's 'Fragment of an "Antigone"', Haemon speaks in unfamiliar tones. He is a despairing accuser

---

[1] We have no complete listing of seventeenth(?)- and eighteenth-century Antigone operas. The short lists given in S. Fraisse, *Le Mythe d'Antigone* (Paris, 1974), and W. Schadewaldt (ed.), *Sophokles Antigone* (Frankfurt-on-Main, 1974), are unreliable, if only because of confusions between operas on Antigone and on Antigono, a wholly different mythological personage, the subject of an exceedingly popular libretto by Metastasio. Copies of a number of the works listed above are to be found in the incomparable collection at the Fondazione Cini in Venice. A good many others appear to have been lost. The whole topic, including the striking popularity of the Antigone material just before and during the French Revolution *in opera*, deserves study.

[2] This work is included in *Drei Bühnenwerke* (Munich, 1902), with illustrations by Adolphe Appia.

not of Creon, but of Antigone! Her communion with death
appalls him (as it clearly did Arnold himself):

> No, no, old men, Creon I curse not!
>   I weep, Thebans,
>   One than Creon crueller far!
> For he, he, at least, by slaying her,
> August law doth mightily vindicate;
> But thou, too-bold, headstrong, pitiless!
> Ah me!—honourest more than thy lover,
>   O Antigone!
> A dead, ignorant, thankless corpse.

The moderns cast a colder eye. Anouilh's Hémon is average
in every fibre. Terrified of solitude, of complete adulthood, he
begs Créon to be the father still, the protector, the rescuer from
bad dreams whom he idolized as a child. Anouilh drives home
this motif of childishness. Turning on Créon in the final horror
of the burial-chamber, Hémon 'n'a jamais tant ressemblé au
petit garçon d'autrefois' ('has never been more like the little
boy of times past'). In Kemal Demirel's highly politicized
Antigone, published in Istanbul in 1973, Haimon does play a
more dynamic part. He is a liberal, championing the cobalt-
miners on the exploitation of whose slave labour Creon is
basing the wealth and power of his state, and whom Polyneices
sought to lead to revolt. Haimon is an enlightened engineer, a
man of rational decency. He urges Antigone to flee with him at
once, to escape from the trial being prepared for her by Creon.
Creon, whose attitude towards Antigone's conviction and execution is subtly vacillating, offers to abdicate. He challenges
Haimon to govern according to democratic and progressive
principles. When Haimon, driven to despair by Antigone's
death, shoots himself, the futility of his gesture is unmistakable.

But was Haemon ever the main object of Antigone's great
force of love?

We have noted that the identities of Eteocles and Polyneices
and the relations between them are, even in terms of archaic
myths, almost indecipherable. In certain mythographies, the
two figures appear to be virtually structural: they are antithetical or interchangeable counters in a seasonal, dynastic
ritual. Elsewhere, Eteocles and Polyneices take on distinct
traits, and legend apportions between them varying degrees of

responsibility for the catastrophe at Thebes. Spartan and Etrurian traditions, connected to questions of family lineage, sought to rescue Eteocles and Polyneices from incestuous parenthood. They are the sons of a marriage which Jocasta contracted with one or another monarch before or even after her union with Oedipus. In *Oedipus at Colonus* Polyneices is the older; in Euripides' *Phoenician Women*, it is Eteocles. However, and very nearly from the outset—one senses that Sophocles is himself drawing on an ancient bias—interest focuses more on Polyneices than on his royal brother. Only Aeschylus, in the *Seven Against Thebes*, assigns to Eteocles a central role.[1] As in the *Persians*, this attribution is profoundly indicative of Aeschylus' insight into guilt, of the lucid piety he brings to imagining the self-punished. In the *Phoenician Women*, perhaps deliberately, Euripides will counterbalance this Aeschylean choice, and make Polyneices much the preferred. This is so despite the fact that the names show that in the original legend Eteocles is good and Polyneices bad! But seen either as a usurper maddened by ἄτη or as a victim of Eteocles' breach of trust, represented either as a suppliant unjustly cursed by unbridled Oedipus or as an intriguer seeking to entrap his blind father in purely political designs, Polyneices looms large in the tradition. He does so not only by virtue of his part in the *Oedipus at Colonus* material, but in his own right. There are 'Polinice' operas and 'Polynice' dramas.

Though Polyneices' functions in respect of Eteocles, of Oedipus, of Creon, of his father-in-law Adrastus, of Argia his wife, and of the six other champions against Thebes are structurally and mytho-poetically manifold, it is of course his relation to Antigone which has concentrated re-creative and interpretative attention. What is this relation?

The tradition whereby Antigone is thought to prefer Polyneices to Eteocles *seems* well established by the time it is echoed in *Oedipus at Colonus* (lines 1414–16) and in the *Phoenician Women* (lines 163 ff.). Early exegetes remarked on the fact that it is Ismene who, in *Antigone*, suggests the ritual motive for Polyneices' burial. It is she who speaks of 'praying for pardon from the dead' whose spirit may have to wander

---

[1] Gabriel Legouvé's *Étéocle* is memorable for the place and date of its first performance, the Théâtre de la République in Paris in 1799. But it is in fact little more than an adaptation of the *Phoenician Women*.

unhoused. Antigone's language is that of intimate immediacy. In a verse of untranslatable moral exposure and vehemence of feeling (line 73), Antigone says that she 'will lie beside Polyneices', beside him 'the dear one'. In line 81, Antigone applies to Polyneices the epithet φιλτάτωι, 'the dearest one', 'the dearly loved'. There is an arresting passage in her death-song: alluding to Polyneices' marriage to Argia, Antigone terms this alliance as fatal to herself. In its lapidary discretion, the text can be, and presumably ought to be, read as signifying that the union with the Argive princess has brought the Seven against Thebes. Is that only the surface meaning? 'Who can lay his hand on his heart and assert with confidence that Sophocles did—or did not—wish to suggest a special relation-ship of deep affection between Antigone and Polynices?'[1] Early in the play, a crucial phonetic echo sets off resonances which will deepen throughout the action. Line 26 tells of 'the corpse (νέκυν) of Poly*neices*.[2] Antigone's subsequent invo-cations of 'a descent into death', of 'a loving reunion with the dead' (νέκυες), enclose the muffled beat of a cherished name. Péguy's 'la fraternelle et coupable Antigone' (in *Toujours de la grippe*, 1900) is concisely ambiguous. In Walter Jens's 'Sophokles und Brecht Dialog', written in conjunction with the staging of Brecht's version at Karlsruhe in 1958, 'Sophocles' confesses that he is not excessively fond of his spiky heroine, that he does not really know very much of her motives. But one thing he does know: 'If Antigone loves anyone, then it is her brother.'[3]

The incest motif is integral to Greek mythology precisely because this mythology encodes the presumably gradual, disputatious evolution of kinship conventions, terms, and taboos; precisely because, as I have suggested, the 'figures' who appear and act in the 'foundational' myths (the myths of linguistic systematization and social ordinance) are also those 'figures of speech' in and through which the root categories of gender, of mutual relation, of exogamic or endogamic status, are made visible and articulate. Greek tragedy came long after. Its uses of myth are reflexive and (notably in Euripides)

---

[1] R. P. Winnington-Ingram, *Sophocles, An Interpretation* (Cambridge University Press, 1980), 130.

[2] Cf. M. S. Santirocco, 'Justice in Sophocles' *Antigone*', *Philosophy and Literature*, iv. 2 (1980), 193.

[3] W. Jens, *Zur Antike* (Munich, 1978), 419.

critical. Nevertheless, the fertile intimations of primal chaos do continue to press on the tragic personae. Great shadows are cast backward. They enfold the Orestes–Electra relation as it is dramatized, with a fascinating diversity of perspectives and, possibly, with a certain measure of reciprocal professional awareness, by Aeschylus, Sophocles, and Euripides. Electra's crazed longing for Orestes, her collapse at the (false) news of his death, the epiphany of nascent recognition as brother and sister meet at last, are charged with erotic potentialities. To a greater or lesser degree, poets and dramatists, painters and composers, have afforded these potentialities free play. Thus an entire legacy of ambiguity is gathered into the fine-spun but overpowering sensuality of the Strauss–Hofmannsthal version. Richard Strauss's ear for the tidal advance of feelings between men and women was acute. In a letter of 22 June 1908 he instructs his librettist to provide a major 'point of repose', of ecstatic stillness, after Electra's stunned, tremulous, thrice-reiterated cry *Orest!* The poet responded:

> [*flüsternd*] Es rührt sich niemand. [*zärtlich*] O lass Deine Augen
> mich sehen. Traumbild, mir geschenktes! schöner
> als alle Träume! unbegreifliches entzückendes Gesicht, o bleib bei
>   mir
> lös nicht in Luft dich auf, vergeh mir nicht —
> es sei denn, dass ich jetzt gleich sterben muss
> und Du Dich anzeigst und mich holen kommst:
> dann sterb ich seliger als ich gelebt!

> ([*whispering*] No one stirs. [*tenderly*] O let your eyes
> look upon me. Dream-vision, bestowed on me! more beauteous
> than all dreams! inconceivable,
> enrapturing countenance, o stay with me
> do not dissolve in air, do not fade from me—
> unless it be that I must die now, at once,
> and that you have disclosed yourself and come for me:
> then I die more blissful than I lived!)

The disturbing quality of the passage, even prior to Strauss's silken setting, its inescapable hints of a *Liebestod*, grow out of 'vergeh mir nicht'. For in *vergehen* there is, simultaneously, 'evanescence' and 'violation'. Only instants before, the beggared Electra had bidden the Stranger not to 'rummage in her torn clothes with his eyes'.

No less than in the case of Electra–Chrysothemis, echoes and suggestions from the mythical, dramatic treatments of the House of Atreus carry over into *Antigone*. The Orestes theme, either distantly or by declared analogy, colours that of Antigone's love for Polyneices. The extreme inference is made by an early scholium on Statius' *Thebaid* (XI. 371): 'propter amorem Polynicis dicitur enim cum eo concubisse.' That *dicitur* is intriguing. Who had so interpreted the Theban cycle; how early had this reading been put forward? It may be that the notion of incest between brother and sister is structurally unavoidable in the figural–semantic fabric of the Oedipus tangle. In this perspective, an Antigone–Polyneices pairing, albeit alien to Sophocles' intent and presentation, would pertain to that logic and economy of recursion as we find it in so many myths.

Direct intimations of incest (such as those of the scholiast), let alone representations, are extremely rare in the 'Antigones'. But often, in encounters between Antigone and Polyneices, the idiom, the aura, of the incestuous, are active immediately beneath the surface. We have seen this to be the case throughout Hegel's experiencings of the Sophoclean text. The pressures of the hidden absolute against the rhetorical surface can be shown in a sequence drawn from French drama and philosophy.

Rotrou is worth quoting at some length. His florid but metrically unsteady style is more open to sexual intonations than will be the transparency of the neo-classics who come after him. Antigone is pleading with Polynice to desist from his military–political designs:

> ANTIGONE. Voilà donc cette sœur qui vous était si chère,
>   Éconduite aujourd'hui d'une seule prière,
>   Et quoi! cette amitié qui naquit avec nous,
>   De qui, non sans raison, Étéocle est jaloux,
>   Et par qui je vois bien que je lui suis suspecte,
>   Ne pouvant l'honorer comme je vous respecte;
>   Cette tendre amitié reçoit donc un refus!
>   Elle a perdu son droit et ne vous touche plus!
>   Au moins si de si loin vous pouviez voir mes larmes,
>   Peut-être en leur faveur mettriez-vous bas les armes:
>   Car je n'oserais pas encore vous reprocher
>   Que vous soyez plus dur et plus sourd qu'un rocher.

Encore à la nature Étéocle défère;
Il se laisse gagner aux plaintes de ma mère;
Il n'a pas dépouillé tous sentiments humains,
Et le fer est tout prêt à tomber de ses mains:
Et vous, plus inhumain et plus inaccessible,
Conservez contre moi le titre d'invincible;
Moi dont le nom tout seul vous dût avoir touché,
Dont depuis votre exil les yeux n'ont point séché;
Moi qui, sans vous mentir, trouverais trop aisée
Quelque mort qui pour vous pût m'être proposée;
Moi malheureuse, enfin, qui vous prie à genoux,
Moins pour l'amour de moi que pour l'amour de vous.
POLYNICE. Si quelque sentiment demeure après la vie,
Que je vous saurais gré de me l'avoir ravie!
Plutôt, ma chère sœur, que de me commander
Ce que ma passion ne vous peut accorder,
Venez m'ôter ce fer, oui, venez; mais sur l'heure
Plongez-le dans mon sein et faites que je meure;
Pour vous ma déférence ira jusqu'au trépas;
Mais je ne saurais vivre et ne me venger pas.

(ANTIGONE. Here, then, is that sister once so dear to you,
Brought here today by a single prayer.
What! that loving friendship which was born with us,
Of which, not without reason, Eteocles is jealous,
And for which, I perceive, I am suspect to him
(Being unable to honour him as I respect you)—
This loving friendship meets with a rebuff!
It has lost its rights, it no longer moves you!
At least, if from so far off you can see my tears,
Perhaps for their sake you will lay down your weapons:
For I would not yet dare reproach you
For being harder and more deaf than stone.
Eteocles as yet defers to nature,
He lets hĭmself be won over by my mother's laments;
He has not set aside all human feelings,
And the sword is ready to fall from his hands.
But you, more inhuman and inaccessible,
Retain towards me an invincible stance—
I, whose mere name ought to have touched you,
Whose eyes have not been dry since your exile,
I who, in very truth, would find all too much ease
In whatever death on your behalf might be suggested to me,
I, wretched, who beg you on my knees,
Less for love of myself than for love of you.

POLYNICE. If any feelings endure beyond our death,
How grateful would I be if you deprived me of life!
Rather, my dear sister, than command me do
That which my passion cannot grant,
Come, take this blade from me, come. But, at once,
Plunge it into my breast, and see to it that I die.
My obeisance to you will reach unto dying,
But I cannot live and not seek vengeance.)

Amitié, tendre amitié, respect, titre d'invincible, ravie, déférence, are terms and turns of phrase which belong to the baroque politics of eros, to that characteristic overlap between amorous and public arts of persuasion. The language and gesture of the sword-blade—ready to fall, to be seized by the beloved, to be plunged in the lover's breast—are conventionally phallic. No seventeenth-century ear would miss the intimate *galanterie* of Antigone's appeal, or fail to note the appropriateness of Étéocle's jealousy. The duplicity of levels, erotic and sisterly, which stylizes the whole discourse, is perfectly rendered by the fluid motion and dual meaning of Antigone's 'Moins pour l'amour de moi que pour l'amour de vous'—in which 'love of/for you' carries either a familial–sacrificial or an erotic weight or both.

Survivor of his far greater brother (the poet André Chénier), Marie-Joseph Chénier adorned the cultural bureaucracy of both Revolution and Empire. His imitations of Sophocles appeared posthumously, in 1820, but were certainly written a good deal earlier. In a manner characteristic of the aesthetics of the 1790s and Napoleonic period, *Œdipe-Roi, Œdipe à Colone,* and the incomplete *Élèctre* seek to combine the ideals of the radical enlightenment with those of a resurgent Christian–stoic piety. Antigone, who embodies filial compassion and the universality of love, reconciles Œdipe and Polynice. Despite this moment of grace, Polynice, on entering the sacred precincts at Colonus, is met by a fearful vision of his fratricidal future. The parallel with Orestes and Electra, when Orestes glimpses the Furies, is close. 'Open your arms to me, my sister, defend me,' cries Polynice. Antigone's arms are open to him. Like another Iphigenia, she can assuage his terrors. Antigone urges Polynice to stay at her side, to put the whole of Greece between himself and fatal Thebes. He cannot do so, but knows that 'Du moins sur mon tombeau je sentirai tes pleurs' ('At least upon my tomb I shall feel your tears'). There is no particular brio or invention here; only a confirmation of that 'special relationship of deep affection' which binds Antigone and Polyneices in the main tradition.

On 2 January 1933 Gide wrote in his journal: 'There is in the pleasantries, trivialities, and incongruities of my play something like a constant need to alert the public: you have Sophocles' play and I do not set myself up as a rival; I leave pathos to him; but here is what he, Sophocles, could not see or understand, and which nevertheless was offered by his theme; and which I do understand, not because I am more intelligent, but because I belong to another era; and I intend to make you see the reverse of the stage-set, at the risk of hurting your feelings, for it is not they which matter to me or to which I address myself. I intend, not to make you shiver or weep, but to make you think.' This quasi-Brechtian programme refers to Gide's *Œdipe*, written in 1930, and first staged two years later. The play had failed to please. Its dry humour and unsparing intellectuality were felt to be arbitrary. Where was the high immensity of the theme, as it came through even in Cocteau's sometimes parodistic pastiches?

It may be that Gide's novels, parables, plays, stem from one basic impetus: that of 'loathing of the family', as it is proclaimed in one of his best-known aphorisms. Or rather, that they stem from the impulse to 'literalize', and thus ironize, the possibilities of human commerce—incestuous, homoerotic, criminally collusive—which the taboos of family life and of societies based on the family have distorted or repressed (*refouler* is one of the few words which Gide accepts from Freud). To any such strategy, the House of Laius beckons.

André Gide's Antigone is one of those young women of cloistered radiance whom we meet also in *La Porte étroite* and the *Symphonie pastorale*. Her 'enclosedness' is literal: Antigone wishes to become a nun, to return to those who have schooled her towards God. Gide's Polynice, on the contrary, is a budding immoralist:

POLYNICE. Antigone, listen . . . Don't blush at what I shall ask you.
ANTIGONE. All right, I blush in advance, But ask, none the less.
POLYNICE. Is it forbidden to marry one's sister?

ANTIGONE. Yes, most certainly; forbidden by men and by God. Why do you ask me this?

POLYNICE. Because if I could marry you completely, I believe that I would let myself be led by you to your God.

ANTIGONE. How, doing evil, can one hope to reach good?

POLYNICE. Good, evil . . . You have nothing but those words in your mouth.

ANTIGONE. No word reaches my lips which has not, before that, been in my heart.

It is a key exchange, not only with regard to Gide's version of the Antigone–Polyneices relation, but when we remember the whole of Gide's pursuit of a morality of truth beyond conventional criteria of good and evil.

Shortly after this dialogue, Eteocles confides to Polyneices that he is seeking in 'books', this is to say in the free play of speculative thought, some licence, some 'approbation of indecency', which will allow him to sleep with Ismene. The symmetry of outrage is complete. Oedipus has overheard his sons. His objection to their desires is thoroughly Gidean: 'That which touches us too nearly is never a profitable conquest. In order to grow, one must look far away from oneself.' The ironies are grim. Oedipus conquered nearer to himself than any man. His far-sightedness will be out of blind eyes.

Rotrou's lushness and Gide's austerity are alternate constants in French rhetoric. The hermetic virtuosities of the 'semiotic', 'deconstructive' movements of the 1960s and 1970s can, I think, be seen as a recrudescence of the baroque, but of a baroque energized by the word-games and psychological sophistication of the Surrealists. The 'Gongorists', the *précieux* of the sixteenth and seventeenth centuries, would take delight in the arcane sports which Jacques Derrida has with myths and texts. They would recognize the labyrinths, mazes, mirror-galleries in which he enfolds and splinters established meanings.

I have referred already to *Glas*, and to the arabesques which Derrida weaves around what he defines and uses as the 'pre-texts' in Sophocles' *Antigone* and the 'Antigones' of Hegel. Derrida's interpretation of the fratricidal functions of Eteocles and Polyneices cites the death of Hegel's brother in Russia in 1812. 'How can two beings of the same sex cohabit in the same household?' asks Derrida, playing on a dubious equation between 'house' and 'tomb' in the word οἶκος. 'In a stand-off, two brothers can do nothing but kill each other. . . . The one must plunge, must fall on the other' (*s'abattre sur* is cunningly suggestive, having both active and passive, polemic and possibly erotic connotations).[1] Antigone must now save Polyneices' corpse from 'the probably cannibalistic violence of the unconscious desires of the survivors'.[2] But hers is not only a generalized piety, it does not only represent the transcendent femininity whereby women are custodians of men's flesh. 'Antigone est aussi le frère ennemi d'Étéocle' ('Antigone is also a brother-enemy to Eteocles', *frère ennemi* being a specific allusion to the subtitle of Racine's *La Thébaïde*).[3] Antigone's mortal closeness to Polyneices is not, as Hegel contended, a universal. It is, on the contrary, 'une singularité singulière' ('a singular singularity'). Mother and father are in Hades. Eteocles has been taken from Antigone by the state. Only Polyneices remains. Orphanage and brother–sister love turn on the same axis. Derrida's terms of reference are structuralist and psychoanalytic. Yet in spirit and rhetorical technique his dramatized discourse is baroque, and even Senecan.

Ultimately, it may be that Antigone's famous self-definition as one 'for whom love of kindred is, as to all true human beings, second nature' is most compelling in respect neither of Haemon nor of Polyneices. It is clairvoyant as to the loving fascination she exercises on western thought and sensibility. M. Derrida's profession is no less ardent (and moving) than those I have quoted from Shelley or from Hofmannsthal:

we have been fascinated by Antigone, by that incredible *rapport*, that powerful *liaison* without desire, that immense impossible desire which could not live, capable only of overthrowing, of paralysing or surpassing a system and a history, capable only of interrupting the conceptual life, of taking away the breath of the conceptual or, which comes to the same thing, of sustaining it from the outside or the inward of a crypt.[1]

[1] J. Derrida, *Glas*, p. 198.   [2] Ibid. 165.
[3] Ibid. 197.   [4] Ibid. 187.

5

Readers of Greek tragedy, students, performers, know that the chorus lies at the formal roots and centre of the art.[1] The Greek tragic chorus is a matchlessly supple instrument. Its role in the play can vary between utter involvement and indifference. The views voiced by the chorus can deploy every nuance of perception or myopia, of psychological acuity or unctuous blindness. The chorus can alter its very nature in the course of the drama (most strikingly in Aeschylus' *Eumenides*). Far beyond any turning stage or proscenium arch, the chorus is a device whereby the antique playwright can exactly calibrate and modulate the distances, the sight-lines, between audience and myth, between spectator and scene. The chorus literally reaches back into the obscure instauration of ritual–dramatic performances. It also reaches forward, first into the section of the πόλις from which it is recruited, then into the audience as a whole, which is to say the body politic. Thus it acts as a kind of drawbridge which the dramatist can raise or lower, shorten or lengthen at will by metrical and choreographic means. Via the chorus, the spectator can be drawn on to the stage or distanced from it; he can be virtually enmeshed in the scenic situation or barred from (naïve) access to it. Twentieth-century experiments, aiming either at 'audience participation', for example through the covert location of actors in the pit and balconies, or at 'audience alienation', such as Brechtian placards and 'objective' commentators, are primitive compared to the formal and conceptual range of effects achieved by the chorus in Greek tragedy. In Sophocles, this range is masterfully exploited.[2]

The question of why it is that choral modes very largely disappear from the western spoken theatre after the early Renaissance, of why we find them surviving only in such special constructs as Milton's *Samson Agonistes*, Shelley's *Hellas*, or T. S. Eliot's *Murder in the Cathedral*, would take us to the heart of our political and social history. It would require the clarification of central, but, perhaps, intractable issues in the evolution towards individuality of the western persona, in

---

[1] The classic treatment remains W. Kranz, *Stasimon* (Berlin, 1933).

[2] For a recent survey cf. R. W. B. Burton, *The Chorus in Sophocles' Tragedies* (Oxford, 1980).

the concomitant loosening of collective–communal habits of identity, utterance, and gesture. It would, I think, necessitate an understanding of the gradual shift from speech-acts to music and gestural forms of certain primary religious, affective, communal impulses and semantic conventions in the West, a long retreat, as it were, from the individuation, the privacies, and the rationality of the word. Whatever the deep-lying reasons, T. S. Eliot's wry finding in reference to his *The Family Reunion* remains true: however much intelligence and discipline has been invested, choruses on the modern western stage turn out either as figures out of some ghastly/ghostly pantomime or as a pack of rugby players in improbable entwining. What this signifies is that an absolutely fundamental presence and executive resource in Sophocles' *Antigone*—a play in which the choral odes reach a pitch of intellectual force and lyric beauty unsurpassed in literature—have, in all but a few instances, lapsed from the legacy of re-creation. Or, more precisely, they have been essentially lost to spoken drama.

The chorus was the pivot of a composite of music and of dance of which we have only conjectural imaginings. Vase-paintings give us information as to masks worn in Greek drama. They give only tantalizing hints of the musical accompaniment and choreography which were basic elements in the performance. The richly differentiated, precisely coded metrics of dramatic monologue, dialogue, and choral ode are, themselves, a 'notation', a verbal correspondent to musical markers and choreography. We do not know how much of any given play was sung or intoned according to exactly accentuated metrical–vocal prescriptions. We do not know how often, or according to what mimetic–metrical 'semantics', the chorus was in motion. What we do know is that Greek tragic drama was a theatrical genre much closer to opera, as we are familiar with it, than to our spoken plays.[1]

All that has survived of the 'music' to a play are five 'notes' on a second-century BC papyrus fragment of a choral antistrophe in Euripides' *Orestes* (lines 338–44). We possess no single dance notation. It would not be unfair to equate our knowledge of the total fabric and effects of Greek tragedy with that which we would glean from the piano transcription and

---

[1] Cf. M. Pintacuda, *La musica nella tragedia greca* (Cefalù, 1978), for a survey of the extant evidence.

summarized libretto of a Verdi or Wagner opera. Vital questions are insoluble. What is the weight, what is the possibly contrastive feebleness or absurdity of Creon's taunt (line 883) that sung laments, that threnodies, have never arrested death? In what measure (literally), how forcibly, did the music and motion of the chorus emphasize, subvert, qualify internally, such immensely important but also arguable passages as the first stasimon, the ode to Eros, the apparent 'quarrel' with death-bound Antigone, or the wildly mistaken(?) hymn to Bacchus in the fifth stasimon? What are the primary relations of meaning in Sophocles' *Antigone* as between what is spoken and what is sung, between personages present but at rest and those who 'dance their purpose'?[1]

It was, however, around a realization, partly scholarly, partly intuitive, of the operatic nature of antique tragedy, that the 'Orphic' and Neoplatonic academies and *camaratas* of sixteenth-century Florence and Venice, of Rome and of Mantua, 'invented' opera or, to use the more informative French designation, *drame lyrique*. The pioneering works of Jacopo Peri, of Monteverdi, were conceived with antiquarian passion. Here, at last, was the theatre of Dionysus restored to its ancient glories. In such restoration, the chorus occupies a central place.

The history of musical settings of the choral odes in *Antigone* is an integral part of any study of the metamorphic 'Antigones' in the western inheritance. A setting of a text is as radical an act of interpretation as are translation, commentary, or performance. To compose a *Lied*, to set to music a libretto, to write a cantata on a liturgical or secular text, is to make hermeneutics dynamic. I have referred already to the longlasting success of Mendelssohn's suave, amply mellifluous settings of the *Antigone* choruses. Half a century later, the theme was again in vogue. It was given in competitive examination for the 1893 Prix de Rome. A year later, the Comédie Française produced *Antigone* with scenic and choral music by Saint-Saëns. Not surprisingly, the coloration of the music is more austere than Mendelssohn's, more academically aware of the antique source.

But it is in the twentieth century that musical interpretations

---

[1] For a precise illustration of this point, cf. W. J. Ziobro, 'Where was Antigone? *Antigone*, 766–883', *American Journal of Philology*, xcii (1971).

and re-creations of the chorus in *Antigone* have been most searching. *Antigone* (1927) is Arthur Honegger's masterpiece. If it has failed to establish itself in the repertoire, the reason may be that Honegger adhered too closely to Cocteau's pallid, idiomatic—therefore, rapidly dated—adaptation of Sophocles in his *Antigone* of 1922. Honegger's music cannot, at all points, bring its book to life. But anyone who saw the work revived at Angers, in the spring of 1981, will have been persuaded by its musical force. In what he felt to be the genuine style of the musical components of Greek tragedy, and with some reference to Bach's settings of the Passions, Honegger composed a severely 'syllabic' score. The music, he tells us, springs from the meaning and contour of the word, from the 'pitch and rhythms of sense' in dramatic speech. Honegger limits his vocalizations to the middle range of the scale. He resists the temptations of cantilena and melodic elevation. Wherever possible, the musical stress coincides with the natural accentuation of the word. No less than Stravinsky's *Oedipus Rex* (here Cocteau's Latin–Senecan text is cunningly apposite), Honegger's *Antigone* is a choral drama. The protagonists detach themselves temporarily from the omnipresent collectivity of the chorus, from the binding tessitura of its chant. Beyond the immediate catastrophe vibrates the humanity of the massed chorus, implying the durance of the city.[1]

By the mere fact that it sets Hölderlin's version, Carl Orff's *Antigonae* of 1949 belongs decisively to the philosophic, poetic, political fortunes of the Antigone motif in German history and feeling. It relates to those Hegelian readings, to the debates which follow on Hegel and Hölderlin, to Nietzsche's theories of tragedy, as I have cited them in the first chapter. Orff's work has been the occasion of critical–psychological malaise. Many have found it seductively brutal. Others, merely brutal. In *Antigonae*, the chorus and Leader of the chorus carry monumental weight. Their mode of utterance is, like that of the score as a whole, brusquely syncopated, percussive, and textually articulative to a degree which verges on *Sprechgesang*. Whereas Honegger orchestrates traditionally, the timbre and texture of Orff's orchestra aim at 'neo-ritualistic' and 'ethnographic' effects. Batteries of pianos sound the dominant beat. Xylophones, marimbas, stone-drums, carillons, tambourines,

[1] Cf. M. Landowski, *Honegger* (Paris, 1978), 90–4.

castanettes, Javanese gongs, an anvil, a congeries of African drums, Turkish cymbals, give to the choral speeches and odes a hammering, a febrile, yet also a flatly metallic, almost translucent, quality. These are the quivering, captious, yet also portentous and, at times, inspired old patricians of Thebes as Sophocles may have seen them declaiming, chanting, and dancing. Personally, I would say that there are episodes in Orff's *Antigonae* which come closer to suggesting the lost totality of the original than does any other variant or imitation.[1]

Certainly, one can say this: to set side by side Mendelssohn's, Saint-Saëns's, Honegger's, and Orff's scorings of the first stasimon in Sophocles' *Antigone*, or of the chorus's parting exchanges with the heroine, is to go to the heart of our theme. It is to hear, to re-experience in detail, 'Antigone and her sad song' across the resonance of successive needs and recognitions.[2]

As I noted above, the Sophoclean chorus tends to fall away from spoken 'Antigones' after the sixteenth century and such scholarly treatments as Garnier's. There are exceptions. Among the most intriguing is Dominik Smolé's Slovene *Antigone*, first staged in 1960. Here, the heroine never appears. It is via the chorus and several secondary personae that we experience the terror and moral–political meaning of her fate. Generally, however, the multiple dramatic and lyric functions of the Greek chorus are redistributed. In the 1866 *Antigone* of Adolf von Wilbrandt, in Hasenclever's version of 1917 (it was turned into an opera a year later), the choral presence is that of the crowd or 'mob', acting either in unison or fragmented into turbulent groups and single voices. Gerhard Schultze's *Antigone* (1911) replaces the Sophoclean chorus with councillors to Creon who enter and speak individually. Among recent solutions, Anouilh's has become the best known. The commentary on the action, the key exchanges with Antigone, the premonitions, the pronouncements of finalities, which

[1] Cf. W. Keller, *Orffs Antigonae* (Mainz, 1950), and R. Münster (ed.), *Carl Orff: das Bühnenwerk* (Munich, 1970).

[2] I have been unable to either hear or see the music composed by the highly original André Jolivet for the staging of Sophocles' *Antigone* in Paris in 1951 and 1960. Nor have I heard Reginald Smith Brindle's *Death of Antigone*, a chamber opera for voices, wind instruments, and percussion, written in 1969 and given a concert performance in London in December 1978.

Sophocles assigns to the chorus of elders, are apportioned by
Anouilh among *Le Prologue*, who can be seen as the chorus-
leader, the Guards, and the *Chœur* itself, whose tone is one of
bleak, faintly unctuous witness. What is lost in all these
variants is the lyric centre and pacing of Sophocles' play.

Bertolt Brecht was too fine a poet not to know this. He felt,
moreover, that the sociology and poetics of a chorus were ideal
means towards the didactic use of classical myths. Through its
collective and, broadly considered, 'populist' character, the
chorus could provide the modern, very possibly unlettered,
audience with direct access to an otherwise remote, 'élitist'
imbroglio. On the other hand, the chorus's own distance and
self-distancings from the regal terrors enacted before it would
help to achieve just those effects of alienation, of critical
dispassion, which Brecht aims at.

On 16 December 1947 Brecht noted that very gradually,
and via work in progress, a 'highly realistic folk-legend' was
emerging out of the 'ideological mist' of the Antigone legend.
In this emergence, Brecht's conception of the chorus was
seminal. He saw that in the Sophocles–Hölderlin text choral
odes were sometimes so riddling and lyrically obscure as to
defy ready understanding. But when *durchstudiert*, when
'studied in depth', these same odes unfolded greater and greater
loveliness. This study in depth, as important to the Brechtian
theatre as is performance itself, makes of the choral parts an
exercise of stringent virtuosity. Brecht's and Caspar Neher's
work-notes for the stagings of *Antigone* in Chur and Berlin,
together with records of rehearsals, show the concentrated
insight and drill which went into the training of the four-man
chorus of *Männer von Theben*.[1]

But Brecht did more than call to scenic life the Sophocles–
Hölderlin text, within the framework of a drama of anti-Fascist
resistance. He added certain choral passages of his own. These
are crucial to his reading and 'modelling' of Antigone (where

[1] Bertolt Brecht, *Die Antigone des Sophokles. Materialien zur 'Antigone'* (Frankfurt-on-
Main, 1976), contains the essential documentation. For Brecht's handling of the
chorus, cf. his letter to Neher of 7 February 1948, as reprinted in the *Bertolt Brecht–
Caspar Neher* catalogue of the exhibition on the work of the two men held in the
Hessisches Landesmuseum, Darmstadt, 1963. Pp. 323 ff. in K. Völker, *Brecht: A
Biography*, trans. J. Nowell (New York, 1978), contain additional reports on rehearsals
and the circumstances, both familial and professional, surrounding the composition
and production of the play.

'modelling', as in the *Modellbuch* of the play issued in 1948, signifies both 'shaping' and 'providing an exemplary, prescriptive pattern'). As Antigone is escorted to her death, *die Alten* come forward:

> Wandte sich um und ging, weiten Schrittes, als führe sie
> Ihren Wächter an. Über den Platz dort
> Ging sie, wo schon die Säulen des Siegs
> Ehern errichtet sind. Schneller ging sie da;
> Schwand.
> Aber auch die hat einst
> Gegessen vom Brot, das in dunklem Fels
> Gebacken war. In der Unglück bergenden
> Türme Schatten: sass sie gemach, bis
> Was von des Labdakus Häusern tödlich ausging
> Tödlich zurückkam. Die blutige Hand
> Teilt's den Eigenen aus, und die
> Nehmen es nicht, sondern reissen's.
> Hernach erst lag sie
> Zornig im Freien auch
> Ins Gute geworfen!
> Die Kälte weckte sie.
> Nicht ehe die letzte
> Geduld verbraucht war und ausgemessen der letzte
> Frevel, nahm des unsehenden Ödipus
> Kind vom Aug die altersbrüchige Binde
> Um in den Abgrund zu schauen.
> So unsehend auch hebt
> Thebe die Sohle jetzt, und taumelnd
> Schmeckt sie den Trank des Siegs, den viel-
> Kräutrigen, der im Finstern gemischt ist
> Und schluckt ihn und jauchzt.

> (Turn, she did, and went with a striding step, as if it was
> She who led on the guard. Across the square, over there,
> She went, where already the bronze pillars are set
> In victory's honour. There she went faster;
> Vanished.
> But this woman also once ate
> Of the bread that is baked in the dark rock.
> In the misery-masking shadow of the towers—
> She sat cosily. Until that which went out
> Murderously from the houses of Laius
> Came home murderously. The bloodstained hand
> Divides it among its own, and these

Do not take it, they tear at it.
Only *after* that did she lie incensed
In the open,
Hurled into goodness!
The cold woke her.
Not till the last patience was spent,
And the final blasphemy meted out,
Did the child of unseeing Oedipus
Take the senile blindfold from her eyes
To look into the abyss.
So unseeing also, Thebes now lifts its feet
And, tottering, laps the brew of victory,
The much-spiced brew, which is mixed in darkness.
And swallows it, and exults.)

The play ends on a choral fugue of four voices. The old men follow Creon 'nach unten', 'into the depths'. The 'zwingbare Hand', 'the coercive hand' of state power, has been hewn off. All this sorrow and waste will profit none but the enemy who is coming to destroy the city. 'Nimmer genügt', 'never suffices' the acquisition of wisdom in old age. A characteristic Brechtian corrigendum to Sophocles. But Brecht has replaced the chorus at the hub of *Antigone*, and done so with a lyric subtlety which matches his source.

The commentary which Brecht provides in his work-notes (*Anmerkungen zur Bearbeitung*) for the second stasimon is lapidary: 'Man, monstrously great (*ungeheuer gross*), when he reduces nature to subjection, becomes, when he reduces his fellow man to subjection, a great monster.' Like Hölderlin before him, Brecht translates τὰ δεινά as *Ungeheuer*, a densely packed word which comports 'what is monstrous', 'what is uncanny', 'what is strangely, hauntingly excessive both in respect of the positive and the negative'. It was not to Brecht's purpose to go into the metaphysics, into the social anthropology of the ode. So many had already done so. Between Martin Opitz's version, in his *Antigone* translation issued in 1636, and today, we know of roughly one hundred German translations and imitations. This sequence may well constitute the richest, the most penetrating 'radioactive tracer' available to us if we seek to follow the inward genesis of German philosophic–social sensibility and the history of the language. It would not be sophistry to argue that the πολλὰ τὰ δεινά passage in Sophocles (lines 332–83) forms the heart of 'the house of being' in German literature, beyond, paradoxically, any text out of Luther's Bible—there being few important Scriptures in German since—or out of native poetry. In other literatures and interpretative traditions also, of course, this second stasimon towers.[1]

I have referred already to the central role which it assumes in Heidegger's ontology and poetics. It seems to have been for Heidegger the inherent talisman, the proof that 'Being', so largely lapsed from western life and thought, was radiantly immanent in certain speech-acts, and recapturable. Explicit allusions to the ode are frequent in Heidegger, implicit ones ubiquitous. We cannot know the full weight and exposition of Heidegger's readings until the publication, in the *Gesamtwerk* now in progress, of the monograph on 'the figure and destiny of Antigone', *Gestalt und Geschick der Antigone*. What we do have is the gloss which Heidegger puts forward in his *Introduction to Metaphysics*, a set of lectures given in 1935 and published in 1953.[2] These observations, together with the translation(s) by Hölderlin which they presume and internalize, make for the most vivid encounter we know of between the Sophoclean chorus and the western imagination after Athens.

Heidegger is seeking to elucidate the statement of Parmenides that thought and being are one. He is seeking to define the image of man which this equation entails. To do so, he turns to 'the thinking poetry', itself supremely representative of 'thought in being', in the second stasimon of the *Antigone*.

[1] To list the literature which has accumulated around the second stasimon in *Antigone* would be to establish a bibliography of studies in Sophocles. It would also be a useful attempt to trace, in miniature but representatively, the history of western classical hermeneutics. From A. W. Schlegel's lectures on dramatic poesy and Wilamowitz-Möllendorff's analyses of Greek metre onward, the πολλὰ τὰ δεινά choral ode has been at the centre of criticism and scholarship. The following are illustrative of the varying approaches: W. Schmid, 'Probleme aus der sophokleischen Antigone', *Philologus*, lxii (1903), 14 ff.; W. Kranz, *Stasimon*, p. 219; M. Untersteiner, *Sofocle* (Florence, 1935), i. 111–23; G. Perrotta, *Sofocle* (Milan, 1935), 66 ff.; E. Schlesinger, 'ΔΕΙΝΟΤΗΣ', *Philologus*, NS xlv (1936–7), 59–66; A. Bonnard, *La Tragédie et l'homme*, p. 45; R. F. Goheen, *The Imagery of Sophocles' Antigone* (Princeton University Press, 1951), 58–64; G. Müller, 'Ueberlegungen zum Chor der Antigone', *Hermes*, lxxxix (1961), 400–2; D. A. Hester, 'Sophocles the Unphilosophical: A Study in the *Antigone*', *Mnemosyne*, xxiv. 4 (1971), 26; G. H. Gellie, *Sophocles, A Reading*, pp. 35–7; W. Jens, *Zur Antike*, p. 425; R. W. B. Burton, *The Chorus in Sophocles' Tragedies*, pp. 96–8.
[2] Available in English as Martin Heidegger, *An Introduction to Metaphysics*, trans. R. Manheim (Yale University Press, 1959).

δεινότερον is the word which shatters 'at the outset all everyday standards of questioning and definition'. Man is 'the strangest', 'the most uncanny'. He contains the ultimate and the abysmal, and this duality is revealed 'only to poetic insight'. Uniquely, the language of ancient Hellas, so far as it dwelt still in reach of primordial 'Being', cuts across the antinomies which are made inert and false in our logic. If δεινόν signifies 'the terrible', it also means, says Heidegger, 'that which is violent in the inborn, necessary drive towards man's exercise of mental and physical power'. In the concept of 'strangeness, uncanniness, unhousedness', Sophocles concentrates his overwhelming perception: man is δεινότερον 'because he is the violent one, who, tending towards the strange in the sense of the overpowering, surpasses the limits of the familiar'.

The second strophe tells us that man, in the unhoused violence of his wanderings, is cast out of his natural and familial framework. Specifically, he is severed from the πόλιc. 'πόλιc is usually translated as city or city-state. This does not capture the full meaning. πόλιc means, rather, the place, the there, wherein and as which historical being-there is.' It is, in Heideggerian parlance, the existential matrix for man. Torn from this matrix, man is ἄπολιc, an epithet whose terror is manifest in *Antigone* and further heightened in Heidegger's political anthropology.

Now Heidegger reverts to the opening of the ode and examines the meanings to be attached to man's brilliant conquests of the sea, of the earth, of the animal orders. To cross the winter waves, to break open the earth with the sharp ploughshare, to net the birds of the air, is to enact the central motion of violent departure in man. A wanderer out of his own housed self, man uproots, constrains, and distorts the delicate cadences, the just 'precincts' of organic life.

At this point, Heidegger rejects any reading of the stasimon as a historicist analysis or critique of progress (as we might find it in Rousseau). No, argues Heidegger: like the pre-Socratics, Sophocles knew that man's enormity, his leap to power and alienation, must be located at the very outset. 'The beginning is the strangest and mightiest.' Our own ecological vandalism is a degenerate, fated consequence of 'the strangeness at the start'. This 'strangeness' and the power it begets precede man. In a reading which exactly parallels Pound's great outcry in

Canto LXXXI, 'it is not man | Made courage, or made order, or made grace', a Canto which is Sophoclean to the heart, Heidegger renders ἐδιδάξατο (line 356) not as 'invented', but as 'found his way towards'. Language, understanding, passion are older and greater than man. They 'speak, they think *him*' (a cardinal Heideggerian principle). But in so far as he is the locus of their being, violence of deed and violence of speech are indissolubly a part of his existence. And it is this pressure of violence on all human creativity and conception which justifies the description of man as δεινότερον. 'The *violent one*, the creative man, who sets forth into the un-said, who breaks into the un-thought, compels the un-happened to happen, and makes the un-seen appear'—this uncanny, will-driven being stands always in peril of ἄτη, of furious error. In him, pre-eminently, 'the centre cannot hold'.

To show the full Sophoclean treatment of this antinomy, Heidegger undertakes a third reading of the ode. He now formulates his hermeneutic method: 'The actual interpre-tation must show what does not stand in the words and is nevertheless said.'

Man's disasters, foreshadowed in the ode, demonstrated in Sophoclean tragedy, result from an inevitable, ontological collision. The 'violence against the preponderant power of Being' by which man asserts his essence *must* shatter. Man is 'hurled into affliction', but this projection stems immediately from the entrance of man into the historicity, into the existential actualities of his 'being-there'. The hearth, the familiar, the homecoming, which are incomparably inferred in this second stasimon, are there, says Heidegger, so that 'they may be broken out of, and so that which is overpowering may break into them'. To man, 'disaster is the deepest affirmation of the overpowering'. Heidegger's conclusion leaves open the paradoxical immensities of the tragic: 'We shall fail to understand the mysteriousness of the essence of being-human, thus experienced and carried back poetically to its founda-tions, if we snatch at value-judgements.' Each time we encounter, to the utmost of our awareness, the πολλὰ τὰ δεινά chorus, the 'mysteriousness of the essence of our being-human' is made deeper and clearer.

Heidegger's idiom, the tidal strategy of his readings, are singularly his own. Here 'strangeness' speaks to 'strangeness' in a vein as dramatic, as poetically re-creative as any in the entire Antigone tradition. Yet the spirit of interpretation is not far removed from that of one of the most 'classic' of readers, E. R. Dodds:

It was above all Sophocles, the last great exponent of the archaic world-view, who expressed the full tragic significance of the old religious themes in their unsoftened, unmoralized forms—the overwhelming sense of human helplessness in face of the divine mystery, and of the *ate* that waits on all human achievement—and who made these thoughts part of the cultural inheritance of Western Man.[1]

6

The fascination of 'Antigone', the pressure which the myth has exercised on poetics and politics, are inseparable from the presence of Creon. Antigone herself is, in fact, absent from much of Sophocles' play. After her exit into night, the drama is Creon's. Pondering the dual or 'broken-backed' architecture of Sophocles' dramaturgy, commentators have repeatedly suggested that 'Antigone and Creon' would be a more just title. In the elaborations of and variations on the theme after Sophocles, the role of Creon has been as densely argued as that of the heroine. The intimacies of conflict have knit and delineated their identities.

The provenance of Creon, his formal and structural functions in the Theban cycle, are of utmost obscurity. A focus, possibly very ancient, may reside in rivalries between Lacedaemonia and Thebes. Creon would be a man of war who had seized power in the city of Cadmus, an outsider seeking legitimacy. A scholiast on Euripides' *Phoenician Women* knows of Creon as a shadowy predecessor of luminous Oedipus, as a ruler over Thebes who has lost his own son, Haemon, to the devouring Sphinx, and who has proved himself unable to free his subjects from the visitations and exactions of the monster. But even at the outset, parallels between Creon and Oedipus make themselves insistent. Oedipus' denunciation of Creon and Teiresias exactly foreshadows Creon's attack on the seer. Both rulers turn in fury on their sons. Both are led by imperious, wilful rationality into unreason and self-destruction.

[1] E. R. Dodds, *The Greeks and the Irrational* (University of California Press, 1951), 49.

The obscurities and suggestions of structural reiteration, however, do not lie solely in the mythical background and in our loss of the epic material.

The appearances of Creon in Greek tragedies, extant and fragmentary, are multiple. It is not, at all points, possible to reconcile the differing versions of his persona. We cannot tell whether Creon, as referred to in Aeschylus' *Seven Against Thebes* (line 474), is or is not related to Laius and Oedipus. Creon is by no means identical in Sophocles' *Oedipus Rex*, where he plays a part of true innocence and nobility, and in *Oedipus at Colonus* and *Antigone*. Almost nothing can be said with any certainty as to Euripides' *Antigone*, though one tradition at least depicts Creon, under the influence of a *deus ex machina*, forgiving Haemon and Antigone and recognizing their child as a legitimate heir.[1] In the *Phoenician Women*, a play which is, together with Statius' epic, the main source for 'Creons' from the late Middle Ages on, the personage becomes intricate almost to the point of self-contradiction.

Here Creon is, as we would expect, Eteocles' maternal uncle. He is also counsellor and strategist to the doomed prince. It is he who suggests, for the defence of the imperilled city, the device of the seven champions at the seven gates. Eteocles is possessed by precise intimations of fatality. Should he perish, it is Creon who must gather the reins of power. It is he who must guard his royal sister Jocasta, and who must assure the marriage of Haemon to Antigone. As to Oedipus, blind and raging behind the walls of the palace, 'it may be that his maledictions will destroy us all'. Thereupon comes a key touch, which may point to Euripides' wish to challenge, contrastively, the Sophoclean version: it is Eteocles who orders Creon to deny burial to Polyneices. If the latter falls in battle, let him never find sepulchre in Theban earth. 'And be it a friend—let whoever inters him suffer death'—where the term for 'friend' is φίλων, with all its resonances out of Sophocles' *Antigone*. After which, Creon is dismissed.

But hideous irony awaits him. He has summoned Teiresias to learn from him how best the city may be saved. The prophet enters with Menoeceus, Creon's other son. It is he who must be

---

[1] For a discussion of this lost *Antigone*, cf. T. B. L. Webster, *The Tragedies of Euripides* (London, 1967), 181–4. The publication of the Oxyrhynchus papyrus may have rendered Webster's speculative account untenable.

sacrificed if Thebes is to withstand the Argive onslaught. Haemon is affianced to Antigone; therefore, he lacks the virginal apartness required of a sacrificial victim. It is Menoeceus, 'the young stallion', who must die. 'Choose between two destinies: to save either your son or the city' (παῖδα and πόλιν are set at merciless odds in the construction and rhythm of the line). The intimations, at this juncture, may be among the most archaic in Greek drama. Ares, god of war, must be propitiated. He has not forgiven Cadmus, who slew the primeval, earth-bound dragon, out of which slaying sprang armed Thebes. Blood calls for blood. The 'golden-helmeted' warriors, Creon's kin, were born of the teeth of the dragon. Now let there be restitution. (Does the designation of Menoeceus as 'a young stallion' point to some indistinct remembrance of the sacrifice of horses, sacred to Ares?)

Creon's reaction is one of outraged humanity and paternity. 'Let no man come to glorify me (εὐλογείτω) by slaying my children.' This Euripidean line is a concentrated but total repudiation of the characterization of Creon in Sophocles' *Antigone*. It denies that characterization categorically. Creon goes further: he declares himself ready and willing to die in his son's place. He is father first, and heroic statesman second. He bids Menoeceus flee from the accursed city. The boy feigns agreement. But when Creon goes to battle, Menoeceus tells the chorus that he is resolved to save Thebes at the price of his own life. With almost ironic terseness, the Messenger, intent upon chronicling the totemic savagery of the duels at the seven gates, reports Menoeceus' suicide, high on the battlements. Creon will suffer. But what is such proud pain compared to victory and the salvation of the πόλις?

Euripides' melodrama grows ever more turbulent. Eteocles and Polyneices perish at each other's crazed hands. Aged Oedipus stumbles out of the literal past, out of the haunted discretion of his enforced retreat. His curses have borne unspeakable fruit. He and Antigone intone their lament. Creon enters and cuts them short. He is now master in the stricken polity. Eteocles has bestowed on him the legacy of power. Polyneices is to be left unburied outside the borders of Theban territory (precisely the proscription we have seen applied to banished traitors in Attic law and usage). Antigone is to marry Haemon and ensure dynastic continuity. Oedipus

must from hence. Teiresias has made clear that Thebes can
never prosper so long as it houses this polluted 'outsider'. 'I do
not say this out of insolence or enmity.' Thebes has known too
much horror since Oedipus' hidden birth and homecoming.
With Oedipus' departure, opines Creon, the ancient anathema
may, at last, be lifted. Antigone interposes, and the dialogue
which ensues (there may be corruptions in our text) differs
instructively from that in Sophocles.

The polemic is muted. Euripides' tone and cadence suggest
utter weariness. The protagonists are at the limits of mental
and nervous endurance. Creon, in whose very name we hear
the root of 'power', comes near to negotiating. The interdict on
Polyneices' bestowal is not his, but Eteocles'. It is plain piety
and good sense to respect such an injunction. Creon orders his
guards to seize the mutinous child of Oedipus. But when she
takes her stand, defiantly, beside her slain brothers, Creon
solicits: 'Child, daughter, higher agencies oppose you.' She, in
turn, moderates her demands. It will be solace enough if she is
permitted to cleanse Polyneices' corpse, if she can bind up its
terrible wounds, if she is simply granted a farewell kiss. And
when Antigone proclaims that she must accompany Oedipus
into exile, that she will slay Haemon if forcibly wed, Creon
responds by one of the most tautly controlled, equitable verses
in the play: he observes that Antigone's lofty impulses are not
untouched by folly, by destructive obsession (μωρία). Having
said this, Creon simply tells Antigone to leave the land of
Thebes.

The epilogue is marked by uncertainties and, possibly,
lacunae in our text. Line 1744 seems to imply that, after
Creon's exit, guards have come to remove and cast out
Polyneices' remains. Antigone repeats her resolve to give
burial to her disgraced brother. But if this resolve is to be
fulfilled beyond Theban bounds, there is no necessary challenge to Creon. This equivocation is suggestive of Euripides'
fluid treatment of the myth. The only certain note is that of
exhaustion.

We know little of the *Antigone* of Astydamas which, together
with two other, thematically unrelated dramas, won a first
prize for its author in 342–1 BC.[1] Clearly, the work was

[1] Cf. the discussion of Astydamas' play in G. Xanthakis-Karamanos, *Studies in
Fourth-Century Tragedy* (Athens, 1980), 48–53.

influenced by Euripides. Indeed, it may be the case that
Hyginus, to whose plot summary I have already referred, is
recounting the Euripidean version and not that of Astydamas
at all. As he tells it, the drama went as follows. Antigone has
interred Polyneices. Creon orders Haemon to kill her. Haemon
conceals his bride among shepherds (a structural counterpart
to the fate of Oedipus). Haemon informs his father that his
orders have been carried out. But many years later, Maion,
whom the hidden Antigone has borne to Haemon, returns to
compete in Theban festive games. Creon recognizes the boy
(how?) and commands the execution of both Haemon and
Antigone. Heracles, with whose adventures and cults the figure
of Creon may, at its opaque origins, have been associated,
intervenes and brings about reconciliation. So, at least,
conclude scholars familiar with the rights of divine interposition in Greek drama. Hyginus, however, says that Haemon
slew his beloved Antigone, and then himself. The role of Creon
is that of a murderous despot.

It would appear to have been via Lucius Accius' adaptation
of Sophocles, in the second century BC, that Virgil knows of
Antigone. Later antiquity, Alexandria and Byzantium in
particular, turns more often to the *Phoenician Women*. From
Seneca onward, epic or rhetorical–dramatic variants on the
Theban cycle, such as in the twelfth-century *Roman de Thèbes*,
in Boccaccio's *Teseida*, and its two English imitations,
Chaucer's 'Knight's Tale' and Lydgate's 'The Story of
Thebes', contain distant elements of Sophocles, but derive
primarily from the *Phoenician Women* and from the uses of
and ornamentations on Euripides in Statius. The pluralities of
tone and value in Creon, as Euripides and Statius picture him,
the uneasy amalgam of military prowess, statecraft, ambi-
tious intrigue, weakness, and exemplary ruin, allowed the
imagination liberties.

In Statius, Creon urges Eteocles on to his fratricidal duel
with Polyneices because he is himself maddened by the self-
sacrifice of his son. In Racine, as we have seen, Creon becomes
suitor to his bereaved niece. It is in the cause of his explicit
humanitarianism, and even stoic 'republicanism', that Alfieri
makes of Creon the very type of the tyrant. Creon's actions are
not even a reasoned apologia for *raison d'état*; they spring from
the unbridled will of a megalomaniac. The departure from this

view, the revaluation of Creon, with its implicit return to
orders of complexity present in ancient myth and in Sophocles'
version, pivot, naturally, on the Hegelian analysis, and on the
extensive debates to which this analysis gave rise. There is,
unquestionably, a Creon after Hegel. Already the celebrated
Tieck–Mendelssohn staging of *Antigone* presents Creon as a
noble, tragically constrained, defender of the law. A long
rehabilitation or, more precisely, a closer questioning had
begun.

This questioning engages philologists and critics, political
theorists and legal historians, connoisseurs of rhetoric and of
the psyche. Though the judgements passed on Creon are, as a
rule, less personal, less emotive than those elicited by Antigone,
they are, often, more closely argued and in conflict.

The central dispute in Sophocles' play has frequently been
perceived as one between archaic, familial usage and codes of
sentiment on the one hand, and the new public rationality of
the Periclean moment on the other. In the light of this
interpretation, Creon's idiom, his legalistic stringency, his
tactics in debate, have been qualified as 'sophistic'—not so
much in a moral as in a technical and historical sense. In
opposition to the 'death-rooted transcendentalism' of Antigone
stands the secular 'enlightenment' of Creon. The catastrophe
of the clan of Laius demonstrates that hoary irrationalities and
obsolete manias have been at work. The abstraction, the civic
impersonality, of Creon's governance represents the promise of
a cooler but more lucid future. No doubt, the actual dramatic
presentation of Creon does suggest Sophocles' doubts and
unease as to such 'progress'. The poet is, himself, too sharply
cognizant of the irremediable authority and sanctity of
darkness in man. Nevertheless, we find in *Antigone*, no less than
in Plato's dialogues, a searching, by no means unreservedly
negative, consideration of the stance of the 'sophist'.[1]

Exactly the contrary thesis is urged with equal conviction. It
is Creon who is the conservative, the conscious custodian of
those long-sanctioned norms of civic life which are reflected, as
we have seen, in such prescriptions against the burial of traitors
in native ground as we have found them in Plato's *Laws* and
Attic observance. Antigone's provocation stems not from

[1] Cf. W. Schmid, 'Probleme aus der sophokleischen Antigone', pp. 6–9, and
R. F. Goheen, *The Imagery of Sophocles' Antigone*, p. 92.

antique tradition. It is, instead, a fragile intimation of humanistic ideals, of a categorical private ethic along Socratic, proto-Christian, and, ultimately, Kantian lines. When Antigone invokes the 'unwritten laws', she is summoning up futurities of conscience and individual compulsion alien to the norms and cohesion of the πόλις.[1] Creon's conservatism, his refusal to entertain the probing play of innovative, 'sophistic' sensibility, align him with the 'reality principle'. The Antigones, on the contrary, are the 'forward imaginers' (Ernst Bloch's phrase) who cannot, who must not, endure the weight and logic of the status quo.[2]

One of the most influential commentaries, that of Karl Reinhardt, sees in Creon the very type of intellectual, emotional limitation. He is a man circumscribed to the point of blindness within the bounds of his mediocrity.[3] Even the bizarre chain of misfortunes which undoes his good intentions at the close of the play is a result of his inadequacies. He is a man destined 'to come too late'.[4] Yet this same Creon is felt by another reader to be the embodiment of tragic awareness: 'As he stands at the end externally broken, internally humbled, and at last fully conscious of the depth of his responsibility, it is . . . Creon who draws most fully on our sympathy and who comes closest to embodying in himself a full attitude towards the tragic world we have seen unfolded.'[5]

Wrong, say others. In his final hour, 'the pasteboard tyrant becomes the most ordinary, if the most unhappy, of men'.[6] Of 'coarse fibre, commonplace mind, and narrow sympathies',[7] Creon is neither a great rhetorician in the new rationalist vein nor a severe statesman, but a politician seduced by vulgar power. Yet in his elucidation of the drama, an elucidation haunted by the pertinence of *Antigone* to twentieth-century conditions, Gerhard Nebel terms Creon *begeistert*,

[1] Cf. H. Höppener, 'Het begrabenisverbod in Sophokles' "Antigone"', *Hermeneus*, ix (1937), and H. J. Mette, 'Die Antigone des Sophokles', *Hermes*, lxxxiv (1956), 131–4.

[2] Cf. A. Lesky, 'Sophocle, Anouilh et le tragique', *Gesammelte Schriften* (Bern, 1966), 162–7.

[3] Cf. K. Reinhardt, *Sophokles*, p. 78.

[4] Ibid. 102.

[5] R. F. Goheen, op. cit. 53. Cf. also G. Méautis, *Sophocle, Essai sur le héros tragique* (Paris, 1957), 186.

[6] R. P. Winnington-Ingram, *Sophocles, An Interpretation*, p. 127.

[7] Ibid. 126.

'spirit-possessed'. Only such possession can account for the unbending, suicidal convictions which compel him to consign
to extinction his own house and dynastic hopes. No less than
other protagonists in certain Greek tragedies, Creon is a man
in the hands of the daemonic.[1] Some interpret this state as, in
some sense, metaphoric; it stems from a pathological con-
sequentiality, a *follia logica*.[2] Others again perceive a literal
madness. The folly which harrows the House of Laius, the
madness of Eros visited upon Haemon, take on, in Creon, the
concrete form of megalomania. Creon's reason succumbs to his
fixation on the half-understood glamour 'of a great, imperious,
regal personality (Oidipous)'.[3] He is simply not of a size to
wrestle with that overwhelming shadow.

Most readers and producers will, however, prefer to consider
the figure of Creon in reference to the general equilibrium of
the play. If some commentators have insisted on the factitious-
ness of Creon's role and have denied him serious stature,[4] the
great majority have registered the wondrous polarity of
Sophocles' design. Creon *is* a commensurate counterpoise to
Antigone. The problem lies in the true nature of their
dialectical parity.

Are they not, in fact, profoundly similar? Are their characters not hewn to precisely the same 'sharp edges'?[5] Does
Antigone's treatment of hapless Ismene not closely correspond
to Creon's treatment of herself and of Haemon? The polemic
intimacy between Creon and Antigone results from a clash of
'existential freedoms', poised, as it were, to a nicety. Neither
can yield without falsifying his essential being.[6] Each reads
himself in the other, and the language of the play points to this
fatal symmetry. Both Creon and Antigone are *auto-nomists*,
human beings who have taken the law into their own keeping.
Their respective enunciations of justice are, in the given local
case, irreconcilable. But in their obsession with law, they come

---

[1] Cf. G. Nebel, *Weltangst und Götterzorn: Eine Deutung der griechischen Tragödie*
(Stuttgart, 1951), 181.

[2] Cf. M. Untersteiner, *Sofocle*, i. 131.

[3] G. F. Else, *The Madness of Antigone*, p. 101.

[4] Cf. H. Patzer, *Hauptperson und tragischer Held in Sophokles* (Wiesbaden, 1978), for a
categorical statement. For A. J. A. Waldock, Creon 'does not approach within hail' of
Antigone's stature (*Sophocles the Dramatist*, p. 123).

[5] Cf. A. Bonnard, *La Tragédie et l'homme*, p. 49.

[6] Cf. G. Ronnet, *Sophocle, poète tragique* (Paris, 1969), 187.

very close to being mirror-images.[1] Hence the close concordance of magnitude and tone in their successive catastrophes: 'That which is terrible in them (*Furchtbarkeit*) hurls them onward. They fall like titans into the abyss.'[2]

Yet it is the genius of the play, or of the underlying myth, to make of these undeniable parallels the markers of antithesis. This remains the irreducible marvel of the case. The balance is not, as Hegel would have it, one of matching equities, of final undecidability. Although it is, indeed, complicated by the similarities of vehemence, of stage presence, between Antigone and Creon, a true judgement must seek out the fundamental contrast offered by 'the noble folly of self-sacrifice' on the one hand, and 'the vicious folly' of arbitrary anger and self-infatuation on the other.[3]

But how does Sophocles achieve this dialectic of 'kindred opposites', a dialectic inexhaustible to reflection and re-enactment? 'The conflict between Creon and Antigone is not only between city and house, but also between man and woman. Creon identifies his political authority and his sexual identity.'[4] The play is shot through with intimations of this primordial antinomy, with echoes of the debate, palpable in the *Oresteia*, on the respective functions of the sexes in the determination and transmission of kinship and of lineage. 'It is in keeping with Creon's fierce adherence to the polis and his inferential, abstractive mentality that he leans heavily on patriarchal lineage and authority (639–647; cf. 635). His stress on patriarchy, though illogical in one sense (see 182–3), is congruent with his antifeminine, antimaternal attitude (see, e.g., 569).'[5] In the last analysis, therefore, the conflict is one between the masculine and the feminine conceptions and conduct of human life, this conflict being, like no other, one of paradoxical 'mirrorings' and implacable contrariety. Antigone speaks, literally as it were, 'out of the womb', out of a timeless centrality of carnal impulse and of domesticity with death. Creon's world is that of masculine immanence, of a willed

[1] Cf. M. S. Santirocco, 'Justice in Sophocles' *Antigone*', p. 186.
[2] E. Eberelein, 'Über die verschiedenen Deutungen des tragischen Konflikts der Tragödie "Antigone" des Sophokles', p. 30.
[3] I. M. Linforth, *Antigone and Creon*, p. 259.
[4] C. Segal, *Tragedy and Civilization, An Interpretation of Sophocles* (Harvard University Press, 1981), 183.
[5] Ibid. 184.

at-homeness in a sphere of political action and futurity. As Charles Segal emphasizes, in his fine reading, Creon envisions the earth in a dual perspective: it is a political terrain, and a place to be seeded and ploughed. Hence the aptness of Creon's retort to Ismene in line 569: after Antigone's death, Haemon will find 'other fields to plough'. (This phrasing is usually taken as evidence of Creon's brutality. It may, however, echo a normal formula of betrothal—'I give you my daughter for the ploughing of legitimate children'—in use as late as the end of the fourth century.) For Antigone, on the contrary, the earth is the house of mysterious engendering and of the dead. Thus a sexual polarity, which reaches beyond even the enormity of the explicit moral–political collision, holds Sophocles' drama and the continued vitality of the myth in tensed balance. The organic conflicts are given harrowing representation in the final tableau: Creon, left both naked and shattered in his manhood, stands between the corpses of his wife and of his son.[1]

7

But the lives of Creon extend far beyond scholarship and the continuous commentaries on Sophocles or Euripides. His ambiguous persona has attracted the political imagination both within and outside formal literature. The year 1948, for example, witnessed not only Brecht's vehement repudiation of the Hegelian defence of Creon, but a far more drastic critique and reversal of values. In his tract, part verse, part lapidary prose, *Antigone vierge-mère de l'ordre*, the eighty-year-old Charles Maurras totally inverted the customary understanding of the polemic between Creon and Antigone. In line with speculative paradoxes put forward by seventeenth- and eighteenth-century monarchists, Maurras proclaimed what had been his insight 'since boyhood'. Accepted interpretations of Sophocles' *Antigone* are 'un contresens complet' ('a total misprision'). The old lion has reread the immortal text. Now 'there can be no doubt': the rebel against civic law and order is *not* Antigone:

It is Creon. Creon has against him the gods of Religion, the fundamental laws of the Polis, the feelings of the living Polis. This is

[1] J. Goth, *Sophokles Antigone: Interpretationsversuche und Strukturuntersuchungen* (Tübingen, 1966), 201.

the very spirit of the play. This is the lesson which derives from it:
Sophocles did not wish to portray for us the surge of fraternal love,
nor even, in the personage of Haemon, Antigone's betrothed, that of
love pure and simple. What he sets out to show also is the punishment
of the tyrant who has sought to free himself from laws divine and
human.

Thus it is Creon, not Antigone, who will destroy the city, an
act the more transgressive as it contradicts the custodianship,
the instruments of conservation, inherent in legitimate sovereignty. It is Creon, not Oedipus' child, who brings on the
ruin of authority and of dynastic succession. Creon's edict
against Polyneices is 'unconstitutional'. Such usurpation
distinguishes the despot from the true king. It is, argues
Maurras, 'a monstrous illegality'. Considered in depth,
moreover, such despotism is a manifestation of anarchy in the
spirit and acts of the ruler. We must, concludes Maurras,
revise our entire millennial misreading of *Antigone* and of the
moral–political issues to which it gives rise. It is Antigone,
'virgin-mother of order' (the Catholic inferences are obvious),
who incarnates 'the closely concordant laws of Man, of the
Gods, of the City. Who violates and defies all these laws?
Creon. It is he the anarchist. It is only he.'[1]

The Dreyfus Affair, the division of loyalties during the Occupation, the success of Anouilh's *Antigone* and the controversy generated by the play,[2] have made French sensibility
peculiarly alert to the claims of Creon. A generation after
Maurras, but with no less casuistic edge and gusto, these
are taken up by the *philosophe*-publicists of the 'new right'.
Creon, affirms Bernard-Henri Lévy, is no spokesman for a
frigid *raison d'état*. It is he, on the contrary, who incessantly
invokes the patronage of the deities. This prince of Thebes is

---

[1] This pamphlet was printed in Geneva in 1948 under the imprint *Cahier des trois
anneaux*. It was presented to Maurras by followers indignant at his condemnation and
imprisonment after the Liberation of 1944. It is somewhat rare.

[2] The history of Anouilh's play, the reactions to it in France during the Occupation,
the questions of policy and public opinion which these reactions involve, are the object
of an exhaustive monograph by M. Flügge, *Refus ou Ordre Nouveau. Politik, Ideologie und
Literatur im Frankreich der Besatzungszeit 1940–44 am Beispiel der 'Antigone' von Jean Anouilh*
(Rheinfelden, 1982). But despite Dr Flügge's authoritative labours, certain points
remain to be cleared up. The somewhat delayed ruling of German censorship in favour
of the play, a ruling which seems to entail an acutely penetrative, sophisticated
evaluation of Creon 'at the close', could well have involved referral to one or two of the
great Sophoclean scholars then active in the Reich. Is this so? If so, are there any
traces of their commentary on Anouilh?

also, and foremost, 'a priest'. 'And the truth is that he is . . . the only priest in the play, alone circumscribing the whole sphere of the sacred as it was conceivable in a city like Thebes at the end of the fifth century—not "law" versus "faith", but the one joined to the other in that "law-of-faith" which is proper to Greek religion.'[1] It follows that Antigone's opposition to the priest-king is a challenge to the cosmic order. Beyond debate, her fault is a metaphysical one. It makes of her not only an outlaw, but a being *hors l'ordre du monde* ('outside the pale of the world'). Without the gods of Creon, of Ismene, of the chorus, declares Lévy, there can only be waste and silence. Appropriately, therefore, Antigone's death is a literal annihilation, a return to zero. By taking her solipsistic stand, by asserting (as did Oedipus) the sufficiency of her ego, Antigone has broken the primary contract in Sophoclean ethics. Sophocles 'repatriates all conscience inside the enclosure of that which is social (*la socialité*)'.[2] *We* may find such 'repatriation' abhorrent and sterile. *We* may see in the discipline of the Greek πόλις and in Plato's programme for such discipline an ill-omened apotheosis of servility. But this is not Sophocles' perspective. This is not the vision which can elucidate the realities of sacred kingship in fifth-century Thebes. Bernard-Henri Lévy's finding is unequivocal: *Antigone* is 'a play written entirely from Creon's point of view, if not indeed to his glory'.[3]

Observe how this 'scandalous' pronouncement relates to Maurras. The *nouvelle droite* reclaims Creon—*rapatrier* is a verb charged with conservative resonance. Antigone is, once again, the outlaw. But the reading of Sophocles' drama as a hymn to civic–religious unison, the image of Creon as priest-king, are simply a reversal of identical terms and concepts in Maurras. The argument reaches back unbroken to such high advocates of divine right as Bossuet. Creon is a Bourbon.

What is, in a sense, an even deeper echo to Maurras may be heard in Alfred Döblin's voluminous novel, *November 1918*. Written in 1937–43, Döblin's *roman-fleuve* offers a kaleidoscope of Germany in the weeks of imperial collapse and attempted revolution. Severely wounded, young Dr Friedrich Becker returns to teach classics in the Gymnasium which he left as an

[1] B.-H. Lévy, *Le Testament de Dieu* (Paris, 1979), 87.
[2] Ibid. 89.
[3] Ibid. 87.

exalted soldier in 1914. The text to be taught is Sophocles'
Antigone. With the exception of one 'leftist', the class is
resolutely for Creon. It expects Becker to concur, indeed to
register in such an attitude an ardent tribute to his own
sacrificial loyalty to the fatherland. A good soldier, a man
wearing the Iron Cross, is living proof of the validity of Creon's
ethic.

Dr Becker first disappoints, then scandalizes, his students:
Antigone is brave, 'but she is no rebel. She is, in fact, the very
opposite of a revolutionary. If anyone in the play is an
insurgent, it is—do not be astonished—Creon, the King.
Haven't you noticed? Yes, it is he, in his actual tyrannical will,
in his pride at being, at last, victor and king, who believes that
he can set himself above sanctified traditions and accepted
truths as old as time.' The 'unwritten laws' cited by Antigone
are inscribed both in the hearts of men *and* in the usages of
civilized humanity. This is Charles Maurras's reading precisely. But Dr Becker's class is unconvinced. Kleist's *Prinz von
Homburg*, with its mystique of sacrificial obeisance to the
imperatives of the state, is invoked in aid of Creon. Perhaps
some remote, 'exotic' Greeks did feel otherwise. For a true
German reader, in 1918, Becker's interpretation is offensive
and inadmissible.

Dr Becker denies that the fundamental issue is that between
individual conscience, rooted in pious tradition, and the fiat of
arbitrary power. The real question is this: 'How is the world of
the living to conduct itself towards the world of the dead?' The
genuine 'hero' or protagonist of the drama is Polyneices. The
dead Polyneices has a *right* to a transcendent presence and
commemoration among the living. It is just this right which
Antigone defends and takes upon herself. If the state is a
reality, so, in no lesser degree, is death. It is Creon's stance
towards the existential weight of death which is flagrantly
inadequate and which entails catastrophe both for himself and
the πόλιc.

It may be that Döblin was drawing on an essay by the
great theologian Rudolf Bultmann.[1] Creon's principles,
says Bultmann, are neither 'foolish nor erroneous'. He is no

---

[1] R. Bultmann, 'Polis und Hades in der Antigone des Sophokles'. (First published in
1936, in a Festschrift for Karl Barth's fiftieth birthday, it is reprinted in *Glauben und
Verstehen*, ii [Tübingen, 1952], and H. Diller [ed.], *Sophokles* [Darmstadt, 1967]).

power-crazed hypocrite. But his creed is 'reiner Diesseits-
glaube'—'pure immanence', 'a pure belief in worldliness'. He
fully recognizes the domain of death, but strives to include it
within the normative bounds of the body politic. The mortal
polemic is one between a secular, legalistic humanism on the
one hand, and the 'extraterritorial' agencies of Hades and Eros
on the other. But let there be no mistake: if Creon's end is one
of exemplary ruin, there is no transfiguration, no triumphant
release in that of Antigone. 'The might of death is the might of
darkness and of horror.'

In the classroom, shaking to the sound of Spartacist gunfire,
such interpretations carry no weight. In words which ring with
the notes of the National Socialist idiom to come, the head of
the class (*Primus*) brutally rejects Becker's views. What the
German nation needs, if it is to survive, are living men, in the
mould of Creon, not subversive ghosts.

Dr Conor Cruise O'Brien knows his Maurras. His own
perception of politics and of the theatre as closely related
structures in which the inherent ambiguities in human action
are played out has often looked to the relations of Creon and
Antigone. O'Brien's labyrinthine career as scholar, publicist,
educator, politician, can be fairly traced in respect of the
two Sophoclean personae. A much-discussed lecture, which
O'Brien gave in Belfast in October 1968, ponders the agony of
Ulster in terms of Antigone's challenge to Creon.[1] The act of
'non-violent civil disobedience' whereby Antigone sets out to
inter Polyneices breeds utmost violence: it brings on her own
suicide, Haemon's attempt to slay his father and his suicide,
the suicide of Eurydice, Creon's wife, and the devastation of
Creon's personal existence and political authority. 'A stiff
price', comments O'Brien, 'for that handful of dust on
Polyneices.' O'Brien, in whose temper both Burke's dis-
enchanted, stoic conservatism and Yeats's weakness for fatal
gestures are vividly at work, weighs Creon. If his decree is
'rash', so is disobedience to this decree. 'It was Antigone's free
decision, and that alone, which precipitated the tragedy.
Creon's responsibility was the more remote one of having
placed this tragic power in the hands of a headstrong child of

---

[1] This lecture is reprinted in the *Listener* (BBC Publications, London), October
1968. The text as included in *States of Ireland* (London, 1972) makes certain significant
omissions.

Oedipus.' This is, by all odds, an arresting gloss. Creon's 'remoteness' is, presumably, that of the 'state' which, in turn, takes on certain privileges of anonymity even where actual power is vested in the will and person of the prince. Antigone 'perpetually challenges and provokes' Creon. But Creon's obligatory 'remoteness' makes impossible and, one infers, undesirable any immediacy or hurried flexibility of response. 'Without Antigone, we could attain a quieter, more realistic world. The Creons might respect one another's spheres of influence if the instability of idealism were to cease to present inside their own dominions, a threat to law and order.' Conor Cruise O'Brien will continue to rethink this ominous equivocation in the light of the terror in Northern Ireland. Predictably, he will come to look more and more to Ismene. Is it not Ismene's 'commonsense and feeling for the living' which hold out what hopes there are in situations of irreconcilable obsession? Yet in no subsequent analysis has O'Brien denied his conception of Creon as a 'more than individual' and institutionalized being whose conduct is both justified and handicapped by constraints beyond those of common morality.

These constraints are teased out in a poem which O'Brien may well have known: Donald Davie's 'Creon's Mouse'.[1] 'When once that dangerous girl was put away', Creon reverts to a natural timorousness and even self-loathing. His fearsome collision with the clan of Oedipus has brought on 'A self-induced and stubborn loss of nerve'. The execution of Antigone and its attendant horrors have made Creon wary of volition. Looking back, he senses that 'He might have managed to amend' both Antigone's unbending will and his own. Now Creon is 'humble'. The mouse can scurry and nibble safely behind his wainscot.

Such tired charities do not extend to the portrayal of Creon in Henri Ghéon's *Œdipe*. Most probably written in 1938, 'Oedipus or the Twilight of the Gods' was not staged until 1951. The text represents a syncretic impulse which we have met before: Greek myths are re-enacted as if they were a secret prefiguration and even annunciation of the coming of Christ. The remarkable point is that Ghéon nevertheless dramatizes the Theban cycle in a manner which, in respect of incident and

[1] The poem is included in Donald Davie, *Brides of Reason* (London, 1955).

technique, remains Euripidean. The meditations on destiny throughout the play, the 'oratorio' of compassion, of reconciliation between the living and the dead at the finale, are instinct with Ghéon's Catholicism. But the drama itself remains a direct heir to the *Phoenician Women* and to the conception of Creon in Statius.

Long and bitterly widowed, Jocaste awaits the young hero who shall vanquish the Sphinx and claim her for his royal bride. Créon is a puritan ironist, whose political ambitions, whose readiness for power, are spurred on by what he genuinely senses to be the ancient swamp-fever in the House of Laius. He interprets the Sphinx as being a divine guardian of the city and a warning against Jocaste's indecent longings for a second marriage. Jocaste had been 'like a mother' to Créon in his childhood. He finds intolerable the pulsing mystique of her reawoken, matronly sensuality. Créon accuses Jocaste of having sent Laius on his fatal journey. He hints darkly at her motives: she could not forgive Laius the unwanted birth, the subsequent exposure on the naked mountains, of the enigmatic 'lost son'. Now, says Créon, she waits for a new husband 'young enough to be her son'. (The Freudian presence is tangential, but also unmistakable, in such versions as Ghéon's and Hofmannsthal's.)

Events take their dread course. When we see Créon again, he is master in the fratricidal, war-worn πόλιϲ. He now can accomplish the Cromwellian purpose which he declared at the outset: 'I have come into this house to drive out pollution, falsehood, sacrilege . . .' He has now 'picked up' the crown. Let Étéocle be buried with high civic honours; let Polynice be fed to the vultures. As in Euripides, but in a tonality which suggests the dawn-light of Christian *caritas*, Œdipe and Antigone oppose Créon's decree. Créon's solution is at once condescending and pragmatic: 'The gods are hard and men are hard. We shall be harder than they. The earth is hard. We shall break it open. That's a king's job (*C'est le métier d'un roi*).' But Œdipe can have the mangled bodies of his sons. Let Œdipe and Antigone bury them far away. Thus an accursed blood and lineage will no longer threaten Thebes.

'That's a king's job'—one suspects that Ghéon's formulation, and particularly the stress on *métier*, were known to Anouilh. This stress is, of course, the essence of his presentation and defence of Creon.[1] Anouilh's *Antigone* is too well known to require further discussion. I want to make only two points, because they are often overlooked.

In Anouilh's version, whose stagecraft, whose argumentative cunning, far exceed what is a fundamentally tawdry, reductive treatment of the Antigone theme, Créon *wins*. Of this there can be no real doubt. At the apex of the great debate, he discloses to Antigone that there is no way of distinguishing between the remains of Étéocle and of Polynice. Both cadavers have been trampled into obscene mud by the hoofs of the charging Argive cavalry. Having taken in this fact, Antigone puts her resolve into the past tense: it 'might *have been* better for her to have died, even in so absurd a cause'. 'Moi, je croyais'—'I believ*ed*'. Beaten, the girl says that she will now return to her room in the palace. This is exactly the solution demanded by Créon. No divine commandment, no ethical absolute, bids otherwise. Créon's insidiously paced dialectic has sapped the existential foundations of Antigone's action. The stage direction is graphic: Antigone 'moves like a sleep-walker'. But she has been jolted out of her puerile dreams of heroism and political impact.

Her decision, a few moments later, to defy Créon nevertheless, to bury what may be left of Polynice after all, has nothing to do with the substantive issues of the legend or of Sophocles' play. Antigone's second revolt springs from a more or less modish and contingent psychological twist. She is nauseated by Créon's avuncular, patronizing insistence on happiness, on the mundane routine which awaits her in married life. Antigone flinches hysterically from domestic bliss. She elects to die in virginal immediacy, unsullied by the unctuous compromises of bourgeois life. Nothing of this in any way weakens Créon's case against the 'hooligan' Polynice and against Antigone's 'absurd' rebellion.

The second point is this: in Sophocles, and throughout much of the tradition, Creon is left in hideous solitude. There is around him, at the end, nothing but familial devastation. He is abandoned to the aloneness of the beast. Not in Anouilh. The closing touch, derived, I would think, from a closely similar

---

[1] For a political apologia for Creon even more thoroughgoing than Anouilh's, cf. W. M. Calder III, 'Sophokles' Political Tragedy, *Antigone*', *Greek, Roman and Byzantine Studies*, ix (1968).

moment at the end of Montherlant's *La Reine morte*, is famous: a young page-boy enters. He reminds Créon that the ruling council is scheduled to meet at five o'clock. Créon gently teases the child. It is madness, he tells him, to want to grow up. 'One ought never to become an adult.' And the man to whom the chorus has just proclaimed his utter abandonment exits leaning on the shoulder of a young boy. Not only is Créon's punitive isolation broken, but the contact with childhood is, inevitably, suggestive of a larger re-entry into life. Might not this have been the trait, in a play eerily poised between the contrary commitments of its two protagonists and the politics which these commitments entail, which determined German acceptance of the text and of its staging?

The distance from Sophocles is subtle but definitive. We are on the way to that dour epilogue proposed by Dürrenmatt in his essay on 'Problems of the Theatre' in 1955. Today, it is 'Creon's secretaries who deal with the case of Antigone'.

8

The presences of Antigone–Creon in the arts and in argument, across languages and cultures, extend far beyond those I have touched on. All I have done is to select. As I said at the outset, no complete catalogue of the explicit and implicit lives of the Antigone theme, from its mythical, 'pre-epic' origins to the present, has been or can be drawn up. The field is too vast.

But even on strictly literary grounds, an inclusive survey would have to go far outside the texts I have cited.

It would examine the recurrent references to the Theban cycle among Alexandrian mythographers and grammarians such as Callimachus, and the interpretations of Antigone's destiny as these surface among such Byzantine scholiasts as Aristophanes. I have touched only in passing on Statius and omitted altogether any discussion of the confused but influential mythological material to be found in such collections of fables as the first-century AD 'Pseudo-Apollodorus'. I lack the competence required to deal with the obscure but vital problem of the transmission of Sophoclean texts and plot summaries by such Byzantine commentators as Eustathius of Salonika (in *c.*1200). N. G. Wilson's recent survey of the

Scholars of Byzantium (London, 1983) throws much light on this subject. But there continue to be gaps in even the best scholarship. Received wisdom has it that specifically literary works were excluded from the legacy of Greek thought and learning which Islam carried to the West. Is our evidence on this really conclusive? When the name 'Antigone' comes to light in medieval Europe, are we quite certain that some of its blurred resonances do not derive from contact with the Arab world?

I have only mentioned *Le Roman de Thèbes* and said nothing of the haunting invocation of the loveliness of Antigone in the late-twelfth-century 'Salute to his Lady' by the Provençal poet Arnaut de Mareuil. Antigone appears in Christine de Pisan's *Cent Histoyres de Troie* (late thirteenth century) and, of course, in chapters twenty-three and twenty-seven of Boccaccio's immensely influential and incessantly imitated *De claris mulieribus*. Nor have I done more than allude to Chaucer, in whose 'Knight's Tale' the women of Thebes denounce Creon, the tyrant, who 'for despit and for his tirannye' has fed the bodies of their slain husbands to the dogs 'To do the dede bodyes vileynye'. Once the actual text of Sophocles' play reaches Italy in 1423, once a printed version is made available in Venice in 1502, the history of the dissemination and forces of suggestion of *Antigone* becomes too manifold for any single scholar to master.

In Italy, the early history begins with Giovanni Rucellai's imitation of the *Antigone* plot in his *Rosamunda* (performed in 1516). It goes on to the full-scale dramatization of the Theban myths in Ludovico Dolce's *Giocasta* of 1554 and to Giovanni Paulo Trapolini's ornately allegoric *Antigone* of 1581. Via mimesis and translation, Italian models spread across Europe. First evoked by Chaucer, the story of Antigone and her doomed brothers reaches England in an adaptation of Euripides and Dolce: George Gascoygne's *Iocasta*, acted at Gray's Inn in 1566. We know of an early, unpublished French translation of Sophocles' *Antigone* by one Calvy de la Fontaine as early as 1542. Garnier's treatment proved so prestigious as to provide almost a new starting-point. Numerous 'Antigones' in northern Europe, and notably in Holland, were ramifications of *Antigone ou la piété*. Meanwhile, hybrid versions, out of Euripides, Seneca, Statius, and, gradually, Sophocles himself, were being written and produced in Portugal, Spain, Dalmatia.

I have all but neglected the prehistory of *Antigone* in Germany. There would be passages worth remembering in Hans Sachs's retelling of the tale during the 1550s and 1560s, in Martin Opitz's translation, and even in the bizarre, melodramatic narration of the fate of Antigone which Anton Ulrich, duke of Brunswick, introduced into his picaresque– historical fiction, *Die römische Octavia*, in 1677. The road to Hegel and Hölderlin was a long one.

Any attempt at a comprehensive register would need to include Thomas May's somewhat distant adaptation of Garnier, *The Tragedy of Antigone, the Theban Princesse*, published in London in 1631. It could not omit the *Antigone* of the Abbé Claude Boyer, produced in Paris in 1686 (under the pen-name of Pader d'Assézan). Consideration would extend as well to the close interactions between such 'Euripidean–Statian' 'Antigones' as those of 'Merindo Fasanio' (Fr. Benedetto Pasqualigo) and Fr. Gaetano Roccaforte on the one hand, and rococo music and choreography on the other. And could one really pass under silence, on grounds of its title alone, M. de la Tournelle's *Œdipe et toute sa famille* (Paris, 1731)?

I have referred frequently to Alfieri's *Antigone*. Its actual impact, however, fell far short of that obtained by Marco Coltellini, whose *Antigone* was set to music by Tommaso Traetta in 1767 and, as I have indicated, was sung from Madrid to St Petersburg. Though it was only published in 1921, Jean Reboul's *Antigone* of 1843–4 was much admired by Lamartine and remains noteworthy for its focus on a roman- tically exalted, solitary Creon. And if my linguistic competence extends to such texts as W. Frohne's compaction of the whole tragedy of the House of Laius into a single *Antigone* in 1833, to Louis Perroy's commemorative–patriotic *Antigone* of 1922, or to the German translation of the Swedish of Selma Lagerlöf's *Nils Holgersens* of 1906 (a folk-tale version of the Antigone– Polyneices motif), it fails altogether with respect to many other national traditions.

I can say nothing of Shigeishi Kure's *Antigone* (Tokyo, 1956, 1960), of successive Russian adaptations, beginning with that of I. Martinov in 1823–5. I lack access to *Antigone a tí druhí*, by the Slovak writer Peter Karvaš. Published in Bratislava in

1961, this play (by all accounts remarkable) is set in a concentration camp. Antigone is seen as one of a whole group of inmates who are seeking to organize resistance to the 'Creon'-Kommandant. Samizdat 'Antigones', perhaps comparable to the spirit of Karvaš's drama, have been circulated in Poland, Hungary, Romania.

The tide shows no sign of abating. As I write this paragraph, a fresh handling of Sophocles' *Antigone* reaches me from the theatre workshop of the Théâtre Populaire des Flandres. The manifesto which accompanies the script is eloquent: the mines in northern France are shutting down; men and women stand helpless against remote, arbitrary edicts; Antigone is the 'raw material of energy'; in her blazes the *combustible* of fundamental human outrage.

Only in the case of Hölderlin have I looked at those acts of transformative appropriation which we call 'translation'. But it is, naturally, through these acts that Antigone has conducted her several lives from Roman antiquity to W. B. Yeats. Any study aiming at completeness would have to establish the modes of grammatical and semantic transfer at work in Renaissance versions of Sophocles. It would, in particular, seek to analyse the more or less conscious but thoroughgoing Latinization of Sophocles and Euripides in sensibilities formed by Seneca or Statius. A sixteenth-century humanist such as Jean Lalamant translates *Antigone* into Latin and Latinized French virtually simultaneously (1558). It was one Dupuy's prose rendition of Sophocles' play in Pierre Brumoy's *Le Théâtre des Grecs* of 1730 which largely inspired eighteenth-century responses to the original both in France and in the German neo-classical movement. The distance which separates Gilbert Murray's translation of *Antigone* from the 'Antigones' proposed under pressure of Ezra Pound's vision and practice of translation is one of the radical moments in the history of the Antigone material itself. The music of meaning has altered.

I have not even attempted to do justice to the pathos and polemics which surround the figure of Antigone in the recent literature of feminism and 'women's liberation'.[1]

But, however central, texts are only a part of the story.

---

[1] For an incisive, caustic review of some of this literature cf. M. R. Lefkowitz, 'Princess Ida, the Amazons and a Women's College Curriculum', *Times Literary Supplement* (London), 27 November 1981.

Drama is born and reborn in performance. Each production of
Sophocles' *Antigone* since the first is a dynamic enactment of
understanding. The Antigones which throng the imagination
across more than two millennia are, in significant measure, the
creations and re-creations of actors, stage designers, and
producers. I have pointed to the Tieck–Mendelssohn staging
or to the famous presentations by Mounet-Sully at the Théâtre
Antique in Orange during the summer of 1894. No less
important to the genesis of intellectual interpretation and
imaginative embodiment are productions such as
Stanislavsky's (Moscow Art Theatre, 1899), the Living
Theatre performances of 1967, or Piet Drescher's *Antigone* as it
was staged in Leipzig in 1972.[1] Masaaki Kubo's open-air
production in Tokyo in 1959 is said to mark a date in the
complex unfolding of Japanese perceptions and transmutations
of western experience. I have said nothing of either the
'archaeological' or 'innovative' stagings of *Antigone* in classical
or modern Greek in Greece itself since the late nineteenth
century. This chapter alone deserves full study. Antigone's
return to native ground has repeatedly touched a central nerve
in Greek politics and in Greek conflicts of national identity.

I have alluded, but only superficially, to the fortunes of
Antigone and Creon in opera and ballet.

The iconography included in this book is only a small
sample.

Nevertheless, I hope that I have given a sufficient sense of
the dimensions of the Antigone theme to justify the question:
how can we read, how can we 'live' *Antigone* now? What kinds
of understanding are possible under the weight of the hermeneutic inheritance, of the sum of preceding commentary
and poetic–performative interpretation? If this problem is
rightly posed, it will, I think, allow an approach to the central
issue in this study. It will lead us to look again at the unique,
unmatched compulsion which Greek myths and personae
exercise on the roots of our being. It will make sharper the
challenge posed by the fact that no fictive–discursive construct
after ancient, perhaps after archaic, Hellas, not even

---

[1] Professor Hellmut Flashar of the University of Munich is currently engaged on a
full-scale study of productions and performances of ancient Greek drama in Germany
since the turn of the century. I am grateful to him for the material which he has put at
my disposal.

Shakespeare's, exhibits a comparable genius for renewal. Antigones past and present have proved beyond inventory. Already, there are so many gathering in the twilight of tomorrow.

CHAPTER THREE

I

To 'understand' a text in classical Greek, to 'understand' any
text in any language as formally and conceptually dense as is
Sophocles' *Antigone*, is to oscillate between poles of immediacy
and of inaccessibility. If we read well, if we make ourselves
answerable to the text intellectually, if we discipline our
sensibility to scrupulous attentiveness, if, in the final analysis,
we make of our reading an exercise of moral trust, rendering
our own risks of feeling concordant to those of the poet (though
on a more modest, secondary level), this oscillation will find
points of stability. It will, more or less consciously, come to rest
in a general sense of the shapes of meaning. It will align local
detail with the landscape, with the 'tonic' conventions of
the work as a whole. But such 'coming to rest' is always
provisional. It is a tensed, momentary poise between degrees of
established perception and the creative uncertainties, even
outright fallacies, which lead to re-vision—literally, to 'a new
sighting'.

Where it addresses itself to a text of the order of the *Antigone*,
'understanding' is, as we have seen, historically and presently
dynamic. It is a process of accord and dissent as between the
cumulative, selective authority of received opinion and the
challenge of individual supposition. Reading is never static.
Meaning is always mobile. It unfolds—though 'unfolding' is
too smooth, too programmatic a term—in the semantic space
mapped, we have seen, by grammarians and critics, by actors
and producers, by music and the visual arts as these 'set' or
image the play. With successive generations, the larger climate
of politics and of social style presses on every fibre of
interpretation. This pressure can alter the conditions and
ideals of understanding. In a marginal note to the *Athenaeum* of
the brothers Schlegel, which he set down in 1804, that master
reader, Coleridge, uses an apt simile. Between us and the
text runs 'a *draw-bridge* of communication'. The implication

is graphic. Such a bridge can be lifted. If it is, the text is made mute.

But can we hope to cross the drawbridge to Sophocles' *Antigone* without knowing classical Greek?

This question seems to me technically and psychologically more punishing than is often allowed. I have directed much of my work and personal life to the study and exposition of the history, of the poetics, of the philosophic–linguistic aspects of translation. The translator is the mail-man of human thought and sentiment. At every single node in time and place, the currents of energy in civilization are transmitted by translation, by the mimetic, adaptive, metamorphic interchange of discourse and codes. Without translation, our acts of spirit and of form would soon be made inert. No polyglot, however far-reaching his linguistic antennae, can touch on anything but a minute fraction of those languages in which have been thought, felt, expressed, the fundamentals and the dynamic variants which constitute literacy. Draw up even the most crassly reductive of 'basic book lists', include in it Homer and Scripture, Dante and the religious teachers of the Orient, Shakespeare and Goethe, Flaubert and Tolstoy—and such a primer of awareness will stand or fall by virtue or failure of translation. Translation *is* that drawbridge across which men after Babel have crossed into what Heidegger has called 'the house of their being'.

This is self-evident.

So is the truism that *no* translation is wholly commensurate with the original, that even in the greatest translation there are hair-line cracks where source and receiver interlock. This essential inadequacy is rooted in the genius of language itself. The genius of language, the existential and formal singularity of every speech-act, can, indeed, be most clearly defined by saying that no translation will be total, that none can transfer to another tongue the entire sum of implication, tonality, connotation, mimetic inflection, and inferred context which internalize and declare the meanings in meaning. Something will get lost or have been elided; something else will have been added by the impulse to paraphrase; subtle but decisive magnitudes will have altered scale; there will be transpositions from those 'key-patterns' and deep-buried cadences which, unrecapturable to analysis, make of each language, of the

speech-habits of each individual, a 'dialect', a more or less
circumscribed uniqueness in the spectrum of communication.
Speech, uttered or unspoken, is as intimate to the pulse of
man's being, is as much the live context of normal human
existence, as is breath. No man can reduplicate perfectly, can
substitute for, another man's breath. This, perhaps, is why
πνεῦμα and λόγος, 'the breath which inspires, which blows us
into being' and 'the word', are so closely meshed in theological
and metaphysical speculations on the essence of the human
person.

This, too, is evident.

I. A. Richards qualified the transfer of full meanings
between semantic codes, between different languages and the
ambience of association and inference in which languages
develop, as 'the most complex type of event yet produced in the
evolution of the cosmos'. Even at humbler levels, this 'event' is
always under twofold pressure. The vast majority of translations are bad. They are imprecise, sloppy, inflationary, short
on stylistic and conceptual competence, at ease in error.
'Through a glass darkly' (a phrase which, itself, poses arduous
problems for the translator) comes near to summarizing our
lifelong encounters with discourse and with texts in languages
which we, ourselves, do not know. But sheer inadequacy,
particularly where it exhibits itself to the listener or reader, is
not the most damaging. More falsifying is 'great' or 'high'
translation interposing its obscuring radiance and virtuosity
between ourselves and the original. Self-conscious translation
will transfigure its source, as do those orchestral transcriptions
of Bach through which the late nineteenth and earlier
twentieth centuries sought to enhance an ancient nakedness. It
will augment and adorn; it will deflect meaning into
'beauty'—'beauty', that is, as experienced and formulated by
the transposer and his contemporary aesthetic milieu. Witness
the marvels of reinvention, of modulating echo, of transformative mimesis, in Dryden's version of Horace, *Odes* III. 29—
one of the undoubted exercises of genius in the long history of
Horatian–European transmission.

The upshot of all this is banal but consequential. When we
read a translation, *whatever its quality*, we are reading the
translator. He can be the hack next door; he can be Hölderlin
or W. B. Yeats. The fact of second-handedness, of individual

and cultural *Ersatz* or synthetic surrogate, remains unalterable. Can one seriously approach Sophocles' *Antigone* on these
terms? Can one hope even to set foot on 'the drawbridge'
without knowing ancient Greek?

But what, in this context, does 'know' really signify? Let us
set aside (though one can never do so in actual practice) the
whole gamut of text problems, the lacunae, errors of transcription, editorial manipulations—some going back to Hellenistic
recensions—which render the literal status of an ancient Greek
drama always questionable. Let us abstract the isolation of
individual plays from the format of the relevant trilogy and
from the lost corpus of Aeschylus', Sophocles', and Euripides'
production. Constraining as they are, these handicaps of loss
and uncertainty are only external. The heart of the difficulty is,
of course, the fact of language. No man after Alexandria has had
direct personal access to Aeschylean or Sophoclean Greek. No
generation speaks precisely the same speech as its predecessors,
except by virtue of willed archaism. With time, the immediacies of identification and implicit reference recede from
the subconscious. They become, inevitably, an object of
deliberate retrieval, of conservation, of interpretation. Modern
scholarship is millennially distant from the text. Even
those who 'know' classical Greek best stand at the present
end of a tunnel through time which is loud with interference,
with false echo and distortion. No man can learn to *speak*
ancient Greek in any customary or meaningful sense of the
term.

Thus, even the masters of classical philology and textual
criticism, an Eduard Fraenkel, an Edgar Lobel, a Rudolf
Pfeiffer, thus, even those whose linguistic–archaeological tact
allows brilliant feats of emendation and recapture, possess a
'knowledge' of Periclean Greek incomparably thinner, incomparably more contrived, than that of the most uncouth natural
speaker in the Athens of Sophocles. The life of resonance, the
vital shorthand of the implicit and the self-evident, the codes of
intonation, of inflectional stress or understatement, as between
social classes, age-groups, genders—all that surrounds individual words and phrases in a living spoken tongue with
exact or diffuse values, is very nearly as lost to the scholar as it
is to the layman. Ruskin notes cheerily in his *Praeterita* that a
mere glance at what were taken to be Anacreon's odes proved

to him 'that the Greeks liked doves, swallows, and roses just as well as I did'. Quantitatively this might be so, albeit that writers of odes need not be the soundest witnesses to their society. But with regard to psychological tenor, to usages of sensibility, to expressive modes, ancient Attic 'likings' may well have differed radically from those of the Victorians. In certain pointed cases—attitudes towards and perceptions of erotic relations, slavery, the concept of determining fate, the readings of illness—we can arrive at some rough sense of such difference. Where the material is primarily literary, where it is deceptive precisely through its immediacy of appeal, traps abound. The roses of Anacreon are *not* those of a nineteenth-century European Christian who, consciously or not, has internalized the symbolic role and values assigned to the flower by the iconographers, troubadours, and theologians of the twelfth century.

Philological authority is no talisman. The great scholar does read with manifest responsibility. Someone whose Greek is (like mine) lame and derivative, someone who can approach Sophocles *only* in translation, leans heavily and thankfully on the scholar's verdict and supposition. But the difficulty is this: the mental set, the equipment of awareness and feeling of classical scholars, grammarians, editors are, in themselves, highly specialized and incisively reductive agents. They narrow in depth. They bring to the elucidation of the poet a more or less conscious bias towards the lexical norm and the rationale of a canonic syntax—though such a norm and rationale may be of their own devising. Housman deemed the combination in the same individual of philological rigour and literary finesse to be even rarer than poetic genius. Yet linguistic determination and literary judgement can never be separated. Housman's own perception of 'the lofty character of Creon', to which I have already referred, stems from, bears upon, his subjective emendation of the second word in *Antigone*, line 746. The letter does not necessarily determine or deny the spirit. But in the scholar-editor it generates a particular sort of 'spirit', a particular sort of 'truth-value'. In consequence, there are celebrated editions of, commentaries on, Greek tragedy either devoid of a sense of poetry and of theatre or arbitrary in their treatment. Knowledge becomes 'knowing', in the slippery sense of the term.

Hence the perennial, insoluble conflict between the qualified classicist and the literary critic or poet-translator (who may, scandalously, have no personal competence in the language of the original). Hence the unsettling, but also bracing, paradox of such intuitive seizures of unmastered material as Pound's *Cathay*, which Chinese readers and scholars find truer to the source than any versions by qualified western sinologists.

Finally there is this: the most learned classical scholar and the layman with his fallible translation are *both* the products of a massive history of inheritance. They come long after. Whether or not they are explicitly aware of the fact, the aggregate of preceding editorship, exegesis, staging, and criticism presses upon their own understanding. There is a distinction, certainly, which needs to be drawn between the legacy of scholarship and the heritage of criticism. There is in the textual-exegetic process a cumulative and collaborative advance. Some errors get cleared up; better manuscripts may be discovered. Criticism is, on the other hand, an essentially synchronic, self-subverting enterprise in which Plato's negation of the poets, Aristotle's catharsis simile, and John Jones's emphasis on the economics of the House of Atreus, are, in some respects, contemporary with each other. But in both the scholarly and the critical spheres the past is an active embodiment within current judgement. It is, organically, at work in each act of new insight. As it comes to us from Sophocles' *Antigone*, 'meaning' is bent out of its original shape just as starlight is bent when it reaches us across time and via successive gravitational fields. It is the creative as well as the obscuring aspects of this distortion, it is the effects such distortion has on reading Sophocles now, which are the theme of this study.

Every element of the challenge is merciless in the first line of *Antigone*.

2

The masked male actor who impersonates Antigone addresses the masked male actor who impersonates Ismene. He does so in verse whose metrical units, based on syllabic lengths, are

underwritten by a complex system of tonal values. A dactylic
hexameter is far more than a metrical convention. It reaches
back into the particular expressive world of the epic. Homeric
resonances give to the discourse of Greek tragic drama much of
its monumental impetus. In turn, the dactylic hexameter is
sometimes under pressure from a more 'demythologized' and
even prosaic idiom—a pressure registered in Aristophanes'
satire on tragic rhetoric. The actual metrics of the lines spoken
in the prologue to Sophocles' *Antigone* (lines 1–99) are
accessible to us; but not the relation of these lines and of their
pattern of pitch and stress to any musical material in the
presentation of the play. All that remains to us are the words in
fifth-century Attic Greek whose transcription by contemporary
or later scribes, notably in lines 2–5, already seemed suspect to
Byzantine scholiasts. *Totus locus vexatus* is the grim finding of a
recent editor.[1]

Context and subsequent reference make clear that the
two personae are meeting in front of the royal palace at
Thebes. Their encounter takes place before daybreak. This is
vital in the general symbolism and taut management of the
play. After the Renaissance, our curtained stages in the West
will simulate dawn. In the theatre of Dionysus, the hour, the
meaningful temporalities of action, must be read out of the
words of the play. There is no half-light on the scene or on the
acting platform; only the white brilliance and knife-edge
shadows of an Attic noon. Inevitably, the fictive moment—the
uncertain end of a harrowed night—must have played against
the absolute sunlight in which 'Antigone' and 'Ismene' first

[1] The reader who, in respect of *Antigone*, seeks 'the art of reading slowly' (an
expression coined by the Russian critic Mikhail Gerschenson) will want to avail
himself of the following: editions of the play by R. C. Jebb (3rd edn., Amsterdam,
1962); A. C. Pearson (first published in 1924, and reprinted by Oxford University
Press, 1955); R. D. Dawe (Leipzig, 1979). He will want to consult F. Ellendt, *Lexicon
Sophocleum*, revised by H. Genthe (Olms, 1958). All serious editions deal with textual
problems. The most recent collation is that of R. D. Dawe in *Studies on the Text of
Sophocles* (Leiden, 1978), 99–120. Commentaries, on the play in general as well as on
points of detail, are, as we have seen, numerous. I have found the following of
particular help: G. Müller, *Sophokles. Antigone* (Heidelberg, 1967); J. V. O'Brien, *Guide
to Sophocles' Antigone* (Southern Illinois University Press, 1978); J. C. Kamerbeek, *The
Plays of Sophocles. Commentaries*, Part III. *The Antigone* (Leiden, 1978). Seth Benardete's
three-part 'A Reading of Sophocles' *Antigone*', *Interpretation: A Journal of Political
Philosophy*, iv. 3, v. 1, v. 2 (1975), is stimulating and invites fruitful disagreement. I
have already cited, throughout this study, the discussions of the play by Karl
Reinhardt, R. P. Winnington-Ingram, H. D. F. Kitto, Hugh Lloyd-Jones, C. H.
Whitman, and Charles Segal.

appear. The inherent 'distancings', the demands made upon
the transformative sensibilities of the vast audience, the extent
to which familiarity with the relevant myth or other scenic
variants thereof helped the spectator to meet these demands,
are factors largely unrecapturable for us.

The opening line consists of five words of which two, 'O' and
'Ismene', are straightforward. The other three have been the
object of voluminous exegesis. The semi-darkness in which they
are spoken seems to cling to them. Literally—and 'literally'
always begs the question—we read *something* like this: 'O my
very own sister's shared, common head of Ismene.' Hölderlin,
as we saw, transposes unflinchingly. He acquiesces in the clotted
strangeness of Antigone's summons, producing a verse ominously near to Housman's parody of the Greek tragic mode.
The textual critic, the scholar-interpreter, the ordinary reader
or spectator, gropes. κοινόν is a seminal term in the history of
language, of religious thought and institution, of anthropology.
A fertile duplicity inhabits the word. It signifies 'common' in
the sense of 'ordinary', 'general', 'widely diffused' (as in κοινή,
meaning 'common speech' or 'vulgate'). It also means 'related
by blood', 'generically bound'. It is a crucial paradox or
duality of the human condition that kinship is, in one respect,
the most universal, ordinary of biological–social facts, yet in
another the most irreducibly singular and individually specific.
In the mouth of Antigone, as Kierkegaard sensed, κοινόν is
fatally charged.

Originally, and the concept of 'origins' is itself in part a
mythical one, much of mythology may have been a compelling
formulation of the uncertainties, of the atavistic embarrassments attached to the sources of kinship and of familial
organization via incest. Antigone and Ismene are the sisters
and children of Oedipus. This dark knot links them with the
monstrous necessities of human origins (whom but their sisters
could Cain and Abel wed?). But this anarchic commonalty, in
its turn an enormity, cuts them off from the accepted norms of
evolved mankind. Within the context of the myth, their kinship
is an outrage. It is precisely this, however, which knits them
close as no other sisters are knit, which makes them 'common to
one another' and, as it were, fused (the which fusion distinguishes them, fascinatingly, from the very similar pairing of
Electra and Chrysothemis in Sophocles' drama). The pendulum

motion of meaning in Antigone's κοινόν is truly dialectical. It modulates from intimations of primordial indistinction and 'con-fusions' of consanguinity to a singularity of social apartness so drastic that it makes of Oedipus' two sister-daughters a single, a 'common', being.

'Of the earth earthy', says Charles Lamb, seeking to make palpable a certain Shakespearean touch. 'Of sisterhood, of sorority sisterly' might, as Goethe felt, come in range of αὐτάδελφον. Ismene's existence on this Theban doomsday is that of being her sister's sister. This attribute is both the sum and summoning of her identity so far as this identity can still be perceived and realized existentially. Again, Antigone's 'provocation', for every syllable in this opening speech is simultaneously a calling and a challenge, aims at the unique scandal and sanctification of kinship in the lineage of Oedipus. Antigone and Ismene are daughters of Oedipus and Jocasta. They are, at the same time, Jocasta's granddaughters. Equally they are sisters to the son of Laius. This triple bond makes the fastness of their sorority matchless. 'Most sisterly of souls' was Goethe's paraphrase. Joined to κοινόν, αὐτάδελφον renders the blood-relation of Antigone and Ismene concretely hyperbolic.

That Ἰσμήνης κάρα has the literal meaning 'head of Ismene' is inescapable. This meaning can be attenuated to that of a periphrasis: 'identity of Ismene', 'essence, spirit of Ismene' (we speak of 'heads of state' in reference to persons). Or it can be allowed its vehement anomaly. Both physically and metonymically, the head of an individual is taken to incarnate his or her individuality. In the shadow-light before dawn, Antigone recognizes Ismene by the shape or bent of her head. To claim this head as being 'common to us both' and as 'shared in the totality of sisterhood', is to negate, radically, the most potent, the most obvious differentiation between human presences. As one commentator puts it: Ismene's head is made 'nothing but a sister's'.[1] In its imperious awkwardness, in its stylized carnality which is at once Aeschylean (αὐτάδελφος will be found in both the *Seven Against Thebes* and the *Eumenides*) and older than Aeschylus, Antigone's prolusion strives to compact, to 'ingest', Ismene into herself. She demands a 'single-headed' unison. In twilight, shadows melt into a compounded mass. (Did the one masked head draw the other to him/her?)

[1] S. Benardete, 'A Reading of Sophocles' *Antigone*, I', p. 148.

This little we can assert with mild confidence. Line 1 of Sophocles' *Antigone* does not, at least, provide the sort of lexical and grammatical tribulations which, in reference to lines 2 and 3, reduce a recent annotator to declare: 'I can see no solution, and write this note only to show that the difficulties of this notorious passage may be even greater than we had imagined.'[1]

But my remarks on Antigone's opening words only scratch the surface. The challenges to understanding, to the achievement of a past presentness which does not violate the integral autonomy of that past, are central and arduous. How are we to grasp the dynamics of inwoven reference, the pointers to social–psychological conventionality or debate, implicit in such a passage? Such grasp is shallow if it is merely archaeological. How may we best hear, from within the music and meanings in the original text, those insistences on human exposure, on the conflictual conditions of human experience, which have initiated and sustained incessant echo across the millennia? In other words, how are we to reach through this echo to the voice, while knowing that these are, at our linguistic–historical–psychological remove, inseparable? It is the absolutely synchronic strangeness and presence in the source, in the original, often irretrievable, play of meanings, which compel and elude adequate response.

The provocation to Ismene, but also to us, turns on the contradictions between the dignities and liberal values of individuation, on the one hand, and the more archaic but perennially recursive ideals and reflexes of community on the other. In the Sophoclean text, this conflict—or, more precisely, the indeterminacies of feeling and of expression which it engenders—finds an exact syntactic form. When Antigone invokes the afflictions which Zeus is unleashing and will unleash upon 'us both', she uses the dual. This is a grammatical marker, in common colloquial use, as we know from Aristophanes, for the endings of those verbs, nouns, and adjectives used only where *two* subjects are acting, are being designated, or are being qualified. We are unable to reproduce this particular linguistic instrument. It is, nevertheless, pivotal. After Ismene's initial refusal to help bury Polyneices, Antigone will not again resort to any dual forms. In the opening lines,

[1] R. D. Dawe, *Studies on the Text of Sophocles*, p. 99.

furthermore, her uses of the dual seem to extend beyond the manifest pairing Antigone–Ismene. The immediate context, referring as it does to the hideous inheritance of sorrows bequeathed by Oedipus to his children, vividly suggests that the two sisters, welded, as it were, into one resolute being, are coupled with that other oneness in simultaneous, reciprocally inflicted death which is constituted by Polyneices–Eteocles. Four doomed personae are, in a sense both spiritual and bodily, made two. This fusion to duality, with its concise enactment in Antigone's syntax, ominously but also ecstatically perpetuates the unspeakable cohesions of kinship in the House of Laius.

The *Hinterland* to Antigone's formulation, the genetic–social conflicts and indecisions which must have attended the very gradual evolution of western concepts of distinct individuality (the tenebrous aetiology of the ego), lie wholly beyond our reach. It is solely in the pathologies and metaphoric suggestions of autism on the one hand and of schizophrenia on the other that such primordial instabilities surface. Indeed, the mystique of familial bonding on which Antigone draws may have had resonances as lost to Periclean Athens and even to Sophocles himself as they are to us. Such temporal 'fade-outs' or 'close-ups' of perception are far subtler than any chronology. What matters is the evident truth that the exponential pressure of the Antigone theme on subsequent imaginings and the concentration, at once integral and insoluble, of these pressures in Sophocles' play, are such as to engage our sense of immediacy without losing the genius of their origins, without relinquishing, easily or altogether, their part of night.

Literally and figuratively, Antigone's writ to Ismene springs at her sister and at ourselves out of receding darkness. It queries, it indicts the new discretions of human privacy (that which is 'discrete' being also, by definition, 'separated' and 'fragmented'). It is Ismene who persistently puts forward the first person pronoun and the singular possessive. Polyneices is also '*my* brother' (ἐμόν). But it is just on this meagre singularity of brotherhood that Antigone brings to bear the ironic fury of her 'dualism'. If Polyneices is 'only' Ismene's brother, he is indeed yielded to the exile of dishonoured death and desecration. Polyneices is, he must be felt and seen to be, the brother whom Antigone and Ismene share in total symbiosis. The newer

syntax of egotism, of individual apartness, which is ours still,
cuts across the mysteries and claims of blood. Sensing but
failing to apprehend these mysteries, Lear will resort to the
obscuring term 'propinquity'. The grammar of Antigone lies
prior to our classifications. When, in lines 71 and 72, with their
vehement enjambment—'him I | Shall bury'—and their (rare)
sense-break after the verb, Antigone uses ἐγώ, the word is a
bitter concession. 'I' is now her marker of solitude, of that
enforced break with unisons of kinship, of familial or clannish
collectivity, which made possible, which necessitated, fusions
of feeling, of purpose, of action. Of these fusions, the Greek
tragic chorus may itself have been a late vestige.

Ismene's rejoinder, in line 90, is celebrated: 'you are
enamoured   of,   you   strive   after,   the   impossible'—
ἀμηχάνων ἐρᾶις. In the play, words built around the stem
μηχαν- (our 'mechanical') are used three times by the chorus,
with its often cautionary idiom, and three times by Ismene
herself. Once, the word is used by Creon (line 175). The
'mechanical' denotes that which pertains appropriately to the
range of productive mundanity. ἀμήχανος conveys notions of
unreality, of unmasterdness, of anarchic disorder. In line 90
the use of the term is intentionally spacious: it points in at least
two directions. On the plane of actuality, Antigone's plan to
bury Polyneices, by herself alone if need be, is a practical
impossibility. On a fundamental level, moreover, that which
is no longer possible, yet which Antigone uncompromisingly
demands, is the welding, the seamless meshing, of individuals—Antigone–Ismene,   Antigone–Ismene–Polyneices—
into an organic oneness. A 'mechanistic' reality is a reality of
Cartesian individual volitions and individual perceptions.
Two lines later, Ismene reiterates her charge: Antigone
'hunts after impossibilities' (τἀμήχανα). Her longing for lost,
nocturnal modes of total kinship has turned to the hunter's
destructive and self-destructive pursuit. As we know, from the
Oedipus Rex and *Electra*, such references to the chase are not,
in Sophocles, comforting.

Throughout the rest of the play, we can follow the
contrapuntal stress on mechanistic individuality on the one
hand, and on more ancient currents of generic and psychic
ecumenism on the other. The chorus oscillates uneasily
between both. In the magical fifth stasimon, the chorus sings

10. *Antigone* (film), 1961,
directed by George
Tsavellas. Antigone:
Irene Papas; Creon:
Manos Katrakis. (*Top
left*) The soldiers find
Antigone by the corpse.
(*Top right*) The
confrontation of
Antigone and Creon.
(*Bottom left*) Antigone
enters the cave/marriage
chamber. (*Bottom right*)
Creon with the body of
his son.

11. *Antigone*, ballet in one act, music by Mikis Theodorakis, choreography by John Cranko. First performed at Covent Garden, London, 1959. Antigone: Svetlana Beriosova; Creon: Michael Soames.

and 'dances itself' into a dithyrambic openness to the imminence of the god. Dionysus is like a bolt of pure energy which
welds into unison the dance of the stars and that of mortal men.
Much of the inexhaustible depth of the first stasimon, the 'Ode
on Man' as it is sometimes referred to, resides in the elusive,
anguished delicacy of the chorus's movements between motifs
of inspired, creative egotism—man's mastery over the possible,
his extension of possibility to the very limits of the material and
organic worlds—and motifs of homecoming to the concentric
circles of his πόλιϲ and of his hearth. The dialectically insoluble
quality of such homecoming stems from the fact that the hearth
is, by virtue of historical development, no longer that of a pre-
social or totemic collectivity, but is itself, in part at least, a
private institution guaranteed by civic ordinance.

Pleading out of the receding edge of night, striving to draw
Ismene's 'shared' head into her own being, Antigone comes as
close as 'modern' speech is able to a consciousness, to a
rearticulation, of those osmotic tides which can, at moments,
negate individuality, dissolve the first person singular, and let
human beings 'flow into one another'. (One recalls Keats's
witness to the entry of other human presences into his own
psychic and, indeed, corporeal self.) It is in a return to
darkness, to that night of the rock-tomb blacker even than the
night of fratricidal slaughter and retributive injustice which
immediately precedes the action of the drama, that Antigone
may find the primal collectivity, the in-gathering of her own
persona into the Oedipus–Polyneices–Eteocles triad, denied to
her in the daylit constraints of the possible. But Antigone is by
no means certain that death will not turn out to be a solitude, a
'discreteness' even sharper than that which she must endure
after Ismene's refusal to be 'one with her', to enact the
grammar of the dual. She, in whom palpable, if indefinable,
impulses towards human interfusion are so intense, is, by virtue
of Ismene's monitory realism and the ambivalences of the
chorus, made the most solitary, individual, anarchically
egotistical of agents. Therein lies the bottomless irony and
falsehood of Antigone's fate.

The wealth of Sophocles' questionings presses on us today.
The magnetism of the collective is unmistakable in our
fragmented societies. Beyond the erosion of formal religiosity,
beyond the shibboleth of 'alienation', one observes nascent

counter-currents of communal existence. Privacies, the nucleus
of the ego, are now under pressure of Utopian, of group-
therapeutic, of mystical nostalgias for symbiosis. The commune, the therapies of 'encounter', of bodily contact and
shared hallucination, are in part artificial but in part authentically atavistic endeavours to claw one's way out of the proud
prison of the self. We recognize in Antigone's attempt to
cradle, to interpenetrate with, 'Ismene's beloved head', as in
Henry Moore's drawings of the meshed, anonymous bodies
seeking each other's warmth and plural strength in the air-raid
shelters, an immensity of need. The sovereignties of individuality, as they are proclaimed by the Renaissance, by
Cartesian methodology, by Puritan and liberal personalism,
seem to many to have left men naked. Great art, music above
all, can set off within each of us those oscillations between self-
consciousness on the one hand and subterranean intimations of
a negation or a transcendence of the 'I' on the other. Primal
collectivities seem to flow towards us out of the fount of dreams
(blurred as they are, Jung's readings of the choral nature of
art and of myth are far more persuasive than Freud's). It is
the pulsing exploration of the 'dual mode'—grammatical,
spiritual, psychological—which, as I have suggested earlier,
makes of the Ulrich–Agathe chapters in Musil's *Man Without
Qualities* the finest 'translation of' and commentary on the first
line of *Antigone* available to us. In both, the voices of blood-
kinship emerge from and seek a homecoming to the solac-
ing indeterminacies of night.

Virtually every line in the play invites reflections and
provisional elucidations of this sort. Commentary is always
latent with unendingness. The breeding of exegesis out of
previous exegesis is menacing in so far as it occludes the
primary text. The proliferation of interpretation threatens to
bury the poem. Yet it is via the hermeneutic process of better
understanding that the text is ensured survivance. I see no
ready way out of this contradiction. Very likely, one ought to
distinguish between categories of essentially textual–critical
analyses (themselves discursive and parasitical) and those
means of 'commentary in action' represented by translation,
stage-production, musical setting, and graphic illustration. But
as I have argued throughout, a translation of *Antigone* by
Hölderlin or Yeats, a setting to music of this or that part or of

the whole of the play by Mendelssohn or Orff, a radically
penetrative staging, be it by Tieck or Meyerhold, are,
inevitably, metamorphic acts of interpretation. They are often
as illuminating as any but the rarest of philological–critical
glosses. Yet these glosses, also, must be attempted in every
generation and context of sensibility, if only to make their
inadequacies fruitful, to fall short in ways which clarify.

Let us stand in the way of other passages.

3

Lines 198–206 seem to call for only trivial emendations. Our
reading, moreover, is more or less ensured by the fact that the
lines are quoted in a parody from antiquity. Together, these
eight verses make up a single overwhelming sentence. Its
construction is reiterative (anaphoric), and Creon's meaning is
plain as a hammer. He addresses his fury to 'that Polyneices'.
Already the syntax dehumanizes. Creon hurls a triple accusation. The 'banished' Polyneices, which epithet makes of his
mere return a gravy felony, had come back to Thebes to 'put
to the torch', to ravage, the land of his father and of his father's
deities. Polyneices had come αἵματος . . . πάcαcθαι, 'to drink,
to feed upon, kindred blood'. Thirdly, says Creon, it had been
Polyneices' resolve to lead the surviving Thebans into slavery,
to annihilate the civic status of his own countrymen.

This is the fratricidal, traitorous, and tyrannical ruffian who
is to be left unburied, carrion for birds and dogs. Subsequently,
in lines 286–7, Creon elaborates on the first charge. Polyneices
purposed to burn, to lay waste, the temples of the gods and the
divine laws. In this passage the grammar is so densely woven
that we can, that we are meant to, equate those 'votive
offerings' which Polyneices will destroy when he puts the
temples to the torch with the laws themselves. For are such
laws not, in turn, 'divine gifts'? Creon's challenge is massive: is
it not blasphemy against piety as well as against ordinary
human good sense to afford the bestial slayer and rebel
Polyneices the same rites of sepulchre as those which are to
be bestowed on Eteocles, the valorous (ἀριcτεύcαc, ἀρίcτοιc)
defender of a πόλιc of which he was the legitimate ruler?

The questions pressed upon us are these: are we to believe
Creon's indictment? At what levels of meaning are we to

interpret the three accusations? If we do believe Creon, this does not, to be sure, signify that we need concur in the edict against Polyneices' remains. The open ground for moral debate, the extraterritorialities of mercy, lie precisely between premiss and consequence. Nevertheless, Creon's claims cannot be evaded. They will exact diverse degrees of acquiescence or denial.

Mazon is unequivocal: Creon's speech is not only inspired rhetoric but manifests 'une conviction sincère'. Other exegetes see in Creon's formulations of Polyneices' alleged intentions nothing more than tactical cunning and a mendacious, secretly uneasy endeavour to rally chorus and citizenry to a despotic cause. Yet others argue with more finesse. Creon's violent sententiousness cannot be dismissed as mere rhetoric or falsehood. Per se his words are true. But he fatally perverts their ethical and pragmatic application. By acting against Polyneices as Polyneices would, according to Creon's own findings, have acted against his kindred and the city, Creon sets in motion the fatal automatism of hatred and self-ruin.[1] This may or may not be so. One asks still: 'Is Creon giving a just account of Polyneices' purpose?' Did Sophocles want us to believe what Creon propounds, be it merely in terms of the equilibrium and economies of the play?

As it happens, such questions of intentionality are at the very heart of current critical–hermeneutic theory. We are no longer allowed an innocent acceptance of auctoritas, of an author's privileged determination of the meanings, open and covert, in his text. Nor is the advance into sophistication made by the Henry Jamesian strategy of shifting narrative 'points of view' felt to be adequate. It is not enough to say: 'This is how Creon sees it; the words are, finally, his.' The new semantics of deconstruction turn wholly to the text itself; as if it was an autonomous play of grammatological and epistemological impulses open to, soliciting, a boundless counter-play of possible interpretations. Such schools of reading and reception would rule out the 'simplistic' query: 'Did Creon mean what he says, and was it true of Polyneices?'

Most instructively, a work such as Sophocles' Antigone seems

[1] Paul Mazon's readings of Creon can be related to that constant debate about and revaluation of the personage which, as we have seen in the previous chapter, is characteristic of modern feeling in French scholarship and literature.

to rebuke the playful pretensions of deconstruction. The modish axiom of 'pure textuality' is naïve in the face of a composite of mask, music, choreography, and complexly stylized elocution. The linguistic text of a Greek tragedy is not an object set apart. It is only one of the relevant means of emotive–informative executive forms. But a second reason for rejecting deconstructive facilities is inherent in Greek dramatic practice itself. The swift, delicately calibrated shifts of interpretation, the ironies and provisionalities of understanding and of decoding, which are the aim of later-twentieth-century theories of reading, are already, as we have seen, dynamic in the chorus. No outside response is more flexible, no external interpretation of what the protagonists say is more supple and self-subverting, than are the 'hearings' and counter-statements of the chorus. It is the chorus in Greek tragedy which, from text-moment to text-moment, 'deconstructs' and recomposes the intentionalities of dramatic rhetoric, which places and displaces the meanings of meaning.

Therefore, the question we must learn to pose precisely is this: 'In what key does Creon speak at this particular point, to what family of possible truths does the idiom, the cadence, of his accusations against Polyneices refer the listening chorus (and that greater 'chorus' which is made up of the audience in the theatre of Dionysus and, thereafter, of ourselves)?' The 'truth-values' of Creon's charge lie in the specific totality— phonetic, syntactic, possibly gestural—of his eloquence. Can we make our hearing sufficiently acute?

The scholars are of direct help. Creon's register throughout, and most saliently at this point, is that of the epic. There are distinct analogues to Homer in Creon's phraseology. The criminal aims attributed to Polyneices are stated almost formulaically, and with the archaic violence appropriate to epic (perhaps 'primitive') evil. This is especially so of the expression 'to feed upon, to drink kindred blood'. It is possible that this grim tag echoes not the Homeric epics so much as it does the language-world of the lost Theban epic cycle. But undoubtedly Creon's style throughout lines 198–206, and the system of recognitions and response which this style articulates, reach back to the *Iliad* and to the immediacies of the *Iliad* in such dramas as Aeschylus' *Seven Against Thebes*. Creon's register and its context are, very precisely, those of war.

It is not easy for us to gauge the role of war in the development of Greek civilization. Hellas derived much of its sense of identity from the *Iliad*. The language(s) of classical Greece, the codes of rhetoric and public conduct, the literary genres, are inseparable from the Homeric precedent. A great war-epic gives to ancient Greece its sense of heroic beginnings. The Persian wars, in turn, bring on a brief but psychologically momentous experience of strategic and ethnic community. Out of the Peloponnesian wars, Thucydides draws the classic concept, which is, very largely, ours still, of history and historicity. The catastrophe consequent on the Peloponnesian wars is a constant undercurrent in the later plays of Sophocles and Euripides. When Heraclitus professed (fr. A 53 Diels–Kranz) that warfare, πόλεμος, 'is the father and ruler of all things', when he said that it was war 'which makes deities of some and men of others, which makes some men slaves and others free', he was giving cosmological totality to a commonplace. The pre-Socratic images of the coming into being of the world are frequently expressive of elemental combat. Greek philosophical argument, the exposition of law and of politics, the dialectical techniques of intellectual and poetic encounter (the 'stichomythia' as used in drama), are 'agonistic'. Like no other body of thought and sentiment before Hegel's, that of ancient Greece reflects and communicates man's experience in conflictual, bellicose terms.

Medieval and Renaissance treatments of the 'matter of Thebes' locate the fortunes of Antigone squarely within the framework of war and of the politics of war. So do Hasenclever and Brecht in their 'Antigones'. War and enemy occupation are the defining context in Anouilh. We look for that framework to Aeschylus' *Seven Against Thebes* rather than to Sophocles. Yet it is overwhelmingly, if concisely, present in our play.

The first choral song or parodos (lines 100–54) has always been admired for the virtuosity of its anapaestic sections, for the wild brilliance of the agonistic clashes of light and dark, of colour and shade, which it evokes. Whereas Antigone's voice aches out of night, private and desolate, the chorus surges towards daybreak in loud ecstasy. Sophocles seems to echo Pindar's mythopoeic but also tactile sense of a kinship between the sacred circularity of a πόλις, within its rescued ramparts,

and the white sphere of the divine sun. Sophocles takes over
from Aeschylus and, doubtless, from the epic repertoire which
is the common font of tragedy the motif of the fierce radiance of
the sun as it is reflected by the blanched shields and weapons of
the doomed Argives. Commentators draw attention to the
Sophoclean use, in this parodos, of emblematic, perhaps
originally totemic, touches such as they were developed in the
almost ritual art of the *Seven Against Thebes*. Although editors
know there to be a lacuna at line 112, the central thematic
motion is pellucid. Polyneices, the mercenary host, or both,
had flown over Thebes like an eagle, screaming as it plunges to
seize its prey. But Cadmus' dragon has routed the winged
attacker. Phonetically, metrically, in its skein of imagery—the
white sun burning off the retreating darkness, the hot light of
the torches which were to incinerate Thebes, the white Argive
shields, the white-plumed eagle screaming against the light—
the choral song is a marvel of closely mimed battle.

But the choral song in no way disguises the realities of war.
Zeus and the sun have rescued the πόλιϲ from savage
onslaught, destruction, and enslavement. The god to whom
victory and the trophies of victory are due is Zeus τροπαῖοϲ—
literally, 'the causer of rout'. And these trophies are the
brazen, heraldic panoplies of the slain champions. Ares, god of
war, is, at one point in the ode, the personification (though this
term is too abstract to convey the hybrid complexity and terror
of the original) of the clamour of battle. At another point, Ares
is at once the trace-horse, spearman, and charioteer tearing
through the enemy host. A play which is 'about' the fate of two
corpses on a battlefield springs into lyric life with an evocation
of total war—'total' in precisely the Homeric and the
Heraclitean sense. It engages gods and mortals, the duel of
light and of dark, the blank fury of animals at each other's
throats. In the closing antistrophe, the chorus ascribes to the
persona of Victory an 'immensity of splendour' commensurate
with that of Zeus and of the sun itself. Yet in a sudden
('deconstructive') impulse, the elders of Thebes appear to
flinch from this hyperbole: 'Yesterday's wars are now done; let
us achieve forgetting.' At this exact moment, however, Creon
enters.

A number of editors and producers envision him advancing
in armour, immediate from combat. Others would have him

garbed in his newly donned royal robes; and the chorus does point to him as βασιλεύς, 'king'. The costume is, surely, immaterial. The point is that Creon enters with the winds of war at his back. It is to the carnage of the preceding day and night that he owes his sovereignty over the delivered city. The Argive aggressors are, as it were, still on the horizon. Creon's oration (rhesis), with its metallic grandiloquence and self-aggrandisement, with its striking alternance of static sententiousness and peremptory ordinance, has behind it and pulses with the tumult and sudden, uncanny cessation of hand-to-hand combat. The effects are analogous to those achieved in *Coriolanus*, I. ix. 41–6:

> May these same instruments, which you profane,
> Never sound more: when drums and trumpets shall
> I' the field prove flatterers, let courts and cities be
> Made all of false-fac'd soothing:
> When steel grows soft, as the parasite's silk,
> Let him be made an overture for the warres. . . .

Both Sophocles and Shakespeare show grammar stiffened, monumentalized, and intonation pitched to stentorian brutality, under stress of physical combat and abrupt release. Creon's account of Polyneices' purpose is convincingly that which a man must picture to himself and proclaim unreservedly to his followers if he is to hurl himself into mortal battle. Like the eagle simile in the choral ode, Creon's assertions are a 'war-truth'. They bespeak the fierce twist of the world and its natural nuances in times of battle. Sophocles was himself acquainted with warfare and command. Like Thucydides, he knew of the conscription and arming of language towards necessary hatreds. These hatreds, the concept of discourse as a hand-to-hand and spirit-to-spirit ἀγών, will reach far into the play. Antigone will refuse 'the truths of war'. More exactly, she will seek to circumscribe them narrowly. Her ethic, with its obvious note of femininity, is fundamentally anti-Heraclitean. To her, πόλεμος is neither father nor regent of human relations. Battle is a contingent disaster within a much larger and abiding fabric of kinship and transcendent fidelity. The utter gap between Creon's idiom and Antigone's is that which Shakespeare contracts into the double-edged pathos of Coriolanus' salutation to Volumnia:

'My gracious silence, hail.' In the face of Creon's 'war-truths' and of what they logically entail, Antigone cannot be mute. But observe Sophocles' equity: no one in the play seeks to refute Creon's bitter charge against Polyneices. Creon's Polyneices is what Creon declares him to be.

4

The conventions whereby the preternatural is met with and recounted take us to the heart of a culture and its poetics. Greek attitudes to the irrational have been studied magisterially. What we know very little about, however, are the orders of 'suspended disbelief', of selective credulity, operative in the audience at the dramatic festivals of Dionysus. The problem is more specific than that, so often debated, of the extent and precision of the knowledge of mythology which the Greek tragic playwright could expect from his public. What one would want is some clear notion of the levels of acceptance of the spectators with regard to the 'divine', to the daemonic, and, in general, to the domain of the supernatural. As we know, this domain is significant in many extant plays and, presumably, throughout the classic tragic repertoire.

It is difficult to imagine the art of Aeschylus, Sophocles, and Euripides, as we know it, without its resort, at once spectacular and oblique, manifest and inferred, to oracular voices, to 'ghosts', such as that of Darius in the *Persians*, to miraculous substitutions—Iphigenia in Tauris, Helen in Egypt—to godly apparitions and epiphanies of varying degrees of directness (ranging, say, from the full presence of gods on stage in plays such as *Prometheus* or the *Eumenides*, to the almost imperceptible hint of a divine voice sounding through the lips of otherwise mute Pylades in *Choephoroe*). Certain insistent tonalities and plot constructions in Euripidean drama have been interpreted as strategies of ironic literalism, as rationalistic subversions of a mythological inheritance and apparatus too concretely invoked. But whether or not such an interpretation is valid, the question remains that of the response of the fifth-century audience to the authenticity of enacted or narrated supernatural encounters where these play a vital role in drama, notably in Aeschylus and in Sophocles. To what degree was such material privileged precisely because of the archaic status and indeterminacies of its distant origins? To what extent was the 'miraculous', if this concept applies at all, metaphorized so as to take on essentially psychological values? Moreover, even where such modulations occur, as in the *Bacchae*, a primordial force of naked terror persists. One would dearly wish to know how many men and women, in the noon-light of the theatre, chose to interpret Prometheus' thunderous plunge into the abyss or Heracles' wrestling bout with Death as aesthetic fictions. We do know how urgently the ambiguous relations between revealed religious beliefs or inherited rites on the one hand and their presentment in poetry and drama on the other exercised Plato's moral politics. The several treatments of this relation in the *Ion*, the *Republic*, and the *Laws* suggest that the dilemma had lost none of its acuteness even after the close of the major phase in the Greek tragic theatre. But the rest is, very largely, conjecture.

The supernatural possibility is incised in myths, in those eroded or shadow-myths which underwrite our metaphors and, if my hypothesis is right, in certain non-pragmatic, poetic features of grammar itself—features which correspond, at depths perhaps unrecapturable to formal analysis, to the meetings of sensibility and sense with categories of experience, with phenomenological constructs, 'outside' or tangential to the empirical order. Masters of poetic discourse can bring to the light of articulate speech the solicitations of the uncanny, of the extra-sensory, of the hallucinatory and hypnotic, as these are embedded in and integral to the tenebrous growth of human perceptions and syntax. (Music, as Plato knew and feared, can perform this externalization even more mysteriously and immediately than can language.) The true poet or dramatist will open the doors of speech on significant darkness, yet leave us at liberty to doubt, or to translate his findings into a rational, explicative register. Being, as Hölderlin stressed, one who envisions mortal man as living in resplendent yet perilous proximity to agencies greater, more numinous than himself, Sophocles works close to 'the shadow-line' (Conrad's tale is, at many points, profoundly Sophoclean) between the empirical and the transcendent. The madness of Ajax, the clairvoyance of Neoptolemus, the grove and epiphany at Colonus, are superbly poised constructs of twilight, circum-

scriptions of existential zones bordering equally on reason and
on miracle. No other poet, unless it be Blake, has brought to
bear on lucid, indeed transparent, modes of statement a
stronger inference of secret presences. Here also, a phrase out
of Conrad, 'the secret sharer', is most apposite. And it is such
inference, together with our uncertainties as to the context of
credence in which the dramatist and his audience mesh, that
make 'untranslatable' lines 417–25. Yet which tell us, at the
same time, that in these lines the genius of the play is explicit.

Annotations come fairly thick and technical. Line 418
poses problems of accentuation and comprehension, even
at a superficial level. σκηπτός has Homeric and Aeschylean
authority as signifying a lightning-bolt, but with implications,
as well, of a violent, upward discharge, as from the thrust of a
weapon. How is this range of meanings to be accorded with the
'dust-storm', if it is precisely that, in *Antigone*? The grammatical placing and function of the two final words in line 418
are debated. They do appear to echo line 573 in Aeschylus'
Persians. Read in apposition to σκηπτόν, the phrase would
designate an affliction, a punishing visitation, earth-bred or, at
the least, surging from the earth, albeit of a 'celestial' kind, and
'heaven-sent'. If the words are not to be taken in apposition,
the direction of meaning would be generalized and more
expressly 'of the heavens' (e.g. Mazon's 'un vrai fléau céleste,
qui envahit la plaine', where the use of the word *vrai* all too
clearly signals the scholar-translator's discomforts). The verb
in line 420, which is generally taken to mean 'has been filled',
is echoed in Sophocles' *Electra*, line 713. But editors and textual
critics note the possibility of a variant reading. The syntax in
lines 422–4 is uncommon and does some violence to everyday
logic. However, the paratactic sequence and historic present
seem essential to the poetic–theatrical effect of the passage as a
whole. The closing, crucial word in line 423 is much discussed.
Where Jebb and Mazon read πικρᾶς, where Bothe and Bruhn
emend to πικρῶς, Dawe, in his edition and commentary,
proposes πικρά. The distinction is, in fact, far-reaching: in the
one case, 'bitterness' is a moral–psychological trait of the kind
attributed to Antigone by the speaker or general opinion and
reflected, as it were, in her outcry. Müller's analysis and
Dawe's emendation, on the other hand, make of the word
an adjective pertaining strictly to the bird-like quality of the

cry, to its specific avian shrillness and sharpness. It is this
latter reading which would underwrite the recent Bernard
Knox–Robert Fagles version: 'And she cried out a sharp,
piercing cry.'

But these textual uncertainties are, even in the case of
variant transcriptions and translations, merely symptomatic of
the intended, necessary complication of the dramatic episode
and its recital. The midday sun hammers at the senses of the
watchmen, forcing them to shield their eyes, dazzling their
observance. The 'dust-storm' compels them to close their
eyes altogether and numbs their perceptions with its seeming
'endlessness' (Sophocles' acute psychological touch). The
subtle modulations of verb tenses further blur the material
sequence. The sharpness of the light, abruptly smothered, the
equally abrupt sharpness of sound—the 'bird-cry'—are trans-
posed into, are in turn communicated by, the flickering or
oscillating sentence and verse structure. The echo-crowded
idiom, again richly Homeric and Aeschylean, the play of
sound (note the vowels in lines 422–3), the unconventionalities
in the syntax, are performative of the scene being recounted.

What, then, has transpired? Or, in terms of the play: what is
it that the Guard, with his own ambivalent motives of
imminent terror and relieved self-satisfaction, with his own
personal style, is conveying to Creon, to the chorus, and to us—
a triple focus whose intricate flexibility of placement is, as I
have emphasized, singular to the Greek tragic stage?

The insinuation of the supernatural possibility occurs early
in the play. The moment is a famous illustration of Sophoclean
economy. Having heard the Guard's report of the first,
nocturnal scattering of forbidden earth on the corpse of
Polyneices, having listened to the Guard's insistence on the
total absence of any visible spoors around the ostracized
cadaver, the coryphaeus, in lines 278–9, specifically alludes to
the possibility of divine agency. It is the gods who may have
intervened in mysterious visitation. Creon's withering retort
leaves the issue in ominous abeyance. Now we hear of a sudden
'whirlwind'. It strikes, strangely, in the blaze of noon. We have
seen that the terms chosen by Sophocles and spoken by the
Guard are at once dynamic and obscure. The spinning 'dust-
pillar' springs from the earth, skyward. Earth and air are
violently confounded. At the close of line 417, χθονός carries its

full weight of literal and symbolic meanings: uprooted, the earth, which is the primordial sanctuary of the dead, the locale of justiciaries and custodians older than Zeus, is made spiralling dust. This dust is also that which Antigone strews on the flesh of Polyneices. The mysterious tornado rises from the earth towards the realm of the gods who, by unmistakable implication, are its begetters. But, as S. Benardete acutely notes, decisive discriminations are being made as between the plausibly preternatural phenomenon of the sudden storm and that dust which Antigone has bestowed on her brother before sunrise, and which she will be bestowing once more as the storm recedes:

What distinguishes the two dusts is this. What is unseemly for Polynices' unburied corpse to suffer from birds and dogs is the opposite of the unseemliness that the dust storm inflicted on the foliage in the plain (206, 419). The guard ascribes malicious intent to the storm; and this malice that blasted every vestige of life cannot be the same as the love that Antigone poured into the dust that covered Polynices' corpse. Furthermore, no matter how unelaborate her original arrangements might have been, they might yet have borne the mark of human artifice, which the haphazard swirling of the dust could not duplicate. Perhaps, however, Antigone's ritual dust and whatever dust clung to Polynices' corpse during the storm differ not so much (if at all) because artifice and chance differ as because Antigone has stamped the dust with herself. It carries in the eyes of the loving Antigone her own signature. . . . Antigone's recognition, then, that the storm's dust is not her dust perfectly agrees with the law's prescription that man must bury man.[1]

This is ingeniously argued. But ought we not to look further? In relating the chthonic to the celestial, in undoing Antigone's pious handiwork while, at the same time and in precisely the same motion, giving to Polyneices a 'burial' greater, more numinous than any available to human hands, the 'dust-pillar' (an almost Semitic expression which German *Wettersäule* aptly reproduces) dramatizes the problematic contiguities between the acts of Antigone and those of the gods. As Hölderlin saw, the question of priorities, both absolute and temporal, as between mortal impulse and divine interposition, is central to the tragedy. It may be that human law ordains burial by human hands. But how does this law accord with the larger,

[1] S. Benardete, op. cit., II, p. 4.

often hidden fabric of transcendent and Olympian design? In the uncanny 'twister'—the American designation of a brief tornado is palpably right—the two 'dusts' are as inextricably, as menacingly mingled as are the δαίμων of Oedipus' child and the probable proximity of the gods. The uncertainties in the Guard's narrative are those of the play itself.

Birds play a manifold part in *Antigone*. In the first anti-strophe of the opening stasimon, man's ability to ensnare 'free', 'blithe' birds is cited as a mark of his strange mastery over the natural order. Certain scholars assign to the epithets which Sophocles attaches to birds in this great passage a distinctly feminine tonality. If so, the association with Antigone is latent. The birds of prey, in contrast, the eaters of carrion which are to settle on Polyneices' remains, are evoked in lines 29–30 with a savagery which will increase as the play unfolds. At the close of *Antigone*, in Teiresias' climactic narration and prophecy, birds play a dominant role. Too late, Creon will 'fly away' to attempt to undo the sequence of his murderous feats.

As the dust clears, the sentinels see a young woman hovering over the body. Her piercing cries are those of a bird returning to its nest and finding its fledglings gone. Commentaries refer to a close parallel, and likely source, in Aeschylus' *Agamemnon*, lines 48–51. We have seen that the custody of the unburied dead by 'the robin red-breast and the wren' lies deep in European folklore. Sophocles' simile, tightly wrought but, presumably, traditional, links the 'emptied nest' to an 'orphaned bed'. In human terms, λέχος is a bed. This is no conventional contrast or formal duplication. It is an over-whelming inference of barrenness, of solitude. The desecration of Polyneices determines Antigone's own imminent doom. For her too the nuptial and maternal 'nest/bed' shall be empty and generation laid waste. The language at this point enforces recognitions, transpositions of literal and symbolic markers as central as, yet more poignantly evident than, any put forward by psychoanalysis (though the Sophoclean and the Freudian coincide, as Freud himself insisted). The pathos of Antigone's bird-cry needs no emphasis. But the Guard's account points to areas of experience outside those which are strictly human. And this is the point. Bird-headed anthropomorphic figures, 'women as birds', be they nightingale or harpy, have their functions—consoling, devouring, or ambivalent—throughout

Greek myth and ritual. At its origins, even the Sphinx may very likely have been a bird-woman.[1] Antigone's shrill lament voices instincts and values, older, less rational than man and man's discourse. Can the πόλις, built as it is on essential delimitations between the human and the animal spheres, fundamentally committed as it is to articulate speech, contain, give adequate echo to, such cries?

Both storm and bird-cry stand outside civic reason. But it is precisely the bounds of civic reason, of immanent logic, which delineate Creon's map of the permissible, intelligible world. It is the transgression of just these bounds towards transcendent irrationality on the one side and pristine animality or 'organicity' on the other (observe how animals and the world of the dead are brought into contact, aggressive, totemic, custodial, at so many points in the play) which Creon labours to arrest. The economy of the drama is such that the wind-storm and the cry of the mother bird over her vacant nest precisely intimate those opaque existential areas towards which the chorus in turn advances and from which it recoils. Receptive, by dint of age and of piety, to the phenomenal manifestations of the divine, yet timorously aware that such manifestations, too readily solicited, are as dangerous to the fragile contours of the city as are the inroads of atavistic or anarchic autonomy—the blood-bonds of the clan of Laius—the chorus strains towards middle ground. Only in the fifth stasimon, when it is literally 'beside itself ', will the chorus overstep the *limes* of rationality and of civic Thebes. Its ecstatic summons to Dionysus, the almost distraught annunciations of his coming, and the tumultuous geography of the god's onrush will confound the civic order with the cosmic and shatter reason into song. But what of the sentry? There *are* naturalistic, indeed comic, touches in his style. His fear of Creon, his brute relief at being able to produce the wanted culprit, his spurts of barrack-room revolt against a taxing, inequitable order of things, belong to a realistic plane of speech. But these dramatic tints do not colour his narrative either of the eerie storm or of the discovery of Antigone. Here a crass perception is made transparent.

The convention of narration, of the extended 'message', in Greek tragedy, in Latin, and in neo-classical drama, corresponds to an aesthetic of abstinence. The removal of

[1] Cf. M. Delcourt, *Œdipe ou la légende du conquérant* (Paris, 1944, 1981), ch. III.

spectacle and of violent physicality gives to 'the world behind the stage' a paradoxically intense nearness and pressure. This urgent contiguity overflows into words. Such words and the events which they articulate on the visible scene derive a fierce strength and actuality from the very impact of that which they exclude. The means of discourse and of gesture (so far as we can reconstruct them, and with such evident exceptions as the *Prometheus* or Sophocles' own *Ajax*), are the audible, visible spear-point of a wealth of excluded motion and excluded physical tumult. Only a rhetoric and theatrical form of quite exceptional coherence can abstain from so much or, more exactly, can energize, can buttress, the severities of its own means with that which it narrates but does not mime. Such abstention is, in Greek grammatical and logical terms, the 'privative' and deletionary aspect of the use of a messenger and *nuntius*.

But there is also a positive semantic yield. In such passages as lines 417–25, speech is the actor. The immediacy of action is integral to lexicon and syntax. The coincidence, in the strong sense of the word, of language and reality excludes not only the exits and alarms of physical mimesis—the wind-machine to blow up dust, the actor trying to look or sound bird-like—but the naturalistic particularities of personal idiom. Where the message attains its highest degree and urgency of delivery, the *nuntius* is, himself, a transparency. Far from being un-dramatic, as they are often held to be by a 'Shakespearean' or romantic–realistic dramaturgy, the great tragic narrations and *récits* are the quintessence of drama. For in so far as he 'acts' but does not 'do', in so far as his performance is never performative (Laertes' foil is everlastingly blunt, Gloucester recovers his eyesight when the curtain falls), the actor is the unavoidable, the necessary betrayer of drama. The ideal of drama is that of speech in total action; it is that of a world totally spoken. Where such totality is closely approached, as in the central portion of the Guard's report in *Antigone*, the equivocations of natural and supernatural, of human and divine, of civic and bestial, can be allowed free play—as they cannot in the deterministic naïveties of stage-business. We need only *listen* to hear those other orders of possible meaning and experience which are brought to bear upon language, which are connoted by language when speech is freed from its servitudes to (pretended) action. It is for us to hear whether the god is in the dust-pillar, whether Antigone's fury of bereft womanhood carries her outside, makes her in some way more primitive than, civilized humanity. Creon perceives only meteorology in the storm. He hears only archaic infantilism in Antigone's cry. The chorus is obscurely torn. The narrative of the Guard tests us, as well as Creon and the elders, with its charged innocence of immediacy.

Such innocence is, in a closely comparable configuration, undermined by Euripides and no longer really available to Racine when he turns to Euripides. In the closing moments of *Iphigénie*, Ulysse, the embodiment of Cartesian *bon sens*, delivers his famous *récit* of Iphigénie's miraculous salvation at the altar. Meteorology is emphatic:

> Les dieux font sur l'autel entendre le tonnerre;
> Les vents agitent l'air d'heureux frémissements,
> Et la mer leur répond par ses mugissements;
> La rive au loin gémit, blanchissante d'écume. . . .

The implications—those 'felicitious' winds, the reply of the bovine sea, the plangent echo of the far shore—are so stylized as to lose, to erode into abstraction, their original, animistic content. Correspondingly, the first touch of miracle is so light as to pass almost imperceptibly:

> La flamme du bûcher d'elle-même s'allume. . . .

Such spontaneous combustion lies discreetly in reach of secular explanation (lightning, friction). Indeed, by a swift manœuvre of pragmatic suggestion, Racine points precisely in some such direction:

> Le ciel brille d'éclairs, s'entre-ouvre, et parmi nous
> Jette une sainte horreur qui nous rassure tous.

The couplet is, in its reticent musicality and equipoise, a masterpiece of accommodation. *Le ciel*, in its very neutrality, allows, invites the aura of a dispensation of grace beyond the pagan. This aura is obliquely, yet vividly, reinforced by *sainte horreur*, a phrase almost specific to baroque and later-seventeenth-century Christian rhetoric. But now comes the crux, Diane's epiphany and descent on the altar:

Le soldat étonné dit que dans une nue
Jusque sur le bûcher Diane est descendue,
Et croit que, s'élevant au travers de ses feux,
Elle portait au ciel notre encens et nos vœux.

The tribute paid to Cartesian–Galilean analytic empiricism is, at once, formally astute and conceptually massive. Ulysse shifts to a second, distancing plane of narrative. An 'astonished soldier', his testimony implicitly subverted by his humble rank and anonymity, his powers of observation presumably obscured by 'amazement', *says* (*dit*) that the goddess has lit upon the sacrificial pyre. Ulysse himself merely transmits this report. But even this second-hand, coolly impersonal communication is further undermined. The soldier 'believes' (*croit*) that Diane ascended to the heavens. Discreetly, but unmistakably, Racine insures his text against the rebukes of reason. A twofold interposition, the report of a report and the inference of the common man's dazed credulity, keeps the irrational at a distance. Racine's perfection here has a cautionary bias. His discourse is no longer open to the uncertain epiphanies of the dust-storm around Polyneices. Yet the continuities from *Antigone* to *Iphigénie* are real.

Shakespeare's dramatic speech has a degree of self-awareness, an autonomy of self-deployment, supremely representative of that which divides modern sensibility from the antique. It spirals inward, energizing levels of suggestion which are, in their turn, linguistic, but whose dynamics often lie beneath consciousness and intentionality. At the same time, the language of Shakespeare's plays has an inherent commitment to stage-action, to the plenitude of histrionic device. It is 'theatrical' in the highest sense. It initiates, parallels, counterpoints the mimetic facts of the given scene. Only rarely, as in Enobarbus' very brief account of the recessional music which signifies the departure of divine good fortune from doomed Anthony, do we experience in Shakespeare the willed invocation of the 'unsayable'. Vast as it is, the Shakespearean range, just *because* it presses an incomparable articulacy to the very edges, into every rift and cranny, of human existence, rarely includes a theological–metaphysical transcendence as such. It speaks the sum of our worldly world, and bestows a marvellous substance on certain visitations, spectral, diabolical, elfin, to that world. In Shakespeare, as in the early

Wittgenstein, the limits of language coincide with those of that which is. Hence the naïve but persistent questions about Shakespeare's religious–metaphysical beliefs—if any.

Yet where it is convincing, the *felt* pressure on mortal saying by that which lies 'outside' may well represent the ultimate in thought and in poetry ('of that of which one cannot speak one cannot be silent'). Heidegger, who observes this pressure on the texts of Sophocles, of Hölderlin, and, at moments, of Rilke, marks therein the vestigial presentness, the after-glow of Being itself, of the ontological nucleus which precedes language and from which language, in passages of supreme risk and extremity, derives its numinous validity, its powers to mean so much more than can be said. The Fourth Gospel can fairly be seen to argue throughout the paradoxical concreteness of the transcendent when the latter 'is made flesh'. St John's prologue and certain episodes in his narration are embodiments of the natural supernaturalism of the Word's presence in the word. The Greek of the Fourth Gospel is made translucid to mystery. A comparable translucency, a liberal apprehension of the truths of unknowing, can be found in Sophocles. Matthew Arnold, who seems to have had in mind lines 582 ff., gives voice to this recognition when he evokes Sophocles in seeking to define the bleakness of immanence in 'Dover Beach': 'Sophocles long ago | Heard it.' Such 'hearing' transfigures the Guard's notice and report of Antigone. From it stems the light past understanding which tides towards us in the *récit* of the wonder at Colonus.

5

It has, I believe, been given to only one literary text to express all the principal constants of conflict in the condition of man. These constants are fivefold: the confrontation of men and of women; of age and of youth; of society and of the individual; of the living and the dead; of men and of god(s). The conflicts which come of these five orders of confrontation are not negotiable. Men and women, old and young, the individual and the community or state, the quick and the dead, mortals and immortals, define themselves in the conflictual process of defining each other. Self-definition and the agonistic recognition of 'otherness' (of *l'autre*) across the threatened boundaries of self, are indissociable. The polarities of masculinity and of femininity, of ageing and of youth, of private autonomy and of social collectivity, of existence and mortality, of the human and the divine, can be crystallized only in adversative terms (whatever the many shades of accommodation between them). To arrive at oneself—the primordial journey—is to come up, polemically, against 'the other'. The boundary-conditions of the human person are those set by gender, by age, by community, by the cut between life and death, and by the potentials of accepted or denied encounter between the existential and the transcendent.

But 'collision' is, of course, a monistic and, therefore, inadequate term. Equally decisive are those categories of reciprocal perception, of grappling with 'otherness', that can be defined as erotic, filial, social, ritual, and metaphysical. Men and women, old and young, individual and *communitas*, living and deceased, mortals and gods, meet and mesh in contiguities of love, of kinship, of commonalty and group-communion, of caring remembrance, of worship. Sex, the honeycomb of generations and of kinship, the social unit, the presentness of the departed in the weave of the living, the practices of religion, are the modes of enactment of ultimate ontological dualities. In essence, the constants of conflict and of positive intimacy are the same. When man and woman meet, they stand against each other as they stand close. Old and young seek in each other the pain of remembrance and the matching solace of futurity. Anarchic individuation seeks interaction with the compulsions of law, of collective cohesion in the body politic. The dead inhabit the living and, in turn, await their visit. The duel between men and god(s) is the most aggressively amorous known to experience. In the physics of man's being, fission is also fusion.

It is in lines 441–581 of Sophocles' *Antigone* that each of the five fundamental categories of man's definition and self-definition through conflict is realized, and that all five are at work in a single act of confrontation. No other moment that I know of, in either sacred or secular imagining, achieves this totality. Creon and Antigone clash as man and as woman. Creon is a mature, indeed an ageing, man; Antigone's is the virginity of youth. Their fatal debate turns on the nature of the coexistence between private vision and public need, between ego and community. The imperatives of immanence, of the living in the πόλις, press on Creon; in Antigone, these imperatives encounter the no less exigent night-throng of the dead. No syllable spoken, no gesture made, in the dialogue of Antigone and Creon but has within it the manifold, perhaps duplicitous, nearness of the gods.

In other great literature and in philosophic argument one or several of these binary 'elementals' are set out. Man and woman face each other in immensities of inadmissible and, therefore, destructive need in Racine's *Bérénice*, in Wagner's *Tristan und Isolde*, in Claudel's *Partage de midi* (the three supremely monistic dramas after Sophocles). There is no deeper realization of the irreconcilable intimacies of love and of hatred between the old and the young than *King Lear*. Schiller's *Don Carlos*, Ibsen's *Enemy of the People*, Shaw's *Saint Joan*, are pre-eminent studies of the wars between conscience and community, between the inner light of the individual and the demands of pragmatic order. Could there by any more acute understanding than Dante's or Proust's—so akin in this respect—of the manifold ways in which the worlds of the dead reach into those of the living? Jacob wrestles with the Angel; in the novels of Dostoevsky, such characters as Stavrogin, Kirillov, Ivan Karamazov, are 'God-duellists', tight-knit, in loving detestation, to their adversary. But alone, it seems to me, in the Creon–Antigone confrontation, as it is enunciated and enacted in Sophocles' play, is each of these ultimate pairings made equally manifest.

And they are made manifest with a perfect economy and natural logic. The dialectic of genders, of generations, of private conscience and public good, of life and of death, of mortal and divine, unfolds unforcedly from within the dramatic situation. Thus the structure of conflict is at once universal and local. It is inherent in the context yet wholly transcends it. The radical components of man's arguable humanity, arguable just because it must always be tested and delineated anew by means of its confrontation with *l'autre*, are concentrated into a single, specific collision. This concentration releases immense energies (modern particle physics speaks of 'implosions'). The mature civic masculinity of Creon, his commitment to a rational mundanity and theocracy—the two go readily together—define one half of the possible world; the other half is that determined by Antigone's femininity and youth, by her 'organicism' and privacy, by her intuitions of the transcendent and neighbourhood to death. Had we but this play left in literature, had we, perhaps, only this central scene, the primary lineaments of our identity and history, certainly in the West, would be visible. And because each in this set of five elemental antinomies is, as I have said, non-negotiable (as is one's breath, as is the irreducible core of one's identity), the encounter of Antigone and of Creon remains not only inexhaustible in itself, this is to say in its Sophoclean formulation, but productive of variants to this day.

Let us consider, summarily at least, each of these absolutes in conflict.

That which has in it the seed of all drama is the meeting of a man and of a woman. No experience of which we have direct knowledge is more charged with the potential of collision. Being inalienably one, by virtue of the humanity which distances them from all other life-forms, man and woman are at the same time inalienably different. The spectrum of difference is, as we know, one of most subtle continuum. There are in every human being elements of masculinity and of femininity (each encounter, each conflict is, therefore, also a civil war within the hybrid self). But at some point along the continuum, most men and women crystallize their essential manhood or womanhood. This gathering of the partly divided self to itself, this composition of identity, determines the gap across which the energies of love and of hatred meet.

To locate the sources of western drama, of all theatrical arts anywhere, in ritual, in mimetic ceremonies of a liturgical–civic character, is to focus on a late and formal phase. The original source of the dramatic lies in the paradox of conflict, of agonistic misunderstanding, in language itself. The roots of dialogue, without which there can be no drama, are to be found in the discovery that living beings using the 'same language' can mean entirely different, indeed irreconcilable, things. This paradox of divisive facsimile is present in all speech and speech-acts. It occurs persistently as between men as well as between women. But it is in the exchanges of language between men and women that the antinomies within external concordance, the reciprocal incomprehensions within outward clarity, take on a formidable thrust. Even as practices of translation between mutually incomprehensible tongues dramatize the problems of communication *inside* a single language, so discourse between men and women dramatizes the central psychosomatic duality of all spoken exchanges. It makes palpable the dynamics of non-communication and mutual misprision inherent in the very act of articulation. Men and women use words very differently. Where their uses meet, dialogue becomes dialectic and utterance is drama. The androgyne, the hermaphrodite as Plato conceives of him in his fable of human origins, need speak only to him-/herself, in the perfect peace and transparency of tautology.

The most concentrated dramatic *donnée* in our experience is the meeting of a man and of a woman. It can take place in the most banal setting. The commonest daylight will do. There is no need of costume: when they incur the perils of dialogue, men and women stand naked before each other. Forests in motion, tempests, spectral apparitions, the bustle of crowds and battles are, in respect of tension, of compressed energy (Cleopatra's 'mortal coil'), slight when compared to a man and a woman standing, very still, in a room. Even a chair is unnecessary. Or, rather, the question of whether a chair would not vulgarize, would not diminish to contingency, the absolute purity of collision, the blank space of the irreconcilable between a man and a woman, can itself become the nucleus of supreme drama (as it does in *Bérénice*). The high masters and purists of tragedy have always known this. Agamemnon and Clytemnestra, Tite and Bérénice, Tristan and Isolde, Claudel's Ysé and Mésa, act out the finalities of human confrontation (the mortal 'affront' of our intimacy with otherness). The meetings between these men and women, the immediacies and incommunicados of the words which they speak, whisper, hurl *at* each other, take us to the heart of our divided and polemic condition. These encounters, because they represent the oneness of love and of hatred, of the need for union between man and woman and of the compulsions towards mutual destruction inwoven in that need, are drama in essence. They embody the Manichaean perception of human existence from which dialogue and drama spring.

Shakespeare's pluralistic vitalism, his profound bias towards the tragi-comic, incline to enfold the confrontations of men and of women in the rich, hybrid fabric of surrounding life. The urgent politics of Cyprus, the energies of plume and of trumpet, crowd in even on the withering apartness of Othello and Desdemona. Hamlet and Ophelia are persistently over-heard by others. Shakespeare knows, he would have us know and remember, that mariners are counting their wages or vomiting below deck in the very instant in which Tristan and Isolde believe that they have annulled the world (an annul-ment which Wagner's text and music, in fact, bring about). This Shakespearean perspective may well be true to organic life itself. It will constitute the foundations of the novel. It is not, in the final analysis, that of absolute tragedy or of a tragic sense of the conflictual nature of human speech. In Shakespeare himself, though this is mere speculation, the part of man and of woman may have been so rarely poised, so harmoniously interactive, as to make it possible for him to unify language, to experience language as oneness. No such unification is conceivable between the speech-worlds of Creon and of Antigone.

We know pitifully little of the place of women in either archaic or classical Greek sensibility.[1] The dismissive state-ments as to women's spirituality or aptness for public life which are perennially cited out of Aristotle and Thucydides are suspect precisely because of their vehement generality. What is certain is that we have no realistic insight into the inward history and tenor of sexual codes and reciprocities of percep-tion between men and women in ancient Hellas. The ambi-guous centrality of the erotic, as we know it, as it is manifest in western art, literature, music, and moral argument after the early Middle Ages, is, as has often been observed, a Christian phenomenon. The only primary, seminal myth that western man has added to the basic inventory of attitudes and recognitions set out in Greek mythology is, precisely, that of Don Juan (Faust is latent in Prometheus). Add to this what we know of Attic theatrical practice—the performance by men of all women's roles—and the question naturally arises as to

[1] Cf. S. B. Pomeroy, 'Selected Bibliography on Women in Antiquity', *Arethusa*, vi (1973); P. E. Slater, *The Glory of Hera* (Boston, 1968); S. B. Pomeroy, *Goddesses, Whores, Wives and Slaves* (New York, 1975); M. R. Lefkowitz, *Heroines and Hysterics* (London, 1981); M. R. Lefkowitz and M. B. Fant (edd.), *Women's Life in Greece and Rome* (London, 1982).

whether one can extend to Sophocles the tragic focus of sexual encounter as I have postulated it.

The answer does, I think, lie to hand. In Aeschylus' Clytemnestra, in the three 'Electras' that have come down to us, in Sophocles' Ismene, Antigone, Deianeira, in Euripides' Hecuba, Andromache, Helen, Phaedra, Medea, Alcestis, or Agave—to name only the most obvious examples—Greek tragic drama presents in speech and in action a constellation of women matchless for their truth and variousness. No literature knows of more audacious or compassionate insights into the condition of womanhood. How this achievement relates to domestic and to civic usage, just what conventions or privileges attach to the stage-presentation of femininity in fifth-century Athens, we do not know. But the plenitude of perception is evident. There may be an analogy in the fact that neither the actual status of women in Elizabethan–Jacobean power-relations nor the masculine performance of feminine parts inhibited the range and genius of Shakespeare's treatment of women. But perhaps we can go further.

It may well have been the case that Greek tragedy, at least so far as we know it, was the particular medium in which female agents (though impersonated by masked men) could deploy their unrestricted ἐνθουσιασμός and humanity. It may well have been that those elemental rights of femininity, even of feminine primacy in certain capabilities and situations, which were denied to women in everyday life, in law, in Platonic politics and the Aristotelian classification of organic beings, were one of the impulses behind, and extraterritorial licences of, Greek tragic drama. If this supposition is right, it would tie in closely with the ultimate origins of drama in the dialectic of man and of woman as I have inferred it. The tragedies of Aeschylus, Sophocles, and Euripides retain their archaic force, their intimacy with the primordial, because in them the encounters between men and women reach back to the roots of dramatic form.

But whether or not this is so, there can be no doubt as to the fullness and authority of the realization of masculinity and femininity in the pivotal collision in *Antigone*.

In this scene, the five determinants of human definition which I have cited are implicit and explicit. But they are also deployed throughout the play. Lines 248, 319, and 375 direct us to the unexamined assumption of Creon, of the Guard, and of the chorus that only a man's hand can have scattered forbidden dust on the corpse of Polyneices. Hence the specific touch of scandal, of psychological shock, when Antigone is led in, captive. Editors are uncomfortable about Creon's grammar and meaning in lines 484–5. The difficulty may arise precisely from the contracted vehemence of Creon's assertion of outraged masculinity. If Antigone prevails—'if', to follow Dawe's suggested reading, 'these actions shall lie unpunished'—a twofold inversion of the natural order will ensue. Creon will no longer be a man and, in perfect expression of the logic of reciprocal definition, Antigone will have become one. The word 'man' is said twice, giving to line 484 a threatening symmetry. The masculinity of Antigone's deed, the masculinity of the risks which she has incurred, a masculinity postulated a priori and, in consequence, perceived as self-evident by the ruler of the city no less than by his sentinels and councillors, fundamentally impugns the manhood of Creon.

In his indictment, Creon emphasizes Antigone's unbridled, juvenile femininity. Antigone is a recalcitrant filly whom the rider must master (the implicit metaphor of erotic and domestic power-relations is very nearly a commonplace in Greek lyric verse). Creon's verbal duel with Antigone ends on the word 'woman' (line 525). 'So long as I am alive, no woman shall rule over me.' This imperative and the stichomythia as a whole lay bare terrors and animadversions particular to Creon. Dramatically, it is *he* who is afraid of being thought or made 'womanly'. But the hierarchy of values which he expresses is given a universal claim. The centre of argument comes in the great, difficult passage in lines 677–80. The gravity of Creon's dictum is underwritten by the echoes from comparable pronouncements in both the *Oresteia* and the *Seven Against Thebes*. Creon instructs the assenting chorus that 'we', by which plural he manifestly designates all the men of the city, all males in any given social organism, must 'defend the cause of order, must support all measures taken to support order'. To do so is to make absolutely certain that man shall not, not at any cost, 'yield to a woman' or 'be bested by a woman'. τοῖc κοcμουμένοιc very probably signifies 'the regulations', the 'edicts' whereby order is defined and enforced. Possibly, the phrase can be read to designate the rulers, the bringers of order themselves. What matters is the all-embracing reach and weight of 'the cosmic' as it is contained in the actual word κοςμουμένοιc. Those who speak, those who exercise, those who obey and thus preserve the principles of the social order, are in harmony with the fundamental hierarchies of the natural world. In so far as femininity incarnates the amorphous, the nocturnally anarchic, a woman's assertion of dominance utterly transcends any private, local quarrel. It challenges the rational cosmology of which a well-governed πόλιc is emblematic. It follows that it is infinitely preferable, as being more 'natural', as being more consonant with the disasters to which the cosmic and human order of things is prone, to 'fall, to come to ruin by a man's hand' (Creon's tag is Homeric), rather than to be worsted by a woman or to be seen to fall under her sway. Pentheus will say precisely this in the *Bacchae*.

Creon's rhetoric at this point is undoubtedly sententious; his hyperboles of fear and menace fall leaden. But the articulate seriousness of his position is evident. It strikes chords no less deep, no less demanding of reflection, than those which will, analogously, vibrate in Ulysses' plea for order and degree in Shakespeare's *Troilus and Cressida*.

The furious debate with Haemon further intensifies, but also vulgarizes, Creon's doctrine of male prepotence. The right sequence of lines in the stichomythia has been the object of perennial conjecture and transposition.[1] But the strident insistence by Creon on masculine as against feminine obligations and attitudes is perfectly obvious. By exact instinct or design, Sophocles assimilates Creon's vocabulary to that of warfare, which is the male art *par excellence*. It is abject, says Creon to his son, 'to make of a woman one's ally' in the struggles of public, political action. It is inexcusable 'to place oneself at her command' (somewhere, in obscure reach of this admonition and of parallel passages in Greek political theory and historical writing, may be the bizarre dream or nightmare of the Amazon myth). Haemon's espousal of Antigone's cause makes of him 'a slave-*thing*'—in line 744 or 756, depending on editorial placement, δούλευμα is a neuter noun. γυναικὸc ὕcτερον (line 746) communicates a double outrage: Haemon has yielded precedence to a woman; now he stands morally, substantively,

[1] Cf. R. D. Dawe, op. cit. 109–10.

lower than a woman. It is precisely against any such reversal
that Creon had invoked the hierarchies of values in the cosmos.
Through such submission, the dignity of man is wasted. 'You
shall not use wheedling speech with me,' declares Creon, you
shall not 'cajole me by whining'. The verb is richly suggestive.
It is used, in Anacreon, of a 'twittering' swallow. It has delicate
but insistent overtones of excited, deceitful femininity. It may,
indeed, evoke the Guard's earlier comparison of Antigone to a
bereft bird. Haemon's mere speech is, according to Creon, no
longer that of a man. It betrays that reversion to the spheres of
animality of which woman is, enigmatically, an extension, and
which, if allowed free play, let alone dominion, will undermine
the city *of man*. The unsettling ambiguity in this division of the
masculine and the feminine order is made brutal in Creon's
taunt (if it is that) in line 569: should Antigone perish,
Haemon will find 'other furrows to plough'. Knife-blade and
feminine–maternal earth; male will and supine, receptive eros.
Creon knows that human life requires both. But to him and,
one has every reason to believe, to the very great majority of
Sophocles' audience, the logic of coexistence is one of clear
masculine primacy.

   Antigone's stance is immeasurably subtler. It evolves, moreover, during the course of the drama. Antigone's entry into
the configuration of male values and duties is twofold. She performs burial rites for her brother Polyneices. Such performance
is, as we have seen, traditional to woman. Hegel makes of
the burial and commemoration of the dead, to whom he
always refers, by subconscious definition as it were, as 'men'
(fallen in battle?), a defining attribute of womanhood. The
reflexes of definition and expectation at work here seem to be
deep-seated: what would be our response if Antigone were to
undertake her mortal provocation on behalf of an unburied
sister? Antigone, however, acts not only *for*, this is to say in the
interest of, a man (Polyneices), but inasmuch as her action is
political, is publicly agonistic, she acts *as* a man. She will
emphasize that no other option was open to her. Oedipus and
his sons are dead. Of the withered house, only she and Ismene
are left. If the 'Kierkegaardian' touch in the much-disputed
line 941 is to be trusted—and Sophocles' Electra does come
very close to making the same move—Antigone in fact
becomes the *sole* survivor of the clan of Laius. Failing to join

their sisters in the perilous enterprise of justice and kinship, Ismene in the one case, Chrysothemis in the other, have 'annulled themselves'. They no longer exist meaningfully.

Acting for and, in the perspective of the prevailing conventions of society and of politics, as a man, Antigone exhibits certain masculine traits. Ismene's repeated use of the verb φύω, with its immediate reference to 'the natural order', is explicitly contrastive. She is 'by nature' and 'in her very φύϲιϲ' a wholly feminine being. Ismene's terrors, her stress on bodily weakness in the face of the task which Antigone would set her, the impulses of unconsidered sympathy, compassion, and grief to which Ismene yields as disaster looms, all these are characterized in the play as 'womanly'. At the moment of her sovereign acquiescence in death, in line 464, Antigone refers to herself in the masculine gender. Editors point out that this usage is not infrequent where general or abstract propositions are stated. But taken in conjunction with parallel passages in tragic drama, in Euripides' *Medea* for example, Antigone's syntax has a definite edge.

Yet as the play unfolds, and in a counter-motion of controlled pathos, Antigone's femininity is deepened and affirmed. In this development, Sophocles' dramatic tact and poetry are matchless. Made victim, Antigone grows into essential womanhood. The delicate gravity of the paradox is this: Antigone dies virgin and, therefore, unfulfilled in respect of her sexual identity, of the implicit teleology of her being. Over and over, in her torment and lamentations, Antigone lays stress on this cruel unripeness, on that which shall prevent her from being bride and mother, the crowning conditions of a woman's existence. Lines 915 ff. come near to being unendurable in the precision of their mourning: it is not only the extinction of her young life which Antigone laments, it is the extinction inside herself of those other lives to come which only a woman can engender. If there is, in the symmetries of mortality, any counterpoise to a tomb, it is the bridal bed and the bed of childbearing (so often united in image and metaphor). There is, in the fourth stasimon, a strange, subsersive hint of consolation. The chorus cites crimes committed by mothers on their children or stepchildren. Motherhood may, by itself, be no guarantee of loving felicity.

But Antigone is already out of hearing. She has gone to what

the Messenger will, in his recital of catastrophe, evoke as a
bridal chamber without blessing. Antigone's suicide has
several facets of meaning. But feminine connotations may be
present. Though practised also by men—witness Sophocles'
Ajax—antique sensibility very definitely attaches to suicide an
aura of the feminine. In *Antigone*, such association is swiftly
reinforced by the suicide of Creon's wife, Eurydice. Freely
chosen death is a primordially feminine reply to the loquacious
inhumanity or imperception of men. The symbolic values are,
throughout the presentation of Antigone's incomplete yet
profound womanhood, of the most demanding complexity. In
the Christian order, virgin-birth is seen as the supreme
manifestation of and salutation to woman. In the Antigone
myth, and both Hegel and Kierkegaard seem to have sensed
this, it is virgin-death which, by tragic paradox, leads to the
chthonic centre of that which is woman.

Confrontations between genders are, in essence, non-
negotiable. So they are, as well, between generations. No
literature engages more penetratingly the complicities of love
and of loathing, of intimacy and of estrangement between old
and young, parent and child, than does classical Greek
literature (the distant heirs to this depth of concern are
Turgenev and Dostoevsky). Anthropology has a good deal to
say of this intensity and constancy of awareness, of this self-
consciousness in regard to kinship, which marks Greek sentiment in both the archaic and classical phases of social
organization. But the ubiquity, the special power of the theme
of fathers and sons, of sons and fathers, also has its express
poetic source.

   The more one experiences ancient Greek literature and
civilization, the more insistent the suggestion that Hellas is
rooted in the twenty-fourth Book of the *Iliad*. There are not
many primary aspects of Greek moral, political, rhetorical
practice which are not incipient in and, indeed, given
unsurpassed imaginative formulation by, the night encounter
of Priam and Achilles and the restoration to Priam of Hector's
body. Much of what Greek sensibility knew and felt about life
and death, about the acceptance of tragic fate and the claims
of mercy, about the equivocations of intent and of mutual
recognition which inhabit all speech between mortals, is set out

in this climactic, most perfect part of the epic. Already active in *Iliad* xxiv are those uncertainties, those feral lapses or spontaneous courtesies of heart in reference to the rights of the dead which are central to *Antigone*.

But, above all, it is the Homeric treatment of Priam's old age and of Achilles' youth, of the inexhaustible interplay of enmity and love between two fathers, Priam and Peleus, and two sons, Hector and Achilles, which seems to generate the urgency and wealth of similar confrontations throughout Greek poetry and drama. The meeting in Achilles' tent seems to inform the particular Greek perception of the dual, inescapably anti-nomian character of old age. It is seen as both a benediction and a curse. To be old is to possess an inherent right to honour, to the reverence of those who are younger (a trait which relates a number of Mediterranean conventions, the Hebraic and the Hellenic among them). But it is, at the very same time, to be infirm, to be lamed in civic strength and sexuality, to be at constant risk of ruin and derision—as Sophocles himself was reported to have been in high old age. Hector's death, moreover, and Achilles' imminent doom, the two being, of course, intimately meshed, may have given to the classical Greek image of youth its death-shadow. Often in Greek thought and art death dwells closer to the young than to the old, in whom it has, as it were, lost interest. There have been many other societies and mythologies of doomed young warriors and youthful civic sacrifice. But none as incisively responsive as that of ancient Greece to the symmetries of waste and of glory in the death of the young. The nocturne which gives to the close of the *Iliad* its enigmatic yet coherent finality marks the whole Greek sense of the wonder and waste of generations.

The supposition voiced in *Oedipus at Colonus* that 'it is best never to have been born at all, next best to die young, and that old age is the worst that can befall man', is much older than its famous Sophoclean formulation. It dates back to the sixth century, at least, and the elegiac poet Theognis. It embodies, furthermore, only one element, perhaps a very late element, in the motif of the relations between old and young. There are, before Shakespeare and Turgenev, no more acute studies of the collision between generations than those we find in *Philoctetes* and *Oedipus at Colonus*. What we can gather from the fragments of the lost plays suggests that this same theme is prominent elsewhere in Sophocles and that it belongs, distinctly, to the strongly Homeric tenor of his style. In *Antigone*, the clash between youth and age derives a special density from the fact that four parties are involved: Creon and the chorus of elders on the one hand, Antigone and Haemon on the other.

Again, we lack any certain knowledge of the constraints of expectation, of assumed normality, prevalent in Sophocles' audience. How heavily does Antigone's youth, a quality so intimately inwoven with her virginal femininity, weigh in the overall scandal of her political and public insurgence? Did fifth-century Athenian sentiment register a specific offence in the mere fact that the deeds and words of Antigone are those of a *young* woman, almost of a child? Lines 471–2 may take us near the heart of this guarded play. Having listened to Antigone's great profession of defiance and of readiness for death, the chorus responds with a couplet which—deliberately, one suspects—arrests any ready understanding, let alone translation. Antigone has shown herself to be 'the savage, the uncouth offspring of a savage father and sire'. The chorus uses two different words where one would, ordinarily, serve: γέννημα, signifying 'offspring', the 'one begotten', and παῖς, the customary word for 'child'. The suggestion that this duplication adds pathos or that it, in some manner, corresponds to the divided reflexes of the chorus at other moments in the drama is almost certainly inadequate. Oedipus is formidably present in the semantic and emotive context of the Creon–Antigone duel. The inverted word order in these two lines as well as the implicit discrimination between 'offspring' and 'child' do seem to point towards the monstrous singularity of incestuous begetting. Antigone is the daughter-sister of Oedipus, sprung of an act of generation outside the norms of kinship. But she is also, as she *has* been before returning to Thebes from Argos (in the myth), and as she *will* be in Sophocles' *Oedipus at Colonus*, the most 'daughterly of daughters', the most absolute of children, to an old father. Hence the tense conjunction of the two terms. 'The offspring is savage from the savage father of the girl' is the reading which one commentator proposes for Sophocles' gnarled phrasing.[1] 'Savage' here is ὠμόν. The chorus designates both Oedipus and

---
[1] S. Benardete, op. cit., II, p. 13.

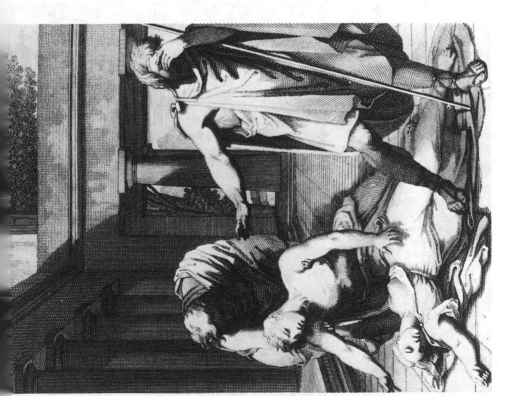

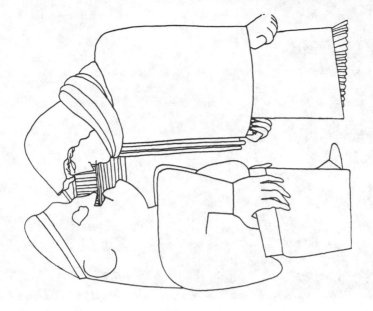

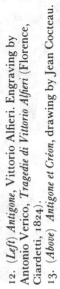

12. (*Left*) *Antigone*, Vittorio Alfieri. Engraving by
Antonio Verico, *Tragedie di Vittorio Alfieri* (Florence,
Ciardetti, 1824).

13. (*Above*) *Antigone et Créon*, drawing by Jean Cocteau.

14. (*Above*) 'Landschaft mit Antigone, die ihren Bruder Polynices beerdigt', 1799, drawing by Josef Anton Koch.

15. (*Right*) 'Antigone strewing dust on the body of her brother', painting by V. J. Robertson.

Antigone as ὠμοί. The word will recur only once in the play, in the compound ὠμηϲτῶν (line 697). There it refers unambiguously to flesh-eating dogs, to those very dogs from whom Polyneices' remains must be preserved. Why this appalling cross-reference? Is her obsession with Polyneices' corpse not wholly innocent of a primal, nocturnal instinct distantly analogous to that of the beasts of prey and of carrion? Such is the obscure strength of these choral lines, so palpable are the ways in which vocabulary and grammar call attention to themselves, that it is difficult to believe, be it at a naïve level, that Sophocles' profoundest moral intuitions were not uneasily implicated.

Creon's persuasions are woodenly patriarchal. In the mounting fury of his exchanges with Haemon, Creon invokes not merely his own manifest seniority, but also that of the chorus. Demanding to know whether men of his age are to be schooled by those of Haemon's, Creon includes the elders of Thebes in his rhetorical outrage. οἱ τηλικοίδε, 'those of our age', comprises both actual years and concomitant civic standing. The full meaning might best be rendered by 'worthies'. Haemon argues the circumspect but not, therefore, negligible rights of youth. The chorus takes a characteristically mixed view of his impassioned exit. It warns, sententiously, of the fierceness which anger unleashes in the young. Some commentators find here an allusion to a possible political rebellion, led by Haemon; others see a premonitory hint at the possibility of the young man's suicide. Often in Greek epic and drama, the rage of the young is self-destructive, the fury of the old self-preserving.

Only one child actually figures in the play, and its role, that of leading aged, blind Teiresias, is purely functional (the pairing exactly mirrors that in *Oedipus Rex*). But the explicit fatality of the relations between young and old dominates the close of *Antigone*. After the double suicide of Antigone and Haemon comes the reference to the earlier death of Megareus. Scholars advert to textual uncertainties in lines 1301–5. And the plain question as to how many in Sophocles' audience could, in full flight as it were, catch the passing allusion to Megareus/Menoeceus remains tantalizingly open. Was the dramatist relying on the expertness in mythology of a small portion of his public? If we knew the answer, we would know far more of Greek classical tragedy than we in fact do. What needs to be noted, and has, so far as I am aware, been passed over in editions and commentaries, is the central importance of the Megareus reference to Sophocles' entire design—an importance which far transcends the textual awkwardness of the passage.

In the moment of her suicide, Eurydice evokes the deaths of *both* her sons. One plausible reading has it that 'the beds of both sons are now empty'. It is not clear whether or not the queen's lament attributes to Creon the guilt for Megareus' sacrificial or self-sacrificial end during the battle for Thebes. The point is immaterial. What matters, what comes through with numbing import, is the epithet παιδοκτόνος, 'son-' or 'child-slayer'. Haemon's death is not the result of an appalling accident—of the fact that Creon reaches the rock-tomb a few instants too late—or of a single incidence of blind misjudge-ment. It is in the nature of the man Creon, in the nature of the power-relations and values which he proclaims and embodies, to bring on the violent deaths of his sons. We are faced, and this is the very key to Sophocles' poised vision of the fated freedom of human action, with a prescriptive norm. Creon is the sort of man who will, who must, sacrifice the lives of his sons to what he deems to be, to what may in fact prove to be, certainly in the case of Megareus, the highest ideals of civic–political preservation. Megareus' self-offering and Creon's acceptance of, or it may be, active participation in, that gesture meant salvation for the besieged city (consider Agamemnon's di-lemma at Aulis). The condemnation of Antigone and the death of Haemon which it unwittingly entailed derive from an absolute sense of the rule of law and of those patriotic pieties which honour the guardian-hero and dishonour the traitorous assailant.

But motive, whether valid or illusory, fades before the particular, 'infanticidal', nature of the man. He is Κρέων παιδοκτόνος. And because this is so, Sophocles will not allow us to localize the meaning and terror of his play in any special sequence of human error or divine malice. With Eurydice's reference to Megareus, the implications of universality over-whelm us. Creon is one of those men who grow old, who gather the instruments of political dominance into their ageing grip, by virtue of the capacity to send the young to their several deaths. Creon's solitary outcry in line 1300, 'o my child', is at once raw and empty. It is in the nature, in the δαίμων of survival, of such older men as Creon to sacrifice to political and strategic abstractions the bodies of the young. This is the strict sense in which the edict of Creon against Polyneices' corpse can be understood as central to his being and as extending well beyond immediate psychological or tactical reflexes. This edict is an exact symbolic and material prefiguration of the homicidal abstractions which Creon will visit upon Antigone and Haemon. There are not many pages in literature or in moral and political philosophy that tell us more of our history, of the ways in which elder statesmen and generals have dispatched the young to their graves.

It would be idle to suppose that one has anything new to contribute to the commentaries on the confrontations between conscience and state in *Antigone*. We have seen throughout this study that this confrontation, as it was 'invented' or formulated by Sophocles, has been a leitmotif in western philosophy, political theory, jurisprudence, ethics, and poetics. More than any other factor, it is the unbounded plenitude and depth of implication in the Antigone–Creon debate which have given to the play its immediate and enduring status. Lines 450 ff. are canonic in our western sense of individual and society. In so far as he is a 'political animal'—the notion is, itself, Greek—it is in these lines that man comes of age. Every textual, historical, conceptual element in Antigone's reply to Creon has been the object of exhaustive inquiry and debate. We have seen what diverse magnitudes of moral and even of metaphysical construction have been put upon the elusive syntax and punctuation of Antigone's opening words. But every line in her discourse and exchanges with Creon solicits, and has often received, a comparable wealth of construction.

What I want to emphasize is simply this: this celebrated dialogue—is there a more intrinsically fascinating and consequential word-clash in any literature?—is, in fact, a *dialogue des sourds*. No meaningful communication takes place. Creon's questions and Antigone's answers are so inward to the two speakers, so absolute to their respective semantic codes and visions of reality, that there is no exchange. Where, in essence, does the chasm lie? Creon's idiom is that of temporality. Like

no other speaker previous, perhaps, to the Fourth Gospel,
Antigone speaks or, rather, endeavours to speak, out of eternity.
And this attempt raises the question: can intelligible discourse
be extrinsic to time?

Translation cannot render nor commentary circumscribe
the network of discriminations and contiguities which comprises the Greek terms Θέμις, Δίκη, and νόμος. The rough and
ready equation with 'right', 'justice', and 'law' not only misses
the shifting lives of meaning in each of these fundamental Greek
words, but fails altogether to translate the interplay in both
Θέμις and Δίκη of pragmatic or abstractly legalistic connotations on the one hand, and of archaic but active agencies of
the supernatural on the other. The stucco or even marble
allegories and statuary of our lawcourts give no corresponding
sense of a transcendent and, at times, daemonic embodiment.
Yet it is within the intensely energized terrain of values and
application covered, bounded by these three terms, that the
worlds of Creon and of Antigone collide.[1]

Linguistically, Θέμις may be the most ancient and originally
localized (northern Greece?). In Homer and in Hesiod, the
'goddess in this word' enunciates, is the high advocate for, the
traditional, inherited right order of things. She seems to
represent a primary comelineness in heaven and on earth.
There are strong hints, throughout the poets and mythographers, that Θέμις has intimate bonds with those exceedingly ancient, formidable, and inherently ambiguous incarnate
concepts known as Eris ('raging struggle'), Nemesis, and
'Ανάγκη ('necessity'). Θέμις would appear to belong to levels of
personification older than the Olympian pantheon. But it is
Δίκη whom the epic poets, fabulists, and dramatists habitually
designate as the 'child of Time'. Again, translation falls short of
the dynamic range of the word and of the images present in it.
Δίκη is 'animate Justice', but also that which constitutes the
aim and the principle of the judicial process as such.
Symbolically and iconographically, the links of this configuration to the Antigone theme are direct. Δίκη appears quite
often on funerary urns in the guise of a virginal young woman

---

[1] The literature here is extensive. I have found the following of particular help:
R. Hirzel, *Themis, Dike und Verwandtes* (Leipzig, 1907); M. Ostwald, *Nomos and the
Beginnings of Athenian Democracy* (Oxford, 1956); J. de Romilly, *La Loi dans la pensée
grecque* (Paris, 1971), 26–34; E. A. Havelock, *The Greek Concept of Justice* (Harvard
University Press, 1978).

of grave, indeed fierce, mien. For she is an intimate of Hades and one concerned, certainly in a number of representations and references, with the just treatment of the dead. νόμος would seem to be the more secular term in the triad. Its relations to the divine or absolute order are not self-evidently intrinsic or figurative. They need to be argued. It may well be that 'the law' is the expression, on the mortal and mundane level, of the cosmology of order and due process which is in the keeping of Θέμις. Δίκη could be conceived of as presiding over and being fulfilled, more or less perfectly, in the νόμοι prescribed and practised by just, law-abiding men. But any such 'triangulation' atrophies and vulgarizes what must have been, to judge by the texts of Greek thinkers and poets, the problematic subtlety of the three clusters of meaning and the wealth of interaction between them.

Θέμις is, vividly, an Aeschylean word. When used in lines 880 and 1259 of *Antigone*, it has a somewhat pale and formalistic cast (something in the vein of our 'if it is right' to do or say this). The Creon–Antigone polemic turns explicitly on Δίκη and νόμος. Much of the depth of provocation in lines 450 ff. lies, precisely, in the transformative pressures which Antigone brings to bear on Creon's use of νόμος, and on the equivalence which she puts forward as between the subterranean authority of Δίκη and the sphere of law among mortals in the πόλις. Antigone, as we know, attaches to *her* usage of νόμιμα the famous epithets 'unwritten' and 'not subject to overthrow or revocation'. Such usage may well contain a strand of antique authority. In one fragment of Heraclitus, if the translation is at all indicative, the 'law' is held to be such only if it is in accord with the divine principle, only if it shares with the divine order the self-evidence of eternal rectitude. Elsewhere, connotations are unsteadier. In the *Protagoras*, 337 d, a passage almost always referred to by scholars when they comment on Antigone's 'unwritten laws', νόμος is perceived very much as if it were, indeed, Creon's instrument, i.e. as a potential 'despot over mankind' and as an agency that can do violence to nature (φύσις). But in the *Laws*, when using the phrase πάτριοι νόμοι, Plato gives to the notion of public law a wholly positive sense. There are laws which must, which do, animate and determine the true spirit of civic existence and mature conduct. In the context, it is made clear that such laws can be promulgated by those in responsible power, and that their temporal and written character need in no way derogate from their worth.

When Aristotle, in turn, cites Antigone in the *Rhetoric*, he inflects her words towards what was to become the whole doctrine and politics of 'natural law'. Bridging the very gap opened in the *Protagoras*, Aristotle equates Antigone's ἄγραπτα νόμιμα with those 'laws of nature' or 'natural laws' shared by all civilized communities. Yet it is not to φύσις that Antigone would bind the true validity and everlastingness of the law: it is to Δίκη. Or, rather, it is to 'nature' in a very special and non-temporal sense. To put it another way: it is only when nature is made free of the compromise of time and change that νόμος, under the direct guardianship of Δίκη, can enter the realm of absolute justice which is that of Θέμις. But we ask (with Creon, as it were): can there be such re-entry in the temporal order of human existence, or only in death?

Time is, truly, of the essence. At the catastrophic close of the action of the play, Creon will, as Teiresias foretells, race vainly against time. Antigone, who has made of herself the accuser of Creon, proclaims that no temporal edict can overrule laws which are immeasurably older than man's willed instrumentalities (such as writing). She postulates a 'natural eternity' of which Δίκη is custodian. She does not flinch from the antinomian inference that that which underwrites the timeless, unalterable legitimacy of 'the unwritten laws' is the sanctified status of the dead. Antigone, in her great counter to Creon, does not name Polyneices. A man's name, however immediate to her cause, belongs to the province of place and of circumstance. Anonymity is, at this point in her challenge and apologia, a tactic of universality. Many have asked: '*If* those "laws" invoked by Antigone are of manifest universality and eternity, why should they not be incised in Creon or the chorus as evidently as they are in her?'

The answer is that for Antigone the πόλις and the category of the historical—of rationally organized and mastered timeliness—have obtruded, irrelevantly and then destructively, upon an order of being, call it 'familial', 'telluric', 'cyclical', in which man was, literally, at home in timelessness. Such at-homeness before or outside history makes of φιλία, of 'loving immediacy', of 'unquestioning care', the rule of human relations. It is in this very definite sense that the unwritten laws of loving care which Antigone cites, and which she places under the twofold aegis of Olympian Zeus and chthonian Δίκη, are 'natural laws'. They embody an imperative of humaneness which men and women share before they enter into the mutations, the transitory illusions, the divisive experiments, of a historical and political system.

Creon does not and cannot answer. For time does not answer or, indeed, bandy words with eternity. There is no possibility of fruitful dialogue between moral conscience in a condition of timeless (Kantian) ethical imperatives, and the morality of the state which must, by honest definition, be timely. The whole force of the Hegelian revision of Sophocles' *Antigone* lies in Hegel's attempt to redress this unbalance and to achieve that form of dialogue which is known as the dialectic. Hegel is determined to give to the necessary timeliness of politics its own rights in eternity.

No such equilibrium is established in the play. As the dialogue of non-communication proceeds, Antigone's refusal of temporality—she will not 'temporize'—takes on an ever more explicit and self-destructive point. Creon's death sentence is, to her, immaterial. It pertains exclusively to the servile sphere of secular time. The sentence of death passed on Antigone is invalid in exactly the sense in which Creon's so closely related edict against Polyneices' remains is invalid. Antigone's death is *not* that which Creon purposes and proclaims—a distinction which Heidegger's doctrine of the existential specificity of individual death helps clarify. The death which Antigone freely, knowingly chooses, has axes of meaning wholly beyond Creon's will or understanding. The Antigone in Sophocles' play is, as it were, the young woman who had learnt at Colonus that only the full acceptance of death can yield a mortal lastingness (the archaic word 'durance' would be most accurate). She has no inkling, she would refuse any such, of that other eternity or suspension of time which is dynamic in the life of institutions and which connects successive generations in and by virtue of an evolving πόλις (a far greater adversary than Creon would be Edmund Burke). Listening to Antigone, we hear the primal, feminine world recorded, in a more modern guise, in Salvatore Satta's novel, *Il giorno del giudizio*. It is a world outside political time, in which the unmarried and the childless are darkly at home.

The presentation of Antigone's anarchic lawfulness in lines 450 ff. is incomparable. But the questioning of temporality to which the text compels us is far from being circumscribed by Antigone's eloquence and heroism.

The subtleties, the metrical variousness of lyric modes available to the tragic chorus, more especially in that musical and choreographic ensemble now lost to us, could transpose, qualify, enrich the discursive argument of a play (or, indeed, as in the *Oresteia*, create an immensely complex 'play within the play'). With the chorus, we move from the overt rhetoric of dramatic oration and exchange, from the temporal directness of narration, into a more 'imagistic', metaphoric, and contrapuntal register. Thus it is that the major choral odes in extant Greek tragedy set into free motion the fundamental undecidabilities of man's condition. Past speech, music and dance contain, though they do not resolve, the contrary currents of myth. The chorus has open to itself both discourse in unison and the option of dialogue via internal division, an option enacted in the responsions of strophe and antistrophe. In consequence, a chorus can be more economical in depth than any other poetic–dramatic instrument that we know of.

Voiced, mimed, sung, and danced, the choral proposition, query, or commentary, the choral expression of ecstasy or of anguish, enlists the whole range of mental and bodily expression. It achieves a semiotic totality. It is, therefore, in the parodos and in the five choral stasima of *Antigone* that the issues of conscience and state, of the individual and of the πόλις, of nature and of history, are given their highest pressure of uncertainty. If there is a Sophoclean bias, it is in the sung and danced thoughts of the chorus that we shall find it.

A significant discrimination is incipient in the brilliant turbulence of the chorus's evocation, one can almost say mimicry, of the battle for Thebes. The celebrated simile of the shrill-screaming eagle, ravening at the city gates, the ritual enormity of the duels to the death between the seven assailants and the seven champions, give to the report of the struggle a deliberately inhuman tenor. The delicate touch, in lines 131 ff., whereby the chorus does not name the giant Capaneus, enforces a sense of superhuman, but also of primitive, almost bestial, onrush. The battle for Thebes is, truly, a 'giganto-machia'. The throbbing anapaestic beat, the wild poetry of the language of birds, of fire, of hatred blasting like a tempest, together with what must, one presumes, have been the mimetic vehemence of the chorus's movements, set the whole episode in the twilit zone outside, prior to, civic reason. The world of the *Seven Against Thebes*, as it is reflected in Sophocles' parodos, is that of titans and half-gods, of miracles and monsters.

But even before Creon's entrance the ode modulates into a historical and civic key. Νίκη, the goddess Victory, is distinctly a political emblem and a civic presence. 'Thebes of the many chariots' is, undoubtedly, an epic formula, but it also infers the material means of ordinary warfare. As Creon nears, the leader of the chorus twice uses the adjective 'new'. A 'new king' enters, one on whom a 'new destiny' or a 'new status' has bestowed power. The hour is that of sunrise, and the chorus guides our imaginings out of a world of titanic and totemic violence into the daylight of the πόλιc.

In the second choral ode or first stasimon, as we know, these polarities are incommensurably deepened. As scholars have pointed out, the πολλὰ τὰ δεινά ode can be understood as contributing to a stream of philosophic–poetic meditation which was, very possibly, initiated by Anaxagoras and by Solon.[1] Anaxagoras saw in the foundation of the law-governed city the most eminent of human devices, the crowning act in man's wondrous assumption of mastery over the natural realm. No less than Sophocles, Solon, in his elegiac poem to the Pierian Muses, celebrates the manifold pursuits of mortal men, their skills as fishermen, ploughmen, craftsmen, and healers. Solon's sense of society is haunted by the fear that the accumulation of wealth will bring with it disaster. Yet although fatalistic—Destiny, says Solon, presides over all actions, and it is Zeus who, in ways often obscure to us, distributes good and ill fortune—Solon's is, fundamentally, a promise of εὐνομία, of a progressive harmony. Sophocles' reading is far more intricate.

In the human inventions which the first stasimon extols, there is a constant oscillation as between solitude and community. The winged vessels on which men cross the perilous

[1] Cf. P. Friedländer, 'πολλὰ τὰ δεινά (Sophokles, Antigone 332–375)', in *Studien zur antiken Literatur und Kunst* (Berlin, 1967), 190–2.

seas point to collective design and manœuvre. The ploughman is both alone and a part of an agricultural system. The snaring of fowl and of fish can be, and customarily is, the act of a man alone; as can be the taming of horse and bull in the wild of the hills. Yet these accomplishments, also, tell of a social order not too far distant. The ambiguities are resolved by the invention of speech. Like the Eleatic thinkers before him, like Isocrates, Sophocles sees in the evolution of human discourse an immediate step towards political society. Lines 354–5 (in Dawe's numeration) entail almost a political theory of speech. Out of language, out of the capacity of language to communicate thought to others, come the instauration and organization of the state. Aristotle's well-known analysis of the intimate bonds between human discourse and the moral fabric of a political society, in *Politics*, i. 2. 12, reads like a gloss on Sophocles. The gains which come of the foundation of the city are decisive: man now finds proper shelter and is armed against the visitations of hostile nature. Only death shall unhouse him. It is this increase in man's strength of being via the πόλιϲ in which Anaxagoras and Pericles exult.

At once, however, and with a gnomic concision available only to supreme poetry, the second antistrophe adverts to the undecidable finalities of conflict at work in *Antigone* and beyond it. As lucid as will be his great student, Freud, Sophocles knows that civilization (the condition of the *civic*) breeds its mortal discontents. He knows that the very construction of a social order, through the genius of speech and of the moral–political reflection which speech articulates, generates constraints. It is now, by unsparing inference, the civic order which 'tames', which 'entraps', the legacy of aloneness, of organic wildness and freedom in man, as did the nets and snares evoked in the first antistrophe. Torn between opposing needs and impulses, man's cunning, his acumen of spirit, may impel him to choose evil and self-destruction rather than good. Such a choice has consequences far beyond individual fate. The cardinal terms of the play are now densely meshed: νόμοϲ, Δίκη, 'the gods', and, above all, in paratactic sequence, ὑψίπολιϲ and ἄπολιϲ.

Few words outside Scripture have drawn more intense commentary or had a more diverse legacy of theoretical and existential enactment. Speculation rises to the ambivalence in both (the first may well be a Sophoclean coinage). He who stands by the laws which he has sworn to uphold, he who honours the civic contract, will 'uphold' the city and/or be 'eminent' within it. Does this signify that Creon's legalism and eminence are representative of a right moral choice? The law-breaker, the evil-doer, on the other hand, is ἄπολις (and we remember Heidegger's draconian gloss on this expression). Yet, once more, the connotations are multiple and potentially contradictory. For the 'cityless man' can be either a culpable pariah, as in line 255 of Euripides' *Medea*; or a political exile and temporary victim of political bad luck, as in several uses of the word in Herodotus; or he can be that most innocent and maltreated of guilty men, Oedipus at Colonus (line 1357). Being ἄπολις, finally, may signify that a man has, by his breach of the social contract, not only left his city but been its destroyer. This being so, can one, in the seven closing lines of the stasimon, altogether escape the hint at Polyneices?

Already, the tension of meanings is extreme. It is pressed even further by the adjuration of the chorus: 'May no such man' (ἄπολις) 'share my hearth' or be a partner 'to my thoughts'. The concentric pattern of the lyric is moving both inward and, temporally, backward. The hearth is a more ancient, familial focus than the πόλις. It tells of an earthy centrality and of the feminine rites and custodies so resonant in the person of Antigone (in the ancient Mediterranean pantheon, the divinity which presides over the hearth is feminine). A man's thoughts, from whose intimacy the ἄπολις is to be banished, are the inmost ('the hearth') of his being. Moreover, as the chorus has sung, speech and shared thought are the builders of cities. Yet solitary thought need not be impotent or base. It can be the life-spring of moral finding and moral decision. Whom, then, shall we keep from our hearth: Creon or Antigone? Which of the two is truly ἄπολις?

When the chorus sings again, after the Antigone–Creon ἀγών, its register is even more Aeschylean than it was in the famous echo of the *Choephoroe* at the outset of the first stasimon. Behind Aeschylus, in turn, stood the language of the epic and, more particularly, one assumes, that of the Theban cycle and its narration of the doom of the House of Laius. The bearing of this third choral ode on the central matter of conscience and of state, of the world prior to the πόλις and of

the civic system of values, is oblique but, I think, unmistakable. The seminal division is made explicit in the
vocabulary and contrapuntal structure of the two strophic
pairs. The keywords in the opening movement are those which
designate or refer to man's lineage, to his roots, to that which
binds him to house and hearth. Line 593 contains the crucial
term ἀρχαῖα, which Jebb translates 'from olden times'. The
second strophic pair invokes time present and time to come. In
the midst of resigned prophecy comes the word 'hope' (ἐλπίς).
The supernatural agencies of anathema and chastisement, as
they have come upon the Labdacidae in the two initial
strophes, seem to belong to the archaic spheres of night, of
blood-vengeance, of an aggressive underworld. The Zeus of
the second strophic set is no less overwhelming in his retributive
justice, but he 'dwells in the radiant light of Olympus', and
there obtains as between human conduct and human suffering
the rationale of guilt, of 'trespass'. In the archaic logic of Necessity, of inherited malediction, as it weighs upon and annihilates
the clan of Oedipus, unwitting crime (Oedipus' parricide and
incest) carries the irremediable consequences of accomplished
fact. There is no escape from the paradox of innocent guilt.
There is no escape either, to be sure, from the judicial
omnipotence of Olympian Zeus or the self-destructive illusions
of human ambition, endeavour, and hope. If the extremely
difficult text of lines 614 ff. can be so read, the man or woman
whom the gods inspire to action is, by that very inspiration,
unavoidably exposed to overweening. But there are deep
differences between the ancient and the new or humanistic
dispensation. A normative principle and truth is now at work.
Heredity does not doom the individual, though it may still
predispose him to exemplary vulnerability. γένος, which, as
commentators point out, signifies 'parentage' and 'kinship' at
the beginning of the stasimon, has, by its close, and in direct
reference to Haemon, taken on a more individualized, secular,
and social tonality. The ebb and flow of ironies, of self-
delusion, and subconscious insight on the part of the chorus are
multiple. They are of a polyphonic indeterminacy consonant
with music and dance. If, as one commentary puts it, 'The
first strophic pair seems to pardon Antigone, the second
to condemn her',[1] the vivid evocation of hubristic energy

---

[1] S. Benardete, op. cit., II, p. 27.

and of the inescapable vengeance of Zeus points, perforce, to Creon.

But the choral inferences, tantalizingly apposite as they are to the given moment in the play, extend much further. Only under Olympian aegis, only within a fabric of rational law—both νόμος and cοφία or 'rational wisdom' figure in the second strophic pair—can there be an advance beyond purely genetic criteria of blood-guilt or innocence. No less than in the *Eumenides*, to which, internally, this second stasimon does appear to address itself, we have here a meditation, albeit instinctive and darkly metaphoric, on the transition, ambiguous yet progressive, from a purely solipsistic and familial code of human relations to one of historicity and civic reason. What is demanded of us is the attempt to think through or, rather, to bring to full life in our moral imagining the enigma whereby the 'cursed' deed of Antigone seems to embody the ethical aspirations of humanity whereas the civic legalism of Creon brings devastation. But to bring an enigma to felt life is not to resolve it. Nothing in the text refutes the implicit, positive motion towards a rational criterion of politics and social order (a motion which would be emphatic if the uncertain third word in line 614 was, indeed, πάμπολις—but this is doubtful).

In his *in memoriam* to Freud, W. H. Auden calls on 'Eros, builder of cities and weeping anarchic Aphrodite'. No summons could, even if by contrast, take us nearer the ambience of the third stasimon. In one antistrophic pair, the chorus, in the sharpening grip of contrary intuitions and of a wildness of feeling which will mount to full force in the closing ode, hymns Eros. The implicit cosmology, as often in moments of passion and bewilderment in Greek tragedy, is archaic, pre-Olympian. Eros is omnipotent. The echoes of the first stasimon are almost ironic: man's uncanny wit has mastered land and sea, has netted or tamed the beasts of the field, the fish, the creatures of the air—but Eros, mastering man, has mastered all. It enslaves, it maddens the man who dwells apart (ἄπολις) as well as the citizen. In its pulsing enormity, Eros overpowers even the immortals. In the preceding choral song, Zeus was hailed as all-powerful in his intelligible, moralistic sovereignty. Now Eros and wilful Aphrodite emerge as supreme.

Lines 796–800 are full of textual and syntactic pitfalls. Are we meant to picture Eros as enthroned beside, as on the same elevation as, the 'supreme laws of the world'? Are we, more concretely and hyperbolically, to think of Eros as 'assessor in the high tribunal of universal law'? But the general thrust of lyric argument is plain. Eros, the begetter of madness and strife, the light in the eye of the bride, the incendiary of hatred between fathers and sons, is beyond good and evil. Again, we seem in reach of a Sophoclean intuition so central that it will not translate adequately out of the elided logic of lyric–choreographic expression and metaphor. Fullness of being, teaches Sophocles, attaches to itself a charged potential of destruction and self-destruction. The quality of action which springs from such fullness—there is no authentic human plenitude without action—*does* have intense bearing on the morality or immorality of man's conduct. But, in the final analysis, this bearing is secondary. It falls short of a certain criterion, of a certain mystery of lived intensity. Where it is great enough, this intensity entails privileges of heroic perception and 'privileges'—again, this same word is paradoxically justified—of transgressive fatality outside, beyond the ethical domain. It is some such intuition of the moral extra-territoriality of pure intensity (an intuition very close to Blake's sense of the holiness of energy) which sets Eros 'beside' or even in judgement over 'the eternal laws'.

How, then, are we to interpret this placement in reference to Antigone's invocation of these very laws? Reflection suggests that Antigone's abstinence from sexual initiation and fulfil-ment, with its concomitant espousal of death, represents the only way open to mortals if they would escape or defy the tyranny of Eros. But such escape or defiance, Sophocles intimates, is, in its own turn, radically aggressive and wilful. Antigone's ideal of φιλία is, for all its aura of humanistic morality or, rather, by virtue of this aura, an offence to life. Unnervingly at work in the third stasimon is the Sophoclean suggestion of an irreconcilable dialectic between eternal moral law and vitality. But in what ways does the omnipotence of Eros in the bounds of the living world relate to the conflict between conscience and state, between the ego of the indi-vidual persona and the rights of the πόλις? Answers to this question, implicit in the choral ode, will be sketched and tested throughout the remainder of the play.

The fourth stasimon is, perhaps, the most elusive in Greek

tragedy. The ode connects, though at many points only tangentially, to the confrontations between man and woman, old and young, the living and the dead, men and gods, which determine the architecture of *Antigone*. But it does not, I think, contribute to the Antigone–Creon polemic, to the debate on family and city, as such. It is in the last choral song, in the vertiginous fifth stasimon, that the fundamental issues in this debate are raised to an ultimate pitch and dimension.

The Theban elders are inebriate with hope, that very narcotic of which they gave warning to themselves and to us in the second stasimon. The dramatic misprision and effects of irony are manifest; the ode looks to joy at the moment in which disaster is imminent. The device is one which Sophocles uses also in the *Ajax*, in the *Women of Trachis*, and *Oedipus Rex*. But this dissociation between mood and fact is only the surface element. Teiresias has prophesied unambiguously. At the rational level, the chorus is cognizant of the doom which must now descend on both Creon and his tragic adversaries. But what matters in this stasimon is the literal ecstasy, the dithyrambic state of mental and bodily possession, in which the old men find themselves. The insinuation into their own psyche of trance-like clarities of insight, of a pounding choriambic beat inside, as it were, their very being, has been strengthening since the third choral ode. Now the god is fully upon them. Every formal component in lines 1115–52 contributes to our sense of this possession. The binary structure of the antistrophic pairs, of which the first enacts the onrush of the god and the second becomes a prayer for the cleansing of the city, plays antiphonally against the triadic organization inside each set of strophe–antistrophe. The vowel sounds interact in a veritable chromatic crescendo.[1] Sophocles' poetry in this ode is of a precise magic. But nowhere in *Antigone* is our total loss of its musical and choreographic matrix more drastic. Here, as in Nietzsche's ideal of argument, thought of fierce rigour and depth was danced. The ritual, the processional images and references in the actual words, must have leapt into motion, setting language 'beside itself' in a wild clarity of tone and of gesture.

Dionysus is 'myriad-named' precisely because the common

---

[1] Cf. G. Müller, *Sophokles. Antigone*, p. 250, for an illuminating analysis of the metrical effects.

logic of designation cannot comprise his transcendent, internally antinomian manifold of phenomenal presences and functions—Dionysus, who is 'also Hades', said Heraclitus (if we translate rightly). In this last choral ode in the play, the sixth, Dionysus (as in the *Bacchae*) has the potential and attributes of both life and death, of instauration and of devastation. He finds expression both in trance and in lucidity. Dionysus is, as we saw previously, termed the 'master of' or 'the one who presides over the cries in the night'. This enigmatic nomination can evoke either the nocturnal sorrows of Antigone or the salute to daybreak in the opening parodos, or both. The chorus now adjures the god to come to Thebes, *his* city, the place of *his* birth. Its dance would have simulated the enormous tread of that homecoming. Yet the allusions to Dionysus' mother, Semele, and the reference to his 'attendant Thyads', signifying the 'delirious ones', recall, past overhearing, the dread first homecoming of the god to his city, with the consequent frenzy of the Bacchae and killing of wretched Pentheus. If the epiphany of Dionysus can bring purification, it can also bring ruin.

This duality is, as Hölderlin taught, incipient in the mere meeting of god and mortal, in the implosive unison of eternally distinct polarities. The fire imagery in the stasimon makes this clear. The lightning-bolt which consumed Semele gave Dionysus lambent birth (hence the epithet, at once festive and menacing, of 'loud-thundering' Zeus in line 1116). The god moves, fire-like, over mountain-crests and seas. The sacrifices brought to him are burnt offerings. The festivals, the ritual processions, which, literally, 'dance him into the city', are torch-lit. The stars which Dionysus leads perform a twofold dance: the circular, harmonic choreography of the cosmos, the 'great dance of being' which was to fascinate Neoplatonism and the Renaissance, and a wild counter-dance, mirroring that of the mortal acolytes. Both are πῦρ πνείοντες. There is immensity in this word. It tells of the fire-breathing dragon whom Cadmus slew when he founded Thebes. It images (cf. *Prometheus*, line 917) the homicidal and life-giving lightning loosed on Semele. It makes of the 'burning stars' torch-bearers to Dionysus. Compellingly, moreover, it takes us back to the beginning of the play. Polyneices, declares Creon, had come expressly to put Thebes to the torch—πυρί, 'fire', is the emphatic climax to line 200. Fire cleanses, but cleanses by destruction.

Thus the entire cosmology of the fifth stasimon is that of Heraclitean fire. But how can such divine incineration be legitimately invited and brought into the city of man?

πάνδαμος πόλις: the phrase, in line 1141, is unambiguous. The *whole* city is polluted. The body politic is infected, as by pestilence (though grammatically difficult, ἐπὶ νόσου clearly means this). Catharsis now lies beyond pragmatic and civic resources. It is not the flames set by invading Polyneices which could have brought purgation. It is the god Dionysus who must blaze through the seven gates and the stars in his train who must set alight the altars. At this summit-moment in *Antigone*, Sophocles confronts the limitations of the city of man, of the state as the genius of man has devised it, with the homecoming of the god, a homecoming compulsively inherent in religious ritual and in the extremity of human supplication. Such epiphany is the ecstatic expectation, the desideratum of the human spirit when this spirit aspires to its own fulfilment, when it strives to return to its own pre-civic sources of being (a striving explicit in Heidegger's metaphor of *Behausung*, of the in-dwelling of man within but also beside himself). But how, except in a destructive fire-storm, is Dionysus to inhabit Thebes? Can there be any coexistence, other than suicidal, between transcendence and *civitas*?

The more one endeavours to live with, to 'live', the parodos and the five inspired stasima in *Antigone*, the more difficult it becomes to dismiss the belief that Sophocles is educating our feelings and understanding towards a specific terror. His dramas, the poetry of his thought, so far as we know them, are penetrated throughout by a sense of the fragility of human institutions. The sources of menace are threefold. Man's animality, the creative–destructive atavisms of the organic and animal kingdom inside his own evolved person, threaten to restore to archaic solitudes and exposures the fabric of human existence. They threaten to subvert and deconstruct the edifice of society and of rule-governed civilization (a word which, of course, has 'the city' within it). At the opposite extreme of the spectrum of perils lie the visitations of the divine. Gods have played diverse, sometimes ambivalent, roles in the foundation and erection of cities—witness the instauration of Troy, of

Rome, of Thebes itself. They are tempted to visit or revisit them. Without the potential of such visitation, the lives of mortal citizens may become merely *urbane*. But the coming of the gods is a consuming favour. The fabric of man's institutions may prove too weak to contain its callers. Like St Augustine after him, Sophocles brings a great weight of questioning to bear on the status of 'the city' in the central simile or contrastive pairing which binds the 'City of God' to the 'city of man'.

The third source of danger is the most difficult to define. It is implicit in *virtus*, in man's bias to action, in the realization that excellence springs from action. From such excellence, in turn, derive ὕβρις, the self-deceptions, the fratricidal rivalries, the dogmatic collisions which can reduce to ash the profoundly beneficent but always labile constructs of communal life. Sophocles' imagination, his vision of the place of man in the context of significant reality, was, so far as we can judge, possessed by intimations of radical fragility. Bestiality and transfiguration, the antithetical yet concomitant threats of the monstrous and the divine (a fusion of contraries embodied in the Sphinx), cast their hungry shadows over human institutions and the hard-won terrain of reason. This is the constant perception in Sophocles' treatment of the madness of Ajax, of the ruin of Heracles in that drama of vengeful animality, the *Women of Trachis*, in his account of the clash between primitive solitude and the politics of collective need in *Philoctetes*, and throughout every facet of the story of Thebes and of the House of Laius. Only Dante, perhaps, manifests a comparable focus on the fragile, externally and internally threatened, wonder of civility. Both he and Sophocles are overcome by the realization of how appallingly easy it is for man to be either reduced to less, or transported to more, than himself—both motions being equally fatal to his just identity and progress.

One comes to grasp that it is not the Hegelian hope of an evolutionary synthesis between the values of conscience and of state in a πόλις cleansed, educated by the Antigone–Creon catastrophe, which best expresses the Sophoclean sense of the play. The fundamental question is not whether Thebes can contain both Creon and Antigone or whether it would be a just and stable city if it housed only Antigone or only Creon (though these subsidiary questions are, indeed, posed). The final, inescapable question is whether it can, whether it should, contain *either*. But if the answer is No, how, then, is man to test the bounds (the 'city-bounds') of his condition? And how, then, is he to be host to the gods?

There is, in Sophocles, no resolution of the dilemma. But there is much in *Antigone* to suggest that Sophocles regarded man's testing of boundaries and man's offer of the hospitality and freedom of his city to the gods as inevitably destructive of the middle ground. And it is on this middle ground, if I apprehend Sophocles rightly, that man labours to acquire the immensely demanding arts of living with his own kind. Sophocles' piety, which encompasses but extends beyond the Antigone–Creon options and collision, is that of a haunted humanism. Behind *Antigone*, behind the fire-breathing ecstasy of the ode to Dionysus, smoulder the never-cooling embers of Troy.

Many, besides Kierkegaard, have observed that the play is death-crowded. Hardly any notable utterance or action by the living does not occur under pressure of the dead. The literal framework of *Antigone* is a battlefield strewn with the slain. The immediate cause of the drama is the corpse of Polyneices. Dead Oedipus and the terror of his leaving overshadow the events of the play from the outset. The successive complications and enrichments of awareness among the characters and ourselves are of a kind to draw the dead nearer and nearer to the sphere of the living.

Starting with Antigone's first speech, the dead are made animate both in their place of darkness and at the uncertain frontiers of life. Eteocles is pictured as receiving his due welcome from the dead (line 25). It is this welcome which properly removes him from Antigone's further anguish and all but cursory mention. Ismene's awesome necrology of the House of Laius, in lines 49–60, achieves a twofold effect. It evokes a massive counter-presence to the living agents in the play, a counterpoise of alternative values and obligations. Secondly, it gives to the ostracism of dead Polyneices, to that decree which inhibits his homecoming to the welcome of the Labdacidae, a particular pathos and isolation.

Antigone's resolve to lie in death beside her brother (lines 72–3) initiates a closely woven sequence of rhetorical and symbolic moves whereby the distance between the quick and the dead is gradually effaced. By line 83, the centres of emotional and of moral gravity are shifting: in her polemic with Ismene, Antigone uses 'life' and the business of continued living as terms of scornful reproach. The dead are rising into action. Ismene (lines 93–4 are textually problematic) will be 'subject' to the hatred of Polyneices, or will have made of him an active enemy. Creon, also, is conscious of the claims of the dead to a notable place in the hierarchy of civic affairs—a claim which will be the central motif of ironic dramatization in Sartre's *Les Mouches*. In lines 209–10 Creon carefully conjoins 'the living and the dead'; both are to be honoured and held in prestigious remembrance if they have shown devotion to the public good. With Creon's edict (lines 217–22), death enters the play, not only as the objective–symbolic pivot—dead Polyneices is to be left unburied—but as the coiled spring of imminent tragedy, for whoever defies this edict shall be subject to death. The words νεκρός, θανεῖν, θανόντων crowd the language of Creon, of the Guard, of the unsettled chorus. But these words are losing the aura, the numinous resonance, won for them, by virtue of utmost poetic and moral insight, in Book xxiv of the *Iliad*. Antigone's task, throughout the remainder of the play, could, concisely, be defined as that of restoring to the vocabulary of death the Homeric, the Socratic dignity of which Creon's political vitalism has stripped it. In the flawless economy of Sophocles' design, it is exactly this 'stripping', this legalistic making naked, which is pressed home by the Guard's account (410 ff.) of the malodorous and decaying condition of Polyneices' remains.

Antigone's riposte and exaltation of death are central to her stance. Her eloquent espousal of early death, in lines 462 ff., is more than a provocation of Creon. It is, at once, a defiance of the living, of those who set life above the eternities of moral law, even where, especially where, the font of these eternities is the abode of Δίκη in Hades, and an assertion of personal freedom. To choose death freely, to choose it early, is to retain mastery and self-mastery in the face of the only phenomenon against which man knows no remedy (line 361). We are not far here from the heroic absolutism which we find in the world of Corneille or in the Hegelian allegory of Master and Slave. It is this declaration of ontological liberty which generates the momentarily anguished, if also contemptuous, query in line 497: 'Would you now do more than seize and slay me?' Confronting Creon's vainglorious fury, Antigone wonders whether it is in his power somehow to demean, to trivialize by arbitrary pain, the death which is *hers*, which she has freely chosen.

But as the debate intensifies, Antigone's exaltation of the ethical and visceral demands of death carries all before it. It is not only that Hades requires equal rites/rights for all the slain, whatever the discriminations grossly made by mundane politics (line 519): it is that 'loving care, the loving humaneness of mortal solidarity' or φιλία, while bridging the ultimately trivial gap between life and death, has its foundations in the realm of eternity. It is φιλία which ensures the salutary pressure of transcendence on the living. There is a spasm of radical impotence in Creon's taunt (lines 524–5): 'If you must love, go love the dead' (φίλει κείνους). But once more, the tensed equity of Sophocles' treatment of the conflict arrests us. In line 555, Antigone flings at Ismene a climactic dichotomy: 'Your choice was to live, mine to die.' With its emphatic connotations of superiority, Antigone's accusation has in it more than a touch of the absolutism, of the pride, which blind Creon. Prematurely, Antigone arrogates to herself the infallibilities of death.

The second half of Sophocles' *Antigone* is a set of variations on the theme of death as elaborate and sustained as any in devotional, baroque, or Romantic literatures. I will look further at Antigone's death-song, the κομμός, and at Teiresias' apocalyptic vision. But it is worth recalling briefly Sophocles' dramatization of the tidal advance of the dead on the dissolving society of the living.

All of Antigone's clan are now guests of underworld Persephone (line 894). It is simply because she is still so markedly of the living that Ismene has, in the context of the children of Laius, ceased to exist. More and more, the hospitality of Hades reaches irresistibly into daylight. It draws after it Antigone, Haemon, Eurydice, and, by implacable association, Megareus. In a play which contains many moments of terror, the crowning enormity is that of line 1173: the Messenger, who has spoken nothing but death, asserts that to be 'of the living' is to be the killer of the dead. Surely, there is here an echoing inversion of the Servant's murderous reply to unknowing Clytemnestra in the *Choephoroe*: 'It is the dead

(inside the house) who have returned to kill the living.' The
barriers between the worlds of the living and of the dead,
barriers whose fragility, whose inadequacy as a safeguard to
the secular city are, as we have seen, a recurrent and
fundamental Sophoclean concern, are now broken. 'Corpse
embraces corpse' (κεῖται δὲ νεκρὸς περὶ νεκρῶι). This line
(1240) fulfils fatally Creon's derisive injunction to Antigone. A
difficult play on words in line 1266 may imply not only that
Haemon has died young, but that Death itself, in implicit
contrast to Creon laid waste, is 'new' and 'young'. The
Messenger's successive revelations rain down on Creon like
homicidal blows. But it is a man 'already dead' or 'as dead'
(line 1288) who is being struck anew. Creon himself calls
wildly on Death. To die now would be both consummation
and final, supreme (ὕπατος) release.

Sententiously, the chorus, old men who are, however, yet
lodged in life, denies him such solace. Closely echoing Creon's
own admonition to self-blinded Oedipus in *Oedipus Rex*, the
chorus bids Creon desist from imperious prayer. The acts and
discourses of human will end in doom. This rebuke enacts a
dread symmetry: Creon, who denied burial to Polyneices, is
now himself barred from entry into the house of the dead. The
ostracism he pronounced against Polyneices has become his.
This equilibrium of fatality is quintessentially Sophoclean. But
it reaches back, as well, to more ancient intuitions of tragic
harmony. In the most famous of the citations ascribed to
Anaximander, at the outset of metaphysical thought, we learn
that all things compensate each other, by force of retribution,
for the ἀδικία, for the 'injustice' which, inevitably, attaches to
their temporal existence. It is a riddling proposition. But its
doctrines of a symmetry of suffering and of the mystery of
inescapable injustice implicit in human actions do seem to
foreshadow the commerce between life and death in our play.

The fifth of the great axes of encounter is that between men
and god(s). A Greek tragedy was performed around an altar.
The religious dimension is explicit in the actual presentation of
the play and implicit in the mythology which is, with very
few exceptions, its material. And even in those rare instances
in which the subject is drawn from recent and secular history,
as it is in Aeschylus' *Persians*, historicity is made mythical

ANTIGONES   267

and the logic of the supernatural applies. Comparative anthropology has been tempted, certainly since the late nineteenth century, to expound analogies between the supplicatory, theophanic, quasi-liturgical elements in Greek tragic drama and such genres of religious dance-drama or sacral mimesis as they are found in India, in south-east Asia (the narrative dance-plays of Bali), or in the medieval Mystery Cycles of western Europe. Such comparisons turn out to be misleading. The fact is that the tragedies of Aeschylus, Sophocles, and Euripides, and what little we can gather of the dramatic texts of their immediate predecessors and successors, are like no other performative act or art, like no other aesthetic realizations of enacted intellect and feeling, of which we have knowledge. It is not even certain that inventions at all like them were made and applied beyond the narrow confines of Athens and of Attic culture.

This singularity relates, unquestionably, to the religious–ritual character of dramatized lament and heroic commemoration at it began on Attic ground with, tradition has it, Thespis. Aristotle's suppositions as to the precise nature of this background are, already, uncertain and, it may be, erroneous. That the presence of the religious and of the supernatural in classical Greek tragedy was, at once, functionally vital *and* unstable, or, indeed, frankly problematic, is suggested both by the uniqueness of the Aeschylean–Sophoclean–Euripidean format, and the extreme brevity of its creative phase. Only some seventy years separate the innovative genius of Aeschylus from the last tetralogies of Sophocles and the rapid decline which, according to ancient witness, set in with the fourth-century epigones. The tension between ritual literalism and internalized, even subversive or questioning, religiosity, between the epiphany of the god and the metaphorization or humanization of his divine powers, between the *deus* and the stage-*machina* from which he steps in his overwhelming but also questionable shape, could be sustained and made formally constructive only briefly.

So far as we are able to judge, the tragic–satyric tetralogy embodies and realizes a profoundly fruitful modulation from conventions of empathic, mimetic, perhaps therapeutic (cathartic) rites to a context of metaphysical–political debates and critiques. The tragic mode itself passes out of collectivity into the radical solitude of poetic doubts and inventions. Roughly, one can place Solon at the inception of this unique motion of spirit, and Socrates at its coda. The notion of brevity, moreover, attaches to the religious substance of Greek tragedy not only in a historical, but also in a formal sense. The axiomatic possibility of divine intervention, the proximate pressure of the gods on mortal words and gestures, allow a rare economy. A Greek tragic trilogy can be almost of the length of a single Shakespearean play. There are tragedies by Aeschylus, Sophocles, and Euripides which do not exceed the length of a single act in *Hamlet, King Lear,* or *Troilus and Cressida.* Each major Shakespearean tragic drama or tragi-comedy must define and communicate its thematic context and, where this applies, the quality of supernatural or theological inference proper to itself. The categories of immanent limitation or transcendence are, always, local. The conveyance to the audience of these particular prescriptions (particular to the given play), the establishment in the actual level and idiom in the play of the relevant categories of speculative enlistment, take time and expository insistence. Witness the expositions of the Ghost in *Hamlet* or of the disincarnate orders in *The Tempest.* A Greek tragedy, in contrast, has at its disposal economies of symbolic deployment as immediate as those of the Mass.

In the brief flowering of a tensed and concise art form, the position of Sophocles is, nearly schematically, median. His treatment of the divine dimension, as we find it both in the extant plays and fragments, does not match the Aeschylean sense of man's close neighbourhood to the gods, a neighbourhood which is, itself, still a function of a 'titanic', pre-civic stage in human evolution.[1] On the other hand, Sophocles seems to avoid—though he comes close to it in the Athena of *Ajax*—the Euripidean duplicity whereby the gods are either irrationalized, made ethically and spiritually more 'archaic' than their mortal victims, or ironized by the play of inquisitive and sophistic uncertainties. Available to Sophocles' temper, so far as we have textual evidence, is neither the direct monumentality of divine struggle and epiphany as we find it in the *Oresteia* nor the disconcerting pathos of man's judgement on and valediction to the gods as these are dramatized in

[1] Cf. the general discussion of this point in W. Bröcker, *Der Gott des Sophokles* (Frankfurt-on-Main, 1971).

Euripides' *Hippolytus* or *Bacchae*. The interrogative meditation
on the very nature of a 'playhouse of the gods' (the theatre of
Dionysus), on the price which a πόλιϲ and a literary genre must
be prepared to pay if they are to enfold the gods—a meditation
manifest in the *Bacchae*, and which seems to make of this drama
the reflexive finale to Greek classical tragedy—lies to one side
of Sophocles' sensibility.

As we saw, Sophocles views the potential actualization of
divine vicinity, realized in Aeschylus, as one of the ebbing yet
still menacing currents of archaic and anarchic pressure on
civility and the slow ripening of reason. No less acute, however,
is his notice of the hubristic crescendo of immanent energies, of
will, of proud positivism, which threatens mankind in a world
either emptied of the gods or in contact with them only by
courtesy of ritual practice. It is, therefore, Sophocles' particular art to suggest the proximity of the gods while, already,
giving to this proximity the incipiently metaphoric, psycho-
logized status of personal and private consciousness. Neither
Aeschylus nor Euripides could, I think, have achieved (even if
they had wished to do so) the mystery of Oedipus' transfiguration at Colonus, that persuasive radiance of suggestion as it
unfolds between contrasting polarities of naked supernatural-
ism and of rational inquiry. The mediate miracle in the sacred
wood springs from an intimation, already almost Virgilian,
that the primal intimacies between men and gods are
fortunately/unfortunately receding out of all but eccentric or,
in some sense, scandalous reach. It was as if the very incest
committed by Oedipus was a dark reminiscence of the greater
incest in the original commerce between gods and men. Hence
my definition of Sophoclean *pietas* as 'a haunted humanism'.

It has been argued that the theatre of Racine depends on a
deus absconditus as its hidden spectator. In Sophoclean tragedy,
the 'hidden god' is a central agent. He makes his appearance
early in *Antigone*: in lines 278–9 the leader of the chorus asks
whether the enigmas which seem to mark the first 'burial' of
Polyneices have not been 'divinely willed' or even 'divinely
performed'.[1] As we have seen, this hint broadens in the

---

[1] Cf. A. Maddalena's argument in *Sofocle* (2nd edn., Turin, 1963), 69–72.
Maddalena sees the first burial as a trap, an ambush (*una trappola . . . una reta, un
inganno*) set for Antigone by the gods. If, argues Maddalena, the gods have trapped
Creon, the net which they have cast over Antigone is even 'worse'.

cognitive and dramatic equivocations on the possible intervention of the supernatural in the 'dust-storm' around the second
burial. Yet the very outset of the play also suggests to us a
distancing of and from the gods. Antigone does not appeal for
divine help in the execution of her pious design. No supplication either to Zeus or to the eternal custodians of the dead
graces her resolve. The successive invocations of 'eternally
all-seeing Zeus' (line 184) comes from the lips of Creon. It is
he who, in his denunciation of city-burning, sacrilegious
Polyneices, introduces into the drama the pantheon of civic
deities and their pillared shrines. But the ritual proprieties of
Creon's formulations are undermined by the pomp and
grammatical torsion of line 304: threatening the Guard with
cruel death if the men 'who did this deed for hire' are not
found, Creon swears by 'Zeus who still has my reverence' or 'as
he still has my reverence'. The Greek does not translate to full
clarity. But the hint of menace, covert though it be, masked as
it is by the furious pitch of Creon's rhetoric, cannot be
overheard.

Creon's view of his relations with Zeus is one of utilitarian
reciprocity, of invocations and honours proffered in the
expectation of condign reward. Now we have noted that a civic
order of religiosity, that the encompassing of worship in the
general politics of decency, are a positive element in the
Sophoclean vision of rightness. The impulse which cheapens
and betrays this vision stems from the coercive nature of
Creon's oath, as well as from the simple fact that this oath is set
in a context of imperious error and injustice. Creon's warning
to Zeus, veiled, as it were, in the syntax of line 304 and in that
arrogant touch of temporality ('still'), lays the ground for
subsequent blasphemy. Already, both Antigone's omission of
prayer and Creon's hectoring fluency of adjuration keep the
divine at a distance. And it is precisely this distance—the gods
are drawn irresistibly towards vacant ground, they cluster near
negation—of which Sophocles is master.

One need not adopt Hölderlin's reading of Antigone as an
Antitheos to be made aware of the extreme sparseness of
reference to the divine in her apologia. πρὸς θεῶν, the formula
of supplication so frequent in Sophocles' other plays, occurs
only once in *Antigone* (in line 838 or 839, depending on
editorial numeration, and there in a polemic context). Zeus

and Dike are cited only once in Antigone's great defence, in an argument whose logic and grammar are, in fact, negative: 'it was *not* Zeus . . . these are *not* the laws prescribed by Dike.' The transcendent absolutes to which Antigone appeals in her debate with Creon are, in a radical sense, secular. They are those of parity in death and of those indiscriminations between past good and evil which give to the dead their claim on familial solidarity. If there is a divine presence in the advocacy for Polyneices' bestowal, it is that of Hades. But here, as well, Antigone's register is one of almost perfunctory self-evidence. We are worlds away from any Homeric or Aeschylean stress on the imminent substantiality of the preternatural. Antigone draws about herself an ethical solitude, a lucid dryness which seem to prefigure the stringencies of Kant. She is abstemious in respect of the transcendent. This, too, is part of her implacable discretion.

Again, and with incomparable dramatic–psychological finesse, it is through the mouth of Creon that Sophocles points to the ambiguous proximities of the divine. Ζεὺς ἑρκεῖος, as Creon calls upon him in line 487, is metonymic of the very essence of 'the family'. His altar stands in the courtyard of the house, the family dwelling (ἕρκος) enfolds it. It is to this specific incarnation of Zeus that the family prays or offers sacrifice in a shared rite which, in turn, defines its own cohesion and identity of kinship. There is, therefore, a complex impropriety in Creon's appeal to the god. He tells us that even if the culprit were nearer to him in parentage than those who worship Zeus at the familial altar, he or she shall not escape doom as prescribed by law. As in line 304, Zeus is harnessed to an act of arbitrary vindictiveness. The 'Zeus of the family' is being invoked, almost parodistically, against those specific ties of kinship and domesticity which he safeguards. But Creon's impropriety or even indecency is made complex and double-edged just because Ζεὺς ἑρκεῖος has *not* been invoked by Antigone in what would have been a most natural turn of spirit and of speech. Once more, Creon seems, instinctively, to appropriate and exploit an emptiness left by Antigone.

The persistently strategic and opportunistic impulse in Creon's religiosity is underlined in lines 658 ff. He yields to Antigone the 'Zeus of blood-kinship' whom he had himself earlier sought to enlist. It is now Zeus βασιλεύς, monarch and

patron of civic–masculine domination, whom Creon adduces
in his own (Creon's) exact image. Yet Haemon's counter-
arguments are as distant from the immediacies of the divine as
were Antigone's. The allusion to the 'honours due to the gods'
(line 745) is made in passing, and the deities of the underworld,
θεῶν τῶν νερτέρων, whom Haemon cites in line 749, are, in the
context, well and truly 'hidden'.

Throughout the major part of Sophocles' *Antigone*, in short,
the dramatis personae keep the gods at arm's length. It is, as I
have tried to show, the choral odes which both solicit and make
probable the coming of the divine. This coming upon man
grows palpable as the actions of the protagonists in the drama
veer out of control. The inadequacies of immanence, be they
those of Antigone's moral monism or be they those of Creon's
selective and officious 'established church', are revealed,
terribly, in the fourth stasimon. Here, I believe, is the fatal
hinge of the play.

Through the elusive turbulence of the ode, the pertinence of
whose three mythological cameos to the present fate of
Antigone has been interminably and inconclusively argued,
pierces the theme of catastrophic intimacies between gods and
mortals. The dread, the uncanny power of fate—and
μοιριδία τις δύνασις δεινά are, it seems to me, the four words
which concentrate the finalities of Sophocles' vision and art—
spares neither the high-born nor even those of divine ancestry.
On the contrary, it is upon *them* that it focuses its terrors. Zeus'
golden visitation incarcerates Danae in a chamber secret as the
grave. Lycurgus of Thrace is hideously chastised for having
doubted the divine birth of Dionysus. Like Pentheus in the
Bacchae, he had foolishly striven to define and maintain the
pragmatic demarcations between the world of the gods and
that of the πόλις. Now Dionysus, himself the mysterious
offspring of an ecstatic–destructive encounter between
immortal Zeus and mortal Semele, crosses the barrier in
vengeance. The bearing of the horrors which befall Thracian
Cleopatra on the choral logic is obscure (Sophocles appears to
have dealt with this savage myth in at least two lost plays). But
again, the motif of intercourse and generation between gods
and men appears. Cleopatra is a child of Boreas, the divine
North Wind. She was nursed in his cavern of tempests. If the
passage is not corrupt (see Jebb's annotation to line 970), the

implication is that Ares watches the blinding of Cleopatra's children with 'cruel joy'.

Antigone, who has denied Eros, who has interposed a sterile purity of moral will between herself and the uncertainties or dilatoriness of divine aid, has been led to her death. In its heightened state of manic perception, the chorus cites, dances, three terror-myths each of which refers to that most intimate and fateful of encounters between gods and mortals, the erotic. As sacrificial blood draws to daylight the spirits of the dead, as honey draws bees, so human conflict and the representation of such conflict in the theatre draw the gods, and hybrid Dionysus in particular. The point is crucial to our grasp of Attic tragedy. The gods are present in the enunciation and miming of the myth. But they come also to the altar in the amphitheatre. Dionysus is present in his playhouse and at his festival. He returns to Thebes not only in the summoning of the chorus's sententious finale (lines 1349–50), but in the greater guise of the play itself, of the terrors and demands which *Antigone* enforces on us.

It is as if this wild stasimon had burst open the secular gates. Supernatural agencies now throng Creon's city. The birds at the place of sacred augury are frenzied and scream barbarously (there is here, perhaps, a sinister echo of Aeschylus' *Agamemnon*, line 1051). Hephaestus, the fire god and, by metonymy, the sacrificial flame itself, refuses his presence. The flame will not kindle. The fat, the entrails do not burn. Such is the macabre rebuke of the gods to those who would honour them in polluted Thebes. The civic altars as well as those of the private hearth have been sullied with carrion ripped by the birds from the unburied flesh of Polyneices. The spasmodic, diffuse causalities and contiguities which normally operate in human affairs have yielded to an instantaneous and implacable symmetry. The birds and dogs whom Creon bade devour the corpse of loathed Polyneices are infecting the πόλις with obscene droppings. The flames denied to the son of Oedipus are now denied to the altars. Creon, who, like Oedipus before him, has seen in Teiresias a corrupt augur, one whom mutinous citizens have bribed with gold so that he shall traffic treacherously (*marchander* renders the precise flavour of the original) with the truth, must now confront the physical omens of divine disgust. He must grapple with the apparent abrogation of the contract of public piety between himself, as legitimate ruler, and the supernatural presences whom he had personally invoked on terms of reciprocity. Creon does so in what I take to be one of the central passages in our text.

In Jebb's version, lines 1039–44 read as follows:

but ye shall not hide that man in the grave—no, though the eagles of Zeus should bear the carrion morsels to their master's throne—no, not for dread of that defilement will I suffer his burial—for well I know that no mortal can defile the gods.

Robert Fagles translates:

> You'll never bury that body in the grave,
> not even if Zeus's eagles rip the corpse
> and wing their rotten pickings off to the throne of god!
> Never, not even in fear of such defilement
> will I tolerate his burial, that traitor.
> Well I know, we can't defile the gods—
> no mortal has the power.

And Mazon:

Non, quand les aigles de Zeus l'emporteraient pour le manger jusques au trône du dieu, même alors, ne comptez pas que, par crainte d'une souillure, je vous laisse l'enterrer, moi. Je sais trop que souiller les dieux n'est pas au pouvoir d'un mortel.

This is not the place at which to do more than merely draw attention to the considerable differences in intonation and literal understanding which these three versions exemplify. It is evident that the Greek resists unequivocal paraphrase. There may be textual problems in line 1040, and various clarifying emendations have been proposed. Some commentaries labour for ambiguity. Creon will not bury Polyneices' remains even under threat of pollution; or, should the eagles bear carrion to the omnipotent throne, the burial would none the less result only from Creon's decision, and not have been imposed on him by Teiresias' portents or mendacities.

But this strikes one as strained elaboration. The pulse of baffled rage—the gods whom he has honoured and whose temples he has victoriously defended against the incendiary Argives are now turning on him—and the blasphemy that erupts out of Creon's fury are emphatic. We have seen how subtly they are prepared for by the undercurrent of unctuous blackmail in line 304. And again, a dire symmetry is at work. Although lines 855-7 are notoriously difficult to interpret, the chorus sees Antigone as overweeningly close to the plinth and throne of Justice, seeking either to embrace it imperiously or even to thrust against it. Mirroring this image, Creon's blasphemy now reaches out, with crass impurity, to the very seat of Zeus.

But, so far as I am aware, no commentary has perceived the challenging depth of Creon's justification— θεοὺς μιαίνειν οὔτις ἀνθρώπων cθένει.

Theologically, psychologically, within but also far beyond the context of the drama, this is a tremendous postulate. Jebb reads the line as a sophism 'of the kind with which a stubborn and wrong-headed man might seek to quiet his conscience'. Others see the statement as evidence that fury has momentarily overcome Creon's prudential piety. Citing, in contrast, the profoundly serious use of this maxim in line 1232 of Euripides' *Hercules Furens*, some exegetes qualify Creon's utterance as purely hypocritical. Thus Erasmus in his *Adagia* (v. 1): 'sententia pia est sed a Creonte impia anima dicta.' Do these readings do justice to the probing, unsettling psychology of Sophocles' construct? Ought we not, rather, to welcome the suggestion put forward by Lewis Campbell, in his edition of Sophocles of 1871, that Creon's sovereign scepticism is genuine and that it anticipates that of the Epicureans?

We must, I think, ponder the context closely. Creon's political theology had officiously gauged the conventionalized and due degrees of contact as between men and gods. Now the rules have been broken by the wild ingress into the city of mystery and hostile portent. Has Creon discovered, in the bleak clairvoyance of his rage, the abyss of 'non-relation' between mortal and divine? Does he now realize, even if only in a barren flash of insight, that his desecration of Polyneices' corpse was a meaningless gesture because man's fate in respect of the transcendent cannot be determined via ritual or the denial of ritual? For if no human pollution can defile the gods, then the non-burial of Polyneices is a trivially immanent act. And Antigone's agonistic reflex becomes simultaneously excessive and reducible to a wholly private, sentimental impulse. The tragedy need not have been.

Arguably, this is to place on line 1044 too great a charge of suggestion. Yet the grandeur of the statement does stand. It echoes forward to attitudes as philosophically and morally consequent as are the ethics of *caritas* and compassion announced by Antigone. And it is just this touch of self-destructive parity as between certain of Antigone's foresights and those of Creon which persuades one.

But it is, of course, too late. Zeus, Dionysus, Hephaestus, and Pluto are abroad in the city of man.[1] It is their presence which gives to each successive disaster its edge of meaning. As Creon and his servants pause to bury the remains of Polyneices, they pray for mercy to Hecate, goddess of crossroads—how fatal are crossroads in the affairs of the House of Laius—and to Pluto, lord of the underworld. As we know, this moment of penitential piety serves to make doubly sure that Creon will no longer reach the rock-tomb in time. It is at the altar of Ζεὺς ἑρκεῖος, that Zeus of the familial hearth whom Creon had tactically invoked earlier, that his wife Eurydice now kills herself. Creon's outcry in line 1284 offers difficulties. Some read it as signifying that no sacrifice can appease all-devouring Hades. Others, more tellingly perhaps, interpret the passage to mean that there is no haven for Creon in death, that the victims he has sent to Hades now choke and pollute its longed-for entrance. What is certain is the overwhelming presentness of the vortex of the underworld. It drags Creon after it into blackness.

It is the meetings between gods and men in *Antigone* which are, finally, the most destructive. *Nemo contra deum nisi deus ipse*, said Goethe. Sophocles knew better. The attempts of the protagonists to keep the divine at a moral or a diplomatic remove fail utterly. At the last, the gods arrive, and civility and the fabric of reason succumb.

But each of the great determinants of collision as they are set out and spring from the debate between Creon and Antigone—between man and woman, between old and young, between society and the individual, between the quick and the dead, between gods and mortals—is, in the final reckoning, non-negotiable and always recursive. It is this timelessness of

---

[1] H. D. F. Kitto's comment, in *Sophocles, Dramatist and Philosopher* (Oxford, 1958), 40—'The gods *are* active in these final scenes of the *Antigone*', but they belong to 'the natural order of events'—is clearly inadequate.

necessary and *insoluble* conflict, as Greek tragedy enacts it, which invites us to assimilate the condition of man on this earth to that of the tragic.

6

Antigone's progress towards death (lines 806–943) comes close to constituting a play within the play. The successive parts of this fourth ἐπεισόδιον are interwoven with consummate art. We have Antigone's lament (the κομμός), the contrapuntal responses of the chorus, Creon's brutal intervention after his entrance at line 883, Antigone's final oration or rhesis in lines 891–928, and the brief invocation which she speaks at her exit. The diversity of metrical means, the manifold virtuosities of rhetoric which characterize *Antigone* as a whole, are concentrated and deployed to their highest pitch around Antigone's rite of death.

It is plausible to suppose that Greek tragic drama evolved out of proto-dramatic exchanges between a chorus and a solo voice. Tensions between organic collectivity and the aloneness of the individual, as he steps out of or against this collectivity, are, therefore, built into the very structure of Greek tragic forms. It is, moreover, probable that these archaic lyric choruses and beginnings of dialogue commemorated the heroic dead in the locale associated by myth or monument with the hero's burial. Thus a κομμός in a Greek tragedy may literally take us back to the ceremonies of lamentation and to the mimetic recall of the hero's fate which lie at the roots of drama. We are taken back to the origins of the dramatic genre also by the fundamental interaction between the choral community and the emergence into contour and apartness of the individual persona.

Sophocles is a master of solitudes. Not before Shakespeare's Timon, the most classically and uncompromisingly tragic of his creations, do we find studies in human isolation to match Sophocles' Ajax, Electra, Philoctetes, or Oedipus at Colonus. Nowhere in literature or moral thought is the existential terror of aloneness, of severance from *communitas*, more acutely rendered than in the 'Ode on Man' in *Antigone*. Thus, more than any other episode in ancient tragedy, excepting the closing, mutilated scenes in the *Bacchae*, Antigone's κομμός comprises in a single recapitulation and unfolding both the actual source of the tragic theatre and its poetic fulfilment.

The δαίμων of Antigone has been one of self-isolation. Hence, we saw, the depth of Kierkegaard's identification with her. When Ismene fails her, the premises of trust which underwrite intimate relationships lapse. Antigone reverts to the solipsistic grammar of Oedipus, the syntax of the ego. The crux in line 941—Antigone's reference to herself as the last child of Oedipus—is a profound dramatic–psychological provocation. By proclaiming herself to be the sole surviving offspring of the Labdacidae, Antigone annuls Ismene from the living. To Antigone, life itself has become equated with a total commitment to the duties and fatalities of kinship. Yet throughout the play Antigone has asserted that these same duties and fatalities transcend good or evil conduct, that they lie outside the shallow jurisdiction of reason or of hatred. How, then, can she deny to Ismene that sense of φιλία which embraces Polyneices and gives validity to her own death? Sophocles gives no answer.

But the play, and the κομμός in particular, direct us towards a feeling of estrangement in Antigone so drastic that her reflexes of isolation affect not only all other human presences— Eteocles, Ismene, Haemon, the chorus—but also herself. Antigone's lament and farewell can best be understood as a desperate endeavour to come home to her own sole truth of being. This endeavour will enlist pathos and sophistry as well as a surpassing nakedness of appeal. If Antigone does not wholly succeed, it is precisely because the vehemence of her dissociations, of her cumulative exits from the compromising fabric of erotic, social, and civic life, have finally made her something of a stranger even to the initial certitudes and firmness of her own ego.

Jebb cites the exquisite paraphrase of Antigone's farewell to the sun in Swinburne's *Erechtheus*:

> People, old men of my city, lordly wise and hoar of head,
> I, a spouseless bride and crownless, but with garlands of the
>   dead,
> From the fruitful light turn silent to my dark unchilded bed.

The scissions she must suffer from organic and social fulfilment are mercilessly set out. Antigone will not know marriage, and her κομμός is, as it were, the mirroring antistrophe to a ὑμέναιον or bridal song. By virtue of supreme irony, Antigone is herself to be deprived of those rites of burial in which she has perceived the only consecration, the only dictate of comeliness, appropriate to her doomed house. The manner of her death will consign her to monstrous limbo: in the lightless chamber, Antigone will be neither of the living nor of the dead. The motif of ostracism, densely foreshadowed by the word ἄπολις in the first stasimon, modulates from a philosophical–political register into one of ontological finality. Though there are textual difficulties, the underlying sense of lines 850–2 is inescapable: Antigone has a home neither on earth nor in the underworld, she can find dwelling neither in the city of the quick nor in that of the departed. The famous keyword is μέτοικος, 'the half-breed', 'the hybrid stranger'.[1] Yet the alienation and exile from social normality which the half-caste condition comports are as nothing when compared with the expulsion out of life-and-death, out of the bounds of primordial humanity, entailed by Antigone's live burial.

Possessing, possessed by so graphic a vision of her impending fate, Antigone is no longer in trusting touch with the springs of her action. Her closing speech, spiralling upon, darting against itself, has the wild truth of contradiction. At the same time, it belongs to the topos of a last flinching before a willed, accepted self-sacrifice. Similar movements occur in the Gospel narratives of the agony in the Garden or in what we know of Joan of Arc's momentary recantation. Without this flinching, there would not be the self-knowledge (αὐτόγνωτος) which gives to self-sacrifice its lucidity and meaning.

Creon is on stage during Antigone's monologue. But her words are directed neither at him nor at the chorus. Antigone addresses those who cannot or will not hear her—the guests of Persephone in the night-world. She speaks to herself and to *her* dead. Three times in lines 898–9 Antigone intones varying forms of her talismanic word, φίλος. In line 902, and this is the only time she does so in the play, Antigone calls directly and by name on Polyneices. There follows the arch-disputed ground of philological, stylistic, and psychological controversy. No lay

---

[1] Cf. the influential study of this entire concept in M. Détienne and J.-P. Vernant, *Les Ruses de l'intelligence — La Métis des Grecs* (Paris, 1974).

reader will have anything to contribute to the arguments and counter-arguments which have, since 1821, divided scholars, textual critics, and students of Greek tragedy as to the authenticity or interpolation of lines 904–20. What the layman *will* note is the light which this irreconcilable debate throws on the limitations of both scholarship and intuition.

My sense of the passage, a sense drawn in part from having seen some productions of the play which included it and others which omitted it, is that it belongs. Antigone is struggling fiercely to keep at bay the inrush of doubt and of despair. Neither subterranean Persephone nor beloved Polyneices has come to her aid. She knows nothing of Haemon's rebellious support. The chorus has queried not only the legal and ethical propriety of her act, but its meaningfulness. In this extremity, it is, in fact, the forced logic and concreteness of Antigone's 'Herodotean' plea, it is the sophistry whereby she would prove the unique status of a dead brother as against all other losses, which ring true. On the knife-edge of total solitude, Oedipus' child reaches towards that shallow but momentarily dazzling rhetorical ingenuity which marked her father's style. And could interpolation really account for δεινὰ τολμᾶν (line 915), that great echo from the 'Ode on Man', which signifies 'to dare terribly'?

But whether or not these lines are genuine, whether Aristotle is right in quoting them as Sophocles' or Goethe in finding such ascription intolerable, what matters is Antigone's manifest incapacity to find peace of mind. The coercive logic (and this, too, is suggestive of authenticity) of her apologia leaves Antigone finally bereft. The 'Gethsemane moment'—Hegel's audacious analogy is not baseless—is upon her.

In a theological scenario, the 'dark night of the soul' precedes intimations or epiphanies of redemption. The theological construct is, in essence, one of melodrama: abandonment, the temptations of despair, come in Act IV. Absolute tragedy is so exceedingly rare a form precisely because it negates the up-beat, the pendulum-swing towards hope which seems to be ingrained in human sensibility. Absolute tragedy, which comprises a handful of Greek tragedies, Marlowe's *Faustus*, Shakespeare's *Timon of Athens* (there are ambiguities of compensation at the close of *Lear*), Racine's theatre of Jansenist retribution, tests the reflex of Capaneus, the blasphemer among the Seven against Thebes, who, even in Dante's *Inferno*, scorns salvation. Tragedy perceives the world as does Ivan Karamazov when he sends back to God his 'ticket of admission'. It extends to Act v the logic of damnation. In very rare instances—and it is these which human imagining finds close to unbearable—tragedy confronts the possibility of nothingness (*nothing* and *never* are, of course, the keywords in *Lear*). Such extension, such probation, make of lines 921–8 in *Antigone* a touchstone of tragedy.

Every word repays attention. Antigone is δύcτηνοc — 'doomed', 'star-crossed' in the Shakespearean sense of one predestined to wretchedness. She is 'god-abandoned'. But Sophocles articulates the discourse so as to compel Antigone to ask herself, and to ask of us, whether it was not her 'autonomy' which chose to do without the gods or, at least, without the Olympians. Formally, δαιμόνων δίκην (line 921) may be the equivalent of θεῶν νόμιμα. Both signify those rules which, according to Antigone, emanate from divine and everlasting justice. But the first phrase, which is the one she actually uses, inevitably connotes her bias towards chthonian night, towards a cosmology older, more ungoverned, than that of Zeus. Antigone harbours no solacing certitudes as to the nature of Hades. As in *Ajax*, so in *Antigone*, the reticence of Sophocles' art is such as to leave open the possibility of 'nihilism', of that abyss of nothingness after life which western religiosity, metaphysical idealism, and the common pulse of the imagination would deny. Antigone envisions herself as entering either upon blank and inconceivable extinction—something like Baudelaire's 'grand trou | Tout plein de vague horreur, menant on ne sait ou'—or as seeking uncertain reunion with the clan of the self-destroyed and fratricidal dead. No Elysium beckons, no Socratic grove.

With the self-lacerating clarity which also characterizes Oedipus when fatality strikes, Antigone spells out, urges the paradox of her undoing: her piety has harvested both the designation and fruits of impiety. Her just deed has generated hideous injustice. Now what moral right, what pragmatic motive, has she to call upon those gods whose manifest failure to intervene on her behalf is *either* incomprehensible *or* a signal that Antigone has acted in error? Unspoken, yet in range of Antigone's bitter casuistry, is the third, most terrible, alternative: that the gods are unjust or impotent, that mortal man, if he insists on acting ethically, according to reason and conscience, must leave the gods 'behind'. We find this view, if the text can be adequately reconstructed, stated all but explicitly at the close of Euripides' *Bacchae*. I take it to be outside Sophocles' world-view. Nevertheless, it is a distant inference which seems to press on the inhuman solitude and self-torment of Antigone's finale. Nothing in her acquiesces in an Aeschylean theodicy, in the acceptance, proposed by the chorus, of unmerited doom or of the absence of divine help in consequence of some hereditary malediction. She wants to *know*. She is Oedipus' child, rebellious in knowledge.

No translation does justice to the grim pathos and casuistical provocation of the closing lines. At one level, there is desperate doubt: *if* the gods have found for Creon, *if* she has been truly doomed for impiety, Antigone will 'know her error'. It is not that Antigone has ceased to believe in the fundamental rightness of her conduct. But to term lines 926–7 as 'at most scornfully concessive', as J. C. Kamerbeek does in his commentary, is to miss the authentic terror of Antigone's position and to overhear the intimations of futility and nothingness which dog her. Chillingly, παθόντες, in line 926, allows the possibility that Antigone will convict herself of error *after* she has been done to death. Before her may stretch an eternity of punishment and self-punishment. ἁμαρτάνουσι (line 927) is fatally ambiguous: it means either the commission of an unwitting, excusable fault, or the perpetration of a culpable deed, or *both*.

But having turned the double-edge upon herself, Antigone now turns it on her cruel enemies. If *they* have sinned, if the ἁμαρτία, here understood as deliberate, as criminally wilful, is *theirs*, then may they suffer 'no greater evil' than that presently being meted out to her. The rhetorical twist—'may their punishment not exceed mine'—the touch of legalistic equivocation at such a moment, are uncannily apposite. It is Antigone speaking, a young woman whose sombre and probing intellect keeps desperation at bay (it is, I have suggested, this same Antigone who fences dialectically in lines 904–20). She is of Oedipus' mettle, even now, in the 'storm-winds of her soul' (line 929).

It is the House of Laius into which Antigone appears to reenter in her lyric farewell (lines 937–43). Figuratively, this homecoming corresponds precisely to her descent into the rock-tomb. The emblematic terms are πατρῷιον, προγενεῖς, βασιλειδᾶν. Thebes is now and above all the land of Antigone's fathers, the *patrimoine* of her race. She, who is being haled away to vile death, is the last 'of the blood royal'. Let the πόλιc of Laius witness at whose base hands Antigone suffers execution (in sovereign contempt, Antigone does not designate Creon by name). Fearful of heaven, she has cast out mortal fear. In Antigone's parting words, the note of confidence is not one of transcendent faith, but of the heroic temper. Come night or nothingness, Antigone is, at the last, every inch regal. But no splendour is allowed to mask or diminish the abyss. Instants before, in line 934, Antigone has cried out in terror when hearing Creon threaten the guards for their slowness in carrying out his sentence. In Sophocles, heroism does not blunt tragedy. It makes it more wasteful.

7

We have seen throughout these readings that much remains unrecapturable. Consider what might be our full sense of Antigone's final exit if the relevant music and motion were available to us; or if we could clearly visualize the conventions of a theatre of masks in the Greek tragic mode. Appeals to Sophocles' intentions, as one finds oneself making them more or less consciously, are, at best, conjectural. Quite apart from the hermeneutic crux as to whether or not the author's intentions, even where there is good evidence for them, carry any prescriptive authority, the attempt to establish what a fifth-century Athenian dramatist had in mind at this or that point in his plays can never be realized. Hence the characteristic modern resort to the notion of 'constraints'. Philology, classical scholarship, schooled reading, seek to determine the limits of possibility within which an Attic mentality of the Periclean age may reasonably be supposed to have operated. They seek to narrow the areas of textual and semantic uncertainty by delimiting the constraints on language, on syntax, on poetic or philosophic statement functional in contemporary discourse and feeling. Historical learning and

ordinary common sense do lead us to believe, indeed they
almost compel us to do so, that there are things which neither
Sophocles nor his dramatis personae could have meant, felt, or
said in *c*.440 BC.

Where reference to actual objects and practices, say in
agriculture or manufacture, is involved, or where actual
historical occurrences and institutions are alluded to, such
constraints are self-evidently present and worth noting. But
these are only the most primitive elements of context. A major
poet is an innovator in language as well as in sensibility. He
may attach to the words which he uses connotations, tonal
values, even meanings outside and often critical of the usages
current in his society. A character in a play may exhibit
categories of perception and modes of expression radically
eccentric to the norm. Drama has been, time and again, the
testing-ground for lost or future potentials of human utterance
and behaviour. Where they are applied to such crucial
nuances and ambiguities as those we have been looking at—
Antigone's possibly contrastive attitudes to Eteocles and to
Polyneices, the religiosity of Creon, the status of masculine and
of feminine styles of being in the myth and in Sophocles'
treatment—arguments from constraint turn out to be intuitive
and approximate. If this were not the case, how then could one
account for the open-ended disputations between scholars of
the same rank, between equally equipped connoisseurs of the
text on (to cite the obvious case once more) the authenticity or
spuriousness of lines 904–20? One need only have heard a
Winnington-Ingram and a Bernard Knox take diametrically
opposite views on this or other points, and argue their
irreconcilable persuasions with equal wealth of supporting
evidence, to know how little we know.

But the reading of a classical text can also elicit exactly the
contrary difficulty. The work or passage will press on us a
claim of seeming immediacy. Far from sounding archaic and
unrecapturable, the Homeric, Aeschylean, or Sophoclean
words, images, and gestures strike us as overwhelmingly
pertinent. They foreshadow, they symbolize, they speak
nakedly to our present condition. Under pressure of 'relevance', the intricate mappings of distance between reader and
classical text, on which responsible interpretation depends, are
annulled. Now obviously it has been successive experiences of

immediacy, successive compulsions of identification between ancient and modern, that make up the afterlife of Hellas. Ciceronian Atticism, the Platonism of the Renaissance, the neo-classicism of the *ancien régime*, the 'Sparta' of the French Revolution, Victorian Hellenism, are characteristic examples of willed recognition. A later climate of feeling, of aesthetics, of political theory or individual style, discovers in ancient Greece that which is most germane, most immediate in depth and justifying precedent, to its own present needs. Marathon and Salamis, observed Matthew Arnold, were more actual to the governing culture of nineteenth-century England than was the Battle of Hastings.

In the twentieth century, such foreshortenings and claims to relevance have taken on peculiar force. I have alluded often to Heidegger's sense of the yet-to-be-apprehended presence of the pre-Socratics in the birth of authentic modern thought. From Frazer to Lévi-Strauss, comparative anthropology and ethnography have, consciously or not, done much to render our view of culture and ritual synchronic. Ancient Greece is made to 'feel' as near to us as, perhaps nearer than, any other anthropologically and sociologically analysable community. Psychoanalysis, after both Freud and Jung, has literally fed on Greek myths. It has made of the archaic the raw material and substance of the continuities of the human psyche. We are, proclaim psychoanalysis and structural anthropology, *les enfants d'Œdipe*. Thus the modern dramaturgy of consciousness and symbolic identifications bids us recognize in Oedipus and Narcissus, in Prometheus and Odysseus, *mon semblable, mon frère*. More and more, we can come to understand in the modernist movements in the West a hunger for 'beginnings', for a return to archaic, essentially Greek, sources.

This will to homecoming, to the fusion of past and present, has been vivid in the representations of the tragic politics of our age. The burning of cities in 1939–45 was seen, almost at once, as cognate with the destruction of Troy. Euripides' dramatizations of defeat and enslavement, of the survivors and the deported, particularly as these are enacted in the lives of women, took on a fierce pertinence. For Sartre and the Living Theatre, during the wars in Algeria and Vietnam, such figures as Andromache, Hecuba, and the Trojan women provided a code of universal presentness. The 'counter-culture' of the

ANTIGONES

addict and the flower-child, of the manic and the schizoid,
found in the *Bacchae* an immediacy of self-recognition, a
fullness of articulate realization, far beyond those in any
contemporary text. Throughout this study, we have seen
something of the lives of Antigone and of Creon in our
time.

That such sensations of overlap, indeed of identity, between
past and present are guarantors of the continued vitality of a
classic is evident. That a text recedes from literature into
epigraphy or mere historical documentation when it is no
longer experienced as somehow relevant, is equally certain.
Walter Benjamin's hermeneutic conceit whereby there is that
in an ancient text which awaits our discovery, that vital texts
perform a millennial pilgrimage towards recognitions and
interpretations yet to come, contains a real methodological
truth and incitement. Nevertheless, the obstacles which relevance poses to understanding are not to be discounted.
Immediacy sets sensibility ablaze. By the same token, it can
make blind.

Let me illustrate this point, briefly, with reference to lines
1064–76.

Editors point to textual problems (notably in lines 1068–71).
They suggest that Teiresias' prophecy is at once precise and
indistinct. It is precise in its foreknowledge of imminent ruin.
It is indistinct in that it kindles in Creon the false hope that evil
may still be undone, that the prompt entombment of
Polyneices will save the royal house and the city. Teiresias
knows, of course, that it is already far too late. Creon can no
longer satisfy the demands of the nether gods for compensation
for the 'absence' of Polyneices, nor that of the gods above who
will demand restitution for the slaying of Antigone. In this
double and symmetrical exaction, the deaths of Haemon and
of Eurydice are implicit. Such is the central enormity of
Creon's actions that Teiresias hardly alludes to Antigone (is
she not, to his clairvoyance, already a corpse?). In the dread
equilibrium of crime and of punishment Antigone has become
almost fortuitous. Creon's evil deeds must be paid for by
Creon's own flesh and blood.

The potential of blinding relevance lies in Teiresias' summation of what it is that Creon has actually brought about.
Fagles translates strongly:

                              you have thrust
to the world below a child sprung from the world above,
ruthlessly lodged a living soul within the grave—
then you've robbed the gods below the earth,
keeping a dead body here in the bright air,
unburied, unsung, unhallowed by the rites.

An emendation may be needed in this difficult passage to get
exactly the right nuance: 'you keep, here on earth, one of those
properly belonging to those below.' But the meaning of
Teiresias, the circle which he draws, are clear.

Creon has not committed some local, limited crime, however savage, He has, in a way one might not have deemed
possible to a mortal man, inverted the cosmology of life and of
death. He has turned life into living death, and death into
desecrated organic survivance. Antigone is to 'live dead' below
the earth; Polyneices is to be 'dead alive' above. The wheel of
being has been turned obscenely full circle. Greek perception
as a whole, and that of Sophocles more especially—witness the
great monologue to the sunlight in *Ajax*—intimately associated
light and life. To be alive is to see and to be seen by the sun; the
days of the dead are unlit. Creon has done final violence to this
equation. Alive, Antigone is thrust into blackness; dead,
Polyneices is left to rot and to reek in the light of the sun.
Teiresias suggests to us the twofold, subtly equivalent, nature
of the outrage. For if the sun is sacred, so is the dark of Hades.
Creon has polluted both the light and the dark, both the day
and the night. 'Death and the sun', said Pascal, 'cannot face
each other.' Concomitantly, the darkness must not be made
host to the agony of living sight.

No poet or thinker, I believe, has found a greater, a more
comprehensive, statement of 'the crime against life'. None has
found a more total image of the continuum from individual to
cosmic evil. Teiresias' words are, none the less, embedded in
the language and the context of the play. When Teiresias tells
Creon that the Erinyes are 'lying in ambush for you' (line
1075), the formula is Homeric. At work throughout the
prophecy are such specific questions as to whether or not the
Olympian gods have any share in the destiny of the dead, and
as to whether, in the perspective of Aeschylus' *Eumenides*, the
Furies which wait on Creon are specially and vengefully
attached to the errant spirit of Polyneices. Any attempt at

careful reading ought to take these elements into precise account.

Yet I find myself almost unable to do so. Teiresias' (Sophocles') vision of the inversion of the worlds of the living and of the dead has taken on for us, today, an overwhelming actuality. It is the lucid delineation of a planet on which massacres or nuclear warfare have left the numberless un-buried dead, and in whose subterranean shelters, caves, or conscripted catacombs the living wait in blackness for their end. Henry Moore's 'shelter drawings', to which I referred earlier, already draw us uncannily close to the imaginings of *Antigone*. But they are as pastoral ornaments compared to the prospects of death-in-life, of life-in-death, now open to man-kind. It is these very prospects, the murder of life itself by the politics of the living, politics which, like Creon's, have their undoubted claims to dignity and to rationality, which Teiresias enunciates. The relevance of his saying negates all cautionary distance between us and the ancient text. The full meaning of Creon's deeds (errors) has come home to us as it cannot have to any spectator or reader before our present danger. It is not 'the light' which, to reverse a compelling image in Christopher Logue's imitations of the *Iliad*, 'screams to us across three-thousand years', it is the dark.

8

In respect of any text longer than a short lyric, the concept of total grasp is a fiction. Our minds are not so constructed as to be able to hold in steady and complete view a language-object of the dimensions and complexities of Sophocles' *Antigone*. We cannot, for purposes of rounded inspection and mental recon-stitution, circumvent a work of literature as we do a piece of sculpture. The angles of perception from which the play can be approached, the principles of selection or emphasis which are brought to bear on the text's multiple components when one seeks to arrive at a working model of unity, are as diverse as are the linguistic sensibilities, the cultural inheritance, the pragmatic interests, of different individuals.

Even where drafts, preliminary sketches, or statements of intention survive, we can hardly hope to reconstruct the

inward process of assemblage and unification as it is experienced and reported (amost invariably after the fact) by the
artist himself. Such famous admissions as that of Tolstoy in
reference to the 'unexpected' and 'unwilled' evolution of the
character of Anna Karenina in the novel suggest that the
genesis of poetic forms is, at certain points at least, produc-
tively resistant and opaque to the previsions and control of the
writer. At some moment in the dynamics of the subconscious,
witness Henry James's notebooks, the initial 'germ', the
incident, memory, felt configuration, from which the work
develops, modulate into a vision or programme of unison. But
whether the poet, dramatist, or novelist truly sees his text as an
interactive whole, or whether the claim to such perception is,
where it is made, itself a necessary fiction, remains uncertain.
We cannot hope to describe what *Antigone* was, what it became
in the course of composition or retrospection, to Sophocles.

Stanislavsky's work-notes and those of other producers show
that the means whereby a particular staging of a play is given
its unifying style, its performative coherence, are the result of
intricate, fluid adjustments between the producer's internal
ideal and the theatrical resources in fact available to him. The
method is one of compromise and of choice between practical
options. Even the most comprehensive production, the production most intentionally faithful to the text, will elide certain
aspects in order to emphasize others. From the nearly boundless range of conceivable constructs, the producer selects a
dominant shape, a key-note and instrumentation. The neo-
classical harmony which Tieck strove for in his staging of
Antigone differs, conceptually and empirically, from the view of
the play taken by Max Reinhardt in 1900. The actor's sense of
the drama is, in its turn, a fascinating collage. Centred on his
own part and on the immediate context of his memorization
and stage-movements, the actor's *Antigone* is an angular,
fragmented digest of a larger, partly hidden text. Creon's play
is never the same as Antigone's; neither will have the same
sense and remembrance of pace or proportion as we would find
it in the play of the Messenger. Drama is more subject to such
varieties of deconstruction than is any other literary genre (a
fact on which Stoppard's brilliant conceit in *Rosencrantz and
Guildenstern* is founded).

It is in the face of such fragmentation and selective

practicalities that the scholar, that the philologist, will advance his claim to a total view. Working letter by letter, word by word, line by line, the philologist and textual scholar aims to exclude nothing and to insinuate no arbitrary priorities. He would see and present Sophocles' *Antigone* 'as it stands'. Yet there is a sense, going far beyond the problem of scholarly disagreements, in which the neutral, disinterested assemblage by the philologist decomposes a literary text more drastically than does any other approach. For in ways which are at once a banality and an enigma, a literary text, a work of art that has in it any genuine authority, is not only more than the sum of its parts. It is, in a palpable sense, the denial of its own assembling. The organic nature of a great poem or play is, to be sure, seen metaphorically. We cannot define rigorously, let alone quantify, the felt analogy to living forms. But we know it to be justified; and we know that the agencies of autonomous being in literature and in art act beyond and even in repudiation of any anatomy of discrete thematic, structural, or technical features. There can be no enumeration of that which makes up the vital whole of Sophocles' *Antigone*. But in their impartiality towards detail, in their obligatory reduction of substance to material embodiment (sense is brought back as closely as possible to lexical–grammatical instrumentality), philology and textual scholarship *are* enumerative. The philological perspective is precisely that which postulates an equation, arduous to resolve but fundamental nevertheless, between the totality of significant presence and the aggregate of distinct formal units. This is why there is an inherent conflict between thought and scholarship, between the positivism of the philological and the recreative, metaphorically underwritten aims of hermeneutics.

This does not mean that the literary critic or the 'slow reader'—whose interests I have sought to represent throughout this study—have any privileged access to a unifying vision. There is no insurance of clear-sightedness in criticism. We have seen that critical readings of *Antigone* are under direct or oblique, implicit or explicit, pressure of occasion, of particular epistemologies, of theoretical and practical orders of priority. The eye of the critic is personal; his focus will be argumentative and strategic, most especially where it invokes alleged principles of canonic generality. The categories of meaning which critical analysis and valuation graft on a text are, at best, clarifying models. They make salient and throw into relief. Honest literary criticism is simply that which makes its purposed constructions most plainly visible and open to challenge.

The successive compositions and decompositions, elucidations and shadings, fragmentations and compactions which the act of reading brings to a written text, are of such delicate multiplicity that we have no normative or verifiable account of them. The pragmatic context, material as well as cultural, is as much a part of the dynamics of reading as is the psychology of the individual reader. Both context and psyche are, in turn, in constant and interactive motion. Rereading the identical passage or book, we are already other than we were. As we recollect or forget, sequent notices and internalizations of a text, layers, sediments of expectation and surprise, of recognition and spontaneous reaction, are deposited not only in the conscious mind, but in the subconscious where the reception of language probably exfoliates and dissolves into a more general coding of images, symbols, and phonetic associations. In the deep-seated and involuntary circulation of consciousness, these more diffuse semantic forms return, as it were, to the surface, to illuminate or obscure the more overt processes of understanding. Master readers are, so far as we can tell, no more frequent than major critics (I would guess that they are, in fact, rarer). And even in a Montaigne or a Borges, the introspective analyses of inspired reading, the testimonials of disinterested encounters between text and consciousness, remain sparse and metaphoric.

It is my own impression that two contrary currents are operative in serious reading, in that (lesser) work of art which is the product of a *lecture bien faite*. As concentration deepens, as noise and scattering are excised, to a greater or lesser degree, from the narrowing beam of attention, it is local detail that forces itself into the foreground of notice. This foreshortening, which is indispensable to our observance of singularity, of executive techniques, of stylistic specificities, inevitably fragments the text. But a counter-current of recomposition is also at work. Even as the eye looks away momentarily from the written passage, even as the local unit of textual material—the word, the sentence, the paragraph, the stanza in the poem, the scene in the play, the chapter in the novel—is receding into more or less retentive recollection, an erosion towards unity occurs. The detail is made less distinct as it enters into a largely subconscious, provisional construct of the whole. A memory trained to art will include within itself the skills of forgetting; it will smooth the sharp edges of the particular as our fingers smooth the edge of the stone before inserting it in the mosaic.

None the less, in even the most scrupulous of slow readings, the view which emerges of the text as a whole is 'angled' and selective. Where it exceeds the bounds of the verse lyric or prose vignette (it is the calculated observance of such dimensions which makes immediately unforgettable and irrefutable certain parables of Kafka), no literary work is held whole and unwavering in attention and memory. With each rereading, moreover, a new construct, a new assemblage is made. Details previously privileged are set in the background or elided; elements previously slighted or altogether unnoticed move into prominence. The sense of the whole may be strong, but it remains kaleidoscopic and subject to change. Tests have shown that the summaries which even the most attentive of readers gives of a work whose organic shape, whose coherence, are vivid to him will, on each occasion, differ.

Several 'Antigones' precede, underwrite, but also contradict the play which I have read in this chapter. There is the Antigone 'story' as my father told it to me when I was a very young child, an 'Antigone' made mesmeric, as I recall, by the matter of live burial. There is the ennobling myth of heroic Antigone as I first read it for myself in a young person's manual of Greek and Roman mythology, whose precise title and the name of whose editor I cannot remember, but whose olive-green binding and endpapers decorated à l'antique remain in my mind's eye. An eccentric, hectoring teacher taught me ancient Greek at the French Lycée in New York during the Second World War. M. B's true passion was seventeenth-century metaphysics, and Descartes in particular. He ranked the Attic philosophers and orators above the poets (the orations of Andocides fill me still with resentment and self-reproach). But the 'Ode on Man' in *Antigone* and Teiresias' prophecy did seem to M. B to possess a moral weight and philosophic reach beyond those of mere literature. He taught

these texts tightly and unforgettably to his three cowed charges
on long Thursday afternoons. What is more, he knit Sophocles'
text to the news of war and of occupation, of hostages and the
unburied dead which, in that school and at that time, came
daily. One of the three *grécisants*, the old proud designation
which goes back to the school syllabus of the Renaissance, left
New York more or less clandestinely to join the Resistance. He
died in the premature, hopeless battle on the heights of the
Vercors. This death (was A.S. more than seventeen?) lives for
me in the play and, emphatically, in Haemon's impatience.

Anouilh's *Antigone* swept through the schools, colleges,
universities, as well as the amateur and professional theatres of
the post-war period. Its corner-of-the-mouth disenchantment,
its anti-heroics and leather coats, precisely captured both the
hysterics and the embarrassments of unmerited survival. The
apparent simplicity of Anouilh's idiom, the fact that the play
can be staged in everyday dress and with a minimum of décor,
made of *Antigone* the house-favourite of 'French clubs', teachers
of French, and little theatres across the Anglo-American
spectrum. I saw, I had some part in, too many productions.
Anouilh's version came to seem to me a libel on Sophocles. It is
not. It is a highly reductive variant, innocent of awe, but with
an intelligence and argumentative poise of its own. It is, at this
point in time, difficult and, perhaps, artificial, to focus on
Sophocles' *Antigone* without keeping Anouilh's critique of the
myth at alert distance.

I then returned to the Greek text both as student and
teacher, and am not certain of being able to order chronologically the 'Antigones' which followed. It was at a bookstore
in Zurich that I acquired one of the first modern printings of
Hölderlin's translation. The impact of darkness, of doors closed
against me which I then experienced, is with me still. But also
the sensation of an overpowering presentness which, as I began
struggling with this incomparable recasting, drew me into
the lives of Antigone throughout German poetry, philosophy,
and politics. I came to Hegel and to Heidegger. I heard
Carl Orff's strident, mechanistic, yet at its 'Creon-points'
defensible, setting of Sophocles–Hölderlin to music. In turn, it
is against this version of hammers and cymbals that I can,
having seen it performed while already at work on this book,
invoke the *Antigone* of Honegger and Cocteau. Its choral sweep,

its rhetoric of protest and of freedom, are inseparable for me from the grey and soft-lit city of Angers where the work was staged. Now 'Antigone's sad song' as Chaucer imagined it retains an accidental but enduring touch of the Loire. What I am hoping for next is a revival or recording of André Jolivet's *Antigone* music, knowing him to be a composer of exceptional rigour and invention.

The world of textual scholarship, of recension, of philological commentary, is, obviously, of access and of interest mainly to the specialist. But it *is* a world. We have seen how exegesis breeds exegesis, how commentary engenders commentary, how edition follows on edition in augment, correction, and polemic. The energies of scholarship are disputatious and self-generating. Philology and text-criticism are, by their very nature, inflationary. The history and catalogue of previous emendations and opinions are a necessary part of the argument even, and particularly, where this argument seeks to break new ground (as this study goes to press, classicists at Oxford have announced that they are preparing a text of *Antigone* which will improve on Dawe's edition).

I remarked at the outset that a bibliography of the scholarly, monographic publications on Sophocles' *Antigone* would, of itself, constitute a voluminous enterprise. At every stage, moreover, we have seen that philological and contextual analyses are not value-free. Even at their most severely lexical or grammatical, glosses on *Antigone* are acts of more or less conscious, of more or less declared, restatement and interpretation. Academic conventions tend to be arcane. I recall the ironic insistence with which a great classical scholar, at the Institute for Advanced Study in Princeton, set out to persuade me that it was solely in footnotes to footnotes that the truth was to be found. But the specialized and the esoteric do exercise a persistent, cumulative influence on general literacy. In the case of any classical text, this influence is, in the final analysis, causal. Take the 'worst' edition, the sloppiest translation, available of a classical Greek tragedy; take the paperback version off the rack of some book or stationery emporium. It may have few notes, or notes which are wildly misleading. It may be riddled with textual errata and mistranslations. Nevertheless, such a text does result, at the ignoble end of the spectrum, from acts of selection and derivation whose ultimate source lies in the history of scholarship. Behind even the most populist version extends a continuum of philology and exegetic criticism. A comic-strip *Antigone* can exist because classical studies have, since the Renaissance, ensured the transmission and canonic status of Sophocles' drama.

But the influence of commentary, particularly where it is of a philosophic or political tenor, also acts indirectly. Not very many general readers will have come across Hegel's *Antigone* interpretations at first hand. But the Hegelian reading of the play as a dialectical conflict of equal opposites has been widely disseminated in the climate of literacy as well as that of theatrical presentation. Jacques Lacan's remarks on *Antigone* (in the seminar sequence entitled *L'Éthique de la psychanalyse*) may not, as yet, be generally accessible. But his view of Creon as the 'denier of desire', as one whose refusal of the *discours du désire* entails the choice of death, will, by osmosis of fashion, be diffused.

The question is this: to what extent is one's personal experience of Sophocles' *Antigone* a product of the palimpsest of commentaries and judgements which now overlie the 'original', to which, indeed, we owe what personal access we have to this 'original'? Is there any way of going upstream to the source?

Again, the answer must vary with each individual reader/spectator. The absolute grammarian—and he knows ecstasies as intense as any described in current theories of the *jouissance*, of the eros of reading—may come to conceive of, to love, even a text such as Sophocles' *Antigone* as the locus of cruces. The play will come to life in his sensibility by virtue of the syntactic or metrical problems and debates to which it has given prestigious rise. At the opposite pole stands the 'innocent', the man or woman who chances across an extract from, a performance of, *Antigone*, unaware of the concentric spheres of commentary and text-criticism that surround it. The reader of the play, the theatrical audience for whom I am writing, would, I presume, find themselves somewhere past the centre of the scale. They are nearer to philology than to innocence, but will (this, of course, being my own case) have had no hand in the conservation and establishment of the Sophoclean canon.

As I have pointed out, however, there is no complete

modern innocence in the face of the classics. The mere notion
of the 'classic' tells us as much. No twentieth-century public or
reader comes upon Sophocles' *Antigone* wholly unprepared.
The play is, unavoidably, embedded in the long history of its
transmission and reception. Because this history is so extensive,
because variants and adaptations have been both so numerous
and of significant quality, Sophocles' text runs the danger of
receding into context. It can only be by a deliberate and, more
or less, fictive exercise of purification, not unlike that of a
restorer removing levels of varnish and previous restorations
from a canvas, that one can attempt to isolate the Sophoclean
play from the interpretations and uses made of it. The analogy
with the restorer is, moreover, deceptive. It is quite often
possible to bring the original design and coloration back into
view. But no *Ur-Antigone* can exist for us. No stripping away of
interpretative accretions can take us back to the première of
the drama, to the phenomenology of its purpose and impact in
the 440s BC.

   It is, I believe, far more realistic for the 'slow reader' to
acknowledge that judgements and uses of *Antigone*, from
Aristotle to Lacan, will form some part of his own experience of
the work. Even as Freud's 'Oedipus complex' and Lévi-
Strauss's anti-Freudian account of Oedipus as a hero limping
between 'nature' and 'culture' have become active elements in
the myth, so the 'Antigones' of Hegel or of Kierkegaard or of
the clandestine feminine 'brigade' which, in Germany, is seeking to avenge the refusal of the authorities to return to their
families the bodies of slain Baader and Meinhof (Böll's
treatment of *Antigone* springs from this identification) are more
than merely extrinsic to Sophocles. The currently modish term
would be 'metatexts'. But this term communicates nothing of
the symbiotic processes whereby a strong commentary, an
inspired staging, an act of symbolic–political *montage*, a setting
of Sophocles' *Antigone* to, as it were, the present music of the
mind, become a living extension of the original. It is these
processes which allow us to define 'a classic'.

   The classic is a text whose initial, existential coming into
being and realization may well be unrecapturable to us (this
will always be true of the literatures of antiquity). But the
integral authority of the classic is such that it can absorb
without loss of identity the millennial incursions upon it, the

accretions to it, of commentary, of translations, of enacted variations. *Ulysses* reinforces Homer; Broch's *Death of Virgil* enriches the *Aeneid*. Sophocles' *Antigone* will not suffer from Lacan.

The development of metamorphic unity is open-ended. New textual and critical readings of *Antigone*, new scenic, musical, choreographic, and cinematographic renditions, new variants on and adaptations of 'the story', are being produced at this very moment. But each in turn will have to test the strength of its being against that of its Sophoclean source. And very few will survive to become that enigmatic but undeniable phenomenon, an echo that has life.

My understandings of *Antigone* are provisional. They will change with age, with my renewed experience of the text, with my encounter with fresh critical opinions and productions of the play. But such changes are no guarantee of a clearer, more adequate grasp. Insights are lost or spuriously amended (the young Hegel is sometimes a more observant witness to Sophocles than the later philosopher of religion and of power). It is of the nature of the study of philosophy and of the arts— distinct, in this regard, from that of the sciences—that time and age do tend to bring with them a better-informed, a more balanced, view of their object. But neither the questions one poses nor the answers one puts forward are necessarily progressive. The work, that at which we worry and which worries us, becomes more inward to our perceptions. But this intimacy can become one of possession, and thus lodge too deep for clarity. Consciously or not, we may confuse our personal involvement in a great work and the impact of this work on our memories and self-representation with the facts of the case. To reread is to recollect subjectively, across the interpositions, as it were, of the self. It is to ask again or to formulate new questions. These need not, as in the logic of the exact or natural sciences, be 'better' or more economical.

As I come to the formal close of this monograph, whose inadequacies, at least, are now plainer to me than they were during work in progress, a further 'Antigone' invites aware-ness, indistinctly as yet, but with a hint of compulsion, as might an image when it starts to acquire contour and mass in the developer in the dark-room.

I sense in Sophocles' play an undeclared tragedy of the

dissociations between thought and action, between understanding and practice. The ascription to action of manifest pre-
eminence, of an existential worth greater than any other, is a
marked element in Periclean and Aristotelian concepts of
human conduct. Drama itself, as has often been said, is a
stylized expression of this preference. It locates in the individual person those privileges and fatalities of 'doing' which
the preceding, generative tradition of epic poetry had,
assuredly at its origins, placed in ethnic and collective enter-
prises (the clans of Greece sailing to Troy). But experiencing
and re-experiencing *Antigone*, I find it difficult to dismiss the
possibility that Sophocles queried this morality of the deed; or,
more tentatively, that there are not within the play as we know
it certain aspects, traversed, left behind, but consequent, of a
critique of action.

I mean by this that Sophocles tested the cost of deeds which,
whatever their intrinsic obligation and merit, overrule and
dissociate themselves from the provisional largesse of thought.
Nothing, to be sure, is more banal than the notion of actions
performed in blind or coercive contradiction to better insight.
The very word ὕβρις would seem to point in some such
direction of generic human infirmity. I have in mind something more specific. It is Sophocles' probing of the ways in
which dramatic form, the play as a construct of discourse and
of deed, isolates the very different, possibly irreconcilable
functions of intelligibility on the one hand and of the
abstention from adequate understanding on the other (an
abstention which makes action possible).

The unmatched economy of terror in *Oedipus Rex* stems from
the enforced homecoming of Oedipus to his naked identity.
The etymology of 'persona' (itself not Greek) relates directly to
'mask'. In Sophocles' *Oedipus*, the masks by which we necessarily live, the 'personifications' through which we maintain a
customary distance both from our stripped selves and from
others, are successively flayed away. Oedipus' self is made one
with his skin and with that beneath the skin which civilization,
shame, the need for a certain *Lebensraum*—literally a space for
the manœuvres and evasive actions of a social being—would
have us conceal from ourselves as from others. In Oedipus, this
dread reversion to the naked centre proceeds by virtue of a
perfect but also unnatural coincidence between understanding

and action. The action performed by Oedipus is his progressive understanding of his actual self. The normal separations between total intelligibility and performance which, in the common order of life, is selective, tentative, self-deceiving, are annulled. Oedipus' questing mind breaks through to its own springs of motive. He thinks his acts to inescapable finality; he acts his thoughts to the liminal logic of absolute self-perception which is, also, and of necessity, blindness. There is in this perfect intellection, of which Freud's self-analysis was a conscious mimesis, an incest more radical than that of blood. It is only in the *Oedipus at Colonus* that Oedipus' mastering thought yields to the summons of mystery, of that which, very precisely, lies beyond the intelligible; and that Oedipus' *virtus*, his δαίμων for action, surrenders to passivity, to the trance-like motion which transports him beyond doing. It is only in the sacred wood that understanding and deed are again set apart and given peace.

It is the particular genius of these two plays which induces one to ask whether there is not in the *Antigone* a latent challenge to the received wisdom enunciated in a famous line of Euripides' *Hippolytus*. As Phaedra says: 'We understand what is right and proper, we know it, but we do not perform it in our acts.' But 'challenge' is too peremptory. There is, rather, the very delicate yet insistent possibility that Creon's intelligence is of a kind which might lead him to apprehend the necessary claims of Antigone's stance; that Antigone is possessed of a force of empathy which might lead her to perceive the rationale of Creon's position. I do not suppose for a moment that Sophocles could have subscribed to the conclusion arrived at by Coleridge when he wrote in a notebook entry for 1802 'there is something inherently mean in action'. But the waste of unheeded persuasion in *Antigone* seems, at moments, to exceed any rhetorical art or tactic of theatrical symmetry. The behaviour of the protagonists, and this is true also of Haemon, does seem almost extravagantly wasteful of the opportunities for reciprocal intelligibility offered by the dramatic discourse.

In reach of the tragedy as we know and experience it, there lies (or so I now sense) an intimation of inaction, of the deed arrested by the acknowledged gravity, density, and inhibitions of mutual insight. Such a play would not be a 'drama' in the proper sense, the very word, as we have seen, signifying 'action'. The suspension of the deed, the abstinence of the doer in the face of the complexities and doubts revealed, proffered to him by thought, would make for a kind of stasis, for a kind of lasting hesitation alien to the dramatic (before, say, Milton's *Samson Agonistes* or the immobilities of Beckett). Perhaps only drama set to music, music-drama in the true sense of the word, can realize the suspension of the existential compulsion to choose, to be partial, to narrow and sharpen consciousness towards action. The exchange of clairvoyant, undeceived generosities at the close of Mozart's *Figaro* exactly illustrates what I have in view. We need only recall this scene, and the role of the Countess in particular, to know that such mercy of understanding, and the renunciations of action which it brings with it, have their own infinite sadness.

It may be that subterranean to Sophocles' most demanding play is a meditation on the tragic partiality, on the fatal interestedness, of even the noblest deed. An untapped stillness of understanding is present in Antigone, in the aura of that secrecy which has drawn to her poets, artists, philosophers, political thinkers. But there may be hints of such a stillness, of a perceptive weariness also in Sophocles' Creon. As I move nearer the play, leaving behind aspects emphasized in this study, it is the laying waste of stillness, of understanding heard but not listened to, that is beginning to feel central. A phrase out of the Book of Daniel, *ostensio secretorum*, 'the showing of the secret', presses on me. As yet, I can put it no other way.

9

Why the unbroken authority of Greek myths over the imagination of the West? Why should a handful of Greek myths, that of Antigone among them, recur in the art and thought of the twentieth century to an almost obsessive degree? Why is there no end to Oedipus, to Prometheus, to Orestes, to Narcissus, no laying to rest in archaeology? Explicitly and implicitly, this has been the question underlying this study.

Poets, philosophers, anthropologists, psychologists, and even theologians have answered. Many of their answers are fascinating. Because Greek myths encode certain primary biological and social confrontations and self-perceptions in the history of man, they endure as an animate legacy in collective remembrance and recognition. We come home to them as to our psychic roots (but why, then, are they not, strictly speaking, universal and of equal import to *all* cultures, East or West?). The very foundations of our arts and civilization, we are assured, are mythical. Having taken from ancient Hellas the essentials of western rationality, of political institutions, of aesthetic forms, we have taken also the mythology from which these essentials drew their symbolic history and validity. Theologians say that the epiphany and passion of Christ represent the crowning symbolic act of the western imagination. After Christ, who is the Word, God does not address the mortal imagination directly; but because Christ is also the truth, his boundless inheritance is that of belief, of iconic representation, of personal *imitatio*, rather than that of myth.

One can also theorize on a humbler level. Greek literature is the first we recognize and experience as such. Its identification with myths is so immediate and fertile that Greek mythology has become a constant centre or pivot of reference for all subsequent poetic invention and philosophic allegory. The Greek myths are a shorthand whose economy generates unlimited variations but which does not, in itself, need to be reinvented. Compare our alphabet or numerical notations. There *are* addenda: the symbol for zero, the Don Juan motif. But these are exceedingly rare. Heidegger puts it more simply still: for western man, 'myth itself is Greek'.

But why? Why, to adapt Nietzsche's image, this 'eternal return'?

When a question proves too difficult, it may be possible to blunt the fact by asking an equally or even more difficult one. But I do believe that some access to the central, canonic permanence of Greek myths may be found, contrastively, if we consider Shakespeare.

Very close on four centuries have passed since his works were created. Much about Shakespeare has the aura of the anonymous, of one concerning whose personal individuality little is known or needs to be known. In many respects, Shakespeare's inventions and speech, his dicta, similes, symbols, pervade our whole culture. But although there are—in Musset's *Lorenzaccio*, in German and Russian poetry and prose fiction—a considerable number of transpositions from *Hamlet*, and although

Edward Bond's *Lear* is a telling experiment and Ionesco's
Macbett has its moments, the world of Shakespeare remains his.
It has engendered no afterlives, no reprises, of the manifold,
continuous kind or quality we associate with the legacies of the
Oresteia, of Euripides' *Medea* or *Hippolytus*, of Sophocles' dramas
on Oedipus and Antigone. Ought there not, I have asked, by
now to be a legion of 'Macbeths', of 'Othellos', of 'Lears'?

   The sovereignty of Shakespeare is among the very few
genuinely taboo subjects in our cultural discussions. No real
doubts can be argued, except on the plane of angry perversity
(Tolstoy) or on that of merriment and exhibitionism (Bernard
Shaw on *Cymbeline*). The extreme unevenness in Shakespeare,
the puerility of many episodes and intrusions, notably in the
comedies, the verbal prolixity of texts which producers cut
almost as a matter of evident routine, are problems observed,
as it were, in passing. The supremacy of the Shakespearean
achievement as a whole is felt to be such as to override, indeed
to transmute into strengths, what would, in any other writer,
be serious failings. Because the Clown in *Othello* is so patently
intolerable, he is simply elided from commentary and
production.

   Only a man to whom the articulation of personal convictions
is a moral absolute can set down fundamental perplexities
about the begetter of *Hamlet* or of *Lear*. In his *Vermischte
Bermerkungen* (published, it is true, posthumously), Ludwig
Wittgenstein notes that he has never been able 'to make much
of . . . to understand' Shakespeare. The clamorous universality
of adulation fills him with profound distrust. 'War er vielleicht
eher ein *Sprachschöpfer* als ein Dichter?' The distinction is very
difficult to translate. It is, in essence, that between a supreme
virtuoso and creator of language, of expressive devices, and one
whose work leads to 'the truth'. 'Er ist *nicht* naturwahr,' says
Wittgenstein of Shakespeare, '*not* true to nature' or, perhaps,
'of a natural truth'. No one could speak of 'Shakespeare's great
heart', as they can of 'the great heart of Beethoven'. It is,
according to Wittgenstein, Shakespeare's 'supple hand' which,
incomparably, has invented new 'Naturformen der Sprache',
'natural forms' or 'species of language', rather than producing
what Wittgenstein would recognize as substantive, truth-ful
presences.

   It may take a very long time to elucidate fairly, to place in their whole context, Wittgenstein's observations (though, already, their relation to the Kierkegaardian distinctions between the aesthetic and the ethical, and their echoing of Tolstoy, are evident). But the main point is this: Wittgenstein concedes to Shakespeare a unique command over language. This command does not ensure, indeed it may militate against, the striving after and statement of 'truth', be it philosophical or theological. The Shakespeare-world is impartial, perhaps indifferent, in regard to God. It is remote from that which Walter Benjamin posits when he says that 'the theological' is, both in language and supreme art, the only guarantor of felt meaning.

In Greek tragedy, the dimension of transcendence is of the essence. It is openly deployed and addressed in both Aeschylus and Sophocles; it is sometimes subverted, sometimes overwhelming, in Euripides. Myth embodies the potential of finality while postponing, through ambiguity, error, and conflict, its fulfilment. In myth there is always an 'awaiting' of meaning, messianic or anti-messianic—witness the *Bacchae*, witness that anonymous 'Annunciation' in the Brussels Museum in which there is, behind the Virgin, as she receives the angelic message, a painting of the crucifixion.

This unresolved expectation gives rise to Greek tragedy and makes it inexhaustibly open to our needs of understanding. Shakespeare drew on history, folklore, legend, the fairy-tale, the *fait divers* in chronicles of passion. He did not, with the problematic exception of *Troilus and Cressida*, draw on myth. Some marvellous intuition kept him from doing so. His pluralism and liberality, his tragi-comic bias, his attention to the child in man, refuse any unification of reality and with it the intolerant immensity of the mythical moment. The *Oresteia*, *Oedipus Rex*, *Antigone*, the *Bacchae*, but also Wagner's *Tristan und Isolde*, lie outside Shakespeare's kaleidoscopic, *secular* humanity.

But it is myth and its commitment to transcendence which generate, which compel, the dynamics of recursion, of repetition (that 'asking again') across time.

The other direction in which I want to look is that summarily stated in a previous chapter: my hypothesis that the principal Greek myths are imprinted in the evolution of our language, and of our grammars in particular. If my hunch is right—and here everything remains to be shown—we speak organic vestiges of myth when we speak. Hence the indwelling in our mentality and culture of Oedipus and of Helen, of Eros and of Thanatos, of Apollo and of Dionysus.

But these are conjectures and books as yet unwritten. All I can be certain of is this: what I have tried to say is already in need of addition. New 'Antigones' are being imagined, thought, lived now; and will be tomorrow.

INDEX OF PROPER NAMES